WORLD TRADE ORGANIZATION

Dispute Settlement Reports

1996

Volume I
Pages 1-284

CAMBRIDGE
UNIVERSITY PRESS

PUBLISHED BY THE PRESS SYNDICATE OF THE UNIVERSITY OF CAMBRIDGE
The Pitt Building, Trumpington Street, Cambridge, United Kingdom

CAMBRIDGE UNIVERSITY PRESS
The Edinburgh Building, Cambridge CB2 2RU, UK   http://www.cup.cam.ac.uk
40 West 20th Street, New York, NY 10011–4211, USA   http://www.cup.org
10 Stamford Road, Oakleigh, Melbourne 3166, Australia
Ruiz de Alarcón 13, 28014 Madrid, Spain

Printed in the United Kingdom at the University Press, Cambridge

French edition and Spanish edition paperbacks of this title are both available directly from WTO Publications, World Trade Organization, Centre William Rappard, 154 rue de Lausanne, CH-1211 Geneva 21, Switzerland   http://www.wto.org

ISBN 0 521 78095 0 hardback
ISBN 0 521 78581 2 paperback

THE WTO DISPUTE SETTLEMENT REPORTS

The *Dispute Settlement Reports* of the World Trade Organization (the "WTO") include Panel and Appellate Body reports, as well as Arbitration Awards, in disputes concerning the rights and obligations of WTO Members under the provisions of the *Marrakesh Agreement Establishing the World Trade Organization*. The *Dispute Settlement Reports* are available in English, French and Spanish.

This volume may be cited as DSR 1996:I

TABLE OF CONTENTS

UNITED STATES - STANDARDS FOR REFORMULATED AND CONVENTIONAL GASOLINE

Report of the Appellate Body
WT/DS2/AB/R

Adopted by the Dispute Settlement Body on 20 May 1996

United States, Appellant	Present:
Brazil, Venezuela, Appellees	Feliciano, Presiding Member
European Communities, Norway,	Beeby, Member
Third Participants	Matsushita, Member

I. INTRODUCTORY

The United States appeals from certain conclusions on issues of law and certain legal interpretations contained in the Panel Report, United States - Standards for Reformulated and Conventional Gasoline, WT/DS2/R, 29 January 1996 (the "Panel Report"). That Panel had been established to consider a dispute between the United States, on the one hand, and Venezuela, later joined by Brazil, on the other. The dispute related to the implementation by the United States of its domestic legislation known as the Clean Air Act of 1990 (the "CAA") and, more specifically, to the regulation enacted by the United States' Environmental Protection Agency (the "EPA") pursuant to that Act, to control toxic and other pollution caused by the combustion of gasoline manufactured in or imported into the United States. This regulation is formally entitled "Regulation of Fuels and Fuel Additives - Standards for Reformulated and Conventional Gasoline", Part 80 of Title 40 of the Code of Federal Regulations,[1] and is commonly referred to as the Gasoline Rule.

A. Procedural Matters

On 21 February 1996, the United States notified the Dispute Settlement Body of its decision to appeal certain conclusions on issues of law and legal interpretations in the Panel Report pursuant to Article 16 of the Understanding on Rules and Procedures Governing the Settlement of Disputes (the "DSU")[2] and simultaneously filed a Notice of Appeal with the Appellate Body, pursuant to Rule 20 of the Working Procedures for Appellate Review (the "Working Proce-

---

[1] 40 CFR 80, 59 Fed. Reg. 7716 (16 February 1994).
[2] WT/DS2/6.

dures").[3] Thereafter, on 4 March 1996, the United States filed its Submission as Appellant.[4] Venezuela in turn filed, on 18 March 1996, its Appellee's Submission; Brazil filed on the same day its Appellee's Submission.[5] The third participants followed, the European Communities and Norway filing Submissions, on 18 March 1996.[6]

The complete record of the Panel proceedings was duly transmitted to the Appellate Body.[7]

The oral hearing contemplated by Rule 27 of the Working Procedures was held on 27 and 28 March 1996.[8] At the hearing, oral arguments were made respectively by the participants and the third participants. Questions were put to them by the Members of the Appellate Body hearing the appeal. Most of these questions were answered orally, and some were responded to in writing with the responses being furnished both to the Appellate Body and the other participants and third participants.[9] In addition, the participants and third participants were invited to provide, and did provide, the Appellate Body and each other with final written statements of their respective positions.[10] All the participants and third participants responded positively and punctually, which was a source of satisfaction for the Appellate Body.

B. The Clean Air Act and its Implementation

The CAA and its implementation by the Gasoline Rule, are described fully at paragraphs 2.1- 2.13 of the Panel Report. However, it may be convenient to recall a number of the Panel's factual findings at this stage.

The CAA established two gasoline programs[11] to ensure that pollution from gasoline combustion does not exceed 1990 levels and that pollutants in major population centres are reduced. The first program concerns ozone "nonattainment areas", consisting of (i) nine large metropolitan areas that have experienced the worst summertime ozone pollution and (ii) various additional areas included at the request of the state governors concerned. All gasoline sold to consumers in these nonattainment areas must be "reformulated." The sale of conventional gasoline in nonattainment areas is prohibited. The second program concerns "conventional" gasoline, which may be sold to consumers in the rest of the United States. The implementation of both programs, which apply to gasoline sold by domestic refiners, blenders and importers, was entrusted to the EPA. As a result, the EPA adopted the Gasoline Rule, which relies heavily on the use of

---

[3]   WT/AB/WP/1, 15 February 1996.
[4]   Pursuant to Rule 21(1) of the *Working Procedures.*
[5]   Pursuant to Rule 22(1) of the *Working Procedures.*
[6]   Pursuant to Rule 24 of the *Working Procedures.*
[7]   Pursuant to Rule 25 of the *Working Procedures.*
[8]   The oral hearing was originally scheduled for 25 March 1996 but had, for exceptional and unavoidable reasons, to be deferred to 27 and 28 March 1996.
[9]   Rule 28 of the *Working Procedures.*
[10]   Rule 28(1) of the *Working Procedures.*
[11]   Section 211(k).

1990 baselines as a means of determining compliance with the CAA requirements.

1.   The Reformulated Gasoline Program

The CAA established certain compositional and performance specifications for reformulated gasoline.[12] Thus, the oxygen content must not be less than 2.0 per cent by weight, the benzene content must not exceed 1.0 per cent by volume and the gasoline must be free of heavy metals, including lead or manganese. The performance specifications of the CAA require a 15 per cent reduction in the emissions of both volatile organic compounds ("VOCs") and toxic air pollutants ("toxics"), and no increase in emissions of nitrogen oxides ("NOx"). Section 80.41 of the Gasoline Rule sets out two methods by which entities can certify their gasoline as meeting these requirements. From 1 January 1995 to 1 January 1998, domestic refiners, blenders and importers may use an interim method of certification called the "Simple Model", which requires compliance with fixed specifications   concerning Reid Vapour Pressure, oxygen, benzene and toxics performance. In addition, compliance is required with certain "non-degradation requirements" by maintaining sulphur, olefins and T-90 qualities at or below 1990 baseline levels, on an average annual basis. As of 1 January 1998, these entities must comply with the "Complex Model", which more accurately predicts emissions performance. The Complex Model is not in issue in the present dispute.

2.   The Conventional Gasoline Program

In order to prevent the "dumping" of pollutants extracted from reformulated gasoline into conventional gasoline, the CAA requires that conventional gasoline sold by domestic refiners, blenders and importers in the United States remains as clean as 1990 baseline levels.[13] Unlike the Simple Model for reformulated gasoline, the "non-degradation" from 1990 baseline requirements for conventional gasoline applies in respect of all conventional gasoline qualities, and not only sulphur, olefins and T-90. Compliance is measured by comparing emissions from the conventional gasoline sold by domestic refiners, blenders and importers against emissions from a 1990 baseline and is assessed on an annual average basis.[14]

3.   Baseline Establishment Rules

In respect of both reformulated gasoline (for sulphur, olefins and T-90 requirements under the Simple Model) and conventional gasoline (for all requirements), 1990 baselines are an integral element of the Gasoline Rule enforcement process. Accordingly, the Gasoline Rule contains detailed baseline

---

[12] Section 211(k)(2)-(3).
[13] Section 211(k)(8) of the CAA.
[14] Section 80.90 of the Gasoline Rule.

establishment rules.[15] Baselines can be either individual (established by the entity itself) or statutory (established by the EPA and intended to reflect average 1990 United States gasoline quality), depending on the nature of the entity concerned.

(i) domestic refiners

Any domestic refiner which was in operation for at least six months in 1990 must establish an individual baseline representing the quality of gasoline produced by that refiner in 1990. The Gasoline Rule provides three methods of establishment to be used for this purpose. Under Method 1, the domestic refiner must use the quality data and volume records of its 1990 gasoline. If Method 1 data is not available, the domestic refiner must use its 1990 gasoline blendstock quality data and 1990 blendstock production records (Method 2). In the event that Method 2 data is not available, the domestic refiner must establish an individual 1990 baseline on the basis of its post-1990 gasoline blendstock and/or gasoline quality data modeled in the light of refinery changes to show 1990 gasoline composition (Method 3).

Domestic refiners that were in operation for at least six months in 1990 are not permitted to forego their individual baseline and use the statutory baseline established by the EPA. However, domestic refiners that commenced operations after 1990, or operated for less than six months during 1990, are required to use the statutory baseline established by the EPA.

(ii) blenders

Blenders are required to establish an individual baseline representing the quality of their 1990 gasoline using Method 1 above. Failing this, they must use the statutory baseline established by the EPA. Blenders may not apply an individual baseline using Methods 2 or 3.

(iii) importers

Importers of foreign gasoline are required to establish an individual baseline in respect of gasoline imported by them during 1990, using Method 1. Like blenders, importers become subject to the statutory baseline if, as anticipated by the EPA, the data necessary for Method 1 is unavailable.

The Gasoline Rule does not provide for foreign refiner individual baselines, although the possible use of individual baselines for foreign refiners was examined by the EPA while drafting the Gasoline Rule. Indeed, the EPA continued to examine the possible use of individual baselines for foreign refineries after the adoption of the Gasoline Rule, and prepared its May 1994 proposal[16] as a result. The May 1994 proposal provided for limited use by importers of individual baselines established for foreign refineries in order to demonstrate that gaso-

---

[15]   Section 80.91.
[16]   40 CFR 80, 59 Fed. Reg. at 22 800 (3 May 1994).

line produced at that foreign refinery complied with the reformulated (but not conventional) gasoline standards. The individual baselines would be determined using Methods 1, 2 or 3, as for domestic refineries under the Gasoline Rule. However, the use of individual baselines in such cases would be conditioned and limited in a number of ways. The EPA's May 1994 proposal never entered into force, as the United States Congress enacted legislation in September 1994 denying the funding necessary for its implementation.

C. The Panel Report: Its Findings and Conclusions

The Panel's overall conclusions and its recommendation are set out in the following terms:

> 8.1   In the light of the findings above, the Panel concluded that the baseline establishment methods contained in Part 80 of Title 40 of the Code of Federal Regulations are not consistent with Article III:4 of the General Agreement, and cannot be justified under paragraphs (b), (d) and (g) of Article XX of the General Agreement.

> 8.2   The Panel *recommends* that the Dispute Settlement Body request the United States to bring this part of the Gasoline Rule into conformity with its obligations under the General Agreement.[17]

On route to its overall conclusions, the Panel made the following principal findings:

> (i)   that the Panel's terms of reference were established after the 75 per cent rule had ceased to have any effect, and the rule had not been mentioned in the terms of reference, and that, in any case, it was unnecessary, in view of findings (ii), (iv), (v) and (vii) below, to determine whether the measure at issue was inconsistent with Article I:1 of the *General Agreement on Tariffs and Trade 1994* (the *"General Agreement"*);[18]

> (ii)   that imported and domestic gasoline were "like products" and that since, under the baseline establishment rules of the Gasoline Rule, imported gasoline was effectively prevented from benefitting from as favourable sales conditions as were afforded domestic gasoline by an individual baseline tied to the producer of a product, imported gasoline was treated "less favourably" than domestic gasoline. The baseline establishment rules of the Gasoline Rule were accordingly inconsistent with Article III:4 of the *General Agreement;*[19]

---

[17]   Panel Report at paras. 8.1-8.2.
[18]   Panel Report, para. 6.19.
[19]   Panel Report, para. 6.16.

(iii)   that, in view of finding (ii), it was not necessary to examine the consistency of the Gasoline Rule with Article III:1;[20]

(iv)   that the "aspect of the baseline establishment methods" found inconsistent with Article III:4 was not justified under Article XX(b) of the *General Agreement* as "necessary to protect human, animal or plant life or health";[21]

(v)   that the "maintenance of discrimination between imported and domestic gasoline" contrary to Article III:4 was not justified under Article XX(d) as "necessary to secure compliance with laws or regulations which are not inconsistent with the provisions of [the General] Agreement";[22]

(vi)   that clean air was an exhaustible natural resource within the meaning of Article XX(g) of the *General Agreement*;[23]

(vii)   that the baseline establishment rules found to be inconsistent with Article III:4 could not be justified under Article XX(g) as a measure "relating to" the conservation of exhaustible natural resources;[24]

(viii)   that it was unnecessary, in the light of finding (vii), to determine whether the measure at issue was "made effective in conjunction with restrictions on domestic production or consumption";[25]

(ix)   that it was unnecessary, in the light of finding (vii), to determine whether the measure at issue met the conditions in the introductory clause of Article XX (sometimes referred to as the chapeau of Article XX);

(x)   that it was unnecessary, in view of findings (ii), (iv), (v) and (vii), to determine whether the measure at issue was inconsistent with Article XXIII:1(b) as having nullified and impaired benefits accruing under the *General Agreement*;[26] and

(xi)   that it was unnecessary, in the light of findings (ii), (iv), (v) and (vii), to determine whether the measure at issue was inconsistent with Articles 2.1 and 2.2 of the *Agreement on Technical Barriers to Trade* (the "*TBT Agreement*").[27]

---

[20]   Panel Report, para. 6.17.
[21]   Panel Report, para. 6.29.
[22]   Panel Report, para. 6.33.
[23]   Panel Report, para. 6.37.
[24]   Panel Report, para. 6.40.
[25]   Panel Report, para. 6.41.
[26]   Panel Report, para. 6.42.
[27]   Panel Report, para. 6.43.

II.   ISSUES RAISED IN THIS APPEAL

A.   *The Claims of Error by the United States*

It is important to focus upon the subject matter of this appeal. We seek to do this first by identifying the issues which have been raised by the Appellant, the United States. In what follows we highlight those same issues by listing certain other issues dealt with in the Panel proceedings but which have *not* been brought before the Appellate Body in this appeal, and which we accordingly exclude from consideration in this Appellate Report.

In its Notice of Appeal, dated 21 February 1996, and its Appellant's Submission, dated 4 March 1996, the United States claims that the Panel erred in law, firstly, in holding that the baseline establishment rules of the Gasoline Rule are not justified under Article XX(g) of the *General Agreement* and, secondly, in its interpretation of Article XX as a whole.

More specifically, the United States assigns as error the ruling of the Panel that the baseline establishment rules do not constitute a "measure" "relating to" the conservation of clean air within the meaning of Article XX(g) of the *General Agreement*. Consequently, it is also the view of the United States that the Panel erred in failing to proceed further in its interpretation and application of Article XX(g), and in not finding that the baseline establishment rules satisfy the other requirements of Article XX(g) and the introductory provisions of Article XX.

The sharply limited scope of this appeal is underscored by noting the number of findings which the Panel had made but which have not been appealed from by the United States. Very briefly, the United States does not appeal from the findings or rulings made by the Panel on, or in respect of, the consistency of the baseline establishment rules with Article I:1, Article III:1, Article III:4, and Article XXIII:1(b) of the *General Agreement* and the applicability of Article XX(b) and Article XX(d) of the *General Agreement* and of the *TBT Agreement*. Understandably, the United States has also not appealed from the Panel's ruling that clean air is an exhaustible natural resource within the meaning of Article XX(g) of the *General Agreement*.

B.   *The Claims of the Appellees and the Arguments of the Third Participants*

The Appellees, Venezuela and Brazil, submit that the Appellate Body should dismiss the United States' appeal and uphold the Panel's findings and conclusions concerning Article XX(g). In particular, Venezuela and Brazil support the Panel's finding that the measure at issue before the Panel was not one "relating to" the conservation of exhaustible natural resources. Venezuela also states that a measure can only be "relating to" or "primarily aimed at" conservation if the measure was both: (i) primarily intended to achieve a conservation goal; and (ii) had a positive conservation effect.

Venezuela argues that, as the United States has not met its burden with respect to the "relating to" requirement of Article XX(g) in this appeal, the Appellate Body may uphold the Panel Report on this issue alone, and it is not necessary to address the additional requirements of Article XX(g), nor the requirements in the Article XX chapeau.

If the Appellate Body overturns the Panel's findings on the "relating to" component of Article XX(g) and does proceed to examine the other requirements of Article XX(g), Venezuela and Brazil submit that the United States has also failed to demonstrate that those requirements have been satisfied. They argue that the measure in issue is not "made effective in conjunction with restrictions on domestic production or consumption" as the restrictions are not imposed as direct limits on the production or consumption of clean air, but rather upon the consumption of certain kinds of gasoline. They further submit that clean air does not qualify as an "exhaustible natural resource" within the meaning of Article XX(g).

With regard to the requirements in the chapeau to Article XX, Venezuela and Brazil submit that the measure is applied in a manner which constitutes "arbitrary or unjustifiable discrimination between countries where the same conditions prevail." Venezuela argues that the measure constitutes a "disguised restriction on international trade" as well.

The Appellees also raise the conditional argument that, if the Appellate Body were to overturn the Panel's findings on Article XX(g), and not find in favour of Venezuela and Brazil as to the other requirements of Article XX, it would then need to examine their claims under the *TBT Agreement*.

The third participants, the European Communities and Norway, endorse the Panel's interpretation of "relating to" and the Panel's findings under Article XX(g). They find it difficult to accept the United States' arguments that the measure at issue was "made effective in conjunction with restrictions on domestic production or consumption," as the measure in issue did not impose restrictions on clean air. With regard to the Article XX chapeau criteria, the European Communities and Norway both submit that the measure is applied in a manner constituting "arbitrary or unjustifiable discrimination between countries where the same conditions prevail" and a "disguised restriction on international trade."

C.   The Preliminary Question

A preliminary question was raised by the United States at the oral hearing concerning arguments made by Venezuela and Brazil in their respective Appellees' Submissions on the issues of whether clean air is an exhaustible natural resource within the meaning of Article XX(g) and whether the baseline establishment rules are consistent with the *TBT Agreement*. The gist of the preliminary question is that the above issues and the related arguments made by Venezuela and Brazil were not properly brought before the Appellate Body in this appeal in accordance with the *Working Procedures*. It was underscored by the United States that Venezuela and Brazil had not appealed from the ruling of the Panel on the clean air issue or from the non-ruling of the Panel on the applicability of the *TBT Agreement*. Venezuela and Brazil had not filed Appellants' Submissions under Rule 23(1) of the *Working Procedures*. Neither had Venezuela nor Brazil filed separate appeals under Rule 23(4) of the *Working Procedures*.

Their arguments on these two matters had been made in their Appellees' Submissions pursuant to Rule 22 and, as Appellees, Venezuela and Brazil could not challenge the Panel's finding on the clean air issue and its non-finding on the *TBT Agreement*'s applicability.

At the oral hearing, in response to questions posed by the Appellate Body, Venezuela and Brazil confirmed that they, indeed, were not appealing the mentioned two matters. They went on, however, to state that they believed it would be within the scope of authority of the Appellate Body, if it found it necessary to do so, to address the results of the Panel's examination of those two issues.

In its Post-Hearing Memorandum, the United States asserted, among other things, that were the Appellate Body to take up the above two matters in the present appeal, unfairness would be generated *vis-à-vis* the United States and it would encourage a disregard of the *Working Procedures*. Such disregard by the Appellate Body would, it was further stated, create difficulties for third parties who would have to make up their minds to become third participants or not on the basis of the issues raised on appeal as set out in the Notice of Appeal and the Appellant's Submission. The United States itself had not raised the clean air issue and the applicability of the *TBT Agreement* in its appeal, and the United States was the only Appellant in AB-1996-1.

We find the United States' submissions on this preliminary question persuasive. The arguments raised by Venezuela and Brazil on the clean air and TBT issues may be seen to be, in effect, conditional appeals, that is, conditional on the Appellate Body's overturning the Panel's overall findings on Article XX(g) and not finding in favour of Venezuela and Brazil as to the other requirements of Article XX. This condition is not fulfilled. Even if this condition had been fulfilled, the Appellate Body would have been most reluctant to pass upon these two issues. We observe, in the first place, that the issues in fact raised by the Appellant, the United States, are not of the kind which cannot be decided without at the same time necessarily resolving the clean air issue or the applicability of the *TBT Agreement*. In the second place, to deal with those two issues, under the circumstances of this appeal, would have required the Appellate Body casually to disregard its own *Working Procedures* and to do so in the absence of a compelling reason grounded on, for instance, fundamental fairness or *force majeure*. Venezuela and Brazil could have appealed the Panel's finding and non-finding on the two matters by taking advantage of Rules 23(1) or 23(4) of the *Working Procedures* and thereby placing the Appellate Body in a position to dispose of those issues directly in one and the same appellate proceeding.

The acceptance by Venezuela and Brazil of the *Working Procedures*, and their commitment to them, is not in question. We have no option, however, but to find that the route they chose for addressing the two issues in question is not contemplated by the *Working Procedures*, and therefore, these issues are not properly the subject of this appeal.

III.   THE ISSUE OF JUSTIFICATION UNDER ARTICLE XX(G) OF THE GENERAL AGREEMENT

Article XX(g) needs to be set out in full:

Article XX

General Exceptions

Subject to the requirement that such measures are not applied in a manner which would constitute a means of arbitrary or unjustifiable discrimination between countries where the same conditions prevail, or a disguised restriction on international trade, nothing in this Agreement shall be construed to prevent the adoption or enforcement by any contracting party of measures:

. . .

(g)   relating to the conservation of exhaustible natural resources if such measures are made effective in conjunction with restrictions on domestic production or consumption;

. . .

A.   *"Measures"*

The initial issue we are asked to look at relates to the proper meaning of the term "measures" as used both in the chapeau of Article XX and in Article XX(g). The question is whether "measures" refers to the entire Gasoline Rule or, alternatively, only to the particular provisions of the Gasoline Rule which deal with the establishment of baselines for domestic refiners, blenders and importers.

Cast in the foregoing terms, the issue does not appear to be a live one. True enough the Panel Report used differing terms, or terms of shifting reference, in designating the "measures" in different parts of the Report. The Panel Report, however, held only the baseline establishment rules of the Gasoline Rule to be inconsistent with Article III:4, to the extent that such rules provided "less favourable treatment" for imported than for domestic gasoline. These are the same provisions which the Panel evaluated, and found wanting, under the justifying provisions of Article XX(g). The Panel Report did not purport to find the Gasoline Rule itself as a whole, or any part thereof other than the baseline establishment rules, to be inconsistent with Article III:4; accordingly, there was no need at all to examine whether the whole of the Gasoline Rule or any of its other rules, was saved or justified by Article XX(g). The Panel here was following the practice of earlier panels in applying Article XX to provisions found to be inconsistent with Article III:4: the "measures" to be analyzed under Article XX are the same provisions infringing Article III:4.[28] These earlier panels had not interpreted "meas-

---

[28]   *Canada - Administration of the Foreign Investment Review Act*, BISD 30S/140, adopted 7 February 1984; *United States - Section 337 of the Tariff Act of 1930*, BISD 36S/345, adopted 7 November 1989; *United States - Taxes on Automobiles*, DS31/R (1994), unadopted.

ures" more broadly under Article XX to include provisions not themselves found inconsistent with Article III:4. In the present appeal, no one has suggested in their final submissions that the Appellate Body should examine under Article XX any portion of the Gasoline Rule other than the baseline establishment rules held to be in conflict with Article III:4. No one has urged an interpretation of "measures" which would encompass the Gasoline Rule in its totality.[29]

At the oral hearing and in its Post-Hearing Memorandum, the United States complained about the designation of the baseline establishment rules in the Panel Report and by the Appellees Venezuela and Brazil, in such terms as "the difference in treatment", "the less favourable treatment" or "the discrimination." It is, of course, true that the baseline establishment rules had been found by the Panel to be inconsistent with Article III:4 of the *General Agreement*. The frequent designation of those provisions by the Panel in terms of its legal conclusion in respect of Article III:4, in the Appellate Body's view, did not serve the cause of clarity in analysis when it came to evaluating the same baseline establishment rules under Article XX(g).

B. "relating to the conservation of exhaustible natural resources"

The Panel Report took the view that clean air was a "natural resource" that could be "depleted." Accordingly, as already noted earlier, the Panel concluded that a policy to reduce the depletion of clean air was a policy to conserve an exhaustible natural resource within the meaning of Article XX(g). Shortly thereafter, however, the Panel Report also concluded that "the less favourable baseline establishments methods" were *not* primarily aimed at the conservation of exhaustible natural resources and thus fell outside the justifying scope of Article XX(g).

The Panel, addressing the task of interpreting the words "relating to", quoted with approval the following passage from the panel report in the 1987 *Herring and Salmon* case:[30]

> as the preamble of Article XX indicates, the purpose of including Article XX:(g) in the General Agreement was not to widen the

---

[29] Although, in earlier submissions to the Appellate Body, the United States suggested that "the Gasoline Rule" should be examined in the context of Article XX(g), in its Post-Hearing Memorandum, dated 1 April 1996, the United States confirmed its understanding that the "measures" in issue are the baseline establishment rules contained in the Gasoline Rule.

Brazil stated, in its final submission to the Appellate Body, dated 1 April 1996, that "the 'measure' with which this appeal is concerned is the baseline methodology of the Gasoline Rule, not the entire rule itself." This would suggest a position similar to that adopted by the United States. Thereafter, Brazil continued to state that "Brazil and Venezuela did not challenge all portions of the Rule; they challenged only the discriminatory methods of establishing baselines."

Venezuela stated, in its summary statement, dated 29 March 1996, that "the measure to be examined is the discriminatory measure, that is, the aspect of the Gasoline Rule that denies imported gasoline the right to use the same regulatory system of baselines applicable to U.S. gasoline, namely, the system of individual baselines."

[30] *Canada - Measures Affecting Exports of Unprocessed Herring and Salmon*, BISD 35S/98, para. 4.6; adopted on 22 March 1988, cited in Panel Report, para. 6.39.

scope for measures serving trade policy purposes but merely to ensure that the commitments under the General Agreement do not
hinder the pursuit of policies aimed at the conservation of exhaus-
tive natural resources. The Panel concluded for these reasons that,
while a trade measure did not have to be necessary or essential to
the conservation of an exhaustible natural resource, it had to be
primarily aimed at the conservation of an exhaustible natural resource to be considered as "relating to" conservation within the
meaning of Article XX:(g). (emphasis added by the Panel)

The Panel Report then went on to apply the 1987 *Herring and Salmon*
reasoning and conclusion to the baseline establishment rules of the Gasoline Rule
in the following manner:[31]

The Panel then considered whether the precise aspects of the
Gasoline Rule that it had found to violate Article III -- the less favourable baseline establishments methods that adversely affected
the conditions of competition for imported gasoline -- were primarily aimed at the conservation of natural resources. The Panel
saw no direct connection between less favourable treatment of imported gasoline that was chemically identical to domestic gasoline,
and the US objective of improving air quality in the United States.
Indeed, in the view of the Panel, being consistent with the obligation to provide no less favourable treatment would not prevent the
attainment of the desired level of conservation of natural resources
under the Gasoline Rule. Accordingly, it could not be said that the
baseline establishment methods that afforded less favourable
treatment to imported gasoline were primarily aimed at the conservation of natural resources. In the Panel's view, the above-noted
lack of connection was underscored by the fact that affording
treatment of imported gasoline consistent with its Article III:4 obligations would not in any way hinder the United States in its pursuit of its conservation policies under the Gasoline Rule. Indeed,
the United States remained free to regulate in order to obtain whatever air quality it wished. The Panel therefore concluded that the
less favourable baseline establishments methods at issue in this
case were not primarily aimed at the conservation of natural resources.

It is not easy to follow the reasoning in the above paragraph of the Panel
Report. In our view, there is a certain amount of opaqueness in that reasoning.
The Panel starts with positing that there was "*no direct connection*" between the
baseline establishment rules which it characterized as "less favourable treatment"
of imported gasoline that was chemically identical to the domestic gasoline and
"the US objective of improving air quality in the United States." Shortly thereafter, the Panel went on to conclude that "*accordingly, it could not be said that the*

---

[31] Panel Report, para. 6.40.

baseline establishment rules that afforded less favourable treatment to imported gasoline *were primarily aimed at* the conservation of natural resources" (emphasis added). The Panel did not try to clarify whether the phrase "direct connection" was being used as a synonym for "primarily aimed at" or whether a new and additional element (on top of "primarily aimed at") was being demanded.

One problem with the reasoning in that paragraph is that the Panel asked itself whether the "less favourable treatment" of imported gasoline was "primarily aimed at" the conservation of natural resources, rather than whether the "measure", i.e. the baseline establishment rules, were "primarily aimed at" conservation of clean air. In our view, the Panel here was in error in referring to its legal conclusion on Article III:4 instead of the measure in issue. The result of this analysis is to turn Article XX on its head. Obviously, there had to be a finding that the measure provided "less favourable treatment" under Article III:4 before the Panel examined the "General Exceptions" contained in Article XX. That, however, is a conclusion of law. The chapeau of Article XX makes it clear that it is the "measures" which are to be examined under Article XX(g), and not the legal finding of "less favourable treatment."

Furthermore, the Panel Report appears to have utilized a conclusion it had reached earlier in holding that the baseline establishment rules did not fall within the justifying terms of Articles XX(b); i.e. that the baseline establishment rules were not "necessary" for the protection of human, animal or plant life. The Panel Report, it will be recalled, found that the baseline establishment rules had not been shown by the United States to be "necessary" under Article XX(b) since alternative measures either consistent or less inconsistent with the *General Agreement* were reasonably available to the United States for achieving its aim of protecting human, animal or plant life.[32] In other words, the Panel Report appears to have applied the "necessary" test not only in examining the baseline establishment rules under Article XX(b), but also in the course of applying Article XX(g).

A principal difficulty, in the view of the Appellate Body, with the Panel Report's application of Article XX(g) to the baseline establishment rules is that the Panel there overlooked a fundamental rule of treaty interpretation. This rule has received its most authoritative and succinct expression in the *Vienna Convention on the Law of Treaties* (the "*Vienna Convention*")[33] which provides in relevant part:

Article 31

General rule of interpretation

1.   A treaty shall be interpreted in good faith in accordance with the ordinary meaning to be given to the terms of the treaty in their context and in the light of its object and purpose.

---

[32]   Panel Report, paras. 6.25-6.28.
[33]   (1969), 8 *International Legal Materials* 679.

The "general rule of interpretation" set out above has been relied upon by all of the participants and third participants, although not always in relation to the same issue. That general rule of interpretation has attained the status of a rule of customary or general international law.[34] As such, it forms part of the "customary rules of interpretation of public international law" which the Appellate Body has been directed, by Article 3(2) of the *DSU*, to apply in seeking to clarify the provisions of the *General Agreement* and the other "covered agreements" of the *Marrakesh Agreement Establishing the World Trade Organization*[35] (the "*WTO Agreement*"). That direction reflects a measure of recognition that the *General Agreement* is not to be read in clinical isolation from public international law.

Applying the basic principle of interpretation that the words of a treaty, like the *General Agreement*, are to be given their ordinary meaning, in their context and in the light of the treaty's object and purpose, the Appellate Body observes that the Panel Report failed to take adequate account of the words actually used by Article XX in its several paragraphs. In enumerating the various categories of governmental acts, laws or regulations which WTO Members may carry out or promulgate in pursuit of differing legitimate state policies or interests outside the realm of trade liberalization, Article XX uses different terms in respect of different categories:

"necessary" - in paragraphs (a), (b) and (d); "essential" - in paragraph (j);

"relating to" - in paragraphs (c), (e) and (g); "for the protection of" - in paragraph (f);

"in pursuance of" - in paragraph (h); and "involving" - in paragraph (i).

It does not seem reasonable to suppose that the WTO Members intended to require, in respect of each and every category, the same kind or degree of connection or relationship between the measure under appraisal and the state interest or policy sought to be promoted or realized.

At the same time, Article XX(g) and its phrase, "relating to the conservation of exhaustible natural resources," need to be read in context and in such a manner as to give effect to the purposes and objects of the *General Agreement*. The context of Article XX(g) includes the provisions of the rest of the *General Agreement*, including in particular Articles I, III and XI; conversely, the context of Articles I and III and XI includes Article XX. Accordingly, the phrase "relating to the conservation of exhaustible natural resources" may not be read so expansively as seriously to subvert the purpose and object of Article III:4. Nor may

---

[34] See, *e.g., Territorial Dispute Case (Libyan Arab Jamahiriya v. Chad),* (1994), *I.C.J. Reports* p. 6 (International Court of Justice); *Golder v. United Kingdom, ECHR, Series A,* (1995) no. 18 (European Court of Human Rights); *Restrictions to the Death Penalty Cases,* (1986) 70 *International Law Reports* 449 (Inter-American Court of Human Rights); Jiménez de Aréchaga, "International Law in the Past Third of a Century" (1978-I) 159 *Recueil des Cours* 1, p. 42; D. Carreau, *Droit International* (3è ed., 1991) p. 140; *Oppenheim's International Law* (9th ed., Jennings and Watts, eds. 1992) Vol. 1, pp. 1271-1275.

[35] Done at Marrakesh, Morocco, 15 April 1994.

Article III:4 be given so broad a reach as effectively to emasculate Article XX(g) and the policies and interests it embodies. The relationship between the affirmative commitments set out in, *e.g.*, Articles I, III and XI, and the policies and interests embodied in the "General Exceptions" listed in Article XX, can be given meaning within the framework of the *General Agreement* and its object and purpose by a treaty interpreter only on a case-to-case basis, by careful scrutiny of the factual and legal context in a given dispute, without disregarding the words actually used by the WTO Members themselves to express their intent and purpose.

The 1987 *Herring and Salmon* report, and the Panel Report itself, gave some recognition to the foregoing considerations of principle. As earlier noted, the Panel Report quoted the following excerpt from the *Herring and Salmon* report:

> as the preamble of Article XX indicates, the purpose of including Article XX(g) in the General Agreement was not to widen the scope for measures serving trade policy purposes but merely *to ensure that the commitments under the General Agreement do not hinder the pursuit of policies* aimed at the conservation of exhaustible natural resources.[36] (emphasis added)

All the participants and the third participants in this appeal accept the propriety and applicability of the view of the *Herring and Salmon* report and the Panel Report that a measure must be "primarily aimed at" the conservation of exhaustible natural resources in order to fall within the scope of Article XX(g).[37] Accordingly, we see no need to examine this point further, save, perhaps, to note that the phrase "primarily aimed at" is not itself treaty language and was not designed as a simple litmus test for inclusion or exclusion from Article XX(g).

Against this background, we turn to the specific question of whether the baseline establishment rules are appropriately regarded as "primarily aimed at" the conservation of natural resources for the purposes of Article XX(g). We consider that this question must be answered in the affirmative.

The baseline establishment rules, taken as a whole (that is, the provisions relating to establishment of baselines for domestic refiners, along with the provisions relating to baselines for blenders and importers of gasoline), need to be related to the "non-degradation" requirements set out elsewhere in the Gasoline Rule. Those provisions can scarcely be understood if scrutinized strictly by themselves, totally divorced from other sections of the Gasoline Rule which certainly constitute part of the context of these provisions. The baseline establishment rules whether individual or statutory, were designed to permit scrutiny and monitoring of the level of compliance of refiners, importers and blenders with the "non-degradation" requirements. Without baselines of some kind, such scrutiny would not be possible and the Gasoline Rule's objective of stabilizing and pre-

---

[36] *Canada - Measures Affecting Exports of Unprocessed Herring and Salmon*, BISD 35S/98, para. 4.6; adopted 22 March 1988, cited in Panel Report, para. 6.39.
[37] We note that the same interpretation has been applied in two recent unadopted panel reports: *United States - Restrictions on Imports of Tuna*, DS29/R (1994); *United States - Taxes on Automobiles*, DS31/R (1994).

venting further deterioration of the level of air pollution prevailing in 1990, would be substantially frustrated. The relationship between the baseline establishment rules and the "non-degradation" requirements of the Gasoline Rule is not negated by the inconsistency, found by the Panel, of the baseline establishment rules with the terms of Article III:4. We consider that, given that substantial relationship, the baseline establishment rules cannot be regarded as merely incidentally or inadvertently aimed at the conservation of clean air in the United States for the purposes of Article XX(g).

C.   "if such measures are made effective in conjunction with restrictions on domestic production or consumption"

The Panel did not find it necessary to deal with the issue of whether the baseline establishment rules "are made effective in conjunction with restrictions on domestic production or consumption", since it had earlier concluded that those rules had not even satisfied the preceding requirement of "relating to" in the sense of being "primarily aimed at" the conservation of clean air. Having been unable to concur with that earlier conclusion of the Panel, we must now address this second requirement of Article XX(g), the United States having, in effect, appealed from the failure of the Panel to proceed further with its inquiry into the availability of Article XX(g) as a justification for the baseline establishment rules.

The claim of the United States is that the second clause of Article XX(g) requires that the burdens entailed by regulating the level of pollutants in the air emitted in the course of combustion of gasoline, must not be imposed solely on, or in respect of, imported gasoline.

On the other hand, Venezuela and Brazil refer to prior panel reports which include statements to the effect that to be deemed as "made effective in conjunction with restrictions on domestic production or consumption", a measure must be "primarily aimed at" making effective certain restrictions on domestic production or consumption.[38] Venezuela and Brazil also argue that the United States has failed to show the existence of restrictions on domestic production or consumption of a natural resource under the Gasoline Rule since clean air was not an exhaustible natural resource within the meaning of Article XX(g). Venezuela contends, finally, that the United States has not discharged its burden of showing that the baseline establishment rules make the United States' regulatory scheme "effective." The claim of Venezuela is, in effect, that to be properly regarded as "primarily aimed at" the conservation of natural resources, the baseline establishment rules must not only "reflect a conservation purpose" but also be shown to have had "some positive conservation effect."[39]

---

[38]   *Canada - Measures Affecting Exports of Unprocessed Herring and Salmon*, BISD 35S/98, paras. 4.6-4.7; adopted 22 March 1988. Also, *United States - Restrictions on Imports of Tuna*, DS29/R (1994), unadopted; and *United States - Taxes on Automobiles*, DS31/R (1994), unadopted.

[39]   Venezuela's Appellee's Submission, dated 18 March 1996; Venezuela's Statement at the Oral Hearing, dated 27 March 1996.

The Appellate Body considers that the basic international law rule of treaty interpretation, discussed earlier, that the terms of a treaty are to be given their ordinary meaning, in context, so as to effectuate its object and purpose, is applicable here, too. Viewed in this light, the ordinary or natural meaning of "made effective" when used in connection with a measure - a governmental act or regulation -may be seen to refer to such measure being "operative", as "in force", or as having "come into effect."[40] Similarly, the phrase "in conjunction with" may be read quite plainly as "together with" or "jointly with."[41] Taken together, the second clause of Article XX(g) appears to us to refer to governmental measures like the baseline establishment rules being promulgated or brought into effect together with restrictions on domestic production or consumption of natural resources. Put in a slightly different manner, we believe that the clause "if such measures are made effective in conjunction with restrictions on domestic product or consumption" is appropriately read as a requirement that the measures concerned impose restrictions, not just in respect of imported gasoline but also with respect to domestic gasoline. The clause is a requirement of *even-handedness* in the imposition of restrictions, in the name of conservation, upon the production or consumption of exhaustible natural resources.

There is, of course, no textual basis for requiring identical treatment of domestic and imported products. Indeed, where there is identity of treatment - constituting real, not merely formal, equality of treatment - it is difficult to see how inconsistency with Article III:4 would have arisen in the first place. On the other hand, if *no* restrictions on domestically-produced like products are imposed at all, and all limitations are placed upon imported products *alone*, the measure cannot be accepted as primarily or even substantially designed for implementing conservationist goals.[42] The measure would simply be naked discrimination for protecting locally-produced goods.

In the present appeal, the baseline establishment rules affect both domestic gasoline and imported gasoline, providing for - generally speaking - individual baselines for domestic refiners and blenders and statutory baselines for importers. Thus, restrictions on the consumption or depletion of clean air by regulating the domestic production of "dirty" gasoline are established jointly with corresponding restrictions with respect to imported gasoline. That imported gasoline has been determined to have been accorded "less favourable treatment"

---

[40] *The New Shorter Oxford English Dictionary on Historical Principles* (L. Brown, ed., 1993), Vol. I, p. 786.

[41] *Id.*, p. 481.

[42] Some illustration is offered in the *Herring and Salmon* case which involved, *inter alia*, a Canadian prohibition of exports of unprocessed herring and salmon. This prohibition effectively constituted a ban on purchase of certain unprocessed fish by foreign processors and consumers while imposing no corresponding ban on purchase of unprocessed fish by domestic processors and consumers. The prohibitions appeared to be designed to protect domestic processors by giving them exclusive access to fresh fish and at the same time denying such raw material to foreign processors. The Panel concluded that these export prohibitions were not justified by Article XX(g). BISD 35S/98, para. 5.1, adopted 22 March 1988. See also the Panel Report in the *United States - Prohibition of Imports of Tuna and Tuna Products from Canada*, BISD 29S/91, paras. 4.10-4.12; adopted on 22 February 1982.

than the domestic gasoline in terms of Article III:4, is not material for purposes of analysis under Article XX(g). It might also be noted that the second clause of Article XX(g) speaks disjunctively of "domestic production *or* consumption."

We do not believe, finally, that the clause "if made effective in conjunction with restrictions on domestic production or consumption" was intended to establish an empirical "effects test" for the availability of the Article XX(g) exception. In the first place, the problem of determining causation, well-known in both domestic and international law, is always a difficult one. In the second place, in the field of conservation of exhaustible natural resources, a substantial period of time, perhaps years, may have to elapse before the effects attributable to implementation of a given measure may be observable. The legal characterization of such a measure is not reasonably made contingent upon occurrence of subsequent events. We are not, however, suggesting that consideration of the predictable effects of a measure is never relevant. In a particular case, should it become clear that realistically, a specific measure cannot in any possible situation have any positive effect on conservation goals, it would very probably be because that measure was not designed as a conservation regulation to begin with. In other words, it would not have been "primarily aimed at" conservation of natural resources at all.

IV.   THE INTRODUCTORY PROVISIONS OF ARTICLE XX OF THE GENERAL AGREEMENT: APPLYING THE CHAPEAU OF THE GENERAL EXCEPTIONS

Having concluded, in the preceding section, that the baseline establishment rules of the Gasoline Rule fall within the terms of Article XX(g), we come to the question of whether those rules also meet the requirements of the chapeau of Article XX. In order that the justifying protection of Article XX may be extended to it, the measure at issue must not only come under one or another of the particular exceptions - paragraphs (a) to (j) - listed under Article XX; it must also satisfy the requirements imposed by the opening clauses of Article XX. The analysis is, in other words, two-tiered: first, provisional justification by reason of characterization of the measure under XX(g); second, further appraisal of the same measure under the introductory clauses of Article XX.

The chapeau by its express terms addresses, not so much the questioned measure or its specific contents as such, but rather the manner in which that measure is applied.[43] It is, accordingly, important to underscore that the purpose and object of the introductory clauses of Article XX is generally the prevention of "abuse of the exceptions of [what was later to become] Article [XX]."[44] This insight drawn from the drafting history of Article XX is a valuable one. The chapeau is animated by the principle that while the exceptions of Article XX may be

---

[43]   This was noted in the Panel Report on *United States - Imports of Certain Automotive Spring Assemblies*, BISD 30S/107, para. 56; adopted on 26 May 1983.

[44]   EPCT/C.11/50, p. 7; quoted in *Analytical Index: Guide to GATT Law and Practice*, Volume I, p. 564 (1995).

invoked as a matter of legal right, they should not be so applied as to frustrate or defeat the legal obligations of the holder of the right under the substantive rules of the *General Agreement*. If those exceptions are not to be abused or misused, in other words, the measures falling within the particular exceptions must be applied reasonably, with due regard both to the legal duties of the party claiming the exception and the legal rights of the other parties concerned.

The burden of demonstrating that a measure provisionally justified as being within one of the exceptions set out in the individual paragraphs of Article XX does not, in its application, constitute abuse of such exception under the chapeau, rests on the party invoking the exception. That is, of necessity, a heavier task than that involved in showing that an exception, such as Article XX(g), encompasses the measure at issue.

The enterprise of applying Article XX would clearly be an unprofitable one if it involved no more than applying the standard used in finding that the baseline establishment rules were inconsistent with Article III:4. That would also be true if the finding were one of inconsistency with some other substantive rule of the *General Agreement*. The provisions of the chapeau cannot logically refer to the same standard(s) by which a violation of a substantive rule has been determined to have occurred. To proceed down that path would be both to empty the chapeau of its contents and to deprive the exceptions in paragraphs (a) to (j) of meaning. Such recourse would also confuse the question of whether inconsistency with a substantive rule existed, with the further and separate question arising under the chapeau of Article XX as to whether that inconsistency was nevertheless justified. One of the corollaries of the "general rule of interpretation" in the *Vienna Convention* is that interpretation must give meaning and effect to all the terms of a treaty. An interpreter is not free to adopt a reading that would result in reducing whole clauses or paragraphs of a treaty to redundancy or inutility.[45]

The chapeau, it will be seen, prohibits such application of a measure at issue (otherwise falling within the scope of Article XX(g)) as would constitute

(a)   "arbitrary discrimination" (between countries where the same conditions prevail);

(b)   "unjustifiable discrimination" (with the same qualifier); or

(c)   "disguised restriction" on international trade.

The text of the chapeau is not without ambiguity, including one relating to the field of application of the standards its contains: the arbitrary or unjustifiable discrimination standards and the disguised restriction on international trade standard. It may be asked whether these standards do not have different fields of ap-

---

[45]   *E.g., Corfu Channel* Case (1949) *I.C.J. Reports*, p.24 (International Court of Justice); Territorial Dispute Case (Libyan Arab Jamahiriya v. Chad) (1994) *I.C.J. Reports*, p. 23 (International Court of Justice); 1966 *Yearbook of the International Law Commission*, Vol. II at 219; *Oppenheim's International Law* (9th ed., Jennings and Watts eds., 1992), Volume 1, 1280-1281; P. Dallier and A. Pellet, *Droit International Public*, 5è ed. (1994) para. 17.2); D. Carreau, *Droit International*, (1994) para. 369.

plication. Such a question was put to the United States in the course of the oral hearing. It was asked whether the words incorporated into the first two standards "between countries where the same conditions prevail" refer to conditions in importing and exporting countries, or only to conditions in exporting countries. The reply of the United States was to the effect that it interpreted that phrase as referring to both the exporting countries and importing countries and as between exporting countries. It also said that the language spoke for itself, but there was no reference to third parties; while some thought that this was only between exporting countries *inter se,* there is no support in the text for that view. No such question was put to the United States concerning the field of application of the third standard - disguised restriction on international trade. But the United States put forward arguments designed to show that in the case under appeal, it had met all the standards set forth in the chapeau. In doing so, it clearly proceeded on the assumption that, whatever else they might relate to in another case, they were relevant to a case of national treatment where the Panel had found a violation of Article III:4. At no point in the appeal was that assumption challenged by Venezuela or Brazil. Venezuela argued that the United States had failed to meet all the standards contained in the chapeau. So did Norway and the European Communities as third participants. In short, the field of application of these standards was not at issue.

The assumption on which all the participants proceeded is buttressed by the fact that the chapeau says that "*nothing in this Agreement* shall be construed to prevent the adoption or enforcement by any contracting party of measures ..." The exceptions listed in Article XX thus relate to all of the obligations under the *General Agreement*: the national treatment obligation and the most-favoured-nation obligation, of course, but others as well. Effect is more easily given to the words "nothing in this Agreement", and Article XX as a whole including its chapeau more easily integrated into the remainder of the *General Agreement*, if the chapeau is taken to mean that the standards it sets forth are applicable to all of the situations in which an allegation of a violation of a substantive obligation has been made and one of the exceptions contained in Article XX has in turn been claimed.

Against this background, we see no need to decide the matter of the field of application of the standards set forth in the chapeau nor to make a ruling at variance with the common understanding of the participants.[46]

---

[46] We note in this connection that two previous panels had occasion to apply the chapeau. In *United States - Imports of Certain Automotive Spring Assemblies,* BISD 30S/107; adopted on 26 May 1983, the panel had before it a ban on imports, and an exclusion order of the United States' International Trade Commission, of certain automotive spring assemblies which the Commission had found, under Section 337 of the Tariff Act of 1930, to have infringed valid United States patents. The panel there held that the exclusion order had *not* been applied in a manner which would constitute a means of "arbitrary or unjustifiable discrimination against countries where the same conditions prevail," because that order was directed against imports of infringing assemblies "from all foreign sources, and not just from Canada." At the same time, the same order was also examined and found *not* to be "a disguised restriction on international trade." Id., paras. 54-56. See also *United*

"Arbitrary discrimination", "unjustifiable discrimination" and "disguised restriction" on international trade may, accordingly, be read side-by-side; they impart meaning to one another. It is clear to us that "disguised restriction" includes disguised *discrimination* in international trade. It is equally clear that *concealed* or *unannounced* restriction or discrimination in international trade does *not* exhaust the meaning of "disguised restriction." We consider that "disguised restriction", whatever else it covers, may properly be read as embracing restrictions amounting to arbitrary or unjustifiable discrimination in international trade taken under the guise of a measure formally within the terms of an exception listed in Article XX. Put in a somewhat different manner, the kinds of considerations pertinent in deciding whether the application of a particular measure amounts to "arbitrary or unjustifiable discrimination", may also be taken into account in determining the presence of a "disguised restriction" on international trade. The fundamental theme is to be found in the purpose and object of avoiding abuse or illegitimate use of the exceptions to substantive rules available in Article XX.

There was more than one alternative course of action available to the United States in promulgating regulations implementing the CAA. These included the imposition of statutory baselines without differentiation as between domestic and imported gasoline. This approach, if properly implemented, could have avoided any discrimination at all. Among the other options open to the United States was to make available individual baselines to foreign refiners as well as domestic refiners. The United States has put forward a series of reasons why either of these courses was not, in its view, realistically open to it and why, instead, it had to devise and apply the baseline establishment rules contained in the Gasoline Rule.

In explaining why individual baselines for foreign refiners had not been put in place, the United States laid heavy stress upon the difficulties which the EPA would have had to face. These difficulties related to anticipated administrative problems that individual baselines for foreign refiners would have generated. This argument was made succinctly by the United States in the following terms:

> Verification on foreign soil of foreign baselines, and subsequent enforcement actions, present substantial difficulties relating to problems arising whenever a country exercises enforcement juris-

---

States - Prohibition of Imports of Tuna and Tuna Products, BISD 29S/91, para. 4.8; adopted 22 February 1982.

It may be observed that the term "countries" in the chapeau is textually unqualified; it does not say "foreign countries", as did Article 4 of the 1927 League of Nations *International Convention for the Abolition of Import and Export Prohibitions and Restrictions*, 97 L.N.T.S. 393. Neither does the chapeau say "third countries" as did, *e.g.*, bilateral trade agreements negotiated by the United States under the 1934 *Reciprocal Trade Agreements Act*; *e.g.* the *Trade Agreement between the United States of America and Canada*, 15 November 1935, 168 L.N.T.S. 356 (1936). These earlier treaties are here noted, not as pertaining to the *travaux préparatoires* of the *General Agreement*, but simply to show how in comparable treaties, a particular intent was expressed with words not found in printer's ink in the *General Agreement*.

diction over foreign persons. In addition, even if individual baselines were established for several foreign refiners, the importer would be tempted to claim the refinery of origin that presented the most benefits in terms of baseline restrictions, and tracking the refinery or origin would be very difficult because gasoline is a fungible commodity. The United States should not have to prove that it cannot verify information and enforce its regulations in every instance in order to show that the same enforcement conditions do not prevail in the United States and other countries ... The impracticability of verification and enforcement of foreign refiner baselines in this instance shows that the "discrimination" is based on serious, not arbitrary or unjustifiable, concerns stemming from different conditions between enforcement of its laws in the United States and abroad.[47]

Thus, according to the United States, imported gasoline was relegated to the more exacting statutory baseline requirement because of these difficulties of verification and enforcement. The United States stated that verification and enforcement of the Gasoline Rule's requirements for imported gasoline are "much easier when the statutory baseline is used" and that there would be a "dramatic difference" in the burden of administering requirements for imported gasoline if individual baselines were allowed.[48]

While the anticipated difficulties concerning verification and subsequent enforcement are doubtless real to some degree, the Panel viewed them as insufficient to justify the denial to foreign refiners of individual baselines permitted to domestic refiners. The Panel said:

> While the Panel agreed that it would be necessary under such a system to ascertain the origin of gasoline, the Panel could not conclude that the United States had shown that this could not be achieved by other measures reasonably available to it and consistent or less inconsistent with the General Agreement. Indeed, the Panel noted that a determination of origin would often be feasible. The Panel examined, for instance, the case of a direct shipment to the United States. It considered that there was no reason to believe that, given the usual measures available in international trade for determination of origin and tracking of goods (including documentary evidence and third party verification) there was any particular difficulty sufficient to warrant the demands of the baseline establishment methods applied by the United States.[49]

---

[47] Para. 55 of the Appellant's Submission, dated 4 March 1996. The United States was in effect making the same point when, at pages 11 and 12 of its Post-Hearing Memorandum, it argued that the conditions were not the same as between the United States, on the one hand, and Venezuela and Brazil on the other.

[48] Supplementary responses by the United States to certain questions of the Appellate Body, dated 1 April 1996.

[49] Panel Report, para. 6.26.

. . .

In the view of the Panel, the United States had reasonably available to it data for, and measures of, verification and assessment which were consistent or less inconsistent with Article III:4. For instance, although foreign data may be formally less subject to complete control by US authorities, this did not amount to establishing that foreign data could not in any circumstances be sufficiently reliable to serve U.S. purposes. This, however, was the practical effect of the application of the Gasoline Rule. In the Panel's view, the United States had not demonstrated that data available from foreign refiners was inherently less susceptible to established techniques of checking, verification, assessment and enforcement than data for other trade in goods subject to US regulation. The nature of the data in this case was similar to data relied upon by the United States in other contexts, including, for example, under the application of antidumping laws. In an antidumping case, only when the information was not supplied or deemed unverifiable did the United States turn to other information. If a similar practice were to be applied in the case of the Gasoline Rule, then importers could, for instance, be permitted to use the individual baselines of foreign refiners for imported gasoline from those refiners, with the statutory baseline being applied only when the source of imported gasoline could not be determined or a baseline could not be established because of an absence of data.[50]

We agree with the finding above made in the Panel Report. There are, as the Panel Report found, established techniques for checking, verification, assessment and enforcement of data relating to imported goods, techniques which in many contexts are accepted as adequate to permit international trade - trade between territorial sovereigns - to go on and grow. The United States must have been aware that for these established techniques and procedures to work, cooperative arrangements with both foreign refiners and the foreign governments concerned would have been necessary and appropriate. At the oral hearing, in the course of responding to an enquiry as to whether the EPA could have adapted, for purposes of establishing individual refinery baselines for foreign refiners, procedures for verification of information found in U.S. antidumping laws, the United States said that "in the absence of refinery cooperation and the possible absence of foreign government cooperation as well", it was unlikely that the EPA auditors would be able to conduct the on-site audit reviews necessary to establish even the overall quality of refineries' 1990 gasoline.[51] From this statement, there arises a strong implication, it appears to the Appellate Body, that the United States had not pursued the possibility of entering into cooperative arrangements with the governments of Venezuela and Brazil or, if it had, not to the point where

---

[50] Panel Report, para. 6.28.
[51] Supplementary responses to the United States to certain questions of the Appellate Body, dated 1 April 1996.

it encountered governments that were unwilling to cooperate. The record of this case sets out the detailed justifications put forward by the United States. But it does not reveal what, if any, efforts had been taken by the United States to enter into appropriate procedures in cooperation with the governments of Venezuela and Brazil so as to mitigate the administrative problems pleaded by the United States.[52] The fact that the United States Congress might have intervened, as it did later intervene, in the process by denying funding, is beside the point: the United States, of course, carries responsibility for actions of both the executive and legislative departments of government.

In its submissions, the United States also explained why the statutory baseline requirement was not imposed on domestic refiners as well. Here, the United States stressed the problems that domestic refineries would have faced had they been required to comply with the statutory baseline. The Panel Report summarized the United States' argument in the following terms:

> The United States concluded that, contrary to Venezuela's and Brazil's claim, Article XX did not require adoption of the statutory baseline as a national standard even if the difficulties associated with the establishment of individual baselines for importers were insurmountable. Application of the statutory baseline to domestic producers of reformulated and conventional gasoline in 1995 would have been *physically and financially impossible because of the magnitude of the changes required in almost all US refineries; it thus would have caused a substantial delay in the program.* Weighing the feasibility of policy options in economic or technical terms in order to meet an environmental objective was a legitimate consideration, and did not, in itself, constitute protectionism, as alleged by Venezuela and Brazil. Article XX did not require a government to choose the most expensive possible way to regulate its environment.[53] (emphasis added)

Clearly, the United States did not feel it feasible to require its domestic refiners to incur the physical and financial costs and burdens entailed by immediate compliance with a statutory baseline. The United States wished to give do-

---

[52] While it is not for the Appellate Body to speculate where the limits of effective international cooperation are to be found, reference may be made to a number of precedents that the United States (and other countries) have considered it prudent to use to help overcome problems confronting enforcement agencies by virtue of the fact that the relevant law and the authority of the enforcement of the agency does not hold sway beyond national borders. During the course of the oral hearing, attention was drawn to the fact that in addition to the antidumping law referred to by the Panel in the passage cited above, there were other US regulatory laws of this kind, *e.g.*, in the field of anti-trust law, securities exchange law and tax law. There are cooperative agreements entered into by the US and other governments to help enforce regulatory laws of the kind mentioned and to obtain data from abroad. There are such agreements, *inter alia*, in the anti-trust and tax areas. There are also, within the framework of the WTO, the *Agreement on the Implementation of Article VI of GATT 1994*, (the *"Antidumping Agreement"*), the *Agreement on Subsidies and Countervailing Measures* (the *"SCM Agreement"*) and the *Agreement on Pre-Shipment Inspection*, all of which constitute recognition of the frequency and significance of international cooperation of this sort.

[53] Panel Report, para. 3.52.

mestic refiners time to restructure their operations and adjust to the requirements in the Gasoline Rule. This may very well have constituted sound domestic policy from the viewpoint of the EPA and U.S. refiners. At the same time we are bound to note that, while the United States counted the costs for its domestic refiners of statutory baselines, there is nothing in the record to indicate that it did other than disregard that kind of consideration when it came to foreign refiners.

We have above located two omissions on the part of the United States: to explore adequately means, including in particular cooperation with the governments of Venezuela and Brazil, of mitigating the administrative problems relied on as justification by the United States for rejecting individual baselines for foreign refiners; and to count the costs for foreign refiners that would result from the imposition of statutory baselines. In our view, these two omissions go well beyond what was necessary for the Panel to determine that a violation of Article III:4 had occurred in the first place. The resulting discrimination must have been foreseen, and was not merely inadvertent or unavoidable. In the light of the foregoing, our conclusion is that the baseline establishment rules in the Gasoline Rule, in their application, constitute "unjustifiable discrimination" and a "disguised restriction on international trade." We hold, in sum, that the baseline establishment rules, although within the terms of Article XX(g), are not entitled to the justifying protection afforded by Article XX as a whole.

V. FINDINGS AND CONCLUSIONS

For the reasons set out in the preceding sections of this report, the Appellate Body has reached the following conclusions:

(a) the Panel erred in law in its conclusion that the baseline establishment rules contained in Part 80 of Title 40 of the Code of Federal Regulations did not fall within the terms of Article XX(g) of the *General Agreement*;

(b) the Panel accordingly also erred in law in failing to decide whether the baseline establishment rules contained in Part 80 of Title 40 of the Code of Federal Regulations fell within the ambit of the chapeau of Article XX of the *General Agreement*;

(c) the baseline establishment rules contained in Part 80 of Title 40 of the Code of Federal Regulations fail to meet the requirements of the chapeau of Article XX of the *General Agreement*, and accordingly are not justified under Article XX of the *General Agreement*.

The foregoing legal conclusions modify the conclusions of the Panel as set out in paragraph 8.1 of its Report. The Appellate Body's conclusions leave intact the conclusions of the Panel that were not the subject of appeal.

The Appellate Body *recommends* that the Dispute Settlement Body request the United States to bring the baseline establishment rules contained in Part 80 of Title 40 of the Code of Federal Regulations into conformity with its obligations under the *General Agreement*.

It is of some importance that the Appellate Body point out what this does *not* mean. It does not mean, or imply, that the ability of any WTO Member to take measures to control air pollution or, more generally, to protect the environment, is at issue. That would be to ignore the fact that Article XX of the *General Agreement* contains provisions designed to permit important state interests - including the protection of human health, as well as the conservation of exhaustible natural resources - to find expression. The provisions of Article XX were not changed as a result of the Uruguay Round of Multilateral Trade Negotiations. Indeed, in the preamble to the *WTO Agreement* and in the *Decision on Trade and Environment*,[54] there is specific acknowledgement to be found about the importance of coordinating policies on trade and the environment. WTO Members have a large measure of autonomy to determine their own policies on the environment (including its relationship with trade), their environmental objectives and the environmental legislation they enact and implement. So far as concerns the WTO, that autonomy is circumscribed only by the need to respect the requirements of the *General Agreement* and the other covered agreements.

---

[54] Adopted by Ministers at the Meeting of the Trade Negotiations Committee in Marrakesh on 14 April 1994.

UNITED STATES - STANDARDS FOR REFORMULATED AND CONVENTIONAL GASOLINE

Report of the Panel
WT/DS2/R

Adopted by the Dispute Settlement Body on 20 May 1996
as modified by the Appellate Body Report

TABLE OF CONTENTS

I.   INTRODUCTION

1.1   On 23 January 1995, the United States received a request from Venezuela to hold consultations under Article XXII:1 of the General Agreement on Tariffs and Trade 1994 ("General Agreement"), Article 14.1 of the Agreement on Technical Barriers to Trade ("TBT Agreement") and Article 4 of the Understanding on Rules and Procedures Governing the Settlement of Disputes ("DSU"), on the rule issued by the Environmental Protection Agency on 15 December 1993, entitled "Regulation of Fuels and Fuel Additives - Standards for Reformulated and Conventional Gasoline" (WT/DS2/1). The consultations between Venezuela and the United States took place on 24 February 1995. As they did not result in a satisfactory solution of the matter, Venezuela, in a communication dated 25 March 1995, requested the Dispute Settlement Body ("DSB") to establish a panel to examine the matter under Article XXIII:2 of the General Agreement and Article 6 of the DSU (WT/DS2/2). On 10 April 1995, the DSB established a panel in accordance with the request made by Venezuela. On 28 April 1995, the parties to the dispute agreed that the Panel should have standard terms of reference (DSU, Art. 7) and agreed on the composition of the Panel as follows:

    Chairman: Mr. Joseph Wong

    Members: Mr. Crawford Falconer

                   Mr. Kim Luotonen

1.2   On 10 April 1995, Brazil requested the United States to hold consultations under Article XXII:1 of the General Agreement, Article 14.1 of the TBT Agreement and Article 4 of the DSU on the rule issued by the Environmental Protection Agency on 15 December 1993 entitled "Regulation on Fuels and Fuel Additives - Standards for Reformulated and Conventional Gasoline" (WT/DS4/1). Consultations between Brazil and the United States were held on 1 May 1995 without resulting in a satisfactory solution of the matter. In a communication dated 19 May 1995, Brazil requested the DSB to establish a panel to examine the matter pursuant to Article XXIII of the General Agreement, Article 14 of the Agreement on Technical Barriers to Trade and Article 6 of the DSU. On 31 May 1995, the DSB established a Panel in accordance with the request made by Brazil.

1.3   On 31 May 1995, pursuant to Article 9 of the DSU in respect of multiple complainants, the DSB decided, with the agreement of all the parties, that for practical reasons this matter be examined by the Panel already established at the request of Venezuela on 10 April 1995. The date of the constitution of the Panel, namely 28 April 1995, remained unchanged.

1.4   Due to the additional task given to the Panel, the DSB agreed upon, at the same meeting, the following terms of reference:

> "To examine, in the light of the relevant provisions of the covered agreements cited by Venezuela in document WT/DS2/2 and by Brazil in document WT/DS4/2, the matters referred to the DSB by Venezuela and Brazil in those documents and to make such findings as will assist the DSB in making the recommendations or in giving the rulings provided for in those agreements".

1.5   The Chairman of the DSB recalled Article 9.2 of the DSU which provides that "the rights which the parties to the dispute would have enjoyed had separate panels examined the complaints are in no way impaired".

1.6   Australia, Canada, the European Communities and Norway reserved their rights to participate in the Panel proceedings as third parties. Only the European Communities and Norway presented arguments to the Panel.

1.7   The Panel met with the parties to the dispute from 10 to 12 July 1995 and from 13 to 15 September 1995. It met with the interested third parties on 11 July 1995.

1.8   On 21 September 1995, the Chairman of the Panel informed the DSB that the Panel would not be able to issue its report within six months. The reasons for that delay are stated in document WT/DS2/5.

1.9   The Panel issued its interim report to the parties on 11 December 1995. Following a request made by the United States pursuant to Article 15.2 of the DSU, the Panel held a further meeting with the parties on 3 January 1996.

1.10   The Panel issued its final report to the parties to the dispute on 17 January 1996.

II.   FACTUAL ASPECTS

A.   The Clean Air Act

2.1   The Clean Air Act ("CAA"), originally enacted in 1963, aims at preventing and controlling air pollution in the United States. In a 1990 amendment to the CAA,[1] Congress directed the Environmental Protection Agency ("EPA") to promulgate new regulations on the composition and emissions effects of gasoline in order to improve air quality in the most polluted areas of the country by reducing vehicle emissions of toxic air pollutants and ozone-forming volatile organic compounds. These new regulations apply to US refiners, blenders and importers.

2.2   Section 211(k) of the CAA divides the market for sale of gasoline in the United States into two parts. The first part, which covers approximately 30 percent of gasoline marketed in the United States, consists of the nine large metropolitan areas that experienced the worst summertime ozone pollution during the

---

[1]   42 U.S.C. §7545(k).

period 1987-1989, plus any areas that do not meet national ozone requirements and are added at the request of the governor of the state. These areas are referred to as ozone "nonattainment areas", and in this part of the United States only "reformulated gasoline" may be sold to consumers. In the rest of the United States, "conventional gasoline" may be sold to consumers.

2.3   Section 211(k)(2)-(3) of the CAA established certain compositional and performance specifications for reformulated gasoline. The oxygen content must not be less than 2.0 percent by weight, the benzene content must not exceed 1.0 percent by volume and the gasoline must be free of heavy metals, including lead or manganese. The performance specifications of the CAA require a 15 percent reduction in the emissions of both volatile organic compounds ("VOCs") and toxic air pollutants ("toxics") and no increase in emissions of nitrogen oxides ("NOx"). These requirements are measured by comparing the performance of reformulated gasoline in baseline vehicles (representative model year 1990 vehicles) against the performance of "baseline gasoline" in such vehicles. Section 211(k)(10) of the CAA defines the specifications of baseline gasoline sold in the summer, which is the high ozone season, and leaves the specifications of winter baseline gasoline to be determined by EPA. It provides, however, that the specifications for winter gasoline shall be those of the industry average gasoline sold in 1990. For the year 2000 and beyond, the CAA requires that new reformulated gasoline requirements be developed that require a 20-25 percent reduction in emissions of VOCs and toxics, depending on EPA's considerations of feasibility and cost.

2.4   The CAA also sets requirements for conventional gasoline, which ensure that each refiner's, blender's or importer's conventional gasoline sold in the rest of the country remains as clean as it was in 1990. This programme is known as "anti-dumping rules" because it is designed to prevent refiners, blenders or importers from dumping into conventional gasoline fuel components that are restricted in reformulated gasoline and that cause environmentally harmful emissions. To accomplish this, section 211(k)(8) of the CAA provides that no refiner, blender or importer of gasoline may sell conventional gasoline that emits VOCs, toxics, NOx or carbon monoxide ("pollutants") in greater amounts than the gasoline sold in the United States by that refiner, blender or importer in 1990. In order to implement this provision, separate individual baselines must be established for refiners, blenders or importers based on the gasoline they sold in 1990. That permits determination of whether the emissions from a refiner's, blender's and importer's conventional gasoline (post-1994 gasoline) are greater than the emissions from its 1990 gasoline. If, however, EPA determines that no adequate and reliable data exist regarding the composition of such 1990 gasoline sold by a refiner, blender or importer, the statutory baseline gasoline is applied. The statutory annual baseline values are calculated using a seasonal weighting of the statutory summer baseline, as defined in the CAA, and the statutory winter baseline, as determined by EPA.

B.   EPA's Gasoline Rule

1.   Establishment of Baselines

2.5   The CAA directed EPA to determine the quality of 1990 gasoline, to which reformulated and conventional gasoline would be compared in the future: these determinations are known as "baselines". EPA set historic baselines for individual entities, and established a statutory baseline, intended to reflect average US 1990 gasoline quality, which would be used instead of the historic individual baselines for those entities who were determined to be lacking adequate and reliable data regarding the quality of the gasoline they produced in 1990.

2.6   EPA's final rule[2] ("Gasoline Rule") requires any domestic refiner, which was in operation for at least 6 months in 1990, to establish an individual refinery baseline, which represents the quality of gasoline produced by that refiner in 1990. The rule establishes three methods for the purpose of determining a domestic refiner's individual historic baseline. Under Method 1, the refiner must use the quality data and volume records of its 1990 gasoline. However, as acknowledged by EPA at the time, it was not anticipated that many domestic refiners would have all the data necessary to establish an individual baseline based entirely on actual 1990 data. If Method 1 type data are not available, a domestic refiner must use its 1990 gasoline blendstock quality data and 1990 blendstock production records (Method 2). In the event that neither one of these two methods is available, a domestic refiner must turn to Method 3 type data which consist of its post-1990 gasoline blendstock and/or gasoline quality data modeled in light of refinery changes to show 1990 gasoline composition. Domestic refiners are not permitted to choose the statutory baseline.

2.7   An importer which is also a foreign refiner must determine its individual baseline using Methods 1, 2 and 3 if it imported at least 75 percent, by volume, of the gasoline produced at its foreign refinery in 1990 into the United States in 1990 (the so-called "75 % rule").[3]

2.8   Certain entities are, however, automatically assigned to the statutory baseline. Firstly, refineries which began operation after 1990 or were in operation for less than 6 months in 1990 are required to use the statutory baseline. Secondly, importers and blenders are assigned the statutory baseline unless they can establish their individual baseline following Method 1. If actual 1990 data are not available, which is, as for domestic refiners, anticipated by EPA, importers and blenders are assigned to the statutory baseline. EPA considers that blenders which produce gasoline by combining gasoline blendstocks purchased from many sources cannot determine with accuracy the quality of their 1990 gasoline using Methods 2 and 3. Similarly, EPA considers that importers cannot use Methods 2 and 3, because these methods inherently apply only to refineries and because of the extreme difficulty in establishing the consistency of their gasoline quality over time.

---

[2]   40 CFR 80, 59-Fed. Reg. 7716 (16 February 1994).
[3]   40 CFR 80.91(b)(ii).

2. *Reformulated Gasoline*

2.9   Regarding the implementation of the regulations for reformulated gasoline, EPA proposes a two-step approach. From 1 January 1995 to 1 January 1998, EPA enforces an interim programme called the "Simple Model". Under this programme, reformulated gasoline sold in the United States by domestic refiners will be subject to requirements established with reference to the individual baseline for certain gasoline qualities and requirements specified in the Gasoline Rule for other gasoline qualities. More specifically, the parameters sulphur, olefins and T-90 are measured against each US refiner's individual 1990 baseline and must be maintained at or below these 1990 levels (these are called "non-degradation requirements"). The requirements regarding four other gasoline qualities (Reid Vapour Pressure, oxygen, benzene and toxics performance) are specified by EPA in the Gasoline Rule.[4] Importers of foreign gasoline also have to comply with the requirements set out in the final rule regarding Reid Vapour Pressure, oxygen, benzene and toxics performance. However, importers cannot use individual 1990 baseline for sulphur, olefins and T-90, but have to comply with levels specified in the statutory baseline for these parameters. Under the Simple Model, requirements for sulphur, olefins and T-90 must be met on an annual average basis. EPA adopted the individual baseline approach for these parameters in the Simple Model because at the time it was formulating its regulation, it considered that the available data regarding sulphur, olefins and T-90 did not permit an assessment of the precise effects of these components on the emissions level of gasoline. Given this uncertainty, EPA did not want to require refiners immediately to make refinery changes which might later prove to be unnecessary, given the greater flexibility provided by the Complex Model.

2.10   As of 1 January 1998, EPA will enforce the "Complex Model", which will apply the same emissions reduction requirements to all producers of reformulated gasoline. The individual baselines for sulphur, olefins and T-90 will no longer apply.

3. *Conventional Gasoline (or "Anti-Dumping Rules")*

2.11   The 1990 Amendment to the CAA requires that, as of 1 January 1995, each refiner's, blender's or importer's conventional gasoline sold in the United States be no more polluting than the gasoline sold by that refiner, blender or importer in 1990.[5] EPA requires domestic refiners to measure non-degradation requirements for conventional gasoline against their individual baselines while importers of foreign gasoline are assigned to the statutory baseline. However, in this programme, the non-degradation requirements apply to all conventional gasoline requirements, and not only to sulphur, olefins and T-90. Requirements must be met on an average annual basis. The Gasoline Rule limits ("caps") the volume of conventional gasoline that is subject to an individual baseline to the volume of

---

[4]   40 CFR 80.41.
[5]   42 U.S.C. § 7545 (CAA 211(k)(8)).

gasoline produced in 1990 by that entity; all conventional gasoline produced in excess of the specific volume cap is measured against the statutory baseline.

2.12   Domestic refiners and importers of conventional gasoline, unlike those of reformulated gasoline, will still be subject to different baselines after the entry into force of the Complex Model in 1998.

C.   The May 1994 Proposal

2.13   In view of the comments made by interested parties during the rulemaking process of the final Gasoline Rule, EPA proposed, in May 1994, to amend the reformulated gasoline regulation in order to define criteria and procedures by which foreign refiners could establish individual refinery baselines in a manner similar to that required for domestic refiners.[6] Pursuant to this proposal, foreign refiners would be allowed to establish an individual baseline using Methods 1, 2 or 3. If the individual baseline was approved by EPA, importers could use it for the purpose of certifying the portion of reformulated gasoline imported from that particular refinery into the United States. However, the use of individual foreign refinery baselines would be subject to various additional strict requirements, aiming at ensuring the accuracy and respect of the foreign refinery's individual baseline with respect to gasoline shipped to the United States and verifying the refinery of origin. Furthermore, it would not apply to conventional gasoline. After a public comment period, the US Congress enacted legislation in September 1994 denying funding to EPA for implementation of the May 1994 Proposal.

III.   MAIN ARGUMENTS

A.   General

3.1   Venezuela and Brazil requested the Panel to find that the final rule promulgated by the United States' Environmental Protection Agency ("EPA") on 15 December 1993 and entitled "Fuels and Fuel Additives - Standards for Reformulated and Conventional Gasoline" ("Gasoline Rule") was:

(a)   contrary to Articles I and III of GATT 1994;

(b)   not covered by any of the exceptions under Article XX of GATT 1994;

(c)   contrary to Article 2 of the Agreement on Technical Barriers to Trade.

3.2   Venezuela additionally requested the Panel to find that the Gasoline Rule nullified and impaired benefits accruing to Venezuela under the General Agreement within the meaning of Article XXIII:1(b).

3.3   Accordingly, Venezuela and Brazil asked the Panel to recommend that the United States take all necessary steps to bring the Gasoline Rule into conformity with its obligations under the General Agreement and the TBT Agreement.

---

[6]   40 CFR 80 (59 Fed. Reg. 22800, 3 May 1994).

Venezuela requested the Panel to recommend that the United States amend the Gasoline Rule to provide treatment for gasoline imports no less favourable than that accorded to US produced gasoline.

3.4   The United States requested the Panel to find that the Gasoline Rule was:

(a)   consistent with Articles I and III of the General Agreement 1994;

(b)   falling within the scope of Article XX (b), (d), and (g) of GATT 1994;

(c)   consistent with the Agreement on Technical Barriers to Trade.

B.   The General Agreement on Tariffs and Trade

1.   Article I - General Most-Favoured-Nation Treatment

3.5   Venezuela and Brazil argued that the rule allowing an importer which was also a foreign refiner to establish its individual baseline, provided that it imported into the United States at least 75 percent of the gasoline produced at that refinery in 1990 ("75 % rule"), granted an advantage to gasoline exported from certain third countries in violation of Article I of the General Agreement.

3.6   Venezuela argued that the 75 % rule applied only to a fixed, finite and easily determinable group of countries, determined only by historical facts. Hence, no importer or foreign refiner could take any action that would alter its ability to benefit from this rule. According to information submitted to Venezuela by the United States, refineries based in Canada only were likely to meet the criteria. A previous panel report had found that the European Community's meat quality regulations requiring certification of imported beef by the US Department of Agriculture were inconsistent with Article I of the General Agreement because "[E]xports of like products of other origin than that of the United States were in effect denied access to the EEC market considering that the only certifying agency authorized to certify the meat ... was a United States agency mandated to certify only meat from the United States".[7] As a matter of fact, only certain countries could benefit from this provision. This was, accordingly, a breach of Article I.

3.7   Brazil submitted that the two criteria contained in the 75 % rule, i.e. the owner relationship between the importer and the foreign refiner and the percentage of gasoline it imported into the United States, were not neutral but had been chosen so as to suit a particular category of countries and therefore constituted an "advantage" within the meaning of Article I. These criteria had no link with the characteristics of gasoline as a product. Thus, the 75 % rule applied a different and more favourable standard to imports from some foreign refineries than it applied to imports from refineries in other countries.

3.8   The United States replied that the 75 % rule did not provide an "advantage" to the products of any particular country. The 75 % rule would have ap-

---

[7]   "European Economic Community - Imports of Beef From Canada", BISD 28S/92 (adopted on 10 March 1981), paragraph 4.2(a).

plied to any importer that could meet its two objective criteria, regardless of the country of origin of the gasoline. The United States specified that the 75 % requirement represented the minimally acceptable value to ensure that the importer's individual baseline determined under Methods 1, 2 and 3 would be accurate. (In fact, most foreign refiners were unlikely to export more than 30 % of their gasoline). Secondly, the criterion requiring that the importer and foreign refiner be the same entity eliminated the enforcement concerns arising in relation with the establishment of an individual baseline for a foreign refiner. The United States considered that Venezuela's invocation of the panel report "European Economic Community - Imports of Beef From Canada" was inapposite because, in that dispute, the EC regulation at issue expressly listed the US Department of Agriculture (USDA) as the only certifying authority for the meat in question, and USDA was only authorized to certify US meat. In that case, the certifying process itself guaranteed that only US beef would be certified, thereby expressly favouring US beef over that of all other countries. In contrast, the 75 % rule expressly requires any importer that meets its objective criteria to establish an individual baseline for its gasoline. The United States also noted that the regulatory deadline for individual baseline applications under the 75 % rule had elapsed without any company meeting the criteria. The 75 % rule had no application and could therefore not be inconsistent with any provisions of the General Agreement.

3.9   Venezuela considered that the United States interpreted too narrowly the panel report "EEC - Imports of Beef From Canada" when saying that the favoured country must be expressly identified in order for the regulation to violate Article I. A rule violated Article I when it stipulated, like the 75 % rule, that the products of only some countries could qualify.

3.10   Venezuela and Brazil considered that the fact that the 75 % rule had no application should not prevent the Panel from ruling on it. Venezuela considered that the mere existence of such a regulation might have inhibiting effects on commercial and investment decisions. Thus, the possibility of its future application was sufficient to establish an Article I violation. Brazil added that a clear ruling on the 75 % rule was necessary because it would dissuade countries from designing future standards that, being neutral at first sight, were in fact designed to fit only the precise situation of their own multinationals, thus threatening the integrity of Article I.

2.   *Article III - National Treatment on Internal Taxation and Regulation*

a)   Article III:4

3.11   Venezuela and Brazil stressed that they were not questioning the right of the United States to enact stringent environmental standards and regulations in order to improve air quality within the US territory provided these standards and regulations treated imported products no less favourably than domestic like products.

3.12   Venezuela and Brazil argued that the Gasoline Rule, by denying foreign refiners the possibility to establish an individual baseline, violated Article III:4

because it accorded less favourable treatment to imported gasoline, both reformulated and conventional, than to US gasoline. The Gasoline Rule required imported gasoline to conform with the more stringent statutory baseline when US
gasoline had to comply only with a US refiner's individual baseline. Practically,
this meant that imported gasoline with certain parameter levels above the statutory baseline could not be directly sold in the US market whereas gasoline with
these same qualities produced in a US refinery could be freely sold on the US
market provided that it conformed with that refiner's individual baseline. In order
to accommodate this situation, foreign refiners had two options: (i) make expensive investments and changes to their refineries in order to produce gasoline conforming to the more stringent statutory baseline, or (ii) supply at a lower price
gasoline to an importer that could average that gasoline with other gasolines (if
such other gasolines exist in sufficient amount) in order to meet, over an annual
period, the requirements of the statutory baseline. Both options adversely affected the conditions of competition for imported gasoline and afforded protection to domestic production in a manner contrary to Article III. Furthermore,
these adverse competitive effects were precisely what EPA intended to avoid for
US refiners by granting them individual baselines. Brazil added that it was up to
the United States to demonstrate that its discriminatory system did not treat imports less favourably.

3.13   Venezuela and Brazil held that officials from the US government had acknowledged on various occasions that the Gasoline Rule discriminated against
imported gasoline and accorded more favourable treatment to domestically produced gasoline. Venezuela added that another US government official had pub-
licly stated that such discrimination was intentionally endorsed as a means of
affording protection to US gasoline. These statements showed that the Gasoline
Rule discriminated both in effect and in intent against foreign refiners. Venezuela
and Brazil further argued that EPA's 1994 proposed amendments to the Gasoline
Rule ("1994 Proposal") acknowledged that the discriminatory treatment of imported gasoline was inconsistent with the United States' obligations under the
General Agreement. Venezuela and Brazil argued that the 1994 Proposal would
have partly eliminated the discrimination by providing for the establishment of
individual baselines by foreign refiners of reformulated gasoline; however, the
discriminatory treatment of conventional gasoline would have continued.

3.14   Venezuela noted that "Petroleos de Venezuela, S.A." ("PDVSA") had
already made costly adjustments to its production in order to meet the statutory
baseline requirements and had accelerated its programme of investments with a
view to complying with the Complex Model requirements. These adjustments
had reduced the volume and value of Venezuela's current and anticipated gasoline exports to the United States below the levels that would have prevailed if
PDVSA were allowed to establish its individual baseline. These adjustments in-
terfered with PDVSA's investment programme, obliging it to focus on production
for the US gasoline market and adversely affecting other important investment
projects.

3.15   Brazil stated in addition that application of the statutory baseline to foreign refiners and domestic importers was discriminatory in several respects. First,
the flexibility given to domestic refiners in establishing individual baselines had

the effect that many of them were allowed emissions levels higher than those permitted by the statutory baseline. Secondly, the statutory baseline was more stringent than the average of the individual baselines for refineries located in the Eastern and Gulf Coast states (where virtually all Brazilian gasoline was sold) because of the inclusion in the national average of the strict 1990 Californian standards. The Gasoline Rule also favoured imports by domestic refiners over imports by importers who were not domestic refiners. Domestic refiners whose current production was "cleaner" than their individual baseline could import gasoline with parameter levels above the statutory baseline, could blend it with their own cleaner production and sell it on the US market as long as the mixture conformed with their individual baseline. Importers who were not domestic refiners had to conform to the statutory baseline in all instances. Thus, the Gasoline Rule affected the distribution of gasoline in the United States by channelling imports to domestic refiners who had an incentive to take advantage of their privileged position by demanding lower prices from foreign refiners.

3.16   Brazil stated that the same gasoline that it used to export to the United States market as "finished" gasoline was, since the entry into force of the Gasoline Rule, considered only as "blendstock",[8] which was sold at a lower price. Thus, Brazil had not been able to export "finished" conventional gasoline to the US market since 1 January 1995. Brazilian refiners were not currently producing reformulated gasoline .

3.17   The United States replied that the Gasoline Rule did not treat imported gasoline less favourably than domestic gasoline overall. The environmental goal of the Gasoline Rule was to regulate the overall quality of the gasoline sold in the United States. Each importer had to satisfy on average the statutory baseline, which approximated average gasoline quality consumed in the US in 1990, and domestic refiners had to satisfy on average their 1990 individual baselines, which overall roughly represented 1990 US gasoline quality. Hence, overall domestically produced gasoline had to be at least as clean as foreign gasoline since roughly half of domestic gasoline would be "cleaner" and roughly half would be dirtier than gasoline using the statutory baseline. The United States supplied the Panel with data documenting the number of domestic refiners with baseline values both above and below the statutory baseline for specific parameters and emissions levels upon which compliance with the non-degradation requirements was based. This analysis showed that five domestic refineries had individual baselines that were below the annual statutory baseline for all fuel parameters and emissions levels, and three domestic refiners had individual baselines that were above the annual statutory baseline for all fuel parameters and emissions levels. Thus, most refiners had individual baselines with several parameters above the corresponding statutory values and several below. The United States considered that a previous panel report had recognized that "there may be cases where application of formally identical legal provisions would in practice accord less favourable treatment to imported products and a contracting party might thus have to

---

[8]   Blendstock is unfinished gasoline which has to be blended in order to be sold as finished gasoline.

apply different legal provisions to imported products to ensure that the treatment accorded them is in fact no less favourable".[9] Since the majority of importers did not have the necessary data to use Methods 1, 2, or 3, they would be precluded from supplying the US market as they would be unable to establish an individual baseline. In fact, the Gasoline Rule granted more favourable treatment to imports since identical treatment would have in practice excluded imported gasoline from the US market.

3.18   The United States argued that the Gasoline Rule applied to imported gasoline and not to foreign refiners producing gasoline. Moreover, foreign refiners were not required to produce gasoline that met any baseline at all, but could produce gasoline which was cleaner or dirtier than the statutory baseline. The baseline establishment rule focused on the importer of foreign gasoline because the United States was not attempting to regulate the conduct of foreign companies or those of other overseas entities; the importer was the first entity, within US territory, that had control over the quality of gasoline imported into the United States. Thus, foreign refiners were subject only to the independent purchasing decisions of US importers who had to balance the products of one or more foreign refiners with that of another in order to comply with the statutory baseline. The fact that no single batch of gasoline would be deemed as non-complying provided additional flexibility to both importers and foreign refiners. Moreover, the complainants' focus on equal treatment of individual foreign refiners was misplaced since the General Agreement applied to the imported product and not to the producer.

3.19   The United States argued that gasoline from importers was treated similarly to gasoline from similarly situated domestic parties. For instance, imported gasoline was treated identically to gasoline produced by domestic refiners with limited 1990 operations or to gasoline produced by US blenders whose business entailed a lack of consistency of sources and quality of the gasoline produced. These producers had in common with the importers the inability to establish an accurate individual baseline because their business characteristics or history were such that they could not determine the quality of their gasoline as required by Methods 2 and 3. Although theoretically, the 1990 gasoline quality of an importer might be established by first determining the refineries of origin for all of the gasoline imported by that importer in 1990, and then obtaining accurate and verifiable information on the quality of that subset of 1990 gasoline produced at the refinery and exported to the particular US importer, the United States expected that only a very limited number of importers would be able to establish an individual baseline using such a procedure. In addition, there were significant problems associated with establishing the 1990 gasoline quality of foreign refiners: tracking the refinery of origin of the imported gasoline, establishing the quality of the small subset of gasoline shipped to the United States and lack of adequate enforcement capacity. According to the United States, these factors made it very difficult to verify the accuracy or reliability of claims regarding a

---

[9]   "United States - Section 337 of the Tariff Act of 1930", BISD 36S/345 (adopted on 7 November 1989).

foreign refiner's 1990 gasoline quality for that purpose. On the other hand, gasoline produced by domestic refiners was made from crude oil whose quality could easily be documented, as were the characteristics of the physical plant and operational procedures. Thus, the quality of the gasoline produced at such a domestic refinery could be accurately assessed. The United States further argued that imported gasoline and domestically produced gasoline were in the same position with regard to the flexibility for complying with their respective baselines. As various qualities of gasoline were available in the market, some above and some below the statutory baseline, an importer had complete flexibility to select gasoline from different sources and mix them in order to reach the annual average quality required by the statutory baseline. By contrast, a domestic refiner was constrained by its refinery equipment and crude oil supplies.

3.20   The United States considered that Venezuela was incorrect in its claim that the US government official's statement demonstrated that the Gasoline Rule had a protectionist purpose. The statement in question actually reflected the US government's commitment when it issued the final Gasoline Rule to continue addressing the issue of how imports were treated, and the US government's ongoing concern that environmental protection not be compromised. This statement also showed that the government official's objective was adoption of the best environmental provision that was fair to all parties concerned. The United States equally rejected Venezuela and Brazil's argument that the 1994 Proposal implied recognition that the Gasoline Rule discriminated against imports. The 1994 Proposal was a continuation of EPA's prior attempts to develop criteria that would protect the environment, minimize disruption to producers, and treat similarly situated parties alike. The fact that EPA was willing to make this attempt was neither a determination that the Gasoline Rule was flawed nor a determination that the 1994 Proposal was feasible. This proposal received largely negative public comment and was rejected in the end, including by Venezuela. PDVSA itself had objected that the proposed conditions related to gasoline tracking were basically unworkable.

3.21   The United States disagreed with Venezuela's claim about decreased imports. Data from the US Energy Information Administration showed that current import volumes had not significantly decreased from historical levels. Furthermore, import volume and domestic production fluctuated greatly depending on market conditions, irrespective of US regulatory action. More specifically, Venezuela's share of the US import market rose from 11.5 to 18.5 percent in the first five months of 1995 compared to the same period in 1994. Regarding the claim by Venezuela that the Gasoline Rule had obliged its refineries to make burdensome investments, the United States noted that it was impossible to judge to what extent PDVSA's investments were made in reaction to regulations, such as the Gasoline Rule, in force in any particular export market. If, however, PDVSA's investments were related to the Gasoline Rule, they were more likely due to the need to comply with the Complex Model starting in 1998 than to the 1995-1998 non-degradation requirements' programme. With respect to compliance with the Simple Model requirements, the United States considered that PDVSA could upgrade the portion of its gasoline output sent to the United States by simply adding to it additives such as oxygenates. In addition, the amount of complying gasoline that could be produced, or the cost of producing it, was highly dependent on the fraction of gasoline made to meet a particular specification. While a domestic refiner had to produce all its gasoline output within certain limits, foreign refiners typically produced only a small fraction of their gasoline output for the US market. Thus foreign refiners also had the flexibility to select their cleanest blendstocks for the US market. Such approaches did not require refinery modifications. There was no reason that Brazil could not adjust in the same manner to the Simple Model requirements. The United States also noted that reported internal turmoil in Brazil's refining sector, a month-long strike beginning in November 1994, and apparently recurring labour problems this year suggested that Brazil's decreased exports to the United States could hardly be attributed to US regulations.

3.22   Venezuela agreed with the United States that Article III applied to imported gasoline and not to the foreign refiners. The Gasoline Rule discriminated against imported gasoline by applying the statutory baseline to such gasoline while applying individual baselines to US gasoline. The United States wrongly introduced the concept of "similarly situated parties" as a basis for arguing that imported gasoline and US produced gasoline were not "like product". Imported and domestic gasolines had the same tariff classification, served the same end use and the same end users and were indistinguishable from the commercial standpoint; thus, all gasoline was a like product. The concept "similarly situated parties" was new to GATT and lacked a legal basis. Moreover, Venezuela considered that these parties were not "similarly situated". Importers, who obtained finished gasoline for distribution to other wholesalers or retailers were not "similarly situated" to blenders, who produced gasoline by mixing gasoline components produced by others. It was more appropriate to compare them to "jobbers" who obtained finished gasoline for distribution to other wholesalers or retailers and who used the individual baselines associated with the gasoline they acquired. Foreign refiners were "similarly situated parties" with respect to US refiners in that the reasons given by the United States as to why US refiners can establish their own baselines apply equally to foreign refiners.

3.23   Venezuela argued that the United States did not deny the existence of differential treatment for imported gasoline. Thus, it had to assume the burden of proving that such treatment was no less favourable to the imported product. According to past panel reports, the test was not whether the rules were different but whether such differences accorded no less favourable treatment to imported products. Venezuela considered that such a demonstration had not been made. Venezuela disagreed with the interpretation given by the United States to the panel report "United States - Section 337 of the Tariff Act of 1930" and considered that panels interpreted the words "treatment no less favourable" contained in Article III:4 as calling for effective equality of opportunities for imported products. The United States' assertion that it was "incumbent upon the importer to balance the products of one or more foreign refiners with that of another" was contrary to that established understanding of Article III:4. No such equality could exist if the very ability of a producer/exporter to introduce his product into the importer's market depended on the subsequent decisions of the importer to buy additional product produced and exported by another person. The opportunity to import a like product could not be conditional upon the importer's willingness to run a risk of not finding below-statutory baseline gasoline in order to average it with above-statutory baseline gasoline. Venezuela considered that the reasoning of two previous panel reports[10] regarding the loss of competitive opportunities for imported products was applicable to this case and led to the conclusion that imported gasoline should have the same distribution opportunities available to US produced gasoline, including the ability to be sold directly into commerce with the application of an individual baseline.

3.24   Venezuela considered that the issue at stake was not averaging, a technique which was also available to domestic refiners, but the difference between the requirements imposed on imported gasoline and the requirements imposed on US gasoline. In order to regulate the average quality of gasoline in the United States, the Gasoline Rule regulated every batch of gasoline produced in or imported into the US. The fact that the very same gasoline with identical characteristics would be treated differently under the Rule if produced by a US refiner as opposed to a foreign refiner was precisely the "less favourable treatment" prohibited under Article III:4.

3.25   Venezuela rejected the United States' assertion that a foreign refiner that produced gasoline in 1990 with properties of sulphur, olefins and T-90 above the statutory baseline only had to mix "additives such as oxygenates" to upgrade its gasoline; in fact, the very composition of the foreign gasoline had to change. Venezuela denied the United States' claim that Venezuela had rejected the 1994 Proposal. Venezuela had simply explained why some means by which the EPA proposed to achieve certain ends were not workable from a practical standpoint, and presented alternatives to achieve the same ends in a more practical and workable manner.

3.26   Brazil argued that the alleged benefit to imports deriving from the fact that "roughly half" of the domestic gasoline must be "cleaner" than imported gasoline (which, in Brazil's view had not been demonstrated) did not overcome the less favourable treatment accorded to imports deriving from the fact that "roughly half" of the domestic gasoline was permitted to be "dirtier" than imported gasoline. This statement by the United States implicitly admitted the discrimination contained in the Gasoline Rule which required imported gasoline to be cleaner than half of the domestically produced gasoline. Brazil noted that a previous panel report had rejected any notion of balancing more favourable treatment of some imported products against less favourable treatment of other imported products.[11] The same rationale applied to any notion of balancing more favourable treatment vis-à-vis some domestic products against less favourable treatment

---

[10]   "United States - Measures Affecting Alcoholic and Malt Beverages", BISD 39S/206 (adopted on 19 June 1992), and "Canada - Import, Distribution and Sale of Certain Alcoholic Beverages", BISD 39S/27 (adopted on 18 February 1992).
[11]   "United States - Section 337 of the Tariff Act of 1930", BISD 36S/345, (adopted on 7 November 1989).

vis-à-vis other domestic products. Similarly, another panel report[12] had concluded that the exposure of a particular imported product to a risk of discrimination constituted, by itself, a form of discrimination. The Gasoline Rule exposed all imports to less favourable treatment than the treatment accorded to what the United States had described as "roughly half" of the domestic production. Thus, in this dispute as in previous disputes, the panel should reject the notion of "balancing". Brazil further argued that the United States had not in any event demonstrated that the average of the individual baselines was equivalent to the statutory baseline. Domestic refiners were allowed to use post 1990 (Method 3) data to establish their individual baselines whereas the statutory baseline was presumably established based on actual 1990 data. This contradicted the US argument that importers were subject to an overall average standard which was equivalent to that imposed on domestic refiners because baselines based on data from different time periods could not be considered to be equivalent.

3.27   Brazil argued that United States' reference to the "Section 337" panel report was irrelevant since it had not demonstrated in this particular case that the application of formally identical legal provisions would in practice accord less favourable treatment to imported products. The United States only "believed" that granting individual baselines to foreign refiners would disadvantage them. Similarly, the United States had not demonstrated why US importers would not be able to establish an individual baseline following Method 3, based on post-1990 gasoline blendstock, since according to the United States, importers were blenders and used blendstocks. Finally, the comparison made by the United States between a foreign refiner and a US importer was inaccurate, for a foreign refiner had to be compared with a US domestic refiner.

3.28   Brazil rejected the argument that imported gasoline was treated similarly to gasoline from similarly situated parties. Imported gasoline produced by foreign refiners who had unlimited operations in 1990 was treated like gasoline produced by blenders and domestic refiners who had limited operations in 1990, whereas it should have been treated like gasoline produced by comparable US domestic refiners. Brazil further noted that most US blenders who were not domestic refiners were in fact importers, and hence should not, as argued by the United States, be considered as two separate categories. Thus, discriminating between domestic refiners and domestic importers in practice resulted in discriminating against imports. Moreover, the fact that domestic refiners were allowed to import blendstock, mix it with their own production and measure the compliance of the final product against their individual baseline, whereas neither blenders nor importers were allowed to do this with respect to their own blendstock, showed that the system did not treat like products in a similar way.

3.29   Brazil agreed with the United States that Article III applied to gasoline and not to the producer of gasoline. In this particular case, the standard applied to gasoline had been determined with reference to the producer of gasoline. Brazil

---

[12]   "EEC - Payments and Subsidies Paid to Processors and Producers of Oilseeds and Related Animal-Feed Proteins", BISD 37S/86 (adopted on 25 January 1990).

was not questioning this policy choice as such, but the fact that a different and less favourable standard applied to imported products. In the case of Brazil, this discrimination was illustrated by the fact that the gasoline exported by Brazil as "finished" conventional gasoline until 1 January 1995 was now considered as a mere "blendstock" because it did not meet the statutory baseline requirements. Blendstock gasoline commanded a lower price because the buyer had to mix it with "cleaner" gasoline in order to comply with the statutory baseline. In conclusion, Brazil stated that the fact that the product produced by a Brazilian refiner could not be sold in the United States as finished gasoline while the identical product produced by a US refiner complying with its individual baseline could be sold as finished gasoline constituted precisely the less favourable, discriminatory treatment Article III was intended to prohibit.

3.30   The United States argued that the complainants improperly focused on developing foreign refinery baselines, and had not demonstrated how foreign refiners could accurately ascertain the quality of the subset of their total gasoline production exported to the United States, even if they were able to establish the quality of their total 1990 output by using Methods 1, 2 or 3. Even assuming that this problem could be overcome by Venezuela and Brazil, it remained for other foreign refiners. By focusing on foreign refiners' baselines rather than on the more logical establishment of importers' baselines, the complainants appeared to seek a commercial advantage for their national oil companies over other foreign gasoline suppliers. This could favour those importers who had commercial ties to such refiners over others, and thereby distort competitive conditions among importers. The General Agreement did not require the United States to accord rights on foreign soil to foreign refiners, as opposed to WTO Members, especially if issues relating to imports could better be addressed through regulating importers who were located on US territory.

3.31   The United States further argued that the references made by Venezuela to previous panel reports were irrelevant because the situation currently under examination was different. The question posed to this Panel was not whether imports and domestic products were treated identically (the United States recognized that it was not the case), but whether that treatment was less favourable under Article III. Given the fact that, for the reasons stated above, an identical treatment would have precluded most importers from marketing gasoline in the United States, the specific provisions applying to imports did not violate Article III. The United States also rejected Brazil's claim that blenders were in fact importers and maintained that they did fall into two different categories, even if similarly situated in other respects. (Of the registered entities that were blenders or importers, over a third were solely blenders and over a third were solely importers.) The United States considered that the difficulties supposedly experienced by Venezuela and Brazil to export gasoline to the US market were groundless. Firstly, importers could easily find large amounts of gasoline with low levels of sulphur and olefin, thus "offsetting" Venezuela's high sulphur and olefin content, because of the typical configurations of refineries outside of the United States. This was evidenced by the clean imports of reformulated gasoline this year and by the fact that 1995 exports from Venezuela did not reflect an identifiable impact of the Gasoline Rule. Secondly, Brazil's choice not to export finished gasoline, but to export blendstock instead, was unrelated to US environmental regulations since the Gasoline Rule did not contain any requirements as to whether importers imported gasoline on the one hand, or blendstock on the other. The conventional and reformulated gasoline requirements did not aim at establishing whether a product was or was not gasoline. Rather, to be sold as "gasoline", commercial contracts generally required a product to meet certain standards established by the American Society of Testing and Materials. Regarding the alleged reduced export volumes from the complainants, the United States noted that import levels in a given market were generally sensitive to various factors (US demand, exporting country's supply and demand, refinery cost structure, gasoline market conditions in other competing exporting countries, for instance), and that worldwide exports of gasoline to the United States had been following a downward trend over the last five years. It was equally difficult to know the exact role played by the Gasoline Rule with regard to the investment programme of Venezuelan refineries since any refiner operating at the world level needed a significant reformer capacity. Venezuela's investment in such a reformer unit likely reflected overall Venezuelan market strategy. Moreover, whatever production limitations PDVSA might have with respect to one particular refiner, blending of feedstock from several refineries made higher levels of statutory-quality gasoline on a per-shipment basis possible. In addition, the US government had studied refinery cost structure shortly after passage of the Clean Air Act and found that refiners whose production of reformulated gasoline was about 30% or less of their total gasoline production could produce the reformulated gasoline at little or no incremental cost (i.e. investment costs) because of their ability to select among blendstocks.

3.32   The United States argued that, with respect to the particular baseline to be employed by domestic refiners that import, the Rule's requirement that refiners use their own baselines applied only to conventional gasoline, and up to the volume that the refiner imported in 1990. The purpose of the provision was to prevent a domestic refiner with a baseline more stringent that the statutory baseline from avoiding that stringent baseline by exporting gasoline produced at the domestic refinery and then reimporting that same gasoline under the statutory baseline, a concern raised to EPA in public comments.

3.33   Venezuela argued it was not focusing on foreign refiners but on the situation of imported gasoline. The foreign refiner had become an issue only because the characteristics of US produced gasoline set by the Gasoline Rule was determined, in large part, by the historical quality levels of the individual US producers. Venezuela considered that it was misleading to engage, as the United States did, in a discussion of the relative situation of importers and domestic refiners when comparing the respective treatment of domestic and imported products. The focus of the analysis had to remain on gasoline as a product. The previous panel cases cited by Venezuela were relevant because the situations were similar. Venezuela disagreed with the United States' argument that importers could easily obtain suitable offsetting gasoline for Venezuela's gasoline quality. The data presented by the United States to the Panel regarding the properties of gasoline imported in 1995 suggested exactly the contrary: by showing that the maximum values of sulphur, olefins and T-90 of imported gasoline were essentially at the statutory baseline, these data confirmed that above-statutory foreign gasoline was not purchased by US importers. Thus, foreign refiners were effectively obliged to comply with the statutory baseline requirements if they wanted to sell gasoline in the United States.

b)   Article III:1

3.34   Venezuela and Brazil claimed that discriminatory baseline requirements contained in the Gasoline Rule violated Article III:1 for the same reasons they violated Article III:4. By distorting the conditions of competition for foreign gasoline, both reformulated and conventional, they were applied "so as to afford protection to domestic production". Venezuela also noted that Article III:1 was a more general provision than Article III:4. Thus, it would not insist on the panel ruling on Article III:1 if the Panel found the Gasoline Rule to be inconsistent with Article III:4.

3.35   The United States replied that, for the reasons expressed under Article III:4, the Gasoline Rule did not afford protection to domestic production. Furthermore, since Article III:1 had by itself only an exhortatory character, it was not amenable to a finding of "violation" in a dispute settlement proceeding. A Panel had never found an independent violation of Article III:1.

3.36   Brazil argued that previous disputes,[13] to which the United States had been a party, involved a violation of Article III:1.

3.   *Article XX - General Exceptions*

3.37   The United States argued that the Gasoline Rule fell within the scope of Article XX whether or not it was consistent with other provisions of the General Agreement. Not all measures described by Article XX were inconsistent with the General Agreement. However, if the Panel accepted that the Gasoline Rule was consistent with other provisions of the General Agreement, in particular Article III, it did not need to decide whether the measures at issue also fell under Article XX. Article XX guaranteed in any event that these measures were not inconsistent with the General Agreement.

3.38   Venezuela and Brazil considered that the issue at stake under Article XX was not whether the CAA or the regulations implementing it were necessary, but whether it was necessary to accord foreign gasoline less favourable treatment , which, they argued, was the situation in this case. Venezuela argued further that Article XX provided limited and conditional exceptions from obligations under other provisions of the General Agreement, and the burden was on the party invoking that provision to justify the application of any of the enumerated exceptions. The United States lacked the factual and legal support necessary to carry that burden with respect to any of its claims under Article XX.

---

[13]   "Canada - Administration of the Foreign Investment Review Act", BISD 30S/140 (adopted on 7 February 1984) and United States - Measures Affecting Alcoholic and Malt Beverages" BISD 39S/206 (adopted on 19 June 1992).

4. *Article XX(b)*

a)   "Protection of Human, Animal and Plant Life or Health"

3.39   The United States argued that it was well established that air pollution, and in particular ground-level ozone, presented health risks to humans, animal and plants. Toxic air pollution was a cause of cancer, birth defects, damage to the brain or other parts of the nervous system, reproductive disorders and genetic mutation. It could affect not only people with impaired respiratory systems, but healthy adults and children as well. Ozone was also responsible for agricultural crop yield loss in the United States. Vehicular air toxic emissions accounted for approximately 40 to 50 percent of total air toxic emissions. The Gasoline Rule provisions sought to control toxic air pollution from mobile sources by addressing the fuel that creates these emissions. Thus, its aim was to protect public health and welfare by reducing emissions of toxic pollutants, VOCs and NOx for reformulated gasoline, and to avoid degradation of air quality for emissions of NOx and toxic air pollutants for conventional gasoline. Therefore, the Gasoline Rule fell within the range of policies specified in Article XX(b).

b)   "Necessary"

3.40   The United States argued that the non-degradation requirements for both reformulated and conventional gasoline were necessary to protect human, animal and plant life or health. Using individual baselines for conventional gasoline was the quickest and fairest way to achieve the programme's environmental goal, which was to ensure the maintenance of US 1990 gasoline quality in the cleaner areas without affecting the speedy and cost-effective implementation of the reformulated gasoline programme in the most polluted areas, and without causing major disruptions in the domestic production of conventional gasoline. If a single baseline were used for all conventional gasoline, then all producers whose gasoline was dirtier than this baseline for certain gasoline qualities would need to change the characteristics of their production to meet the standard for those qualities, and those producers whose gasoline was cleaner than the baseline could degrade down to the baseline. The result would be the same overall average for gasoline, but large segments of gasoline producers would have been required to make changes to their conventional gasoline production. Where future production exceeded their 1990 output, refiners must meet the statutory baseline. With respect to reformulated gasoline, individual baselines were used for a three year transition period and applied to three gasoline qualities -sulphur, olefin and T-90- which were required to preserve their average US 1990 levels because EPA lacked data about their precise emission effects. This approach avoided requiring large segments of producers to make changes in their gasoline in order to meet a single requirement, whereas it was not clear whether and how any such change was needed to avoid emissions increases. However, all reformulated gasoline refiners must have begun to adjust their operations in order to meet the new reformulated gasoline requirements that would be in effect in 1998 under the Complex Model. All regulated gasoline qualities would then be measured against the statutory baseline. Thus, the baseline system protected air quality in the most practical and cost-effective manner, while taking the best account of the various producers' characteristics.

3.41   The United States argued that the individual baseline approach was however not possible with all producers, in particular, refiners that were only producing during part of 1990, blenders and importers. These categories of producers were in a different situation since they lacked the data necessary to use Methods 1, 2 and 3, and requiring them to establish an individual baseline, like domestic refiners, would have had the effect of precluding them from the US market. Thus, assigning importers to the statutory baseline ensured that they would not be forced out of the market while treating similarly situated parties alike. Moreover, even if in some cases importers might be able to establish individual baselines derived from foreign refiner information, giving importers a choice as to which baseline to use would inevitably have undermined the air quality objective of the regulation since business incentives would have induced them to use the cheapest and least stringent option, which would also have been the most polluting one. Taking into account these concerns over gaming, EPA had determined that no other option was feasible without having adverse effects on trade. The United States stressed that the Gasoline Rule applied to the importer and not to the foreign refiner. Given that there had traditionally been a variety of gasoline and blendstock qualities available on the market, importers were likely to have the flexibility to import gasoline from various sources, some with levels above and others below the statutory baseline, as long as the annual average for the importer met the statutory baseline.

3.42   The United States argued that it was not feasible to give individual baselines to foreign refiners for various reasons. First, gasoline was a fungible international commodity and a shipment of gasoline arriving in a US port generally contained a mixture of gasoline that had been produced at several foreign refineries. Therefore it would be very difficult, if not impossible, to determine the refinery of origin of a shipment of gasoline for the purpose of establishing an individual baseline. Second, the difficulty of identifying the refinery of origin would also favour potential gaming of the system since the foreign refiner could be tempted to claim the refinery of origin for each shipment of imported gasoline that would present the most benefits in terms of the baseline restrictions. The third reason related to the difficulties of the United States to exercise enforcement jurisdiction over foreign refiners. The Gasoline Rule could not be enforced simply by examining the product at the border but required EPA to audit the facilities of refineries in order to verify, *inter alia*, that the data provided to establish the individual baselines were accurate as well as to ensure future compliance. EPA also needed other enforcement tools such as criminal penalties, civil enforcement proceedings or court warrants, that would not be readily available to use outside US territory against a refinery located on foreign soil. Holding the importer accountable for the conduct of the foreign refiner with whom he has not colluded could have been an unfair solution. The United States recalled that the panel report "United States - Section 337 of the Tariff Act of 1930" had acknowledged that a measure might need to provide apparently less favourable treatment to imports in situations where it "might be considerably more difficult to identify the source of infringing products or to prevent circumvention of orders limited to the products of named persons",[14] than for US products. The present case offered similar differences in enforcement needs and capabilities with respect to the identification of the source of gasoline.

3.43   The United States disagreed with Venezuela's assertion that the May 1994 Proposal demonstrated the feasibility of individual baselines for foreign refiners. This Proposal was a continuation of EPA's efforts to develop criteria that would protect the environment, minimize disruption to producers and treat similarly situated gasoline alike, taking into account the comments and concerns expressed by interested parties. The fact that EPA made this attempt was neither a determination that the Gasoline Rule was flawed nor a determination that the 1994 Proposal was feasible. The 1994 Proposal contained several strict conditions governing the establishment of individual baselines for foreign refiners, which showed that concerns still existed. Moreover, it applied only to reformulated gasoline because the indefinite application of individual baselines for conventional gasoline and the expectation that many more foreign refiners would supply the conventional market indicated that the environmental risk associated with allowing this option were too great to justify even its proposal. In public comments, the 1994 Proposal had been criticised as favouring a small group of importers over all the others. PDVSA and other foreign refiners had objected that the proposed conditions, *inter alia* those related to gasoline tracking, were unworkable. For these reasons, the United States rejected Venezuela's assertion that EPA would have finalized this Proposal except for the action by Congress.

3.44   The United States considered that Venezuela's citation of the testimony of a US government official was inapposite. This testimony reflected the US government's commitment when it issued the final Gasoline Rule to continue addressing the issue of how imports were treated together with the concerns that environmental protection not be compromised and that the provisions be fair to all the parties affected. Contrary to Venezuela's argument, this testimony did not show that protectionism underlay the Gasoline Rule's treatment of imports. The statement of a US government official defending the proposed use of foreign refiner baselines only illustrated that US regulators wished to obtain a mutually satisfactory solution with Venezuela. Moreover, the Rule explicitly stated that its motivation was environmental protection, not protectionism.

3.45   Venezuela argued that Article XX(b) was not applicable because the United States had not demonstrated that there were no less trade-restrictive means to achieve its health policy objectives. The Gasoline Rule's discriminatory baseline requirements were not, therefore, "necessary" within the terms of Article XX(b). Venezuela considered that there were less trade-restrictive alternatives to the Gasoline Rule discriminatory baseline requirements that would achieve the same objective. One such alternative was to authorize the use of individual baselines by foreign refiners for both reformulated and conventional gasoline. Another alternative was to require all US gasoline producers to meet the statutory baseline requirements. A third alternative, in Venezuela's view, would have been

---

[14]   BISD 36S/345, § 5.32, adopted 7 November 1989.

to enforce the Complex Model as of 1995, rather than 1998, so as to treat both US and imported reformulated gasoline equally from the beginning. A fourth alternative would have been to authorize the use of foreign refiner individual baselines and, if compensating emissions reductions were necessary, to spread the burden of such compensation equally across all gasoline, US and imported alike.

3.46   Venezuela considered that, contrary to the US argument, the use of a foreign refiner baseline was feasible. It was feasible for a foreign refiner to develop an individual baseline, relying on the same types of records and data as US domestic refiners. In the case of Venezuela, PDVSA had all the records necessary to accurately determine an individual baseline in conformity with the requirements applicable to the US refiners, as had been confirmed by the firm *Turner, Mason and Co.* which served as an independent, EPA-approved auditor. The foreign refiner's individual baseline would be submitted to EPA for approval and to correct any possible mistakes before the product could be imported into the United States. EPA could then require a foreign refiner, as a requirement for establishing and maintaining its individual baseline, to appear before the agency and/or to make available to it production records and any other reasonable information aimed at ensuring the accuracy of the baseline. Then, enforcement would only be relevant in verifying the characteristics of gasoline as it entered the United States. This kind of verification was routinely performed on many types of imported products and, in the case of gasoline, compliance for each shipment could be determined at the port of entry by testing the shipment and comparing its fuel properties with the individual baseline of the foreign refiner. Furthermore, since the importer was currently liable towards EPA for gasoline that did not conform to the statutory baseline, it was similarly possible to make him liable for gasoline that did not conform to the foreign refiner's individual baseline. Under US customs law, precedents existed where an importer was liable for an imported product that did not meet certain standards, and subject to civil and criminal sanctions. Venezuela cited, *inter alia*, the case of importers being liable for products not meeting the safety standards promulgated by the Consumer Product Safety Commission. This demonstrated that United States' concerns about enforcement mechanisms outside its territory and importer's liability for the conduct of a foreign company were without merit. Venezuela rejected the argument that it was not possible to determine the refinery of origin and noted that during the consultations leading to the 1994 Proposal, PDVSA had suggested several alternatives to deal with this problem. Moreover, the concerns expressed by the United States about foreign gasoline being mixed with "dirty" gasoline before being imported into the United States should apply equally to US produced gasoline being degraded after it left a US refinery. Venezuela also strongly denied the assertion that it had rejected the 1994 Proposal since it had clearly supported EPA's proposal to allow foreign refiners to establish their individual baselines and had continued to work with EPA to that end, presenting alternatives and explaining why particular provisions of the Proposal were unnecessarily burdensome and unworkable.

3.47   Lastly, Venezuela argued that United States' concern about "gaming", which was based on the assumption that foreign refiners with "cleaner" gasoline would select the statutory baseline rather than establishing their own baseline, thus affecting the air quality, was purely speculative for several reasons. EPA had itself recognised that it did not have data about the average quality of gasoline imported in 1990, and thus could not know whether a significant amount of that gasoline imported was "cleaner" than the statutory baseline. Available data indicated that foreign refiners were not likely to "degrade" from their 1990 gasoline quality and the impact of any such activity would at most be *de minimis*. Moreover, US statistics showed that, from January to March 1995, imported gasoline represented less than two percent of total US gasoline consumption. Thus, even accepting (which Venezuela did not) the United States' argument that half of the foreign refiners produced gasoline in 1990 that was below the statutory baseline and half of the foreign refiners produced gasoline that was above the statutory baseline, possibilities for gaming would arise for less than one percent of total US gasoline consumption. The practical impact of gaming was too small to justify discrimination against imported gasoline under Article XX(b). Finally, several aspects of the Gasoline Rule are incompatible with the professed US concern regarding the possible environmental impact of potential "gaming" : for example, the fact that there was no limitation on the volume of reformulated gasoline a US refiner could produce under its individual baseline, or the fact that in a particular geographical area, the emissions from gasoline would vary, depending on which refiners were supplying it, and as a consequence, the emissions levels could exceed the statutory baseline. Moreover, EPA had recently proposed several amendments to the Gasoline Rule, such as provisions permitting upward adjustment in baseline levels because of a US refiner's inability to acquire low sulphur content crude oil that was available in 1990, which equally undermined its environmental objectives. Venezuela concluded that the United States had not met the burden of the proof required by Article XX.

3.48   Brazil did not disagree with the purpose of the United States which was to address the problem of air pollution in order to protect human, animal and plant life and health. However, Brazil considered that the Gasoline Rule programme did not satisfy the requirements of Article XX(b), because the burden of achieving this purpose was placed disproportionately on imported gasoline. All imported gasoline had to meet the 1990 average expressed in the statutory baseline whereas half of the domestic refineries could sell gasoline which did not meet the statutory baseline. The concerns expressed by the United States about the negative impact of imposing a single statutory baseline on domestic refiners could not justify a violation to the national treatment obligation for the following two reasons. First, EPA did not want to impose on domestic refiners whose gasoline was dirtier than the statutory baseline the burden of changing their production characteristics, but it imposed precisely this requirement on foreign refiners. Secondly, the United States had not demonstrated to the Panel why domestic refiners whose production was cleaner than the statutory baseline would downgrade to the baseline. And even assuming that such a downgrade would occur, the overall air quality would not change as long as the refiners with "dirtier" gasoline were required to upgrade to the statutory baseline. Brazil considered that a rule establishing the statutory baseline as a minimum with the additional requirement that those refiners who produced gasoline above the statutory baseline continue to do so was another option which would take care of the downgrading concern while at the same time improving air quality in the United States and eliminating discrimination against imports.

3.49   Brazil further argued that the United States had not explained why importers could not establish an individual baseline, especially using Method 3 since importers presumably maintained records of their imports and thus could have data on their 1990 imports. Even assuming that it was necessary to assign importers to the statutory baseline, this did not explain the failure to provide for individual baselines for foreign refiners. Brazil considered that the United States had not demonstrated that foreign refiners did not have sufficient data to establish their own baselines. In that context, the United States referred only to "difficulties" but, according to Brazil, mere "difficulties" did not create necessity within the meaning of Article XX(b). Moreover, assuming that these difficulties were insurmountable, they would nevertheless not allow the United States to discriminate against foreign gasoline since there was an alternative measure, reasonably available, which was the requirement that all gasoline, domestically produced and imported, meet the same statutory baseline, as Brazil had noted above.

3.50   Brazil considered that the United States had presented no factual basis to support its concern that a foreign refiner would "game" the system if given the choice between the statutory and the individual baseline. Besides, this opportunity for "gaming" could be eliminated by simply assigning all refiners, domestic or foreign, to the same baseline, statutory or individual. Regarding the use of individual baselines by foreign refiners, the United States had never made any attempts to investigate or determine empirically whether the calculation and enforcement of such baselines were possible. However it merely insisted that these problems were insurmountable and, therefore, the statutory baseline had to be applied to imported gasoline. Finally, the fact that numerous parties had objected to particular aspects of the 1994 Proposal did not mean that non-discriminatory baselines for foreign refiners were not possible. Brazil concluded that the United States had not demonstrated why it was not possible to permit foreign refiners of both conventional and reformulated gasoline to use their own baselines.

3.51   Brazil argued that the discrimination under the General Agreement or the TBT Agreement was not justifiable even assuming that the use of foreign refiners' individual baselines was impossible. If it were impossible to assign individual baselines to foreign refiners, the United States would then be justified in using individual baselines for domestic refiners only if no other, non-discriminatory measure were available. A WTO Member was not permitted to review several options, select one in which discrimination was unavoidable, and then plead that the selected option required discrimination. Under Article III of the General Agreement -but also under Article I of the General Agreement and Article 2 of the TBT Agreement- a WTO Member was obliged, when the policy option involved discrimination, to choose another option when one was available. In this particular case, there was such an available alternative, which was to apply the statutory baseline to all producers of gasoline.

3.52   The United States maintained its arguments regarding the impraticability of foreign refiner's baseline. It argued that compliance with requirements based on foreign refinery baselines could not be established only by sampling gasoline on its arrival at a US port of entry, because it would be necessary to determine the refinery of origin for such imported gasoline. This type of determination would be difficult, if not impossible, due to the fungible mixing of gasoline that occurs before arrival in a US port of entry. The enforcement provisions of other US statutes cited by Venezuela to negate this concern were inapposite, because those statutes all involved matters that could be resolved by inspection of the product by Customs officials at the border. The United States also noted that there was no analogous concern with identifying the source of gasoline produced at domestic refineries, because domestic gasoline was regulated at the refinery gate, which left no questions of which refinery produced any particular batch of gasoline. The United States further argued that the potential environmental effect of "gaming" could be, under a reasonable scenario, an annual increase in NOx emissions from imported gasoline by 5.6 to 7 percent (about 115,000 short tons). US analyses of foreign refinery configurations showed that because of low fluid catalyst unit capacity among foreign refiners, sulphur and olefin levels in imports were likely to be low compared to the US statutory baseline, thus leaving ample room for gaming and degradation. Moreover, the "gaming" incentives for foreign "cleaner" refiners were not hypothetical: various changes since 1990 in physical plants and operating procedures could change the economic calculus for producing gasoline of a specified quantity, and the quality of the crude used in refining could change. In these conditions, a refiner might choose to degrade the sulphur, T-90 or other characteristics if it proved to be economical. The United States emphasized that there were no regulatory requirements on foreign refiners, who had ample flexibility, not available to domestic refiners, to select among blendstocks. The United States concluded that, contrary to Venezuela's and Brazil's claim, Article XX did not require adoption of the statutory baseline as a national standard even if the difficulties associated with the establishment of individual baselines for importers were insurmountable. Application of the statutory baseline to domestic producers of reformulated and conventional gasoline in 1995 would have been physically and financially impossible because of the magnitude of the changes required in almost all US refineries; it thus would have caused a substantial delay in the programme. Weighing the feasibility of policy options in economic or technical terms in order to meet an environmental objective was a legitimate consideration, and did not, in itself, constitute protectionism, as alleged by Venezuela and Brazil. Article XX did not require a government to choose the most expensive possible way to regulate its environment. In the case at hand, it was not necessary to assign domestic refiners to the statutory baseline for the non-degradation requirements for the reasons stated above.

3.53   The United States argued that the lack of a volume limitation for the use of individual baselines under the reformulated gasoline programme was not expected to affect the success of that program. US data showed that refineries with the highest olefin and sulphur levels in their baselines (i.e. the dirtiest baselines) as a group had not extended their market share after the start up of the reformulated gasoline programme. This was consistent with EPA's original expectations that the short time period during which individual baselines were used in the reformulated programme would not provide an incentive for refiners to revise their investment and production decisions based on whether their baselines were above or below the statutory baseline. The United States also argued that the various baseline adjustments allowed under the Gasoline Rule either redressed disadvantages occurring as a result of government requirements, or dealt with situations where the US government did not have data for a full year's representative operations.

3.54   Venezuela argued that the examples posed by the United States in the attempt to show an increase of average NOx emissions from imported gasoline because of potential gaming were flawed, leading to exaggerated results because they had relied on the Complex Model, which was not in use for 1995-1997, and on the assumption that half of the imported gasoline in 1990 had properties below and half had properties above the statutory baseline. Regarding this last assumption, the United States had conceded that it simply did not know the properties of the pool of imported gasoline in 1990, and had failed to present evidence that foreign refiners which might have exported to the United States gasoline cleaner than the statutory baseline would have an incentive to degrade down to the statutory baseline. Venezuela rejected this assumption and stated that there was no economic incentive for a refiner to operate its refinery in a less than optimal manner to increase the level of a fuel property such as sulphur or olefins for the sole purpose of making "dirtier" gasoline.

5.   Article XX(d)

3.55   The United States considered the Gasoline Rule's baseline establishment system was necessary to enforce the non-degradation requirements aiming at preventing deterioration of air quality. The non-degradation requirements ensuring that gasoline sold in the United States did not become more polluting than in 1990 were "laws or regulations which are not inconsistent with the provisions of the General Agreement". They were measures for which, pursuant to Article XX(g) and XX(b), "nothing in [the General Agreement] shall be construed to prevent the adoption or enforcement by any contracting party". For the reasons stated under Article XX(b), the baseline establishment rules were necessary to ensure that there was no degradation in gasoline or air quality. If importers were allowed to use several baselines, depending on which foreign refiners chose to use them, "gaming" could occur, and result in a deterioration of overall air quality. Therefore, the Gasoline Rule fell within the scope of Article XX(d).

3.56   Venezuela considered that the United States had not clearly established which were the "laws or regulations" which were not inconsistent with the General Agreement and with which compliance was secured, and hence had failed to demonstrate such consistency. Venezuela noted that a previous panel had found that a measure was deemed to "secure compliance with" only if it was effective to "enforce obligations" under laws or regulations consistent with the General Agreement, as opposed to ensuring the broader attainment of an objective.[15] When stating that "the baseline establishment rules are necessary to ensure that

---

[15]   "EEC - Regulation on Imports of Parts and Components", BISD 37S/132, para. 5.17-5.18 (adopted on 16 May 1990).

there is no degradation in gasoline and air quality", the United States precisely referred to an objective, instead of identifying any obligation of the non-degradation requirements that the discriminatory baseline requirements were necessary to enforce. Moreover, for the reasons expressed under Article XX(b), the Gasoline Rule was not necessary. Thus, the United States did not meet the requirements of Article XX(d).

3.57   Brazil considered that, for the reasons it had already developed under Article XX(b), the United States failed to demonstrate that the Gasoline Rule was "necessary" to secure compliance with the Clean Air Act, within the meaning of Article XX(d). As Brazil had previously indicated, there were non-discriminatory alternatives available to the United States.

6.   Article XX(g)

3.58   The United States argued that, as a programme intended to preserve clean air, the Gasoline Rule fell within the scope of Article XX(g).

a)   "Related to The Conservation of Exhaustible Natural Resources..."

3.59   The United States argued that clean air was an exhaustible resource within the meaning of Article XX(g) since it could be exhausted by the emissions of pollutants such as VOCs, NOx and toxics. In the most polluted areas, it could become chronically contaminated and remain so over long periods of time. Air containing pollutants could move long distances to contaminate other airsheds. Moreover, by stopping air degradation, the CAA also protected other exhaustible natural resources such as lakes, streams, parks, crops and forests, which were affected by air pollution. Thus, the objectives underlying the reformulated and conventional gasoline programmes fell within the range of policies to preserve both clean air and, consequently, other natural resources.

3.60   Venezuela noted that it shared with the United States a concern for the impact of dirty air on health, but claimed that the United States' arguments regarding the applicability of Article XX(g) to this case were both factually and legally erroneous. Recalling past panel reports, Venezuela considered that the exceptions provided for by Article XX had to be interpreted narrowly, in a manner that preserved the basic objectives and principles of the General Agreement.[16] Noting that the original purpose of Article XX(g) was to permit exceptions to otherwise applicable prohibitions or restrictions on the export of tradeable goods that could be exhausted as a result of their exploitation, Venezuela doubted that clean air was an exhaustible natural resource within the meaning of article XX(g). Venezuela considered that clean air was a "condition" of air that was renewable

---

[16]   "United States - Restrictions on Imports of Tuna", DS29/R, 16 June 1994 (unadopted), "Canada - Administration of the Foreign Investment Review Act", BIDS 30S//140, para. 5.20 (adopted on 7 February 1984), "United States - Section 337 of the Tariff Act of 1930", BISD 36S/345 (adopted on 7 November 1989).

rather than a resource that was exhaustible, such as petroleum and coal. There was no textual basis for expanding the scope of Article XX(g) to cover renewable "conditions" of resources as opposed to exhaustible natural resources.

3.61   Venezuela noted that under established GATT jurisprudence, a measure "related to" the conservation of an exhaustible natural resource only if it was "primarily aimed at" conserving that resource.[17] The United States had not even attempted to argue that the Gasoline Rule's discriminatory requirements, which were the measure at issue in the dispute, were "primarily aimed at" conservation, but had merely attempted to justify that the reformulated and conventional gasoline requirements fell under Article XX(g). Furthermore, the United States had identified only the protection of health as the primary objective for the reformulated and conventional gasoline requirements, which was irrelevant to an Article XX(g) analysis. Venezuela noted that it had previously demonstrated to the Panel that the Gasoline Rule methodology contained loopholes which undermined its own conservation objectives, thus confirming that the discriminatory baseline system could not be "primarily aimed at" the conservation of an exhaustible natural resource.

3.62   The United States disagreed with the claim that clean air was not an exhaustible natural resource within the meaning of Article XX(g). The United States maintained that air was undoubtedly a natural resource which could be exhausted if it was rendered unfit for human, animal or plant consumption. This was similar to the recognition in previous panel proceedings that fish were an "exhaustible natural resource" since their populations could be depleted or rendered extinct.[18]

b)   "... made effective in conjunction with restrictions on domestic production or consumption"

3.63   The United States considered that the Gasoline Rule restricted domestic production of gasoline by requiring manufacturers to limit their production of gasoline so that over the course of the year the average of particular components of the gasoline did not exceed certain maximum levels. It also restricted domestic consumption by ensuring that the average of those components of gasoline sold did not exceed certain maximum levels.

3.64   Venezuela rejected this argument because it considered that the United States had not shown that the discriminatory baseline requirements were "primarily aimed at rendering effective" restrictions on domestic production or consumption of clean air, the "natural resource" to be conserved by the Gasoline Rule. The United States had only referred to restriction on domestic production and consumption of gasoline.

---

[17]   "Canada - Measures Affecting Exports of Unprocessed Herring and Salmon", BISD 35S/98, para. 4.6 (adopted on 22 March 1988).
[18]   "Canada - Measures Affecting Exports of Unprocessed Herring and Salmon", BISD 35S/98 (adopted on 22 March 1988) and "United States - Prohibition of Imports of Tuna and Tuna Products from Canada", BISD 29S/91 (adopted on 22 February 1982).

3.65   Brazil argued that, even assuming that clean air was an exhaustible natural resource, the Gasoline Rule did not restrict domestic production or consumption of clean air. At best, the Gasoline Rule sought to increase production if not consumption of clean air, not to restrict it. Moreover, neither the CAA nor the Gasoline Rule restricted in any way the quantity of gasoline that could be produced or consumed in the United States, but merely regulated its quality. Since neither the production nor the consumption of air or gasoline was restricted by the CAA or the Gasoline Rule, the Gasoline Rule did not fall under Article XX(g).

3.66   The United States argued that the Gasoline rule did restrict domestic consumption of clean air through its restriction of emissions that polluted the air. This was similar to restrictions applied on cars in order to conserve fuel. In this case, the Gasoline Rule's application to imports - including the baseline rules- was primarily aimed at rendering effective restrictions on domestic production of dirty air, or conversely the consumption of clean air, through regulation of the gasoline that caused air pollution.

7.   Preamble to Article XX

3.67   The United States argued that, as it had demonstrated in the discussion concerning Article III, the Gasoline Rule applied equally to similarly situated parties. Importers and blenders were required to meet the parameters of 1990 average US gasoline because they could not ascertain the refinery of origin and the quality of the gasoline they marketed in 1990. This avoided the alternatives of either "gaming" problems or excluding most imported gasoline from the market. Unlike domestic refiners, importers had the flexibility to rely on a variety of sources so as to meet an annual average quality of gasoline. Moreover, for each of the requirements, about half of US gasoline produced by domestic refiners had to be cleaner in certain respects than the annual average gasoline quality supplied by importers. In addition, a portion of the US gasoline market was being supplied with gasoline by domestic refiners which had to meet the statutory baseline because their gasoline could not be presumed to have been part of the gasoline pool in 1990. But to the extent that the enforcement conditions differed between the United States and other countries, the "same conditions" did not prevail in the United States and in other supplying countries. Accordingly, any differences in treatment were neither arbitrarily nor unjustifiably discriminatory, but were based on valid, legitimate policy reasons.

3.68   The United States further argued that the Gasoline Rule did not constitute a disguised restriction on trade since its objective was to ensure no degradation from 1990 levels for emissions and air pollutants, a health objective that had nothing to do with a restriction on trade. The provisions were transparent and imposed the same overall requirements, stemming from the same objective, on imported as on domestic gasoline. The evolution of the provisions at issue demonstrated that treatment of imports had nothing to do with the fundamental structure of the part of the rule that was being contested. For conventional gasoline, the CAA prescribed individual baselines on a producer-specific basis for refiners, blenders and importer. At the time the CAA Amendments were introduced, imports did not figure significantly in the debate, not surprisingly in the light of their small (2 to 6 percent) share of the US gasoline market. In view of the uncertainty of the emissions effects of these parameters irrespective of the source of gasoline, in 1991 EPA agreed to regulate, with respect to reformulated gasoline, on the basis of individual baselines for the three non-degradation requirements.

3.69   Venezuela argued that the 75 % Rule which applied to only a few refineries that were historically determined did grant an advantage to gasoline imported by the United States from certain third countries, as opposed to gasoline imported from Venezuela. Thus, the Gasoline Rule constituted a means of arbitrary and unjustifiable discrimination between countries where the same conditions prevailed. Referring to past panel reports,[19] Venezuela considered that the reference "where the same conditions prevail" did not relate to the national treatment obligations, as had been argued by the United States, but only to the most-favoured-nation obligation of the General Agreement. Moreover, as had been previously argued by Venezuela, the discriminatory baseline requirements of the Gasoline Rule were not justified by environmental concerns, but intended to distort the conditions of competition in favour of US gasoline against imported gasoline. Hence, the Gasoline Rule was a disguised restriction on international trade, within the meaning of the Preamble of Article XX.

3.70   Brazil rejected the arguments given by the United States and argued that by discriminating between the United States and all other countries, and by discriminating among third countries based upon the criteria of ownership and quantity of exports, the Gasoline Rule constituted a means of arbitrary or unjustifiable discrimination between countries where the same conditions prevailed. Since the discrimination of imported products was so blatant, Brazil considered that the restrictions on trade were not disguised.

8.   Article XXIII - Nullification and Impairment

3.71   Venezuela argued that, in addition to its violation claim under XXIII:1(a), it was making an alternative claim of nullification and impairment under XXIII:1(b). The discriminatory baseline requirements had resulted in shipments of approximately thirty-three thousand fewer barrels of Venezuelan gasoline to the United States per day than would be possible absent the discrimination. The price of Venezuelan gasoline and its share in the US market, as well as the investment programme for Venezuelan refineries, had also been adversely affected. Venezuela was aware that statistical evidence of adverse trade effects was not the basis for a finding of nullification or impairment under Article XXIII:1(b). Nevertheless, it wished to emphasize that by so affecting trade volumes, prices received for Venezuelan gasoline, Venezuela's share in the US market and PDVSA's investment programme, the Gasoline Rule had distorted the conditions of competition for trade in the United States compared to the conditions reasona-

---

[19]   "United States - Imports of Certain Automotive Spring Assemblies", BISD 30S/107, para. 55 (adopted on 26 May 1983) and "United States - Prohibition on Imports of Tuna and Tuna Products from Canada", BISD 29S/91, para. 4.8 (adopted on 22 February 1982).

bly expected by Venezuela under the General Agreement. Venezuela said that if the Panel found nullification or impairment under Article XXIII:1(a), it needed not make a ruling on non-violation nullification or impairment under Article XXIII:1(b).

3.72   In responding to other claims by Venezuela and Brazil, the United States contested generally the allegation that there was any identifiable impact on 1995 Venezuelan exports attributable to the Gasoline Rule. Venezuela's exports to the United Sates had steadily declined over the last five years, and its decrease in exports in 1995 was entirely consistent with the earlier decline.

C.   *Agreement on Technical Barriers to Trade*

1.   *Article 2 - Preparation, Adoption and Application of Technical Regulations by Central Government Bodies*

a)   Whether or Not the Gasoline Rule is a Technical Regulation

3.73   Venezuela and Brazil submitted that the Gasoline Rule was a "document" which laid down "product characteristics" and "with which compliance was mandatory" for both conventional and reformulated gasoline. Therefore, it was a "technical regulation" within the meaning of Annex I of the TBT Agreement.

3.74   The United States replied that the non-degradation requirements contained in the Gasoline Rule did not specify particular product characteristics, and therefore did not meet the TBT Agreement's definition of a "technical regulation". Shipments of gasoline of widely varying characteristics could be sold by a particular entity, the only requirement being that at the end of the year, the average of certain of their chemical ingredients fell below certain levels. Thus, these provisions were requirements on companies, not on products, and compliance was measured on a company level for importers and blenders, and on a refinery level for domestic refiners, but not on a product basis. These provisions constituted requirements on total annual sales, but were not technical regulations within the meaning of the TBT Agreement. Therefore, the TBT Agreement did not apply to this dispute.

3.75   Venezuela maintained that EPA's regulation implementing the CAA through the baseline setting mechanisms precisely established product characteristics for gasoline consumed in the United States and was therefore a "document which lays down product characteristics" within the meaning of the definition contained in Annex I of the TBT Agreement. Moreover, the United States itself admitted this fact when saying that the Rule dealt with "chemical ingredients". Venezuela was also of the view that averaging did not make any difference for the purpose of the TBT Agreement since any averaging techniques required examination of the properties of each individual gasoline shipment. Excluding from the coverage of the TBT Agreement regulations relying on averaging would open a gaping loophole. Under this interpretation, the obligation of the Agreement could be avoided by averaging. Venezuela considered that the United States wanted to avoid examination under the TBT Agreement in order to escape the requirements contained in Article 2.2.

3.76   Brazil objected to the United States' argument that the Gasoline Rule was not a technical regulation within the meaning of the TBT Agreement. Brazil considered that the language of the CAA and that of the Gasoline Rule, referred to the establishment of product standards for gasoline when determining the fuel properties for the statutory baseline and the individual baselines. These product standards applied to gasoline were mandatory. The fact, argued by the United States, that no particular shipment of gasoline needed to meet any precise standards since the requirements were measured on an annual average basis, and thus that the "product" was the annual quantity of gasoline produced, blended, or imported, rather than each sub-unit, was irrelevant. Annual production in this case was simply the unit of production to which the standard was applied. Brazil noted that if the United States were correct in its assertion that the individual baselines applied to refiners and not to gasoline, the discrimination would then be even more apparent because foreign refiners had no baseline. In this case a mandatory requirement would apply only to imported gasoline while, under the logic of the United States, no requirement would apply to domestic gasoline, as distinct from domestic refiners. However, the enforcement and surveillance system provided for by EPA in the Gasoline Rule in order to regularly check the quality of gasoline and its property at the refinery level argued in favour of a technical regulation setting forth product characteristics. Moreover, the United States' own statements to the Panel acknowledged this fact when declaring that the "requirements" of the Gasoline Rule were "necessary to protect human, animal and plant life or health". In conclusion, Brazil considered that a rule which obliged imported gasoline that did not meet the statutory baseline to be blended with gasoline that exceeded these requirements in order to meet the mandatory statutory requirements was a "document" with mandatory product characteristics.

3.77   The United States argued that the TBT Agreement had been designed to elaborate on the disciplines of Article III of the General Agreement for a very specific subset of measures (technical regulations, standards and conformity assessment procedures). The fact that a measure was in writing, mandatory and applied to products did not make it a technical regulation. Excise taxes, for instance, met all these criteria but were not "technical regulations". Similarly, the term "technical regulation" was not so broad as to cover all government regulatory actions affecting products. For example, government regulations requiring factory smokestacks to have devices to reduce emissions were not technical regulations, though they were in writing, mandatory and specified "characteristics". Contrary to what was argued by the complainants, there were no minimum or maximum content or emissions requirements applied with respect to the non-degradation requirements for individual shipments of either reformulated or conventional gasoline under the Simple Model. A shipment or even sale of gasoline was not required to meet specific product characteristics with respect to the non-degradation requirements at issue. The Gasoline Rule was not setting uniform criteria in terms of gasoline characteristics; standardization was neither the purpose nor the result of the regulation. The United States concluded that the complainants were interpreting the term "technical regulation" out of context and such an interpretation, if accepted, would introduce into the TBT Agreement many measures which were in fact not intended to be covered. The United States also argued that Brazil's view that a "product" in this case be defined as an entire year's production, rather than a shipment or a batch, would be a radical departure from the concept of "product" under the WTO and was without basis in the WTO.

b) Article 2.1

3.78   Venezuela argued that Article 2.1 of the TBT Agreement incorporated the obligations of national treatment and MFN set forth in Articles III and I of the General Agreement. Venezuela and Brazil argued that, as a technical regulation within the meaning of the TBT Agreement, the Gasoline Rule laid down product characteristics for imported Venezuelan and Brazilian gasoline that gave less favourable treatment than that provided to imports from certain third countries and to US gasoline. Thus, it violated the obligations of national treatment and MFN treatment contained in Article 2.1 of the TBT Agreement.

c) Article 2.2

3.79   Venezuela and Brazil claimed that the Gasoline Rule created unnecessary obstacles to international trade in violation of Article 2.2 of the TBT Agreement.

3.80   Venezuela considered that the Gasoline Rule violated Article 2.2 for two reasons. First, there was evidence that this Rule had been "prepared, adopted or applied with a view to ... creating obstacles to international trade". The United States did not intend to discriminate against imported gasoline when it initiated the regulatory process. However, crucial decisions involving the specific discriminatory aspects of the Rule were knowingly made both during the regulatory process and thereafter. The testimony under oath made in April 1994 by a government official to the United States Senate was evidence that the discrimination was intentionally adopted as a means of affording protection to gasoline produced in the United States.

3.81   Second, the Gasoline Rule had the effect of creating an unnecessary obstacle to international trade because the more stringent requirements imposed on imported gasoline were not necessary to fulfil the stated objective of the Rule which is to improve air quality in the United States. In this respect, Venezuela considered that Article 2.2 of the TBT Agreement provided greater guidance with respect to the concept of "necessity" than Article XX of the General Agreement, especially its second sentence which expressly calls for a certain balance. Article XX spoke only of measures that are "necessary", which had been in previous cases strictly interpreted to mean that a measure is not necessary if it is not the least trade-restrictive measure reasonably available.[20] As explained in relation of Article XX(b), the Gasoline Rule clearly pursued a trade-restrictive approach despite the fact that alternatives consistent with the General Agreement were

---

[20]   "United States - Section 337 of the Tariff Act of 1930", BISD 36S/345, adopted on 7 November 1989 and "Thailand - Restrictions on Importation of and Internal Taxes on Cigarettes", BISD 37/200, adopted 7 November 1990.

available, while the risks of non-fulfilment of any legitimate objective had been deliberately exaggerated. EPA itself had acknowledged that less trade-restrictive alternatives of achieving the air quality objective were possible and the 1994 Proposal, though not entirely consistent with the General Agreement, was one such alternative.

3.82   Venezuela further considered that the risks of non-fulfilment of a legitimate objective had to be assessed against "scientific and technical information" which, in the case at hand, had never been provided despite various requests made by Venezuela, in particular under Article 2.5 of the TBT Agreement. Article 2.2 of the TBT Agreement required that the trade-restrictive elements of a technical regulation be eliminated unless "scientific and technical information" or other reliable factual data demonstrate that those elements were necessary to fulfil a legitimate objective. The United States had never submitted scientific evidence or technical data demonstrating that the different baseline requirements were necessary to fulfil the air quality objectives but had always relied on "gaming" as the justification. EPA had never attempted to analyze how much imported gasoline would be susceptible to gaming or whether, in case of gaming, the impact on health objectives would be unacceptable. In that regard, Venezuela recalled that EPA itself had acknowledged that the environmental impact of gaming was speculative because it lacked "clear evidence" regarding the actual average quality of 1990 imported gasoline and did not know whether a significant amount of imported gasoline was "cleaner" than the statutory baseline. Moreover, so little gasoline was imported that the potential differential emissions -between individual and statutory baselines- would not have any significant impact on the average emission quality of the gasoline consumed in the United States.

3.83   Brazil stated that, for the reasons already expressed under arguments relating to Articles I and III of the General Agreement and Article 2.1 of the TBT Agreement, the Gasoline Rule created "unnecessary obstacles to international trade" in a manner contrary to Article 2.2 of the TBT Agreement.

2.   *Article 12 - Special and Differential Treatment of Developing Country Members*

3.84   Venezuela observed that Article 12 of the TBT Agreement imposed certain obligations on the United States with respect to developing countries. Venezuela did not seek any special treatment but merely wanted its gasoline to be held to the same baseline requirements as US gasoline. Venezuela stated that it was not asking for the Panel to rule under Article 12 but intended to point out that the discriminatory treatment affecting Venezuelan gasoline was particularly objectionable in the light of that provision.

IV.   SUBMISSIONS BY INTERESTED THIRD PARTIES

A.   *The European Communities*

4.1   The European Communities (the "EC") stated that, as an exporter to the United States of gasoline for automobiles and other fuel oils, it had a substantial

interest in the matter before the Panel. In 1994, the total volume of EC-12 exports to the United States for gasoline represented 6'423'411 metric tonnes. This
volume had increased since the enlargement of the EC, on 1 January 1995. The
EC declared that it did not contest the right of the United States to enforce legislation whose purpose was to protect human, animal or plant life or health. However, such measures had to be in conformity with the provisions of the WTO
Agreement and not be applied so that imports from third countries were discriminated against, that the domestic industry was afforded protection, or that disguised restrictions were imposed on international trade.

4.2   The EC stated that, while agreeing with the United States that the application of formally identical provisions could, in certain cases, accord in practice
less favourable treatment to imported products, it could not agree with the consequences which the United States seemed to draw from the findings of the panel
report "United States - Section 337 of the Tariff Act of 1930" for the present
case. It could not be concluded from that report that when it was not technically
feasible to apply to imported products the rule applied to domestic products, it
was then sufficient to find a workable rule which was sufficiently close to that
applicable to domestic products, without changing that latter rule. The EC considered that the logic behind Article III of the General Agreement required Members to achieve effective non-discrimination or absence of protection. Such an
objective should be achieved preferably by amending existing rules or re-
formulating new rules which could be applied identically to domestic and imported goods.

4.3   The EC argued that risks of violations of Article III:1 and 4 resulted from
the fact that Methods 2 and 3 of establishing individual baselines were only
available to domestic refiners. The EC did not want to discuss the accuracy of the
arguments developed by the United States with respect to the feasibility of individual baselines for foreign refiners, but assumed, for the sake of argument, that
Methods 2 and 3 could not be applied to imported gasoline in this case. Considering the explanations given by the United States as to what the statutory baseline
represented, and assuming they were correct, the EC failed to see why US refiners could not be subject to the statutory baseline, like importers and blenders.
Such a measure would have been in total conformity with Article III, paragraphs
1 and 4. In addition, it appeared from the information submitted by the main parties to the dispute that barely half of the US refiners had their individual baselines
approved at the time of the entry into force of the Rule. While not affecting the
existence of the violation, this fact proved that the application of the statutory
baseline *erga omnes* would probably not affect significantly the competitive position of US refiners.

4.4   The EC understood the concern expressed by the United States that certain importers and blenders, who had the flexibility to select gasoline from various sources, might have an advantage over US refiners if the statutory baseline
were to be applied to all gasoline producers. However, this potential advantage
was inherent to the averaging mechanism contained in the Gasoline Rule and was

not a sufficient reason to introduce a system which would unavoidably favour certain US producers. Article III required that no less favourable treatment be given to imported products, not the contrary.[21] If one considered that a US refiner might have produced extremely "dirty" gasoline in 1990, the Gasoline Rule did not give an immediate incentive for US refiners to adapt their production, whereas increased access to US market for third country gasoline was dependent on a gradual approximation of their quality compared with the statutory baseline. Therefore, the Gasoline Rule entailed at the very least a serious risk of discrimination, which constituted, by itself, a form of discrimination.[22] According to past panel reports, the United States had to show that, despite the different treatment accorded to imported products, the no less favourable treatment standard of Article III was met.

4.5   Regarding the 75 % Rule, the EC argued that the fact it was based on objective criteria, as argued by the United States, was not sufficient to avoid discrimination in the present case. A *de facto* discrimination in the application of the most-favoured-nation principle was possible, as the criteria used to grant that treatment were based on the situation in 1990. An importer meeting the required criteria after that date could not have invoked it. Hence, the Rule could only benefit certain countries where US companies had invested in local refiners before 1990. As acknowledged by the United States, this could have included Canada, where certain US companies owned refineries at that time. However, this could not have benefitted production of refiners located in countries where, for instance, the petroleum industry was mostly, if not exclusively, owned by the State in 1990. Therefore, the 75 % Rule was *de facto* not based on objective criteria, and hence contrary to Article I of the General Agreement. The EC further argued that the Panel should make a finding on this Rule despite the fact that it could no longer be invoked. A Panel should be guided in its examination by the content of the "matter" -the 75 % Rule in the present case- referred to it.[23] A determination by the Panel on the conformity of that rule with Article I would help avoid this kind of measure being found in the future in the legislation of a WTO Member.

4.6   As to whether the Gasoline Rule fell under the TBT Agreement, the EC stated that it agreed with the United States that the requirements on chemical ingredients did not need to be satisfied by each shipment and also that, the measures at issue being based on a yearly average, the importers remained free to import different varieties of gasoline provided that the annual average met the requirements. However, the EC doubted that a standard should be excluded from the scope of the TBT Agreement only for the reason that it required compliance on a yearly basis instead of on a shipment basis. It was clear that the importer had

---

[21]   "United States - Section 337 of the Tariff Act of 1930", BISD 36S/345 (adopted on 7 November 1989).
[22]   "EEC - Payments and Subsidies Paid to Processors and Producers of Oilseeds and Related Animal Feed Proteins", BISD 37S/86 (adopted on 25 January 1990).
[23]   "United States - Imposition of Countervailing Duties on Certain Hot-Rolled Lead and Bismuth Carbon Steel Products from France, Germany and the United Kingdom", SCM/185, 15 November 1994 (not adopted).

only to balance various qualities of gasoline in order to meet the statutory base-line. From the point of view of the exporting country, the Gasoline Rule created a clear incentive for adapting its production standards if it wanted to maintain or increase its share of the US market. Exporting refiners not adapting their production standards to US requirements (or at least not gradually narrowing the difference down to total compliance) would be unlikely to increase their sales in the US since importers had to blend or balance the "dirty" imported gasoline with "cleaner" gasoline. The "cleaner" gasoline being likely to be more expensive, importers would gradually cease to import "dirty" gasoline, thus obliging foreign refiners to meet the statutory baseline for each shipment. For this reason, the EC could not agree with the United States that the non-degradation requirements did not specify particular "product characteristics". Although no maximum content was set per shipment, the US methodology resulted in pushing the market to apply standards gradually closer to the averages referred to in the rule.

4.7   The EC considered that, in certain circumstances, the US system would impose a clearly defined standard. For example, an exporter setting up its own importation network in the United States was likely to be obliged to immediately adapt its production to US standards in order not to have to import gasoline of different qualities at the same time as its own gasoline (with the related increased costs). Therefore, the EC believed that the Gasoline Rule imposed a technical regulation within the meaning of the TBT Agreement. The EC further considered that, if one were to agree with the US arguments, such an averaging system could represent a potential for circumvention of the TBT Agreement, mainly in the field of chemical products where it was used relatively frequently. If the mere use of an averaging requirement was sufficient to exclude the TBT Agreement from applying to certain environmental standards, then the increased legal protection resulting from Article 2.2 of that Agreement compared, for instance, with Article XX of the General Agreement, would no longer be available for the other Members.

4.8   Referring to the findings of a previous panel, the EC considered that, from a procedural point of view, the United States was entitled to rely on Article III and on Article XX *in the alternative.*[24] However, Article XX, as an exception, had to be interpreted strictly, and the EC was of the view that the Gasoline Rule, in the way it was applied, did not meet the requirements of Article XX but imposed a disguised restriction on trade by allowing US refiners to continue producing "dirty" gasoline meeting their individual baselines, while imposing actual constraints on foreign producers to adapt their production to US standards. Such a protectionist effect would probably not be created if identical baselines were applied to both imported and domestically produced gasoline. Moreover, as demonstrated above, the application of the statutory baseline to both domestic and imported gasoline would have achieved the same aim without introducing discrimination between sources of supply. In any event, measures inconsistent with the General Agreement were not necessary to enforce the 1990 CAA

---

[24]   "United States - Restrictions on Imports of Tuna", DS21/R, 3 September 1991, para. 5.22 (not adopted).

amendment. Therefore, the EC considered that, even if the Gasoline Rule did not constitute a "means of arbitrary or unjustifiable discrimination between countries where the same conditions prevail", it was obviously a means to alleviate the restructuring efforts of the US refining industry while at the same time requiring foreign producers to adapt almost immediately their production. Hence, while officially pursuing environmental objectives, it introduced a disguised restriction on trade. The EC concluded that the baselines system was not proportionate and did not meet the necessity test of Article XX.

B.   Norway

4.9   Norway stated that its reasons for reserving its rights as a third party in this case were in legal and practical terms very similar to those argued by Venezuela and Brazil in their respective requests for the establishment of a panel. The Gasoline Regulation denied national treatment to gasoline imported from Norway. Therefore, Norway supported Venezuela and Brazil's request that the Panel find the Gasoline Rule to be inconsistent with Articles I and III of the General Agreement, and with Article 2 of the TBT Agreement.

4.10   Norway said that the Norwegian State Oil Company ("Statoil") was experiencing a very difficult situation because of the way the Gasoline Rule operated. There was a considerable incentive for Statoil to be able to export to the US market as compared to other markets. In 1989, Statoil built the Mongstad refinery with the objective of selling to the United States some 0.5 millions tons per year out of a total gasoline production of 2,5 millions tons per year. In 1990, Statoil sold a total of about 470'000 tons of gasoline to the United States, out of which about 350'000 tons came from Mongstad refinery. Since December 1994, Statoil had not exported gasoline from Mongstad to the United States.

4.11   Norway argued that changing specifications was in the nature of the refining business. However, like Venezuela's and Brazil's refineries, Statoil was affected by the discriminatory nature of the US regulation. Assigned to the statutory baseline for its exports of reformulated gasoline until 1998 and for conventional gasoline indefinitely, the Mongstad refinery would not competitively be able to produce any volumes of gasoline, based on current refinery configurations and investment plans. Norway considered that, if the Panel ruled in favour of Venezuela and Brazil, Statoil would, as an "Importer of Record" in 1990, be allowed to establish its individual 1990 baseline for the volume sold that year.

V.   INTERIM REVIEW

5.1   On 18 December 1995, the United States requested the Panel to review in accordance with Article 15.2 of the DSU precise aspects of the interim report that had been issued to the parties on 11 December 1995, and to hold a meeting for that purpose. The Panel met with the parties on 3 January 1996 in order to hear their arguments concerning the interim report. The Panel carefully reviewed the arguments presented by the United States and the responses offered by Venezuela and Brazil.

5.2   In respect of the interim report's discussion of Article III, the United States argued that in several respects the interim report dealt with issues that were not disputed by the parties or were unnecessary to the Panel's conclusion that aspects of the Gasoline Rule violated Article III:4. While the Panel did not agree with all the arguments made by the United States, it did revise the report to take into account those arguments with which it agreed and paragraphs 6.5 and 6.9 - 6.11 of the findings reflect the Panel's response.

5.3   In respect of the interim report's discussion of Article XX(b), the United States objected to the Panel's use of specific terms which did not appear in the text of the provision, the description of the US argument, and the Panel's analysis of alternative measures available to the United States. The Panel revised the report where it accepted the US arguments and paragraphs 6.20 - 6.25 and 6.27 - 6.28 of the findings reflect the Panel's response.

5.4   In respect of the interim report's discussion of Article XX(d), the United States objected to the Panel's use of specific terms which did not appear in the text of the provision. The Panel accepted the US arguments and paragraph 6.31 of the revised findings reflects the Panel's response.

5.5   In respect of the interim report's discussion of Article XX(g), the United States objected to the Panel's use of specific terms which did not appear in the text of the provision, and the analysis of alternative measures available to the United States. Venezuela requested a change to the description of its argument under this provision. The Panel revised the report where it accepted the arguments of the US and Venezuela and paragraphs 6.35 - 6.36 and 6.40 - 6.41 of the findings reflect the Panel's response.

5.6   In respect of the interim report's descriptive section, Venezuela and the United States suggested further changes which the Panel took into account in re-examining that part of the report. The Panel revised the descriptive section of the report where it accepted the need for these changes.

VI.   FINDINGS

A.   Introduction

6.1   The Panel noted that the dispute arose from the following facts. The Clean Air Act aims to control and reduce air pollution in the United States. The Act and certain of its regulations (the "Gasoline Rule") set standards for gasoline quality intended to reduce air pollution, including ozone, caused by motor vehicle emissions. From 1 January 1995, the Gasoline Rule permits only gasoline of a specified cleanliness ("reformulated gasoline") to be sold in areas of high air pollution. In other areas, only gasoline no dirtier than that sold in the base year of 1990 ("conventional gasoline") can be sold.

6.2   The Gasoline Rule applies to refiners, blenders and importers of gasoline. It requires that certain chemical characteristics of the gasoline in which they deal respect, on an annual average basis, defined levels. In the Gasoline Rule some of these levels are fixed; others are expressed as "non-degradation" requirements. Under the non-degradation requirements, each domestic refiner must maintain, on an annual average basis, the relevant gasoline characteristics at levels no worse than its "individual baseline" — that is, the annual average levels achieved by that refiner in 1990. To establish an individual baseline, a refiner must show evidence of the quality of gasoline produced or shipped in 1990 ("Method 1"). If that evidence is not complete, then it must use data on the quality of blendstock produced in 1990 ("Method 2"). If these two methods do not result in sufficient evidence, the refiner must also use data on the quality of post-1990 gasoline blendstock or gasoline ("Method 3").

6.3   Importers are also required to use an individual baseline, but only in the case (unlikely, according to the parties to the dispute) that they are able to establish it using Method 1 data. Unlike domestic refiners, they are not allowed to establish an individual baseline by using the secondary or tertiary data specified in Methods 2 and 3. If an importer cannot produce Method 1 data, then it must use a "statutory baseline" which the United States claims is derived from the average characteristics of all gasoline consumed in the United States in 1990. Some other domestic entities (such as refiners with only partial or no 1990 operations, and blenders with insufficient Method 1 data) are also assigned the statutory baseline. Exceptionally, importers that imported in 1990 at least 75 percent of the production of an affiliated foreign refinery are treated as domestic refiners for the purpose of establishing baselines. Since this dispute concerns only the Gasoline Rule's non-degradation requirements, and not reformulated and conventional gasoline as such, the Panel will refer generally to "gasoline" in the course of its findings.

6.4   Venezuela and Brazil claim that the Gasoline Rule violates the national treatment provisions of Article III:1 and 4 of the General Agreement and the most-favoured-nation provision of Article I. Venezuela claims in the alternative that the Gasoline Rule has nullified and impaired benefits under the non-violation provisions of Article XXIII:1(b). Venezuela and Brazil also claim that the Gasoline Rule violates Article 2 of the Agreement on Technical Barriers to Trade (the "TBT Agreement"). The United States rejects these claims and argues that the Gasoline Rule can be justified under the exceptions contained in Article XX, paragraphs (b), (d) and (g), which argument is rejected by Venezuela and Brazil. It also argues that the Gasoline Rule does not come within the scope of Article 2 of the TBT Agreement.

B.   Article III

1.   Article III:4

6.5   The Panel proceeded to examine the claim that the Gasoline Rule violates Article III:4 of the General Agreement, which states:

> The products of the territory of any contracting party imported into the territory of any other contracting party shall be accorded treatment no less favourable than that accorded to like products of national origin in respect of all laws, regulations and requirements affecting their internal sale, offering for sale, purchase, transportation, distribution or use.

The Panel noted that under this provision the complainants are required to show the existence of: (a) a law, regulation or requirement affecting the internal sale, offering for sale, purchase, transportation, distribution or use of an imported product; and (b) treatment accorded in respect of the law, regulation or requirement that is less favourable to the imported product than to the like product of national origin. The Panel agreed with the parties that the Gasoline Rule was a law, regulation or requirement affecting the internal sale, offering for sale, purchase, transportation, distribution or use of an imported product. It proceeded therefore to consider whether the Gasoline Rule accorded less favourable treatment to imported products than to like products of national origin.

6.6   The Panel noted the arguments of Venezuela and Brazil that imported gasoline was "like" domestic gasoline, but received treatment less favourable because imported gasoline was subjected to more demanding quality requirements than gasoline of US origin. The United States replied that gasoline from similarly-situated parties was treated in the same manner under the Gasoline Rule. Gasoline from importers was treated no less favourably than that from other domestic non-refiners such as blenders, or refiners who had only limited or no operations in 1990.

6.7   The Panel observed that Article III:4 deals with treatment to be accorded to like products. However, the text does not specify exhaustively those aspects that determine whether the products are "like". In resolving this interpretative issue the Panel referred, in conformity with Article 3.2 of the Understanding on Rules and Procedures Governing the Settlement of Disputes, to the *Vienna Convention on the Law of Treaties*, which states in Article 31 that "a treaty shall be interpreted in good faith in accordance with the ordinary meaning to be given to the terms of the treaty in their context and in the light of its object and purpose".[25]

6.8   The Panel proceeded to examine this issue in the light of the ordinary meaning of the term "like". It noted that the word can mean "similar", or "identical". The Panel then examined the practice of the CONTRACTING PARTIES under the General Agreement. This practice was relevant since Article 31 of the *Vienna Convention* directs that "subsequent practice in the application of the treaty which establishes the agreement of the parties regarding its interpretation" is also to be considered in the interpretation of a treaty. The Panel noted that various criteria for the determination of like products under Article III had previously been applied by panels. These were summarized in the 1970 *Working Party Report on Border Tax Adjustments,* which had observed:

> With regard to the interpretation of the term 'like or similar products', which occurs some sixteen times throughout the General Agreement, it was recalled that considerable discussion had taken place . . . but that no further improvement of the term had been achieved. The Working Party concluded that problems arising from the interpretation of the terms should be examined on a case-by-

---

[25]   Vienna Convention on the Law of Treaties, Art. 31.

case basis. This would allow a fair assessment in each case of the different elements that constitute a 'similar' product. Some criteria were suggested for determining, on a case-by-case basis, whether a product is 'similar': the product's end-uses in a given market; consumers' tastes and habits, which change from country to country; the product's properties, nature and quality.[26]

These criteria had been applied by the panel in the 1987 *Japan Alcohol* case in the examination under Article III:2 of internal taxation measures. That panel had proceeded on a case-by-case basis, determining whether various alcoholic beverages were "like" on the basis of "their similar properties, end-uses and usually uniform classification in tariff nomenclatures."[27] The Panel considered that those criteria were also applicable to the examination of like products under Article III:4.

6.9   In light of the foregoing, the Panel proceeded to examine whether imported and domestic gasoline were like products under Article III:4. The Panel observed first that the United States did not argue that imported gasoline and domestic gasoline were not like *per se*. It had argued rather that with respect to the treatment of the imported and domestic products, the situation of the parties dealing in the gasoline must be taken into consideration. The Panel, recalling its previous discussion of the factors to be taken into account in the determination of like product, noted that chemically-identical imported and domestic gasoline by definition have exactly the same physical characteristics, end-uses, tariff classification, and are perfectly substitutable. The Panel found therefore that chemically-identical imported and domestic gasoline are like products under Article III:4.

6.10   The Panel next examined whether the treatment accorded under the Gasoline Rule to imported gasoline was less favourable than that accorded to like gasoline of national origin. The Panel observed that domestic gasoline benefitted in general from the fact that the seller who is a refiner used an individual baseline, while imported gasoline did not. This resulted in less favourable treatment to the imported product, as illustrated by the case of a batch of imported gasoline which was chemically-identical to a batch of domestic gasoline that met its refiner's individual baseline, but not the statutory baseline levels. In this case, sale of the imported batch of gasoline on the first day of an annual period would require the importer over the rest of the period to sell on the whole cleaner gasoline in order to remain in conformity with the Gasoline Rule. On the other hand, sale of the chemically-identical batch of domestic gasoline on the first day of an annual period would not require a domestic refiner to sell on the whole cleaner gasoline over the period in order to remain in conformity with the Gasoline Rule. The Panel also noted that this less favourable treatment of imported gasoline induced the gasoline importer, in the case of a batch of imported gasoline not meeting the statutory baseline, to import that batch at a lower price. This reflected the fact that the importer would have to make cost and price allowances

---

[26]   L/3464, adopted on 2 December 1970, BISD 18S/97, 102, para. 18.
[27]   "Japan - Customs Duties, Taxes and Labelling Practices on Imported Wines and Alcoholic Beverages", BISD 34S/83, 115, para. 5.6 (adopted on 10 November 1987).

because of its need to import other gasoline with which the batch could be averaged so as to meet the statutory baseline. Moreover, the Panel recalled an earlier panel report which stated that "the words 'treatment no less favourable' in paragraph 4 call for effective equality of opportunities for imported products in respect of laws, regulations and requirements affecting the internal sale, offering for sale, purchase, transportation, distribution or use of products."[28] The Panel found therefore that since, under the baseline establishment methods, imported gasoline was effectively prevented from benefitting from as favourable sales conditions as were afforded domestic gasoline by an individual baseline tied to the producer of a product, imported gasoline was treated less favourably than domestic gasoline.

6.11   The Panel then examined the US argument that the requirements of Article III:4 are met because imported gasoline is treated similarly to gasoline from *similarly situated* domestic parties — domestic refiners with limited 1990 operations and blenders. According to the United States, the difference in treatment between imported and domestic gasoline was justified because importers, like domestic refiners with limited 1990 operations and blenders, could not reliably establish their 1990 gasoline quality, lacked consistent sources and quality of gasoline, or had the flexibility to meet a statutory baseline since they were not constrained by refinery equipment and crude supplies. The Panel observed that the distinction in the Gasoline Rule between refiners on the one hand, and importers and blenders on the other, which affected the treatment of imported gasoline with respect to domestic gasoline, was related to certain differences in the characteristics of refiners, blenders and importers, and the nature of the data held by them. However, Article III:4 of the General Agreement deals with the treatment to be accorded to like products; its wording does not allow less favourable treatment dependent on the characteristics of the producer and the nature of the data held by it. The Panel noted that in the *Malt Beverages* case, a tax regulation according less favourable treatment to beer on the basis of the size of the producer was rejected.[29] Although this finding was made under Article III:2 concerning fiscal measures, the Panel considered that the same principle applied to regulations under Article III:4. Accordingly, the Panel rejected the US argument that the requirements of Article III:4 are met because imported gasoline is treated similarly to gasoline from similarly situated domestic parties.

6.12   Apart from being contrary to the ordinary meaning of the terms of Article III:4, any interpretation of Article III:4 in this manner would mean that the treatment of imported and domestic goods concerned could no longer be assured on the objective basis of their likeness as products. Rather, imported goods would be exposed to a highly subjective and variable treatment according to extraneous factors. This would thereby create great instability and uncertainty in the condi-

---

[28]   "United States - Section 337 of the Tariff Act of 1930", BISD 36S/386, para 5.11 (adopted on 7 November 1989).
[29]   "United States - Measures Affecting Alcoholic and Malt Beverages", BISD 39S/206, para. 5.19 (adopted on 19 June 1992).

tions of competition as between domestic and imported goods in a manner fundamentally inconsistent with the object and purpose of Article III.

6.13   The Panel considered that the foregoing was sufficient to dispose of the US argument. It noted, however, that even if the US approach were to be followed, under any approach based on "similarly situated parties" the comparison could just as readily focus on whether imported gasoline from an identifiable *foreign* refiner was treated more or less favourably than gasoline from an identifiable US refiner. There were, in the Panel's view, many key respects in which these refineries could be deemed to be the relevant similarly situated parties, and the Panel could find no inherently objective criteria by means of which to distinguish which of the many factors were relevant in making a determination that any particular parties were "similarly situated." Thus, although these refineries were similarly situated, the Gasoline Rule treated the products of these refineries differently by allowing only gasoline produced by the domestic entity to benefit from the advantages of an individual baseline. This consequential uncertainty and indeterminacy of the basis of treatment underlined, in the view of the Panel, the rationale of remaining within the terms of the clear language, object and purpose of Article III:4 as outlined above in paragraph 6.12.

6.14   The Panel then noted the argument of the United States that the treatment accorded to gasoline imported under a statutory baseline was *on the whole* no less favourable than that accorded to domestic gasoline under individual refiner baselines. The United States claimed that the Gasoline Rule did not discriminate against imported gasoline, since the statutory baseline (by the nature of its calculation) and the average of the sum of the individual baselines both corresponded to average gasoline quality in 1990, and that domestic and imported gasoline was treated equally overall. The Panel noted that, in these circumstances, the argument that on average the treatment provided was equivalent amounted to arguing that less favourable treatment in one instance could be offset provided that there was correspondingly more favourable treatment in another. This amounted to claiming that less favourable treatment of particular imported products in some instances would be balanced by more favourable treatment of particular products in others. A previous panel had found that

> the "no less favourable" treatment requirement of Article III:4 has to be understood as applicable to each individual case of imported products. The Panel rejected any notion of balancing more favourable treatment of some imported products against less favourable treatment of other imported products. If this notion were accepted, it would entitle a contracting party to derogate from the no less favourable treatment obligation in one case, or indeed in respect of one contracting party, on the ground that it accords more favourable treatment in some other case, or to another contracting party. Such an interpretation would lead to great uncertainty about the

conditions of competition between imported and domestic products and thus defeat the purposes of Article III.[30]

The Panel concurred with this reasoning that under Article III:4 less favourable treatment of particular imported products in some instances could not be balanced by more favourable treatment of other imported products in other instances. The Panel therefore rejected the US argument.

6.15 The Panel observed that, considered even from the point of view of imported gasoline as a whole, treatment was generally less favourable. Importers of gasoline had to adapt to an assigned average standard not linked to the particular gasoline imported, while refiners of domestic gasoline had only to meet a standard linked to their own product in 1990. Statistics on baselines bore out this difference in treatment. According to the United States, as of August 1995, approximately 100 US refiners, representing 98.5 percent of gasoline produced in 1990, had received EPA approval of their individual baselines. Only three of the refiners met the statutory baseline for all parameters. Thus, while 97 percent of US refiners did not and were not required to meet the statutory baseline, the statutory baseline was required of importers of gasoline, except in the rare case (according to the parties) that they could establish a baseline using Method 1.

6.16 The Panel found that imported and domestic gasoline were like products, and that since, under the baseline establishment methods, imported gasoline was effectively prevented from benefitting from as favourable sales conditions as were afforded domestic gasoline by an individual baseline tied to the producer of a product, imported gasoline was treated less favourably than domestic gasoline.

2. Article III:1

6.17 The Panel then noted the arguments advanced by Venezuela and Brazil that the Gasoline Rule was applied "so as to afford protection to domestic production" contrary to Article III:1. The United States disagreed and argued in the alternative that Article III:1 was only hortatory and could not form the basis of a violation. The Panel examined first whether, after making a finding of inconsistency with Article III:4, it should make a finding under Article III:1. The Panel noted that the panel in the *Malt Beverages* case had examined a claim made under paragraphs 1, 2 and 4 of Article III. That panel had concluded that "because Article III:1 is a more general provision than either Article III:2 or III:4, it would not be appropriate for the Panel to consider [the complainant's] Article III:1 allegations to the extent that the Panel were to find [the respondent's] measures to be inconsistent with the more specific provisions of Articles III:2 and III:4."[31] The present Panel agreed with this reasoning, and therefore did not find it necessary to examine the consistency of the Gasoline Rule with Article III:1.

---

[30] "United States - Section 337 of the Tariff Act of 1930", BISD 36S/345, para. 5.14 (adopted on 7 November 1989).
[31] "United States - Measures Affecting Alcoholic and Malt Beverages", BISD 39S/206, 270, para. 5.2 (adopted on 19 June 1992).

C.   Article I:1

6.18   The Panel proceeded to examine the claim of Venezuela and Brazil that the Gasoline Rule violated the most-favoured-nation provision of Article I:1 by permitting an importer to use secondary evidence to establish an individual baseline, provided that in 1990 it imported at least 75 percent of the production from an affiliated foreign refinery. Venezuela and Brazil claimed that the rule targeted a small number of countries, and that the different treatment was based on criteria (ownership and proportion of product purchased) that had no link to the product, as required under Article I:1. The United States claimed the rule was based on objective criteria and, in any case, it was not applicable because no importer had qualified for the benefit before the deadline.

6.19   The Panel observed that it had not been the usual practice of a panel established under the General Agreement to rule on measures that, at the time the panel's terms of reference were fixed, were not and would not become effective. In the 1978 *Animal Feed Protein* case, the Panel ruled on a discontinued measure, but one that had terminated after agreement on the panel's terms of reference.[32] In the 1980 *Chile Apples* case, the panel ruled on a measure terminated before agreement on the panel's terms of reference; however, the terms of reference in that case specifically included the terminated measure and, it being a seasonal measure, there remained the prospect of its reintroduction.[33] In the present case, the Panel's terms of reference were established after the 75 percent rule had ceased to have any effect, and the rule had not been specifically mentioned in the terms of reference. The Panel further noted that there was no indication by the parties that the 75 percent rule was a measure that, although currently not in force, was likely to be renewed. Finally, the Panel considered that its findings on treatment under the baseline establishment methods under Articles III:4 and XX (b), (d) and (g) would in any case have made unnecessary the examination of the 75 percent rule under Article I:1. The Panel did not therefore proceed to examine this aspect of the Gasoline Rule under Article I:1 of the General Agreement.

D.   Article XX(b)

6.20   The Panel proceeded to examine whether the aspect of the baseline establishment methods found inconsistent with Article III:4 could, as argued by the United States, be justified under paragraph (b) of Article XX. The relevant parts of Article XX were as follows:

> Subject to the requirement that such measures are not applied in a manner which would constitute a means of arbitrary or unjustifiable discrimination between countries where the same conditions

---

[32] "EEC - Measures on Animal Feed Proteins", L/4599, BISD 25S/49 (adopted on 14 March 1978). See also the Report of the Panel on "United States - Prohibitions of Imports of Tuna and Tuna Products from Canada", BISD 29S/91, 106, para. 4.3 (adopted on 22 February 1982).

[33] "EEC - Restrictions on Imports of Apples from Chile", BISD 27S/98, (adopted on 10 November 1980).

prevail, or a disguised restriction on international trade, nothing in this Agreement shall be construed to prevent the adoption or enforcement by any contracting party of measures:

(b)   necessary to protect human, animal or plant life or health;

The Panel noted that as the party invoking an exception the United States bore the burden of proof in demonstrating that the inconsistent measures came within its scope. The Panel observed that the United States therefore had to establish the following elements:

(1)   that the *policy* in respect of the measures for which the provision was invoked fell within the range of policies designed to protect human, animal or plant life or health;

(2)   that the inconsistent measures for which the exception was being invoked were *necessary* to fulfil the policy objective; and

(3)   that the measures were applied in conformity with the requirements of the *introductory clause* of Article XX.

In order to justify the application of Article XX(b), all the above elements had to be satisfied.

1.   Policy Goal of Protecting Human, Animal or Plant Life or Health

6.21   The Panel noted the United States argument that air pollution, in particular ground-level ozone and toxic substances, presented health risks to humans, animals and plants. The United States argued that, since about one-half of such pollution was caused by vehicle emissions, and the Gasoline Rule reduced these, the Gasoline Rule was within the range of policy goals described in Article XX(b). Venezuela and Brazil did not disagree with this view. The Panel agreed with the parties that a policy to reduce air pollution resulting from the consumption of gasoline was a policy within the range of those concerning the protection of human, animal and plant life or health mentioned in Article XX(b).

2.   Necessity of The Inconsistent Measures

6.22   The Panel recalled its finding in paragraph 6.16 that imported gasoline was treated less favourably than domestic gasoline, since, under the baseline establishment methods, imported gasoline was prevented from benefitting from as favourable sales conditions as were afforded domestic gasoline by an individual baseline tied to the producer of a product. The Panel then proceeded to examine whether the aspect of the Gasoline Rule found inconsistent with the General Agreement was necessary to achieve the stated policy objectives under Article XX(b). The Panel noted that it was not the necessity of the policy goal that was to be examined, but whether or not it was necessary that imported gasoline be effectively prevented from benefitting from as favourable sales conditions as were afforded by an individual baseline tied to the producer of a product. It was the task of the Panel to address whether these inconsistent measures were necessary to achieve the policy goal under Article XX(b). It was therefore not the task of the Panel to examine the necessity of the environmental objectives of the Gasoline Rule, or of parts of the Rule that the Panel did not specifically find to be inconsistent with the General Agreement.

6.23   The Panel then turned to the arguments of the parties relating to that aspect of the Gasoline Rule found inconsistent with the General Agreement. The United States argued that not all entities dealing in gasoline could be assigned an individual baseline and, of those who could be assigned such a baseline, not all could use the same types of secondary or tertiary evidence (Methods 2 and 3) to establish it. Certain entities including importers, blenders and refiners which did not have continuous 1990 operations, were simply not in a position to furnish this secondary or tertiary evidence. Venezuela and Brazil argued on the other hand that foreign refiners should be accorded their own individual baselines under the Gasoline Rule using the same types of evidence, as easily available to them as to domestic refiners. Alternatively, they argued that importers should be able to use individual 1990 baselines established for the foreign refiners with whom they dealt. They noted that an EPA regulatory proposal had even been made along those lines in May 1994. The United States countered that such a proposal would not be feasible because of: (1) the impossibility of determining the refinery of origin for each imported shipment; (2) the incentive to "game" the system thereby handed to exporters and importers; and (3) the difficulty for the United States to exercise an enforcement jurisdiction with respect to a foreign refinery, since the Gasoline Rule required criminal and civil sanctions in order to be effective. The United States argued further against the use of foreign refiner baselines by citing "equity concerns" of importers that their use would favour those firms that dealt with Venezuelan product, and the existence of particular competitive conditions in the international market, including the flexibility maintained by foreign refiners.

6.24   The Panel proceeded to examine whether the United States had in fact demonstrated that the inconsistent measures found to violate Article III:4 were necessary to achieve the stated policy objectives of the United States. The Panel noted that the term "necessary" had been interpreted in the context of Article XX(d) by the panel in the *Section 337* case which had stated that:

> a contracting party cannot justify a measure inconsistent with another GATT provision as "necessary" in terms of Article XX(d) if an alternative measure which it could reasonably be expected to employ and which is not inconsistent with other GATT provisions is available to it. By the same token, in cases where a measure consistent with other GATT provisions is not reasonably available, a contracting party is bound to use, among the measures reasonably available to it, that which entails the least degree of inconsistency with other GATT provisions.[34]

---

[34]   "United States - Section 337 of the Tariff Act of 1930", BISD 36S/345, para. 5.26 (adopted on 7 November 1989).

The same reasoning had been adopted by the 1990 *Thai Cigarette* panel in examining a measure under Article XX(b). That panel saw no reason not to adopt the same interpretation of "necessity" under Article XX(b) as under Article XX(d), stating that:

> the import restrictions imposed by Thailand could be considered to be "necessary" in terms of Article XX(b) only if there were no alternative measures consistent with the General Agreement, or less inconsistent with it, which Thailand could reasonably be expected to employ to achieve its health policy objectives.[35]

The Panel also noted that while several past panels examining issues under Article XX had identified alternative measures that were reasonably available and fully consistent with the General Agreement, they had also in other instances identified alternative measures that would be "less inconsistent" with the General Agreement. For example, the panel in the *337* case found that, while a general exclusion order applying to imported products was not "necessary", a limited *in rem* order could be justified even though it too was inconsistent with Article III:4.[36] Recalling its remarks in paragraph 6.22 above, the Panel considered that its task was thus to determine whether the United States had demonstrated whether it was necessary to maintain precisely those inconsistent measures whereby imported gasoline was effectively prevented from benefitting from as favourable sales conditions as were afforded to domestic gasoline by an individual baseline tied to the producer of a product. If there were consistent or less inconsistent measures reasonably available to the United States, the requirement to demonstrate necessity would not have been met.

6.25   The Panel then examined whether there were measures consistent or less inconsistent with the General Agreement that were reasonably available to the United States to further its policy objectives of protecting human, animal and plant life or health. The Panel did not consider that the manner in which imported gasoline was effectively prevented from benefitting from as favourable sales conditions as were afforded to domestic gasoline by an individual baseline tied to the producer of a product was necessary to achieve the stated goals of the Gasoline Rule. In the view of the Panel, baseline establishment methods could be applied to entities dealing in imported gasoline in a way that granted treatment to imported gasoline that was consistent or less inconsistent with the General Agreement. If a single statutory baseline applying to all entities — refiners, blenders and importers — was not the chosen regulatory method, then importers could for example be permitted to use a gasoline baseline applicable to imports derived, when possible, from evidence of the individual 1990 baselines of foreign refiners with whom the importer currently dealt. Although such a scheme could result in formally different regulation for imported and domestic products, the Panel noted that previous panels had accepted that this could be consistent with

---

[35]   "Thailand - Restrictions on Importation of and Internal Taxes on Cigarettes", BISD 37S/200, para. 75 (adopted on 7 November 1990).

[36]   "United States - Section 337 of the Tariff Act of 1930", BISD 36S/345, para. 5.32 (adopted on 7 November 1989).

Article III:4.[37] The requirement under Article III:4 to treat an imported product no less favourably than the like domestic product is met by granting formally different treatment to the imported product, if that treatment results in maintaining conditions of competition for the imported product no less favourable than those of the like domestic product. Further, these conditions of competition referred to those conditions that were established by government measures and would not therefore include factors such as the "flexibility of individual producers" in this case. The Panel noted finally that a regulatory scheme using foreign refiner baselines, to the extent that it did not distinguish between imported gasoline on the basis of its country of origin, would not necessarily contravene Article I or other provisions of the General Agreement, and that the United States, notwithstanding suggestions that certain importers might have equitable concerns, had not established the contrary.

6.26   The Panel noted the claims of the United States that allowing importers or foreign refiners to use individual baselines in such a way was not feasible for the reasons listed in paragraph 6.23. The Panel was not convinced that the United States had satisfied its burden of proving that those reasons precluded the effective use of individual baselines in a manner which would allow imported products to obtain treatment that was consistent, or less inconsistent, with obligations under Article III:4. First, while the Panel agreed that it would be necessary under such a system to ascertain the origin of gasoline, the Panel could not conclude that the United States had shown that this could not be achieved by other measures reasonably available to it and consistent or less inconsistent with the General Agreement. Indeed, the Panel noted that a determination of origin would often be feasible. The Panel examined, for instance, the case of a direct shipment to the United States. It considered that there was no reason to believe that, given the usual measures available in international trade for determination of origin and tracking of goods (including documentary evidence and third party verification) there was any particular difficulty sufficient to warrant the demands of the baseline establishment methods applied by the United States.

6.27   Second, the Panel did not agree that the United States had met its burden of showing that the "gaming" concern was an adequate justification for maintaining the inconsistency with Article III:4 resulting from the baseline establishment methods. It was uncertain if, or to what extent, gaming would actually occur, especially given the small market share of imported gasoline (approximately 3 percent). Moreover, the Panel noted that the Gasoline Rule did not guarantee in its regulation of US entities that gasoline characteristics subject to non-degradation requirements (i.e. those regulated by baselines), would remain at the 1990 average levels. For example, there was no volume cap on the production of reformulated gasoline by individual refineries, which meant that if producers of relatively dirtier gasoline expanded their relative share of production of reformulated gasoline, the national average level of pollutants subject to the non-degradation requirements would be greater than in 1990. Similarly, within the

---

[37]   "United States - Section 337 of the Tariff Act of 1930", BISD 36S/345, para. 5.11 (adopted on 7 November 1989).

1990 volume limitations, if the output of producers of relatively cleaner gasoline fell below 1990 levels, while output of others did not, national average levels of pollutants would be worse. Moreover, specific provisions of the Gasoline Rule permitted some refiners to produce dirtier gasoline than they produced in 1990 (e.g., certain producers of JP-4 jet fuel) and permitted others to request specific derogation from the Rule. The Panel stressed that it was not finding that such events would occur, only that they could under the Rule. Given that the Gasoline Rule did not therefore guarantee that gasoline characteristics subject to non-degradation requirements would remain at 1990 levels, the Panel considered that it was not consistent for the United States to insist that there could be no possible deviation from achieving those levels in respect of imports, when it had not deemed it necessary to be as exacting on its own domestic production. Moreover, slightly stricter overall requirements applied to both domestic and imported gasoline could offset any possibility of an adverse environmental effect from these causes, and allow the United States to achieve its desired level of clean air without discriminating against imported gasoline. Such requirements could be implemented by the United States at any time. The Panel concluded that the United States had not met its burden of showing that concern over gaming was an adequate justification for maintaining the inconsistency with Article III:4 result-ing from the baseline establishment methods.

6.28   Third, the Panel did not accept that the United States had demonstrated that there was no other measure consistent, or less inconsistent, with Article III:4 reasonably available to enforce compliance with foreign refiner baselines, or im-porter baselines based thereon. The imposition of penalties on importers was in the Panel's view an effective enforcement mechanism used by the United States in other settings. In the view of the Panel, the United States had reasonably avail-able to it data for, and measures of, verification and assessment which were con-sistent or less inconsistent with Article III:4. For instance, although foreign data may be formally less subject to complete control by US authorities, this did not amount to establishing that foreign data could not in any circumstances be suffi-ciently reliable to serve US purposes. This, however, was the practical effect of the application of the Gasoline Rule. In the Panel's view, the United States had not demonstrated that data available from foreign refiners was inherently less susceptible to established techniques of checking, verification, assessment and enforcement than data for other trade in goods subject to US regulation. The na-ture of the data in this case was similar to data relied upon by the United States in other contexts, including, for example, under the application of antidumping laws. In an antidumping case, only when the information was not supplied or deemed unverifiable did the United States turn to other information. If a similar practice were to be applied in the case of the Gasoline Rule, then importers could, for instance, be permitted to use the individual baselines of foreign refin-ers for imported gasoline from those refiners, with the statutory baseline being applied only when the source of imported gasoline could not be determined or a baseline could not be established because of an absence of data. In the Panel's view, because allowing for such a possibility was reasonably available to the United States and would entail a lesser degree of inconsistency with the General

Agreement, the United States had failed to demonstrate the necessity of the Gasoline Rule's inconsistency with Article III:4 on this matter.

6.29   In view of the Panel's finding that the aspect of the baseline establishment methods found inconsistent with Article III:4 was not "necessary" under Article XX(b), the Panel did not proceed to examine whether it met also the conditions in the introductory clause to Article XX.

E.   Article XX(d)

6.30   The Panel proceeded to examine whether the aspect of the baseline establishment methods found inconsistent with Article III:4 could, as argued by the United States, be justified under paragraph (d) of Article XX. The relevant parts of Article XX were as follows:

> Subject to the requirement that such measures are not applied in a manner which would constitute a means of arbitrary or unjustifiable discrimination between countries where the same conditions prevail, or a disguised restriction on international trade, nothing in this Agreement shall be construed to prevent the adoption or enforcement by any contracting party of measures:
>
> > (d)   necessary to secure compliance with laws or regulations which are not inconsistent with the provisions of this Agreement, including those relating to customs enforcement, the enforcement of monopolies operated under paragraph 4 of Article II and Article XVII, the protection of patents, trade marks and copyrights, and the prevention of deceptive practices;

6.31   The Panel recalled that the party invoking an exception under Article XX bore the burden of proving that the inconsistent measures came within its scope. The Panel observed that the United States therefore had to demonstrate the following elements:

> (1)   that the measures for which the exception were being invoked - that is, the particular trade measures inconsistent with the General Agreement - *secure compliance* with laws or regulations themselves not inconsistent with the General Agreement;
>
> (2)   that the inconsistent measures for which the exception was being invoked were *necessary* to secure compliance with those laws or regulations; and
>
> (3)   that the measures were applied in conformity with the requirements of the *introductory clause* of Article XX.

In order to justify the application of Article XX(d), all the above elements had to be satisfied.

1. Securing Compliance With Consistent Laws or Regulations

6.32   The Panel proceeded to examine whether the aspect of the baseline establishment methods found inconsistent with the General Agreement secured compliance with a law or regulation not inconsistent with the General Agreement. The United States argued that the non-degradation requirements were laws and regulations not inconsistent with the General Agreement, and that the baseline establishment methods secured compliance with these. Venezuela argued that the United States had not clearly established which laws or regulations were not inconsistent with the General Agreement, and with which compliance was secured. Brazil considered that the US measures at most enforced a policy objective, not an actual obligation as required under Article XX(d).

6.33   The Panel observed that, assuming that a system of baselines by itself were consistent with Article III:4, the US scheme might constitute, for the purposes of Article XX(d), a law or regulation "not inconsistent" with the General Agreement. However, the Panel found that maintenance of discrimination between imported and domestic gasoline contrary to Article III:4 under the baseline establishment methods did not "secure compliance" with the baseline system. These methods were not an enforcement mechanism. They were simply rules for determining the individual baselines. As such, they were not the type of measures with which Article XX(d) was concerned.[38]

2. Other Conditions

6.34   The Panel observed that, in view of its finding that the less favourable treatment of imported gasoline under the baseline establishment methods accorded to importers did not "secure compliance" with the underlying baseline establishment rules, it did not need to consider also whether these methods were "necessary" to secure compliance and met the conditions in the introductory clause to Article XX.

F. Article XX(g)

6.35   The Panel proceeded to examine whether the part of the Gasoline Rule found inconsistent with Article III:4 could, as argued by the United States, be justified under paragraph (g) of Article XX. The relevant parts of Article XX were as follows:

> Subject to the requirement that such measures are not applied in a manner which would constitute a means of arbitrary or unjustifiable discrimination between countries where the same conditions prevail, or a disguised restriction on international trade, nothing in this Agreement shall be construed to prevent the adoption or enforcement by any contracting party of measures:

---

[38]   "European Economic Community - Regulation on Imports of Parts and Components", BISD 37S/132, paras. 5.12 - 5.18 (adopted on 16 May 1990).

> (g)   relating to the conservation of exhaustible natural resources
>   if such measures are made effective in conjunction with re-
>   strictions on domestic production or consumption;

The Panel noted that as the party invoking an exception the United States bore the burden of proof in demonstrating that the inconsistent measures came within its scope. The Panel observed that the United States therefore had to demonstrate the following elements:

> (1)   that the *policy* in respect of the measures for which the provision
>   was invoked fell within the range of polices related to the conser-
>   vation of exhaustible natural resources;

> (2)   that the measures for which the exception was being invoked - that
>   is the particular trade measures inconsistent with the General
>   Agreement - were *related to* the conservation of exhaustible natural
>   resources;

> (3)   that the measures for which the exception was being invoked were
>   made effective *in conjunction* with restrictions on domestic pro-
>   duction or consumption; and

> (4)   that the measures were applied in conformity with the requirements
>   of the *introductory clause* of Article XX.

In order to justify the application of Article XX(g), all the above elements had to be satisfied.

1.   Policy Goal of Conserving An Exhaustible Natural Resource

6.36   The Panel noted the US argument that clean air was an exhaustible resource within the meaning of Article XX(g), since it could be exhausted by pollutants such as those emitted through the consumption of gasoline. Lakes, streams, parks, crops and forests were also natural resources that could be exhausted by air pollution. Measures to control air pollution were therefore measures to conserve exhaustible natural resources. Venezuela disagreed, considering that air was not an exhaustible natural resource within the meaning of Article XX(g); rather, its "condition" changed depending on its cleanliness. Article XX(g) was originally intended to cover exports of exhaustible goods such as petroleum and coal; to expand it to cover "conditions" of renewable resources was not justified.

6.37   The Panel then examined whether clean air could be considered an exhaustible natural resource. In the view of the Panel, clean air was a resource (it had value) and it was natural. It could be depleted. The fact that the depleted resource was defined with respect to its qualities was not, for the Panel, decisive. Likewise, the fact that a resource was renewable could not be an objection. A past panel had accepted that renewable stocks of salmon could constitute an exhaustible natural resource.[39] Accordingly, the Panel found that a policy to reduce the depletion of clean air was a policy to conserve a natural resource within the meaning of Article XX(g).

2.   *Measures "Related to" the Conservation of an Exhaustible Natural Resource; and Made Effective "In Conjunction" with Restrictions on Domestic Production or Consumption*

6.38   The Panel proceeded to examine whether the baseline establishment methods found inconsistent with Article III:4 were "related to" the conservation of clean air. Venezuela argued that past panels had interpreted "related to" to mean "primarily aimed at" the conservation of the resource. According to Venezuela, loopholes in the establishment of the baseline undermined its own conservation objectives, and the measure could not therefore be seen as "primarily aimed" at conservation.

6.39   The Panel noted that the words "related to" did not in isolation provide precise guidance as to the required link between the measures and the conservation objective. However, the Panel agreed with the interpretation of this term in the report of the 1987 *Herring and Salmon* case, where the panel stated that

> as the preamble of Article XX indicates, the purpose of including Article XX:(g) in the General Agreement was not to widen the scope for measures serving trade policy purposes but merely to ensure that the commitments under the General Agreement do not hinder the pursuit of policies aimed at the conservation of exhaustive natural resources. The Panel concluded for these reasons that, while a trade measure did not have to be necessary or essential to the conservation of an exhaustible natural resource, it had to be *primarily aimed* at the conservation of an exhaustible natural resource to be considered as "relating to" conservation within the meaning of Article XX:(g).[40] (emphasis added)

For the same reasons, the *Herring and Salmon* panel decided that

> the terms "in conjunction with" in Article XX:(g) had to be interpreted in a way that ensures that the scope of possible actions under that provision corresponds to the purpose for which it was included in the General Agreement. A trade measure could therefore in the view of the Panel only be considered to be made effective

---

[39]   "Canada - Measures Affecting Exports of Unprocessed Herring and Salmon", BISD 35S/98, para 4.4 (adopted on 22 March 1988). See also the same conclusion with respect to dolphins in the Report of the Panel on "United States - Restrictions on Imports of Tuna", circulated on 16 June 1994, DS29/R, para 5.13, not adopted.
[40]   "Canada - Measures Affecting Exports of Unprocessed Herring and Salmon", BISD 35S/98, para 4.6 (adopted on 22 March 1988).

"in conjunction with" production restrictions if it was *primarily aimed* at rendering effective these restrictions.[41] (emphasis added)

6.40   The Panel then proceeded to examine whether the baseline establishment methods could be said to be "primarily aimed at" achieving the conservation objectives of the Gasoline Rule. The Panel recalled the purpose of Article XX:(g), which had been expressed by the panel in the 1987 *Herring and Salmon* case as follows:

> [T]he purpose of including Article XX:(g) in the General Agreement was not to widen the scope of measures serving trade policy purposes but merely to ensure that the commitments under the General Agreement do not hinder the pursuit of policies aimed at the conservation of exhaustible natural resources.

The Panel then considered whether the precise aspects of the Gasoline Rule that it had found to violate Article III -- the less favourable baseline establishments methods that adversely affected the conditions of competition for imported gasoline -- were primarily aimed at the conservation of natural resources. The Panel saw no direct connection between less favourable treatment of imported gasoline that was chemically identical to domestic gasoline, and the US objective of improving air quality in the United States. Indeed, in the view of the Panel, being consistent with the obligation to provide no less favourable treatment would not prevent the attainment of the desired level of conservation of natural resources under the Gasoline Rule. Accordingly, it could not be said that the baseline establishment methods that afforded less favourable treatment to imported gasoline were primarily aimed at the conservation of natural resources. In the Panel's view, the above-noted lack of connection was underscored by the fact that affording treatment of imported gasoline consistent with its Article III:4 obligations would not in any way hinder the United States in its pursuit of its conservation policies under the Gasoline Rule. Indeed, the United States remained free to regulate in order to obtain whatever air quality it wished. The Panel therefore concluded that the less favourable baseline establishments methods at issue in this case were not primarily aimed at the conservation of natural resources.

6.41   With respect to whether the baseline establishment methods could be said to be primarily aimed at "rendering effective restrictions on domestic production or consumption", the Panel noted that it had not determined that the measures at issue were "restrictions", and whether they were "on" domestic production or consumption. However, in light of its finding in paragraph 6.40, the Panel did not proceed to determine this issue or whether the measure met the conditions in the introductory clause of Article XX.

G.   Article XXIII:1(b)

6.42   The Panel then noted the claim by Venezuela under Article XXIII:1(b) that benefits accruing to it under the General Agreement had been nullified and

---

[41]   Ibidem.

impaired by the application of the Gasoline Rule, whether or not it conflicted with provisions of the General Agreement. In view of the finding by the Panel that the Gasoline Rule violated Article III:4 of the General Agreement, and could not be justified under Article XX (b), (d) and (g), the Panel concluded that it was not necessary to examine this additional claim.

H. *Applicability of the Agreement on Technical Barriers to Trade*

6.43   In view of its findings under the General Agreement, the Panel concluded that it was not necessary to decide on issues raised under the TBT Agreement.

VII. CONCLUDING REMARKS

7.1   In concluding, the Panel wished to underline that it was not its task to examine generally the desirability or necessity of the environmental objectives of the Clean Air Act or the Gasoline Rule. Its examination was confined to those aspects of the Gasoline Rule that had been raised by the complainants under specific provisions of the General Agreement. Under the General Agreement, WTO Members were free to set their own environmental objectives, but they were bound to implement these objectives through measures consistent with its provisions, notably those on the relative treatment of domestic and imported products.

VIII. CONCLUSIONS

8.1   In the light of the findings above, the Panel concluded that the baseline establishment methods contained in Part 80 of Title 40 of the Code of Federal Regulations are not consistent with Article III:4 of the General Agreement, and cannot be justified under paragraphs (b), (d) and (g) of Article XX of the General Agreement.

8.2   The Panel *recommends* that the Dispute Settlement Body request the United States to bring this part of the Gasoline Rule into conformity with its obligations under the General Agreement.

EUROPEAN COMMUNITIES - TRADE DESCRIPTION OF SCALLOPS

(REQUEST BY CANADA)

Report of the Panel
WT/DS7/R

Circulated to Members on 5 August 1996

1.   On 19 May 1995, the Government of Canada requested consultations with the European Communities ("EC") concerning French Order NOR MERP9300051A of 22 March 1993 and its amendments, relating to the official names and permitted trade descriptions of scallops in France. This request was made pursuant to Article XXII:1 of the General Agreement on Tariffs and Trade 1994 ("GATT 1994"), Article 14.1 of the Agreement on Technical Barriers to Trade ("TBT Agreement"), and Article 4 of the Understanding on Rules and Procedures Governing the Settlement of Disputes ("DSU"). In accordance with Article 4 of the DSU, the request was circulated to Members of the World Trade Organization ("WTO") on 24 May 1995 (WT/DS7/1).

2.   Pursuant to Article 4.11 of the DSU, Chile on 31 May 1995 (WT/DS7/2), and Iceland (WT/DS7/3), Japan (WT/DS7/4) and Peru (WT/DS7/5) on 2 June 1995, requested to be joined in the consultations requested by Canada. On 23 June 1995, the EC informed the Dispute Settlement Body ("DSB") that it had accepted these requests (WT/DS7/6). Consultations were held in Geneva on 19 June 1995.

3.   Consultations failed to settle the dispute and, on 7 July 1995, Canada requested the DSB to establish a panel, at its next meeting, pursuant to Article XXIII of GATT 1994, Article 14 of the TBT Agreement and Articles 4 and 6 of the DSU (WT/DS7/7 and Corr.1). Canada requested that the panel consider and find that the French Order and subsequent amendments are:

(a)   inconsistent with Article 2 of the TBT Agreement;

(b)   inconsistent with Articles I and III of GATT 1994; and

(c)   nullifying and impairing benefits accruing to Canada under the WTO Agreement.

4.   On 19 July 1995, pursuant to the request made by Canada, the DSB established a panel with standard terms of reference. The terms of reference of the Panel are the following:

"To examine, in the light of the relevant provisions of the covered agreements cited by Canada in document WT/DS7/7, the matter referred to the DSB by Canada in that document and to make such findings as will assist the DSB in making the recommendations or in giving the rulings provided for in those agreements".

5.   Australia, Chile, Iceland, Japan, Peru and the United States reserved their rights to participate in the Panel proceedings as third parties. All these Members,

except Australia, attended the session for third parties and submitted written communications to the Panel.

6.   The parties to the dispute agreed on 6 September 1995 to the following composition of the Panel:

Chairman: Mr. Michael Cartland

Members: Mr. Peter Palecka

Mrs. Barbara Rigassi

7.   Peru and Chile requested consultations with the EC concerning the same French Order, on 18 and 24 July 1995, respectively. At its meeting on 11 October 1995, in accordance with Article 9 of the DSU, the DSB established a single panel on the same matter pursuant to the requests of Peru (WT/DS12/7) and Chile (WT/DS14/6). At that DSB meeting, Peru and Chile asked for the application of Article 9.3 of the DSU so that the same panelists as those serving in this dispute between the EC and Canada (WT/DS7) would also serve on the single Panel established pursuant to the requests of Peru and Chile. On 12 October 1995, the panelists serving on the Panel between the EC and Canada (WT/DS7) agreed to act as panelists on the Panel established for the dispute between the EC and Peru and Chile. The Panel report of this related dispute is contained in WT/DS12/R, WT/DS14/R.

8.   The Panel met with the parties on 12 and 13 October 1995, on 12 December 1995 and on 5 February 1996. It met with interested third parties on 13 October 1995.

9.   On 6 February 1996, pursuant to Article 12.9 of the DSU, the Chairman of the Panel informed the DSB that the Panel would not be able to issue its report within six months (Article 12.8 of the DSU). The reasons for that delay are provided in document WT/DS7/9.

10.   The Panel issued the Descriptive Part of its report on 19 February 1996. It issued the Interim Report on 14 March 1996.

11.   On 2 April 1996, at the request of the EC, the Panel held a review meeting with the parties pursuant to Article 15.2 of the DSU, to hear the comments of the parties on the Panel's Interim Report.

12.   On 16, 19 and 29 April 1996, the parties requested the Panel to postpone issuance of the Final Report to the parties.

13.   On 2 May 1996, the parties again requested the Panel to postpone issuance of the Final Report to the parties until 10 May 1996 (WT/DS7/10).

14.   On 10 May 1996, the parties requested the Panel to suspend the Panel proceedings in accordance with Article 12.12 of the DSU because they were discussing the terms of a mutually agreed solution (WT/DS7/11).

15.   On 5 July 1996, pursuant to Article 3.6 of the DSU, the parties notified the DSB and the relevant Councils and Committees that they had reached a mutually agreed solution, which was circulated as document WT/DS7/12 on 19 July 1996.

16.   The Panel takes note of this mutually agreed solution between the parties to the dispute and of the provisions of Article 12.7 of the DSU which provide that "where a settlement of the matter among the parties to the dispute has been found,

the report of the panel shall be confined to a brief description of the case and to reporting that a solution has been reached". Accordingly, the Panel concludes its work by reporting that a mutually agreed solution to this dispute has been reached between the parties.

EUROPEAN COMMUNITIES - TRADE DESCRIPTION OF SCALLOPS

(REQUESTS BY PERU AND CHILE)

Report of the Panel
WT/DS12/R, WT/DS14/R

Circulated to Members on 5 August 1996

1.   On 18 July 1995, the Government of Peru to the WTO requested consultations with the European Communities ("EC") concerning French Order NOR MERP9300051A of 22 March 1993 and its amendments, relating to the official names and permitted trade descriptions of scallops in France. This request was made pursuant to Article XXII:1 of the General Agreement on Tariffs and Trade 1994 ("GATT 1994"), Article 14.1 of the Agreement on Technical Barriers to Trade ("TBT Agreement"), and Article 4 of the Understanding on Rules and Procedures Governing the Settlement of Disputes ("DSU"). In accordance with Article 4 of the DSU, the request was circulated to Members of the World Trade Organization ("WTO") on 25 July 1995 (WT/DS12/1).

2.   Pursuant to Article 4.11 of the DSU, on 27 July 1995, Chile (WT/DS12/2) and Canada (WT/DS12/3) requested to be joined in the consultations initiated by Peru. On 31 July 1995, the EC informed the Dispute Settlement Body ("DSB") that it had accepted these requests (WT/DS12/4). Consultations were held on 10 August 1995.

3.   These consultations failed to settle the dispute and, on 18 September 1995, Peru requested the DSB to establish a panel, at its next meeting, pursuant to Article XXIII of GATT 1994, Article 14 of the TBT Agreement and Articles 4 and 6 of the DSU (WT/DS12/7). Peru requested that the panel consider and find that the French Order and subsequent amendments are:

   (a)   inconsistent with Articles 2 and 12 of the TBT Agreement;

   (b)   inconsistent with Articles I and III of GATT 1994; and

   (c)   nullifying and impairing benefits accruing to Peru under the WTO Agreement.

4.   On 24 July 1995, the Government of Chile requested consultations with the EC concerning the same French Order referred to above in paragraph 1. This request was made pursuant to Article XXII:1 of GATT 1994, Article 14.1 of the TBT Agreement and Article 4 of the DSU. In accordance with Article 4 of the DSU, the request was circulated to Members of the WTO on 31 July 1995 (WT/DS14/1).

5.   Pursuant to Article 4.11 of the DSU, Canada on 2 August 1995 (WT/DS14/2), Peru on 11 August 1995 (WT/DS14/3) and Japan on 10 August 1995 (WT/DS14/4) requested to be joined in the consultations initiated by Chile. The EC accepted these requests and consultations were held on 10 August 1995, jointly with the consultations referred to in paragraph 2.

6.   These consultations failed to settle the dispute and, on 25 September 1995, Chile requested the DSB to establish a panel, at its next meeting, pursuant to Article XXIII of GATT 1994, Article 14 of the TBT Agreement and Articles 4 and 6 of the DSU (WT/DS14/6). Chile requested that the panel consider and find that the French Order and subsequent amendments are:

(a)   inconsistent with Articles 2 and 12 of the TBT Agreement;

(b)   inconsistent with Articles I and III of GATT 1994; and

(c)   nullifying and impairing benefits accruing to Chile under the WTO Agreement.

7.   At its meeting on 11 October 1995, pursuant to the requests of Peru and Chile mentioned above in paragraphs 3 and 6 respectively, the DSB established a single panel related to the same matter in accordance with Article 9.1 of the DSU.

8.   At that DSB meeting on 11 October 1995, Peru, Chile and the EC agreed that the Panel should have standard terms of reference. The terms of reference of the Panel are the following:

"To examine, in the light of the relevant provisions of the covered agreements cited by Peru and Chile in documents WT/DS12/7 and WT/DS14/6, the matter referred to the DSB by Peru and Chile in those documents and to make such findings as will assist the DSB in making the recommendations or in giving the rulings provided for in those agreements".

9.   At that DSB meeting of 11 October 1995, Australia, Canada, Iceland, Japan and the United States reserved their rights to participate in the Panel proceedings as third parties. All these Members, except Australia, attended the session for third parties and submitted written communications to the Panel.

10.   At its meeting of 19 July 1995, the DSB had established a panel in accordance with the request made by Canada (WT/DS7/7) concerning the same French Order. Chile and Peru had been joined in the consultations of this related dispute between the EC and Canada pursuant to their requests made and accepted in accordance with Article 4.11 of the DSU (WT/DS7/6). The Panel report of this related dispute is contained in document WT/DS7/R.

11.   At the DSB meeting of 11 October 1995, Peru and Chile also requested the application of Article 9.3 of the DSU so that the same panelists serving on the Panel in the related dispute between the EC and Canada (referred to in paragraph 10 above) would also serve on the single Panel established pursuant to the requests of Peru and Chile (referred to in paragraph 7 above).

12.   On 12 October 1995, the panelists serving on the Panel in the dispute between the EC and Canada agreed to act as panelists for the Panel established for the dispute between the EC and Peru and Chile.

13.   The Panel established pursuant to the requests of Peru and Chile (referred to in paragraph 7 above) was therefore constituted on 12 October 1995 with the following composition:

Chairman: Mr. Michael Cartland

Members: Mr. Peter Palecka

            Mrs. Barbara Rigassi

14.   The Panel met with the three parties on 11 December 1995 and on 5 February 1996. It met with interested third parties in the afternoon of 11 December 1995.

15.   On 6 February 1996, pursuant to Article 12.9 of the DSU, the Chairman of the Panel informed the DSB that the Panel would not be able to issue its report within six months (Article 12.8 of the DSU). The reasons for that delay are provided in document WT/DS12/9, WT/DS14/8.

16.   The Panel issued the Descriptive Part of its report on 19 February 1996. It issued the Interim Report on 14 March 1996.

17.   On 2 April 1996, at the request of the EC, the Panel held a review meeting with the parties pursuant to Article 15.2 of the DSU, to hear the comments of the parties on the Panel's Interim Report.

18.   On 16, 19 and 29 April 1996, the parties requested the Panel to postpone issuance of the Final Report to the parties.

19.   On 2 May 1996, the parties again requested the Panel to postpone issuance of the Final Report to the parties until 10 May 1996 (WT/DS12/10 and WT/DS14/9).

20.   On 10 May 1996, the parties requested the Panel to suspend the Panel proceedings in accordance with Article 12.12 of the DSU because they were discussing the terms of a mutually agreed solution (WT/DS12/11 and WT/DS14/10).

21.   On 5 July 1996, pursuant to Article 3.6 of the DSU, the parties notified the DSB and the relevant Councils and Committees that they had reached a mutually agreed solution, which was circulated as documents WT/DS12/12 and WT/DS14/11 on 19 July 1996.

22.   The Panel takes note of this mutually agreed solution between the parties to the dispute and of the provisions of Article 12.7 of the DSU which provide that "where a settlement of the matter among the parties to the dispute has been found, the report of the panel shall be confined to a brief description of the case and to reporting that a solution has been reached". Accordingly, the Panel concludes its work by reporting that a mutually agreed solution to this dispute has been reached between the parties.

JAPAN - TAXES ON ALCOHOLIC BEVERAGES

Report of the Appellate Body

WT/DS8/AB/R, WT/DS10/AB/R, WT/DS11/AB/R

Adopted by the Dispute Settlement Body on 1 November 1996

Japan, Appellant/Appellee	Present:
United States, Appellant/Appellee	Lacarte-Muró, Presiding Member
Canada, Appellee	Bacchus, Member
European Communities, Appellee	El-Naggar, Member

A. INTRODUCTION

Japan and the United States appeal from certain issues of law and legal interpretations in the Panel Report, *Japan - Taxes on Alcoholic Beverages*[1] (the "Panel Report"). That Panel (the "Panel") was established to consider complaints by the European Communities, Canada and the United States against Japan relating to the Japanese Liquor Tax Law (Shuzeiho), Law No. 6 of 1953 as amended (the "Liquor Tax Law").[2]

The Panel Report was circulated to the Members of the World Trade Organization (the "WTO") on 11 July 1996. It contains the following conclusions:

(i)   Shochu and vodka are like products and Japan, by taxing the latter in excess of the former, is in violation of its obligation under Article III:2, first sentence, of the General Agreement on Tariffs and Trade 1994.

(ii)   Shochu, whisky, brandy, rum, gin, genever, and liqueurs are "directly competitive or substitutable products" and Japan, by not taxing them similarly, is in violation of its obligation under Article III:2, second sentence, of the General Agreement on Tariffs and Trade 1994.[3]

The Panel made the following recommendations:

7.2   The Panel *recommends* that the Dispute Settlement Body request Japan to bring the Liquor Tax Law into conformity with its obligations under the General Agreement on Tariffs and Trade 1994.[4]

---

[1]   WT/DS8/R, WT/DS10/R, WT/DS11/R.

[2]   Norway originally reserved its right as a third party to the dispute but subsequently informed the Panel that it was withdrawing its request to participate as a third party.

[3]   Panel Report, para. 7.1.

[4]   Panel Report, para. 7.2.

On 8 August 1996, Japan notified the Dispute Settlement Body[5] of the WTO of its decision to appeal certain issues of law covered in the Panel Report and legal interpretations developed by the Panel, pursuant to paragraph 4 of Article 16 of the *Understanding on Rules and Procedures Governing the Settlement of Disputes* (the "*DSU*") and filed a Notice of Appeal with the Appellate Body, pursuant to Rule 20 of the *Working Procedures for Appellate Review* (the "*Working Procedures*").[6] On 19 August 1996, Japan filed an appellant's submission.[7] On 23 August 1996, the United States filed an appellant's submission pursuant to Rule 23(1) of the *Working Procedures*. The European Communities, Canada and the United States submitted appellees' submissions pursuant to Rule 22 of the *Working Procedures*, on 2 September 1996. That same day, Japan submitted an appellee's submission pursuant to Rule 23(3) of the *Working Procedures*.

The oral hearing contemplated by Rule 27 of the *Working Procedures* was held on 9 September 1996. The participants presented their arguments and answered questions from the Division of the Appellate Body hearing the appeal (the "Division"). The participants answered most of these questions orally at the hearing. They answered some in writing.[8] The Division gave each participant an opportunity to respond to the written post-hearing memoranda of the other participants.[9]

B.   ARGUMENTS OF PARTICIPANTS

1.   Japan

Japan appeals from the Panel's findings and conclusions, as well as from certain of the legal interpretations developed by the Panel. Japan argues that the Panel erred in its interpretation of Article III:2, first and second sentences of the General Agreement on Tariffs and Trade 1994 (the "GATT 1994"), which is an integral part of the *Marrakesh Agreement Establishing the World Trade Organization* (the "*WTO Agreement*").[10] According to Japan, with respect to both the first and second sentences of Article III:2, the Panel erred in: (1) disregarding the need to determine whether the Liquor Tax Law has the aim of affording protection to domestic production; (2) ignoring whether there is "linkage" between the origin of products and the tax treatment they incur and, in this respect, not comparing the tax treatment of domestic products as a whole and foreign products as a whole; and (3) not giving proper weight to the tax/price ratio as a yardstick to compare the tax burdens.

---

[5]   WT/DS8/9, WT/DS10/9, WT/DS11/6.
[6]   WT/AB/WP/1.
[7]   Pursuant to Rule 21(1) of the *Working Procedures*.
[8]   Pursuant to Rule 28(1) of the *Working Procedures*.
[9]   Pursuant to Rule 28(2) of the *Working Procedures*.
[10]   Done at Marrakesh, Morocco, 15 April 1994 and entered into effect on 1 January 1995.

With respect to the first sentence of Article III:2, Japan argues that the Panel erred by virtually ignoring Article III:1, particularly the phrase "so as to afford protection to domestic production", as part of the context of Article III:2. Japan maintains also that the title of Article III forms part of the context of Article III:2, and that the object and purpose of the GATT 1994 and the *WTO Agreement* as a whole must also be taken into account in interpreting Article III:2. Japan argues that the interpretation of Article III:2, first sentence, in the light of these considerations, requires an examination of both the aim and the effect of the measure in question. Japan also alleges that the Panel erred in placing excessive emphasis on tariff classification in finding that shochu and vodka are "like products" within the meaning of Article III:2, first sentence, arguing that the relevant tariff bindings indicate that these products are not "like".

With respect to the second sentence of Article III:2, Japan asserts that the Panel erred by failing to interpret correctly the principle of Article III:1, in particular, the language "so as to afford protection to domestic production", erroneously placing excessive emphasis on the phrase "not similarly taxed" in the Interpretative Note *Ad* Article III:2. Japan claims further that the Panel erred by failing to examine the issue of *de minimis* differences in the light of the principle of "so as to afford protection to domestic production"; the Panel examined the issue of *de minimis* differences only by comparing taxes in terms of taxation per kilolitre of product and taxation per degree of alcohol.

With respect to the points of appeal raised by the United States in its appellant's submission, Japan responds that the arguments advanced by the United States are not based on a correct understanding of the Japanese liquor tax system. Japan argues that the Liquor Tax Law has the legitimate policy purpose of ensuring neutrality and equity, particularly horizontal equity, and that it has neither the aim nor the effect of protecting domestic production. Japan asserts that it is not correct to conclude that all distilled liquors are "like products" under Article III:2, first sentence, or to conclude that the Liquor Tax Law is inconsistent with Article III:2 because it imposes a tax on imported distilled liquors in excess of the tax on like domestic products.

2.   United States

The United States supports the Panel's overall conclusions, but appeals nonetheless. The United States alleges several errors in the findings of the Panel and the legal interpretations developed by the Panel in reaching its conclusions in the Panel Report. The United States maintains that the Panel erred in its interpretation of Article III:2, first and second sentences, principally as a result of an erroneous understanding of the relationship between Article III:2 and Article III:1. The United States contends that the Panel disregarded Article III:1, which the United States sees as an integral part of the context that must be considered in interpreting Article III:2, and Article III generally. The United States asserts that Article III:1 sets out the object and purpose of Article III and must therefore be considered in any interpretation of the text of Article III:2. The United States argues that the Panel did not look beyond the text of Article III:2 in interpreting Article III:2 and thereby fell into error.

More specifically, with respect to the first sentence of Article III:2, the United States submits that the Panel erred in finding that "likeness" can be determined purely on the basis of physical characteristics, consumer uses and tariff classification without considering also the context and purpose of Article III, as set out in Article III:1, and without considering, in particular, whether regulatory distinctions are made, in the language of Article III:1, "so as to afford protection to domestic production". The United States concludes that the Panel erred in its interpretation of Article III:2, first sentence in: failing to interpret Article III:2, first sentence, in the light of Article III:1, consistently with the analysis in *United States - Measures Affecting Alcoholic and Malt Beverages ("Malt Beverages")*;[11] not finding that all distilled spirits constitute "like products" under Article III:2, first sentence; and drawing a connection between national treatment obligations and tariff bindings.

With respect to the second sentence of Article III:2 and the *Ad* Article thereto, the United States argues that the Panel erred with respect to the *Ad* Article to the second sentence in its interpretation of the term "directly competitive or substitutable products" by not considering whether a tax distinction is applied "in a manner contrary to the principles set forth in paragraph 1 of [Article III]", that is, "so as to afford protection to domestic production". The United States also claims that the Panel erred by using cross-price elasticity as the "decisive criterion" for whether products are "directly competitive or substitutable".

The United States contends as well that the Panel erred in not addressing the full scope of the products subject to the dispute and that there is inconsistency between the Panel's conclusions in paragraph 7.1(ii) of the Panel Report and in paragraphs 6.32-6.33 of the Panel Report. The United States further submits that the Panel erred in incorrectly assessing the relationship between Article III:2 and Article III:4 by stating that the product coverage of the two provisions is not identical.

Finally, the United States claims that the Panel erred in incorrectly characterizing adopted panel reports as "subsequent practice" within the meaning of Article 31(3)(b) of the *Vienna Convention on the Law of Treaties* (the "*Vienna Convention*").[12] According to the United States, adopted panel reports serve only to clarify, for the purposes of the particular dispute, the application of the rights and obligations of the parties to that dispute to the precise set of circumstances at that time. The *decision* to adopt a panel report constitutes a "decision" within the meaning of paragraph 1(b)(iv) of the language incorporating the GATT 1994 into the *WTO Agreement*, however, the adopted panel report as such does not constitute a "decision" in this sense.

With respect to the claims of error raised in Japan's appellant's submission, the United States responds that: the national treatment provisions in Article III of GATT 1994 can apply to origin-neutral measures; Japan's taxation under the Liquor Tax Law does have the aim and effect of affording protection to do-

---

[11]   Panel Report adopted on 19 June 1992, BISD 39S/206.
[12]   23 May 1969, 1155 *U.N.T.S.* 331; 8 *International Legal Materials* 679.

mestic production; and the tax/price ratios cited by Japan are not the appropriate basis for evaluating the consistency of taxation under the Liquor Tax Law with Article III:2.

3.   European Communities

The European Communities support the Panel's conclusions, and largely agree with the legal interpretations of Article III:2, first and second sentences, employed by the Panel. With respect to Article III:2, first sentence, the European Communities submit that the Panel's reasons for adopting the interpretation in the Panel Report, and thus for rejecting a specific test of "aims and effects", are sound and "in accordance with customary rules of interpretation of public international law", as contemplated by Article 3.2 of the *DSU*.[13] The European Communities contend that the Panel made it clear that the essential criterion for a "like product" determination is similarity of physical characteristics and that tariff nomenclatures may be relevant for a determination of "likeness" because they constitute an objective classification of products according to their physical characteristics. The European Communities maintain that the Panel's decision to identify only vodka and shochu as "like products" for purposes of Article III:2 cannot be regarded as arbitrary or insufficiently motivated. Although not entirely satisfied with the Panel's conclusions on the range of products found to be "like" under Article III:2, first sentence, the European Communities claim that those conclusions primarily involve the assessment of facts and, therefore, are not reviewable by the Appellate Body, which is limited to the consideration of issues of law under Article 17.6 of the *DSU*.[14]

With respect to Article III:2, second sentence, the European Communities argue that the Panel did not rule that cross-price elasticity is the decisive criterion for a determination that two products are directly competitive or substitutable, but rather ruled that such elasticity is only one of the criteria to be considered. The European Communities view the Panel's findings on the issue of the tax/price ratios as factual; however, if the Appellate Body nevertheless considers it necessary to rule on this issue, the European Communities argue that tax/price ratios are not the most appropriate yardstick for comparing tax burdens imposed by a system of specific taxes. The European Communities submit further that the Panel was correct in ignoring the linkage between differences in taxation and the origin of products. The European Communities assert that Japan's argument that the Liquor Tax Law is not applied "so as to afford protection to domestic production" of shochu because shochu is also produced in other countries and, there-

---

[13]   Article 3.2 of the *DSU* states in pertinent part:

   ...The Members recognize that [the dispute settlement system] serves to preserve the rights and obligations of Members under the covered agreements, and to clarify the existing provisions of those agreements in accordance with customary rules of interpretation of public international law.

[14]   Article 17.6 of the *DSU* states:

   An appeal shall be limited to issues of law covered in the panel report and legal interpretations developed by the panel.

fore, is not an "inherently domestic product" rests on two wrong propositions: first, that "domestic production" of shochu is not "protected" if the same tax treatment is accorded to foreign shochu; and, second, that the mere fact that shochu is produced in third countries is sufficient to conclude that foreign shochu may benefit from the lower tax as much as domestic shochu and, consequently, that protection is not afforded only to domestic production. The European Communities further contend that the United States is incorrect to attribute to the Panel the statement that the product coverage of Article III:2 and Article III:4 is not equivalent.

With respect to the status of adopted panel reports, the European Communities conclude that the Panel's characterization of them as "subsequent practice in a specific case" is intrinsically contradictory, since the essence of subsequent practice is that it consists of a large number of legally relevant events and pronouncements. The European Communities' view is that one adopted panel report "would merely constitute part of a wall of the house that constitutes subsequent practice". The European Communities, therefore, ask the Appellate Body to modify the Panel's legal terminology on this issue. The European Communities further consider that the *decision* to adopt a panel report constitutes a "decision" within the meaning of paragraph 1(b)(iv) of the language of Annex 1A incorporating the GATT 1994 into the *WTO Agreement*, however an adopted panel report is not itself a "decision" in this sense.

4. Canada

Canada confined its submissions and arguments on appeal to Article III:2, second sentence. Canada supports the Panel's legal interpretations of Article III:2, second sentence, as well as the conclusion of the Panel that the Liquor Tax Law is inconsistent with Article III:2, second sentence. Canada claims that the Panel properly found that the phrase "so as to afford protection" in Article III:1 does not require a consideration of both the aim and effect of a measure to determine whether that measure affords protection to domestic production. Canada argues further that: first, the Panel Report did not create a *per se* test in Article III:2, second sentence, and did not equate the reference to "so as to afford protection to domestic production" with a determination that directly competitive or substitutable products are "not similarly taxed"; second, the Panel had sufficient evidence before it to conclude that differential tax treatment under the Liquor Tax Law favours domestic shochu production; third, the Panel Report considered in detail the issue of the tax/price ratios and assigned them their proper weight in assessing the tax burden on the products in dispute; and, finally, the Panel interpreted the phrase "directly competitive or substitutable" properly and did not identify "cross-price elasticity" as *the* decisive criterion for assessment of whether products are directly competitive or substitutable.

With regard to the status of adopted panel reports, Canada argues that decisions to adopt panel reports under GATT 1947 constitute "decisions" under Article 1(b)(iv) of the GATT 1994.

C.   ISSUES RAISED IN THE APPEAL

The appellants, Japan and the United States, have raised the following issues in this appeal:

1.   Japan

(a)   whether the Panel erred in failing to interpret Article III:2, first and second sentences, in the light of Article III:1;

(b)   whether the Panel erred in rejecting an "aim-and-effect" test in establishing whether the Liquor Tax Law is applied "so as to afford protection to domestic production";

(c)   whether the Panel erred in failing to examine the effect of affording protection to domestic production from the perspective of the linkage between the origin of products and their treatment under the Liquor Tax Law;

(d)   whether the Panel failed to give proper weight to tax/price ratios as a yardstick for comparing tax burdens under Article III:2, first and second sentences;

(e)   whether the Panel erred in interpreting and applying Article III:2, second sentence, by equating the language "not similarly taxed" in *Ad* Article III:2, second sentence, with "so as to afford protection" in Article III:1; and

(f)   whether the Panel erred in placing excessive emphasis on tariff classification as a criterion for determining "like products".

2.   United States

(a)   whether the Panel erred in failing to interpret Article III:2, first and second sentences, in the light of Article III:1;

(b)   whether the Panel erred in failing to find that all distilled spirits are "like products";

(c)   whether the Panel erred in drawing a connection between national treatment obligations and tariff bindings;

(d)   whether the Panel erred in interpreting and applying Article III:2, second sentence, by equating the language "not similarly taxed" in *Ad* Article III:2, second sentence, with "so as to afford protection" in Article III:1;

(e)   whether the Panel erred in its conclusions on "directly competitive or substitutable products" by examining cross-price elasticity as "the decisive criterion";

(f)   whether the Panel erred in failing to maintain consistency between the conclusions in paragraph 7.1(ii) of the Panel Report on "directly competitive or substitutable products" and the conclusions in paragraphs 6.32-6.33 of the Panel

Report, and whether the Panel erred in failing to address the full scope of products subject of this dispute;

(g)   whether the Panel erred in finding that the coverage of Article III:2 and Article III:4 are not equivalent; and

(h)   whether the Panel erred in its characterization of panel reports adopted by the GATT CONTRACTING PARTIES and the WTO Dispute Settlement Body as "subsequent practice in a specific case by virtue of the decision to adopt them".

D.   TREATY INTERPRETATION

Article 3.2 of the *DSU* directs the Appellate Body to clarify the provisions of GATT 1994 and the other "covered agreements" of the *WTO Agreement* "in accordance with customary rules of interpretation of public international law". Following this mandate, in *United States - Standards for Reformulated and Conventional Gasoline*,[15] we stressed the need to achieve such clarification by reference to the fundamental rule of treaty interpretation set out in Article 31(1) of the *Vienna Convention*. We stressed there that this general rule of interpretation "has attained the status of a rule of customary or general international law".[16] There can be no doubt that Article 32 of the *Vienna Convention*, dealing with the role of supplementary means of interpretation, has also attained the same status.[17]

Article 31, as a whole, and Article 32 are each highly pertinent to the present appeal. They provide as follows:

Article 31

General rule of interpretation

1.   A treaty shall be interpreted in good faith in accordance with the ordinary meaning to be given to the terms of the treaty in their context and in the light of its object and purpose.

2.   The context for the purpose of the interpretation of a treaty shall comprise, in addition to the text, including its preamble and annexes:

---

[15]   Adopted 20 May 1996, WT/DS2/9.

[16]   *Ibid.*, at AB/R, DSR 1996:I, 3-28.

[17]   See *e.g.*: Jiménez de Aréchaga, "International Law in the Past Third of a Century" (1978-I) 159 *Recueil des Cours* p.1 at 42; *Territorial Dispute (Libyan Arab Jamahiriya/Chad), Judgment,* (1994), *I.C.J. Reports*, p. 6 at 20; *Maritime Delimitation and Territorial Questions between Qatar and Bahrain, Jurisdiction and Admissibility, Judgment,* (1995), *I.C.J.Reports*, p. 6 at 18; *Interpretation of the Convention of 1919 Concerning Employment of Women during the Night* (1932), P.C.I.J., Series A/B, No. 50, p. 365 at 380; cf. the *Serbian and Brazilian Loans Cases* (1929), P.C.I.J., Series A, Nos. 20-21, p. 5 at 30; *Constitution of the Maritime Safety Committee of the IMCO* (1960), *I.C.J. Reports*, p. 150 at 161; *Air Transport Services Agreement Arbitration (United States of America v. France)* (1963), *International Law Reports*, 38, p. 182 at 235-43.

(a)   any agreement relating to the treaty which was made between all the parties in connexion with the conclusion of the treaty;

(b)   any instrument which was made by one or more parties in connexion with the conclusion of the treaty and accepted by the other parties as an instrument related to the treaty.

3.   There shall be taken into account together with the context:

(a)   any subsequent agreement between the parties regarding the interpretation of the treaty or the application of its provisions;

(b)   any subsequent practice in the application of the treaty which establishes the agreement of the parties regarding its interpretation;

(c)   any relevant rules of international law applicable in the relations between the parties.

4.   A special meaning shall be given to a term if it is established that the parties so intended.

Article 32

Supplementary means of interpretation

Recourse may be had to supplementary means of interpretation, including the preparatory work of the treaty and the circumstances of its conclusion, in order to confirm the meaning resulting from the application of article 31, or to determine the meaning when the interpretation according to article 31:

(a)   leaves the meaning ambiguous or obscure; or

(b)   leads to a result which is manifestly absurd or unreasonable.

Article 31 of the *Vienna Convention* provides that the words of the treaty form the foundation for the interpretive process: "interpretation must be based above all upon the text of the treaty".[18] The provisions of the treaty are to be given their ordinary meaning in their context.[19] The object and purpose of the treaty are also to be taken into account in determining the meaning of its provi-

---

[18]   *Territorial Dispute (Libyan Arab Jamahiriya/Chad), Judgment,* (1994) *I.C.J. Reports*, p. 6 at 20; *Maritime Delimitation and Territorial Questions between Qatar and Bahrain, Jurisdiction and Admissibility, Judgment,* (1995) *I.C.J.Reports*, p. 6 at 18.

[19]   See, *e.g., Competence of the General Assembly for the Admission of a State to the United Nations (Second Admissions Case)* (1950), *I.C.J. Reports*, p. 4 at 8, in which the International Court of Justice stated: "The Court considers it necessary to say that the first duty of a tribunal which is called upon to interpret and apply the provisions of a treaty, is to endeavour to give effect to them in their natural and ordinary meaning and in the context in which they occur".

sions.[20] A fundamental tenet of treaty interpretation flowing from the general rule of interpretation set out in Article 31 is the principle of effectiveness (*ut res magis valeat quam pereat*).[21] In *United States - Standards for Reformulated and Conventional Gasoline*, we noted that "[o]ne of the corollaries of the 'general rule of interpretation' in the *Vienna Convention* is that interpretation must give meaning and effect to all the terms of the treaty. An interpreter is not free to adopt a reading that would result in reducing whole clauses or paragraphs of a treaty to redundancy or inutility".[22]

E.   STATUS OF ADOPTED PANEL REPORTS

In this case, the Panel concluded that,

> ... panel reports adopted by the GATT CONTRACTING PARTIES and the WTO Dispute Settlement Body constitute subsequent practice in a specific case by virtue of the decision to adopt them. Article 1(b)(iv) of GATT 1994 provides institutional recognition that adopted panel reports constitute subsequent practice. Such reports are an integral part of GATT 1994, since they constitute "other decisions of the CONTRACTING PARTIES to GATT 1947".[23]

Article 31(3)(b) of the *Vienna Convention* states that "any subsequent practice in the application of the treaty which establishes the agreement of the parties regarding its interpretation" is to be "taken into account together with the context" in interpreting the terms of the treaty. Generally, in international law, the essence of subsequent practice in interpreting a treaty has been recognized as a "concordant, common and consistent" sequence of acts or pronouncements which is sufficient to establish a discernable pattern implying the agreement of the parties regarding its interpretation.[24] An isolated act is generally not sufficient to

---

[20]   That is, the treaty's "object and purpose" is to be referred to in determining the meaning of the "terms of the treaty" and not as an independent basis for interpretation: Harris, *Cases and Materials on International Law* (4th ed., 1991) p. 770; Jiménez de Aréchaga, "International Law in the Past Third of a Century" (1978-I) 159 *Recueil des Cours* p. 1 at 44; Sinclair, *The Vienna Convention and the Law of Treaties* (2nd ed, 1984), p. 130. See *e.g. Oppenheims' International Law* (9th ed., Jennings and Watts, eds., 1992) Vol. I, p.1273; *Competence of the ILO to Regulate the Personal Work of the Employer* (1926), P.C.I.J., Series B, No. 13, p. 6 at 18; *International Status of South West Africa* (1962), *I.C.J. Reports*, p. 128 at 336; *Re Competence of Conciliation Commission* (1955), 22 *International Law Reports*, p. 867 at 871.

[21]   See also (1966) *Yearbook of the International Law Commission*, Vol. II, p. 219: "When a treaty is open to two interpretations one of which does and the other does not enable the treaty to have appropriate effects, good faith and the objects and purposes of the treaty demand that the former interpretation should be adopted."

[22]   *United States - Standards for Reformulated and Conventional Gasoline*, WT/DS2/9, adopted 20 May 1996, p. 23 ([1996] DSR, 21).

[23]   Panel Report, para. 6.10.

[24]   Sinclair, *The Vienna Convention on the Law of Treaties* (2nd ed., 1984), p. 137; Yasseen, "L'interprétation des traités d'après la Convention de Vienne sur le Droit des Traités" (1976-III) 151 *Recueil des Cours* p. 1 at 48.

establish subsequent practice;[25] it is a sequence of acts establishing the agreement of the parties that is relevant.[26]

Although GATT 1947[27] panel reports were adopted by decisions of the CONTRACTING PARTIES,[28] a decision to adopt a panel report did not under GATT 1947 constitute agreement by the CONTRACTING PARTIES on the legal reasoning in that panel report. The generally-accepted view under GATT 1947 was that the conclusions and recommendations in an adopted panel report bound the parties to the dispute in that particular case, but subsequent panels did not feel legally bound by the details and reasoning of a previous panel report.[29]

We do not believe that the CONTRACTING PARTIES, in deciding to adopt a panel report, intended that their decision would constitute a definitive interpretation of the relevant provisions of GATT 1947. Nor do we believe that this is contemplated under GATT 1994. There is specific cause for this conclusion in the *WTO Agreement*. Article IX:2 of the *WTO Agreement* provides: "The Ministerial Conference and the General Council shall have the exclusive authority to adopt interpretations of this Agreement and of the Multilateral Trade Agreements". Article IX:2 provides further that such decisions "shall be taken by a three-fourths majority of the Members". The fact that such an "exclusive authority" in interpreting the treaty has been established so specifically in the *WTO Agreement* is reason enough to conclude that such authority does not exist by implication or by inadvertence elsewhere.

Historically, the decisions to adopt panel reports under Article XXIII of the GATT 1947 were different from joint action by the CONTRACTING PARTIES under Article XXV of the GATT 1947. Today, their nature continues to differ from interpretations of the GATT 1994 and the other Multilateral Trade Agreements under the *WTO Agreement* by the WTO Ministerial Conference or the General Council. This is clear from a reading of Article 3.9 of the *DSU*, which states:

> The provisions of this Understanding are without prejudice to the rights of Members to seek authoritative interpretation of provisions of a covered agreement through decision-making under the WTO Agreement or a covered agreement which is a Plurilateral Trade Agreement.

Article XVI:1 of the *WTO Agreement* and paragraph 1(b)(iv) of the language of Annex 1A incorporating the GATT 1994 into the *WTO Agreement*

---

[25] Sinclair, *supra.*, footnote 24, p. 137.

[26] (1966) *Yearbook of the International Law Commission*, Vol. II, p. 222; Sinclair, *supra.*, footnote 24, p. 138.

[27] By GATT 1947, we refer throughout to the General Agreement on Tariffs and Trade, dated 30 October 1947, annexed to the Final Act Adopted at the Conclusion of the Second Session of the Preparatory Committee of the United Nations Conference on Trade and Employment, as subsequently rectified, amended or modified.

[28] By CONTRACTING PARTIES, we refer throughout to the CONTRACTING PARTIES of GATT 1947.

[29] *European Economic Community - Restrictions on Imports of Dessert Apples*, BISD 36S/93, para. 12.1.

bring the legal history and experience under the GATT 1947 into the new realm of the WTO in a way that ensures continuity and consistency in a smooth transition from the GATT 1947 system. This affirms the importance to the Members of the WTO of the experience acquired by the CONTRACTING PARTIES to the GATT 1947 -- and acknowledges the continuing relevance of that experience to the new trading system served by the WTO. Adopted panel reports are an important part of the GATT *acquis*. They are often considered by subsequent panels. They create legitimate expectations among WTO Members, and, therefore, should be taken into account where they are relevant to any dispute. However, they are not binding, except with respect to resolving the particular dispute between the parties to that dispute.[30] In short, their character and their legal status have not been changed by the coming into force of the *WTO Agreement*.

For these reasons, we do not agree with the Panel's conclusion in paragraph 6.10 of the Panel Report that "panel reports adopted by the GATT CONTRACTING PARTIES and the WTO Dispute Settlement Body constitute subsequent practice in a specific case" as the phrase "subsequent practice" is used in Article 31 of the *Vienna Convention*. Further, we do not agree with the Panel's conclusion in the same paragraph of the Panel Report that adopted panel reports in themselves constitute "other decisions of the CONTRACTING PARTIES to GATT 1947" for the purposes of paragraph 1(b)(iv) of the language of Annex 1A incorporating the GATT 1994 into the *WTO Agreement*.

However, we agree with the Panel's conclusion in that same paragraph of the Panel Report that *unadopted* panel reports "have no legal status in the GATT or WTO system since they have not been endorsed through decisions by the CONTRACTING PARTIES to GATT or WTO Members".[31] Likewise, we agree that "a panel could nevertheless find useful guidance in the reasoning of an unadopted panel report that it considered to be relevant".[32]

F. INTERPRETATION OF ARTICLE III

The *WTO Agreement* is a treaty -- the international equivalent of a contract. It is self-evident that in an exercise of their sovereignty, and in pursuit of their own respective national interests, the Members of the WTO have made a bargain. In exchange for the benefits they expect to derive as Members of the WTO, they have agreed to exercise their sovereignty according to the commitments they have made in the *WTO Agreement*.

One of those commitments is Article III of the GATT 1994, which is entitled "National Treatment on Internal Taxation and Regulation". For the purpose of this appeal, the relevant parts of Article III read as follows:

---

[30] It is worth noting that the Statute of the International Court of Justice has an explicit provision, Article 59, to the same effect. This has not inhibited the development by that Court (and its predecessor) of a body of case law in which considerable reliance on the value of previous decisions is readily discernible.

[31] Panel Report, para. 6.10.

[32] *Ibid.*

Article III

National Treatment on Internal Taxation and Regulation

1.   The contracting parties recognize that internal taxes and other internal charges, and laws, regulations and requirements affecting the internal sale, offering for sale, purchase, transportation, distribution or use of products, and internal quantitative regulations requiring the mixture, processing or use of products in specified amounts or proportions, should not be applied to imported or domestic products so as to afford protection to domestic production.*

2.   The products of the territory of any contracting party imported into the territory of any other contracting party shall not be subject, directly or indirectly, to internal taxes or other internal charges of any kind in excess of those applied, directly or indirectly, to like domestic products. Moreover, no contracting party shall otherwise apply internal taxes or other internal charges to imported or domestic products in a manner contrary to the principles set forth in paragraph 1.*

Ad Article III

Paragraph 2

A tax conforming to the requirements of the first sentence of paragraph 2 would be considered to be inconsistent with the provisions of the second sentence only in cases where competition was involved between, on the one hand, the taxed product and, on the other hand, a directly competitive or substitutable product which was not similarly taxed.

The broad and fundamental purpose of Article III is to avoid protectionism in the application of internal tax and regulatory measures. More specifically, the purpose of Article III "is to ensure that internal measures 'not be applied to imported or domestic products so as to afford protection to domestic production'".[33] Toward this end, Article III obliges Members of the WTO to provide equality of competitive conditions for imported products in relation to domestic products.[34] "[T]he intention of the drafters of the Agreement was clearly to treat the imported products in the same way as the like domestic products once they had been cleared through customs. Otherwise indirect protection could be

---

[33]   *United States - Section 337 of the Tariff Act of 1930*, BISD 36S/345, para. 5.10.
[34]   *United States - Taxes on Petroleum and Certain Imported Substances*, BISD 34S/136, para. 5.1.9; *Japan - Customs Duties, Taxes and Labelling Practices on Imported Wines and Alcoholic Beverages*, BISD 34S/83, para. 5.5(b).

given".[35] Moreover, it is irrelevant that "the trade effects" of the tax differential between imported and domestic products, as reflected in the volumes of imports, are insignificant or even non-existent; Article III protects expectations not of any particular trade volume but rather of the equal competitive relationship between imported and domestic products.[36] Members of the WTO are free to pursue their own domestic goals through internal taxation or regulation so long as they do not do so in a way that violates Article III or any of the other commitments they have made in the *WTO Agreement*.

The broad purpose of Article III of avoiding protectionism must be remembered when considering the relationship between Article III and other provisions of the *WTO Agreement*. Although the protection of negotiated tariff concessions is certainly one purpose of Article III,[37] the statement in Paragraph 6.13 of the Panel Report that "one of the main purposes of Article III is to guarantee that WTO Members will not undermine through internal measures their commitments under Article II" should not be overemphasized. The sheltering scope of Article III is not limited to products that are the subject of tariff concessions under Article II. The Article III national treatment obligation is a general prohibition on the use of internal taxes and other internal regulatory measures so as to afford protection to domestic production. This obligation clearly extends also to products not bound under Article II.[38] This is confirmed by the negotiating history of Article III.[39]

---

[35] *Italian Discrimination Against Imported Agricultural Machinery*, BISD 7S/60, para. 11.

[36] *United States - Taxes on Petroleum and Certain Imported Substances*, BISD 34S/136, para. 5.1.9.

[37] *Japan - Customs Duties, Taxes and Labelling Practices on Imported Wines and Alcoholic Beverages*, BISD 34S/83, para. 5.5(b); *Canada - Import, Distribution and Sale of Certain Alcoholic Drinks by Provincial Marketing Agencies*, BISD 39S/27, para. 5.30.

[38] *Brazilian Internal Taxes*, BISD II/181, para. 4; *United States - Taxes on Petroleum and Certain Imported Substances*, BISD 34S/136, para. 5.1.9; *EEC - Regulation on Imports of Parts and Components*, BISD 37S/132, para. 5.4.

[39] At the Second Session of the Preparatory Committee of the United Nations Conference on Trade and Employment, held in 1947, delegates in the Tariff Agreement Committee addressed the issue of whether to include the national treatment clause from the draft Charter for an International Trade Organization ("ITO Charter") in the GATT 1947. One delegate noted:

> This Article in the Charter had two purposes, as I understand it. The first purpose was to protect the items in the Schedule or any other Schedule concluded as a result of any subsequent negotiations and agreements - that is, to ensure that a country offering a tariff concession could not nullify that tariff concession by imposing an internal tax on the commodity, which had an equivalent effect. If that were the sole purpose and content of this Article, there could really be no objection to its inclusion in the General Agreement. But the Article in the Charter had an additional purpose. That purpose was to prevent the use of internal taxes as a system of protection. It was part of a series of Articles designed to concentrate national protective measures into the forms permitted under the Charter, i.e. subsidies and tariffs, and since we have taken over this Article from the Charter, we are, by including the Article, doing two things: so far as the countries become parties to the Agreement, we are, first of all, ensuring that the tariff concessions they grant one another cannot be nullified by the imposition of corresponding internal taxes; but we are also ensuring that those countries which become parties to the Agreement undertake not to use internal taxes as a system of protection.

G.   ARTICLE III:1

The terms of Article III must be given their ordinary meaning -- in their context and in the light of the overall object and purpose of the *WTO Agreement*. Thus, the words actually used in the Article provide the basis for an interpretation that must give meaning and effect to all its terms. The proper interpretation of the Article is, first of all, a textual interpretation. Consequently, the Panel is correct in seeing a distinction between Article III:1, which "contains general principles", and Article III:2, which "provides for specific obligations regarding internal taxes and internal charges".[40] Article III:1 articulates a general principle that internal measures should not be applied so as to afford protection to domestic production. This general principle informs the rest of Article III. The purpose of Article III:1 is to establish this general principle as a guide to understanding and interpreting the specific obligations contained in Article III:2 and in the other paragraphs of Article III, while respecting, and not diminishing in any way, the meaning of the words actually used in the texts of those other paragraphs. In short, Article III:1 constitutes part of the context of Article III:2, in the same way that it constitutes part of the context of each of the other paragraphs in Article III. Any other reading of Article III would have the effect of rendering the words of Article III:1 meaningless, thereby violating the fundamental principle of effectiveness in treaty interpretation. Consistent with this principle of effectiveness, and with the textual differences in the two sentences, we believe that Article III:1 informs the first sentence and the second sentence of Article III:2 in different ways.

H.   ARTICLE III:2

1.   First Sentence

Article III:1 informs Article III:2, first sentence, by establishing that if imported products are taxed in excess of like domestic products, then that tax measure is inconsistent with Article III. Article III:2, first sentence does not refer specifically to Article III:1. There is no specific invocation in this first sentence of the general principle in Article III:1 that admonishes Members of the WTO not to apply measures "so as to afford protection". This omission must have some meaning. We believe the meaning is simply that the presence of a protective application need not be established separately from the specific requirements that are included in the first sentence in order to show that a tax measure is inconsis-

---

This view is reinforced by the following statement of another delegate:

... [Article III] is necessary to protect not only scheduled items in the Agreement, but, indeed, all items for all our exports and the exports of any country. If that is not done, then every item which does not appear in the Schedule would have to be reconsidered and possibly tariff negotiations re-opened if Article III were changed to permit any action on these non-scheduled items.

See EPCT/TAC/PV.10, pp. 3 and 33.

[40]   Panel Report, para. 6.12.

tent with the general principle set out in the first sentence. However, this does not mean that the general principle of Article III:1 does not apply to this sentence. To the contrary, we believe the first sentence of Article III:2 is, in effect, an application of this general principle. The ordinary meaning of the words of Article III:2, first sentence leads inevitably to this conclusion. Read in their context and in the light of the overall object and purpose of the *WTO Agreement*, the words of the first sentence require an examination of the conformity of an internal tax measure with Article III by determining, first, whether the taxed imported and domestic products are "like" and, second, whether the taxes applied to the imported products are "in excess of" those applied to the like domestic products. If the imported and domestic products are "like products", and if the taxes applied to the imported products are "in excess of" those applied to the like domestic products, then the measure is inconsistent with Article III:2, first sentence.[41]

This approach to an examination of Article III:2, first sentence, is consistent with past practice under the GATT 1947.[42] Moreover, it is consistent with the object and purpose of Article III:2, which the panel in the predecessor to this case dealing with an earlier version of the Liquor Tax Law, *Japan - Customs Duties, Taxes and Labelling Practices on Imported Wines and Alcoholic Beverages* ("*1987 Japan - Alcohol*"), rightly stated as "promoting non-discriminatory competition among imported and like domestic products [which] could not be achieved if Article III:2 were construed in a manner allowing discriminatory and protective internal taxation of imported products in excess of like domestic products".[43]

(a)   "Like Products"

Because the second sentence of Article III:2 provides for a separate and distinctive consideration of the protective aspect of a measure in examining its application to a broader category of products that are not "like products" as contemplated by the first sentence, we agree with the Panel that the first sentence of Article III:2 must be construed narrowly so as not to condemn measures that its strict terms are not meant to condemn. Consequently, we agree with the Panel

---

[41] In accordance with Article 3.8 of the *DSU*, such a violation is *prima facie* presumed to nullify or impair benefits under Article XXIII of the GATT 1994. Article 3.8 reads as follows:

> In cases where there is an infringement of the obligations assumed under a covered agreement, the action is considered *prima facie* to constitute a case of nullification or impairment. This means that there is normally a presumption that a breach of the rules has an adverse impact on other Members parties to that covered agreement, and in such cases, it shall be up to the Member against whom the complaint has been brought to rebut the charge.

[42] See *Brazilian Internal Taxes*, BISD II/181, para. 14; *Japan - Customs Duties, Taxes and Labelling Practices on Imported Wines and Alcoholic Beverages*, BISD 34S/83, para. 5.5(d); *United States - Taxes on Petroleum and Certain Imported Substances*, BISD 34S/136, para. 5.1.1; *United States - Measures Affecting the Importation, Internal Sale and Use of Tobacco*, DS44/R, adopted on 4 October 1994.

[43] *Japan - Customs Duties, Taxes and Labelling Practices on Imported Wines and Alcoholic Beverages*, BISD 34S/83, para 5.5(c).

also that the definition of "like products" in Article III:2, first sentence, should be construed narrowly.[44]

How narrowly is a matter that should be determined separately for each tax measure in each case. We agree with the practice under the GATT 1947 of determining whether imported and domestic products are "like" on a case-by-case basis. The Report of the Working Party on *Border Tax Adjustments*, adopted by the CONTRACTING PARTIES in 1970, set out the basic approach for interpreting "like or similar products" generally in the various provisions of the GATT 1947:

> ... the interpretation of the term should be examined on a case-by-case basis. This would allow a fair assessment in each case of the different elements that constitute a "similar" product. Some criteria were suggested for determining, on a case-by-case basis, whether a product is "similar": the product's end-uses in a given market; consumers' tastes and habits, which change from country to country; the product's properties, nature and quality.[45]

This approach was followed in almost all adopted panel reports after *Border Tax Adjustments*.[46] This approach should be helpful in identifying on a case-by-case basis the range of "like products" that fall within the narrow limits of Article III:2, first sentence in the GATT 1994. Yet this approach will be most helpful if decision makers keep ever in mind how narrow the range of "like products" in Article III:2, first sentence is meant to be as opposed to the range of "like" products contemplated in some other provisions of the GATT 1994 and other Multilateral Trade Agreements of the *WTO Agreement*. In applying the criteria cited in *Border Tax Adjustments* to the facts of any particular case, and in considering other criteria that may also be relevant in certain cases, panels can only apply their best judgement in determining whether in fact products are "like". This will always involve an unavoidable element of individual, discretionary judgement. We do not agree with the Panel's observation in paragraph 6.22 of the Panel Report that distinguishing between "like products" and "directly competitive or substitutable products" under Article III:2 is "an arbitrary decision".

---

[44] We note the argument on appeal that the Panel suggested in paragraph 6.20 of the Panel Report that the product coverage of Article III:2 is not identical to the coverage of Article III:4. That is not what the Panel said. The Panel said the following:
> *If* the coverage of Article III:2 is identical to that of Article III:4, a different interpretation of the term "like product" would be called for in the two paragraphs. Otherwise, if the term "like product" were to be interpreted in an identical way in both instances, the scope of the two paragraphs would be different. (emphasis added)

This was merely a hypothetical statement.

[45] Report of the Working Party on *Border Tax Adjustments*, BISD 18S/97, para. 18.

[46] The *Australian Subsidy on Ammonium Sulphate*, BISD II/188; *EEC - Measures on Animal Feed Proteins*, BISD 25S/49; *Spain - Tariff Treatment of Unroasted Coffee*, BISD 28S/102; *Japan - Customs Duties, Taxes and Labelling Practices on Imported Wines and Alcoholic Beverages*, BISD 34S/83; *United States - Taxes on Petroleum and Certain Imported Substances*, BISD 34S/136. Also see *United States - Standards for Reformulated and Conventional Gasoline*, WT/DS2/9, adopted on 20 May 1996.

Rather, we think it is a discretionary decision that must be made in considering the various characteristics of products in individual cases.

No one approach to exercising judgement will be appropriate for all cases. The criteria in *Border Tax Adjustments* should be examined, but there can be no one precise and absolute definition of what is "like". The concept of "likeness" is a relative one that evokes the image of an accordion. The accordion of "likeness" stretches and squeezes in different places as different provisions of the *WTO Agreement* are applied. The width of the accordion in any one of those places must be determined by the particular provision in which the term "like" is encountered as well as by the context and the circumstances that prevail in any given case to which that provision may apply. We believe that, in Article III:2, first sentence of the GATT 1994, the accordion of "likeness" is meant to be narrowly squeezed.

The Panel determined in this case that shochu and vodka are "like products" for the purposes of Article III:2, first sentence. We note that the determination of whether vodka is a "like product" to shochu under Article III:2, first sentence, or a "directly competitive or substitutable product" to shochu under Article III:2, second sentence, does not materially affect the outcome of this case.

A uniform tariff classification of products can be relevant in determining what are "like products". If sufficiently detailed, tariff classification can be a helpful sign of product similarity. Tariff classification has been used as a criterion for determining "like products" in several previous adopted panel reports.[47] For example, in the *1987 Japan - Alcohol* Panel Report, the panel examined certain wines and alcoholic beverages on a "product-by-product basis" by applying the criteria listed in the Working Party Report on *Border Tax Adjustments*,

> ... as well as others recognized in previous GATT practice (see BISD 25S/49, 63), such as the Customs Cooperation Council Nomenclature (CCCN) for the classification of goods in customs tariffs which has been accepted by Japan.[48]

Uniform classification in tariff nomenclatures based on the Harmonized System (the "HS") was recognized in GATT 1947 practice as providing a useful basis for confirming "likeness" in products. However, there is a major difference between tariff classification nomenclature and tariff bindings or concessions made by Members of the WTO under Article II of the GATT 1994. There are risks in using tariff bindings that are too broad as a measure of product "likeness". Many of the least-developed country Members of the WTO submitted schedules of concessions and commitments as annexes to the GATT 1994 for the first time as required by Article XI of the *WTO Agreement*. Many of these least-developed countries, as well as other developing countries, have bindings in their

---

[47] *EEC - Measures on Animal Feed Proteins*, BISD 25S/49; *Japan - Customs Duties, Taxes and Labelling Practices on Imported Wines and Alcoholic Beverages*, BISD 34S/83; *United States - Standards for Reformulated and Conventional Gasoline*, WT/DS2/9, adopted on 20 May 1996.

[48] *Japan - Customs Duties, Taxes and Labelling Practices on Imported Wines and Alcoholic Beverages*, BISD 34S/83, para. 5.6.

schedules which include broad ranges of products that cut across several different HS tariff headings. For example, many of these countries have very broad uniform bindings on non-agricultural products.[49] This does not necessarily indicate similarity of the products covered by a binding. Rather, it represents the results of trade concessions negotiated among Members of the WTO.

It is true that there are numerous tariff bindings which are in fact extremely precise with regard to product description and which, therefore, can provide significant guidance as to the identification of "like products". Clearly enough, these determinations need to be made on a case-by-case basis. However, tariff bindings that include a wide range of products are not a reliable criterion for determining or confirming product "likeness" under Article III:2.[50]

With these modifications to the legal reasoning in the Panel Report, we affirm the legal conclusions and the findings of the Panel with respect to "like products" in all other respects.

(b)   "In Excess Of"

The only remaining issue under Article III:2, first sentence, is whether the taxes on imported products are "in excess of" those on like domestic products. If so, then the Member that has imposed the tax is not in compliance with Article III. Even the smallest amount of "excess" is too much. "The prohibition of discriminatory taxes in Article III:2, first sentence, is not conditional on a 'trade effects test' nor is it qualified by a *de minimis* standard."[51] We agree with the Panel's legal reasoning and with its conclusions on this aspect of the interpretation and application of Article III:2, first sentence.

2.   *Second Sentence*

Article III:1 informs Article III:2, second sentence, through specific reference. Article III:2, second sentence, contains a general prohibition against "internal taxes or other internal charges" applied to "imported or domestic products in a manner contrary to the principles set forth in paragraph 1". As mentioned before, Article III:1 states that internal taxes and other internal charges "should not

---

[49]   For example, Jamaica has bound tariffs on the majority of non-agricultural products at 50%. Trinidad and Tobago have bound tariffs on the majority of products falling within HS Chapters 25-97 at 50%. Peru has bound all non-agricultural products at 30%, and Costa Rica, El Salvador, Guatemala, Morocco, Paraguay, Uruguay and Venezuela have broad uniform bindings on non-agricultural products, with a few listed exceptions.

[50]   We believe, therefore, that statements relating to any relationship between tariff bindings and "likeness" must be made cautiously. For example, the Panel stated in paragraph 6.21 of the Panel Report that "... with respect to two products subject to the same tariff binding and therefore to the same maximum border tax, there is no justification, outside of those mentioned in GATT rules, to tax them in a differentiated way through internal taxation". This is incorrect.

[51]   *United States - Measures Affecting Alcoholic and Malt Beverages*, BISD 39S/206, para 5.6; see also *Brazilian Internal Taxes*, BISD II/181, para. 16; *United States - Taxes on Petroleum and Certain Imported Substances*, BISD 34S/136, para. 5.1.9; *Japan - Customs Duties, Taxes and Labelling Practices on Imported Wines and Alcoholic Beverages*, BISD 34S/83, para. 5.8.

be applied to imported or domestic products so as to afford protection to domestic production". Again, *Ad* Article III:2 states as follows:

> A tax conforming to the requirements of the first sentence of paragraph 2 would be considered to be inconsistent with the provisions of the second sentence only in cases where competition was involved between, on the one hand, the taxed product and, on the other hand, a directly competitive or substitutable product which was not similarly taxed.

Article III:2, second sentence, and the accompanying *Ad* Article have equivalent legal status in that both are treaty language which was negotiated and agreed at the same time.[52] The *Ad* Article does not replace or modify the language contained in Article III:2, second sentence, but, in fact, clarifies its meaning. Accordingly, the language of the second sentence and the *Ad* Article must be read together in order to give them their proper meaning.

Unlike that of Article III:2, first sentence, the language of Article III:2, second sentence, specifically invokes Article III:1. The significance of this distinction lies in the fact that whereas Article III:1 acts implicitly in addressing the two issues that must be considered in applying the first sentence, it acts explicitly as an entirely separate issue that must be addressed along with two other issues that are raised in applying the second sentence. Giving full meaning to the text and to its context, three separate issues must be addressed to determine whether an internal tax measure is inconsistent with Article III:2, second sentence. These three issues are whether:

(1)   the imported products and the domestic products *are "directly competitive or substitutable products" which are in competition with each other*;

(2)   the directly competitive or substitutable imported and domestic products *are "not similarly taxed"*; and

(3)   the dissimilar taxation of the directly competitive or substitutable imported domestic products *is "applied ... so as to afford protection to domestic production"*.

Again, these are three separate issues. Each must be established separately by the complainant for a panel to find that a tax measure imposed by a Member of the WTO is inconsistent with Article III:2, second sentence.

---

[52]   The negotiating history of Article III:2 confirms that the second sentence and the *Ad* Article were added during the Havana Conference, along with other provisions and interpretative notes concerning Article 18 of the draft ITO Charter. When introducing these amendments to delegates, the relevant Sub-Committee reported that: "The new form of the Article makes clearer than did the Geneva text the intention that internal taxes on goods should not be used as a means of protection. The details have been relegated to interpretative notes so that it would be easier for Members to ascertain the precise scope of their obligations under the Article." E/CONF.2/C.3/59, page 8. Article 18 of the draft ITO Charter subsequently became Article III of the GATT pursuant to the Protocol Modifying Part II and Article XXVI, which entered into force on 14 December 1948.

(a)   "Directly Competitive or Substitutable Products"

If imported and domestic products are not "like products" for the narrow purposes of Article III:2, first sentence, then they are not subject to the strictures of that sentence and there is no inconsistency with the requirements of that sentence. However, depending on their nature, and depending on the competitive conditions in the relevant market, those same products may well be among the broader category of "directly competitive or substitutable products" that fall within the domain of Article III:2, second sentence. How much broader that category of "directly competitive or substitutable products" may be in any given case is a matter for the panel to determine based on all the relevant facts in that case. As with "like products" under the first sentence, the determination of the appropriate range of "directly competitive or substitutable products" under the second sentence must be made on a case-by-case basis.

In this case, the Panel emphasized the need to look not only at such matters as physical characteristics, common end-uses, and tariff classifications, but also at the "market place".[53] This seems appropriate. The GATT 1994 is a commercial agreement, and the WTO is concerned, after all, with markets. It does not seem inappropriate to look at competition in the relevant markets as one among a number of means of identifying the broader category of products that might be described as "directly competitive or substitutable".

Nor does it seem inappropriate to examine elasticity of substitution as one means of examining those relevant markets. The Panel did not say that cross-price elasticity of demand is "*the* decisive criterion"[54] for determining whether products are "directly competitive or substitutable". The Panel stated the following:

> In the Panel's view, the decisive criterion in order to determine whether two products are directly competitive or substitutable is whether they have common end-uses, *inter alia*, as shown by elasticity of substitution.[55]

We agree. And, we find the Panel's legal analysis of whether the products are "directly competitive or substitutable products" in paragraphs 6.28-6.32 of the Panel Report to be correct.

We note that the Panel's conclusions on "like products" and on "directly competitive or substitutable products" contained in paragraphs 7.1(i) and (ii), respectively, of the Panel Report fail to address the full range of alcoholic beverages included in the Panel's Terms of Reference.[56] More specifically, the Panel's

---

[53] Panel Report, para. 6.22.

[54] United States Appellant's Submission, dated 23 August 1996, para. 98, p.63. (emphasis added)

[55] Panel Report, para 6.22.

[56] The Panel's Terms of Reference cite the matters referred to the Dispute Settlement Body by the European Communities, Canada and the United States in WT/DS8/5, WT/DS10/5 and WT/DS11/2, respectively. In WT/DS8/5, the European Communities referred the Dispute Settlement Body to Japan's taxation of shochu, "spirits", "whisky/brandy" and "liqueurs". In WT/DS10/5, Canada referred the Dispute Settlement Body to Japan's taxation of shochu and products falling "within HS 2208.30 ('whiskies'), HS 2208.40 ('rum and tafia'), HS 2208.90 ('other' including fruit brandies,

conclusions in paragraph 7.1(ii) on "directly competitive or substitutable products" relate only to "shochu, whisky, brandy, rum, gin, genever, and liqueurs," which is narrower than the range of products referred to the Dispute Settlement Body by one of the complainants, the United States, which included in its request for the establishment of a panel "all other distilled spirits and liqueurs falling within HS heading 2208". We consider this failure to incorporate into its conclusions all the products referred to in the Terms of Reference, consistent with the matters referred to the DSB in WT/DS8/5, WT/DS10/5 and WT/DS11/2, to be an error of law by the Panel.

(b) "Not Similarly Taxed"

To give due meaning to the distinctions in the wording of Article III:2, first sentence, and Article III:2, second sentence, the phrase "not similarly taxed" in the *Ad* Article to the second sentence must not be construed so as to mean the same thing as the phrase "in excess of" in the first sentence. On its face, the phrase "in excess of" in the first sentence means *any* amount of tax on imported products "in excess of" the tax on domestic "like products". The phrase "not similarly taxed" in the *Ad* Article to the second sentence must therefore mean something else. It requires a different standard, just as "directly competitive or substitutable products" requires a different standard as compared to "like products" for these same interpretive purposes.

Reinforcing this conclusion is the need to give due meaning to the distinction between "like products" in the first sentence and "directly competitive or substitutable products" in the *Ad* Article to the second sentence. If "in excess of" in the first sentence and "not similarly taxed" in the *Ad* Article to the second sentence were construed to mean one and the same thing, then "like products" in the first sentence and "directly competitive or substitutable products" in the *Ad* Article to the second sentence would also mean one and the same thing. This would eviscerate the distinctive meaning that must be respected in the words of the text.

To interpret "in excess of" and "not similarly taxed" identically would deny any distinction between the first and second sentences of Article III:2. Thus, in any given case, there may be some amount of taxation on imported products that may well be "in excess of" the tax on domestic "like products" but may not be so much as to compel a conclusion that "directly competitive or substitutable" imported and domestic products are "not similarly taxed" for the purposes of the *Ad* Article to Article III:2, second sentence. In other words, there may be an amount of excess taxation that may well be more of a burden on imported products than on domestic "directly competitive or substitutable products" but may nevertheless not be enough to justify a conclusion that such products are "not

---

vodka, ouzo, korn, cream liqueurs and 'classic' liqueurs.)" In WT/DS11/2, the United States referred the Dispute Settlement Body to Japan's taxation of shochu and "all other distilled spirits and liqueurs falling within HS heading 2208".

similarly taxed" for the purposes of Article III:2, second sentence. We agree with the Panel that this amount of differential taxation must be more than *de minimis* to be deemed "not similarly taxed" in any given case.[57] And, like the Panel, we believe that whether any particular differential amount of taxation is *de minimis* or is not *de minimis* must, here too, be determined on a case-by-case basis. Thus, to be "not similarly taxed", the tax burden on imported products must be heavier than on "directly competitive or substitutable" domestic products, and that burden must be more than *de minimis* in any given case.

In this case, the Panel applied the correct legal reasoning in determining whether "directly competitive or substitutable" imported and domestic products were "not similarly taxed". However, the Panel erred in blurring the distinction between that issue and the entirely separate issue of whether the tax measure in question was applied "so as to afford protection". Again, these are separate issues that must be addressed individually. If "directly competitive or substitutable products" are *not* "not similarly taxed", then there is neither need nor justification under Article III:2, second sentence, for inquiring further as to whether the tax has been applied "so as to afford protection". But if such products are "not similarly taxed", a further inquiry must necessarily be made.

(c) "So As to Afford Protection"

This third inquiry under Article III:2, second sentence, must determine whether "directly competitive or substitutable products" are "not similarly taxed" in a way that affords protection. This is not an issue of intent. It is not necessary for a panel to sort through the many reasons legislators and regulators often have for what they do and weigh the relative significance of those reasons to establish legislative or regulatory intent. If the measure is applied to imported or domestic products so as to afford protection to domestic production, then it does not matter that there may not have been any desire to engage in protectionism in the minds of the legislators or the regulators who imposed the measure. It is irrelevant that protectionism was not an intended objective if the particular tax measure in question is nevertheless, to echo Article III:1, "*applied* to imported or domestic products so as to afford protection to domestic production".[58] This is an issue of how the measure in question is *applied*.

In the *1987 Japan- Alcohol* case, the panel subsumed its discussion of the issue of "not similarly taxed" within its examination of the separate issue of "so as to afford protection":

> ... whereas under the first sentence of Article III:2 the tax on the imported product and the tax on the like domestic product had to be equal in effect, Article III:1 and 2, second sentence, prohibited only the application of internal taxes to imported or domestic products in a manner "so as to afford protection to domestic production". The Panel was of the

---

[57] Panel Report, para. 6.33.
[58] Emphasis added.

view that also small tax differences could influence the competitive relationship between directly competing distilled liquors, but the existence of protective taxation could be established only in the light of the particular circumstances of each case and there could be a *de minimis* level below which a tax difference ceased to have the protective effect prohibited by Article III:2, second sentence.[59]

To detect whether the taxation was protective, the panel in the 1987 case examined a number of factors that it concluded were "sufficient evidence of fiscal distortions of the competitive relationship between imported distilled liquors and domestic shochu affording protection to the domestic production of shochu". These factors included the considerably lower specific tax rates on shochu than on imported directly competitive or substitutable products; the imposition of high *ad valorem* taxes on imported alcoholic beverages and the absence of *ad valorem* taxes on shochu; the fact that shochu was almost exclusively produced in Japan and that the lower taxation of shochu did "afford protection to domestic production"; and the mutual substitutability of these distilled liquors.[60] The panel in the 1987 case concluded that "the application of considerably lower internal taxes by Japan on shochu than on other directly competitive or substitutable distilled liquors had trade-distorting effects affording protection to domestic production of shochu contrary to Article III:1 and 2, second sentence".[61]

As in that case, we believe that an examination in any case of whether dissimilar taxation has been applied so as to afford protection requires a comprehensive and objective analysis of the structure and application of the measure in question on domestic as compared to imported products. We believe it is possible to examine objectively the underlying criteria used in a particular tax measure, its structure, and its overall application to ascertain whether it is applied in a way that affords protection to domestic products.

Although it is true that the aim of a measure may not be easily ascertained, nevertheless its protective application can most often be discerned from the design, the architecture, and the revealing structure of a measure. The very magnitude of the dissimilar taxation in a particular case may be evidence of such a protective application, as the Panel rightly concluded in this case. Most often, there will be other factors to be considered as well. In conducting this inquiry, panels should give full consideration to all the relevant facts and all the relevant circumstances in any given case.

In this respect, we note and agree with the panel's acknowledgment in the *1987 Japan - Alcohol* Report:

> ... that Article III:2 does not prescribe the use of any specific method or system of taxation. ... there could be objec-

---

[59] *Japan - Customs Duties, Taxes and Labelling Practices on Imported Wines and Alcoholic Beverages*, BISD 34S/83, para. 5.11.
[60] *Ibid.*
[61] *Ibid.*

tive reasons proper to the tax in question which could justify or necessitate differences in the system of taxation for imported and for domestic products. The Panel found that it could also be compatible with Article III:2 to allow two different methods of calculation of price for tax purposes. Since Article III:2 prohibited only discriminatory or protective tax burdens on imported products, what mattered was, in the view of the Panel, whether the application of the different taxation methods actually had a discriminatory or protective effect against imported products.[62]

We have reviewed the Panel's reasoning in this case as well as its conclusions on the issue of "so as to afford protection" in paragraphs 6.33 - 6.35 of the Panel Report. We find cause for thorough examination. The Panel began in paragraph 6.33 by describing its approach as follows:

> ... if directly competitive or substitutable products are not "similarly taxed", and if it were found that the tax favours domestic products, then protection would be afforded to such products, and Article III:2, second sentence, is violated.

This statement of the reasoning required under Article III:2, second sentence is correct.

However, the Panel went on to note:

> ... for it to conclude that dissimilar taxation afforded protection, it would be sufficient for it to find that the dissimilarity in taxation is not *de minimis*. ... the Panel took the view that "similarly taxed" is the appropriate benchmark in order to determine whether a violation of Article III:2, second sentence, has occurred as opposed to "in excess of" that constitutes the appropriate benchmark to determine whether a violation of Article III:2, first sentence, has occurred.[63]

In paragraph 6.34, the Panel added:

> (i)   The benchmark in Article III:2, second sentence, is whether internal taxes operate "so as to afford protection to domestic production", a term which has been further interpreted in the Interpretative Note ad Article III:2, paragraph 2, to mean dissimilar taxation of domestic and foreign directly competitive or substitutable products.

And, furthermore, in its conclusions, in paragraph 7.1(ii), the Panel concluded that:

[62]   *Japan - Customs Duties, Taxes and Labelling Practices on Imported Wines and Alcoholic Beverages*, BISD 34S/83, para. 5.9(c).
[63]   Panel Report, para 6.33.

> (ii)   Shochu, whisky, brandy, rum, gin, genever, and li-
> queurs are "directly competitive or substitutable products"
> and Japan, by not taxing them similarly, is in violation of its
> obligation under Article III:2, second sentence, of the Gen-
> eral Agreement on Tariffs and Trade 1994.

Thus, having stated the correct legal approach to apply with respect to
Article III:2, second sentence, the Panel then equated dissimilar taxation above a
de minimis level with the separate and distinct requirement of demonstrating that
the tax measure "affords protection to domestic production". As previously
stated, a finding that "directly competitive or substitutable products" are "not
similarly taxed" is necessary to find a violation of Article III:2, second sentence.
Yet this is not enough. The dissimilar taxation must be more than *de minimis*. It
may be so much more that it will be clear from that very differential that the dissimilar taxation was applied "so as to afford protection". In some cases, that may
be enough to show a violation. In this case, the Panel concluded that it was
enough. Yet in other cases, there may be other factors that will be just as relevant
or more relevant to demonstrating that the dissimilar taxation at issue was applied
"so as to afford protection". In any case, the three issues that must be addressed
in determining whether there is such a violation must be addressed clearly and
separately in each case and on a case-by-case basis. And, in every case, a careful,
objective analysis, must be done of each and all relevant facts and all the relevant
circumstances in order to determine "the existence of protective taxation".[64] Although the Panel blurred its legal reasoning in this respect, nevertheless we conclude that it reasoned correctly that in this case, the Liquor Tax Law is not in
compliance with Article III:2. As the Panel did, we note that:

> ... the combination of customs duties and internal taxation in
> Japan has the following impact: on the one hand, it makes
> it difficult for foreign-produced shochu to penetrate the
> Japanese market and, on the other, it does not guarantee
> equality of competitive conditions between shochu and the
> rest of 'white' and 'brown' spirits. Thus, through a combina-
> tion of high import duties and differentiated internal taxes,
> Japan manages to "isolate" domestically produced shochu
> from foreign competition, be it foreign produced shochu or
> any other of the mentioned white and brown spirits.[65]

Our interpretation of Article III is faithful to the "customary rules of interpretation of public international law".[66] WTO rules are reliable, comprehensible
and enforceable. WTO rules are not so rigid or so inflexible as not to leave room
for reasoned judgements in confronting the endless and ever-changing ebb and
flow of real facts in real cases in the real world. They will serve the multilateral
trading system best if they are interpreted with that in mind. In that way, we will

---

[64]   *Japan - Customs Duties, Taxes and Labelling Practices on Imported Wines and Alcoholic Beverages*, BISD 34S/83, para. 5.11.
[65]   Panel Report, para. 6.35.
[66]   Article 3.2 of the *DSU*.

achieve the "security and predictability" sought for the multilateral trading system by the Members of the WTO through the establishment of the dispute settlement system.[67]

I.   CONCLUSIONS AND RECOMMENDATIONS

For the reasons set out in the preceding sections of this report, the Appellate Body has reached the following conclusions:

(a)   the Panel erred in law in its conclusion that "panel reports adopted by the GATT CONTRACTING PARTIES and the WTO Dispute Settlement Body constitute subsequent practice in a specific case by virtue of the decision to adopt them";

(b)   the Panel erred in law in failing to take into account Article III:1 in interpreting Article III:2, first and second sentences;

(c)   the Panel erred in law in limiting its conclusions in paragraph 7.1(ii) on "directly competitive or substitutable products" to "shochu, whisky, brandy, rum, gin, genever, and liqueurs", which is not consistent with the Panel's Terms of Reference; and

(d)   the Panel erred in law in failing to examine "so as to afford protection" in Article III:1 as a separate inquiry from "not similarly taxed" in the *Ad* Article to Article III:2, second sentence.

With the modifications to the Panel's legal findings and conclusions set out in this report, the Appellate Body affirms the Panel's conclusions that shochu and vodka are like products and that Japan, by taxing imported products in excess of like domestic products, is in violation of its obligations under Article III:2, first sentence, of the General Agreement on Tariffs and Trade 1994. Moreover, the Appellate Body concludes that shochu and other distilled spirits and liqueurs listed in HS 2208, except for vodka, are "directly competitive or substitutable products", and that Japan, in the application of the Liquor Tax Law, does not similarly tax imported and directly competitive or substitutable domestic products and affords protection to domestic production in violation of Article III:2, second sentence, of the General Agreement on Tariffs and Trade 1994.

The Appellate Body *recommends* that the Dispute Settlement Body request Japan to bring the Liquor Tax Law into conformity with its obligations under the General Agreement on Tariffs and Trade 1994.

---

[67]   Article 3.2 of the DSU.

JAPAN - TAXES ON ALCOHOLIC BEVERAGES

Report of the Panel
WT/DS8/R, WT/DS10/R, WT/DS11/R

*Adopted by the Dispute Settlement Body on 1 November 1996,
as modified by the Appellate Body Report*

TABLE OF CONTENTS

I. INTRODUCTION

1.1   On 21 June 1995, the European Communities ("the Community") requested consultations with Japan under Article XXII of the General Agreement on Tariffs and Trade 1994 ("GATT") concerning the internal taxes levied by Japan on certain alcoholic beverages pursuant to the Japan's Liquor Tax Law (WT/DS8/1). On 7 July 1995, pursuant to Article 4.11 of the Understanding on Rules and Procedures Governing the Settlement of Disputes ("DSU"), the United States (WT/DS8/2) and Canada (WT/DS8/3) requested to be joined in these consultations. Japan accepted these requests on 19 July 1995 (WT/DS8/4).

1.2   On 7 July 1995, Canada requested consultations with Japan under Article XXII of GATT 1994 concerning certain Japanese liquor taxation laws (WT/DS10/1). On 17 July 1995, pursuant to Article 4.11 of the DSU, the United States (WT/DS10/2) and the Community (WT/DS10/3) requested to be joined in these consultations. Japan accepted these requests on 19 July 1995 (WT/DS10/4).

1.3   On 7 July 1995, the United States requested consultations with Japan under Article XXIII of GATT 1994 regarding internal taxes imposed by Japan on certain alcoholic beverages pursuant to the Liquor Tax Law (WT/DS11/1).

1.4   On 20 July 1995, the Community, Canada and the United States jointly held consultations with Japan with a view to reaching a mutually satisfactory resolution of the matter, but they were unable to reach such a resolution. On 21 July 1995, the United States and Japan consulted under Article XXIII:1, but they did not reach a mutually acceptable resolution of the matter.

1.5   On 14 September 1995, pursuant to Article XXIII:2 of GATT 1994 and Article 6 of the DSU, the Community requested the Dispute Settlement Body ("DSB") to establish a panel with standard terms of reference (WT/DS8/5). The Community claimed that:

> "a)   Japan had acted inconsistently with Article III:2, first sentence, of GATT 1994 by applying a higher tax rate on the category of 'spirits' than on each of the two sub-categories of shochu, thereby nullifying or impairing the benefits accrued to the European Communities under GATT 1994; and that
>
> b)   Japan has acted inconsistently with Article III:2, second sentence, of GATT 1994 by applying a higher tax rate on the category of 'whisky/brandy'[1] and on the category of 'liqueurs' than on each of the two sub-categories of shochu, thereby nullifying or impairing the benefits accrued to the European Communities under GATT 1994.
>
> In the event that the liquors falling within the category of 'spirits' were found by the Panel not to be 'like products' to shochu within the meaning of the first sentence of Article III:2, the [Community] further claimed that:
>
> c)   Japan has acted inconsistently with Article III:2, second sentence, of GATT 1994 by applying a higher tax rate on the category of 'spirits' than on each of the two sub-categories of shochu, thereby nullifying or impairing the benefits accrued to the European Communities under GATT 1994".

1.6   On 14 September 1995, pursuant to Article XXIII of GATT 1994 and Articles 4 and 6 of the DSU, Canada requested the DSB to establish a panel with standard terms of reference (WT/DS10/5). Canada claimed that:

> " ... the higher rates of taxation on imported alcoholic beverages including whiskies, brandies, other distilled alcoholic beverages and liqueurs than on Japanese shochu imposed pursuant to the Japanese Liquor Tax Law are:
>
> > a)   inconsistent with Article III:1 and III:2 of GATT 1994;

---

[1]   In the present Panel report the use of the term "whisky" includes also the term "whiskey" as used in the case of Irish whiskey and Tennessee whiskey.

> b)   nullifying and impairing the benefits accruing to Canada pursuant to the WTO".

1.7   On 14 September 1995, pursuant to Article XXIII:2 of GATT 1994 and Articles 4 and 6 of the DSU, the United States requested the DSB to establish a panel with standard terms of reference (WT/DS11/2). The United States claimed that:

> "... the internal taxes imposed by Japan [pursuant to the Liquor Tax Law] on these beverages, and in particular the preferential tax treatment accorded to shochu, are inconsistent with Article III of GATT 1994, and otherwise nullify and impair benefits accruing to the United States under the GATT 1994".

1.8   At its meeting of 27 September 1995, pursuant to the first request of the three complaining parties and with Japan's acceptance, the DSB established a single panel with the mandate to examine the requests of the Community, Canada and the United States, all of which related to the same matter, in accordance with Article 9 of the DSU (WT/DSB/M/7).

1.9   During the 27 September 1995 meeting of the DSB, Norway reserved its right as a third party to the present dispute. However, on 7 November 1995, Norway informed the Panel of the withdrawal of its request to participate as a third party in the dispute (WT/DS8/7, DS10/7 and DS11/4).

1.10   At the same meeting of the DSB on 27 September 1995, the parties agreed that the Panel should have standard terms of reference as follows:

> "To examine, in the light of the relevant provisions of the covered agreements cited by the EC, Canada and US in documents WT/DS8/5, WT/DS10/5, WT/DS11/2, the matters referred to the DSB by the EC, Canada and the United States in those documents and to make such findings as will assist the DSB in making the recommendations or in giving the rulings provided for in those agreements".

1.11   On 30 October 1995, the Panel was constituted with the following composition:

Chairman: Mr. Hardeep Puri

Panelists: Mr. Luzius Wasescha

Mr. Hugh McPhail

II.   FACTUAL ASPECTS

A.   The Japanese Liquor Tax Law

2.1   This dispute concerns the Japanese Liquor Tax Law (Shuzeiho), Law No.6 of 1953 as amended ("Liquor Tax Law"), which lays down a system of internal taxes applicable to all liquors, which are defined as domestically produced or imported beverages having an alcohol content of not less than one degree and which are intended for consumption in Japan.

2.2   The Liquor Tax Law currently classifies the various types of alcoholic beverages into ten categories and additional sub-categories: sake, sake compound, shochu (group A, group B), mirin, beer, wine (wine, sweet wine), whisky/brandy, spirits, liqueurs, miscellaneous (various sub-categories).

1.   Terminology and Definitions

The Liquor Tax Law defines liquors involved in the present disputes - shochu, whisky/brandy, spirits and liqueurs - as follows:[2]

"Article 3

Paragraph 5

'Shochu' shall mean liquors produced by the distillation of alcohol containing substances. Included in this definition are those produced by adding water, sugar or other substances stipulated in government ordinances to the above-mentioned liquors. They must have an alcoholic strength of 45% vol or less. The liquor must be less than 36% vol in case distilled by a 'continuous still', the definition of which is as follows: a machine that removes fusel oil, aldehyde and other impurities during the process of continuous distillation. The definition of the type of sugar which can be added is given by government ordinances. In case produced by adding substances other than water, the extract of the product ought to be less than 2g/100 ml.0

Note that those enumerated below from (a) through (d) do not fall under the definition of 'shochu'.

(a)   Liquors produced in whole or in part from malted cereals or fruit (including dried fruit or boiled-down or concentrated must, but excluding dates or other fruit as stipulated in government ordinances. The same shall apply hereafter).

(b)   Liquors produced by filtering it through white birch charcoal or other substances specified in government ordinances.

(c)   Liquors produced in whole or in part from saccharized substances (e.g. molasses, sugar, syrup and honey; excluding sugar as defined by government ordinances) and by the distillation at less than 95% vol.

(d)   Liquors produced by flavouring alcohol by way of steeping ingredients of other substances during distillation.

---

[2]   These definitions (translations from the Liquor Tax Law) were submitted by Japan.

Paragraph 9

'Whisky/Brandy' shall mean the following liquors on condition that those listed in (a), (b) and (d) be excluded in case covered by (b) through (d) of Paragraph 5:

(a)   Liquors produced by distillation of alcohol containing substance derived by first saccharifying malted cereals and water and then fermenting them. The above- mentioned liquors must be distilled at less than 95% vol.

(b)   Liquors produced by the distillation of alcohol containing substance derived by first saccharifying unmalted cereals with malted cereals and water and then fermenting them. The above mentioned liquors must be distilled at less than 95% vol.

(c)   Liquors produced by adding alcohol, spirits, flavouring substance, colorants, or water to liquors mentioned in above (a) and (b). Excluded from this provision are those in which the aggregate of the alcoholic contents of the liquors mentioned in above (a) and (b) is less than ten hundredth (10/100) of those of the liquors resulted from the addition of the above enumerated substances.

(d)   Liquors produced by the distillation of alcohol containing substance obtained by the fermentation of fruit / fruit and water, or by distillation of wine (including wine lees). The above mentioned liquors must be distilled at less than 95% vol.

(e)   Liquors produced by adding alcohol, spirits, flavouring substance, colorants or water to liquors mentioned in above (d). Excluded from this provision are those in which the aggregate of the alcoholic contents of the liquors mentioned in above (d) is less than ten hundredth 10/100) of those of the liquors resulted from the addition of above enumerated substances.

Paragraph 10

'Spirits' shall mean liquors other than those as listed from Paragraphs 3 to 9, the extract of which must be less than 2g/100ml. 'Spirits' does not include sparkling liquors made in part from malt other than those produced by the distillation of alcohol-containing substances made partly from malt. The same exclusion shall apply in the next paragraph.

Paragraph 11

'Liqueurs' shall mean liquors made from liquors and other substances such as saccharide (including liquors, but excluding those as stipulated in the government ordinances), the extract of which is not less than 2g/100ml (excluding liquors as listed from Paragraphs 3 to 9), and sparkling liquors made in part from malt, as well as the powdered one which can be dissolved to make a beverage with an alcoholic strength of not less than 1% vol.

Article 4:

> The liquors of the categories as listed in the left column of the following table shall be split into the sub-categories described in the mid-column thereof, and the definition of each sub-category shall be shown at the right-column thereof."

Category	Sub-Category	Definition
Shochu	Shochu A	Shochu which are distilled with a continuous still
	Shochu B	Shochu other than Shochu A

2. Tax Rates

2.3   Pursuant to the Liquor Tax Law, liquors are taxed at the wholesale level. In the case of liquors made in Japan, the tax liability accrues at the time of shipment from the factory, and in the case of imported liquors, at the withdrawal from a customs-bonded area. As explained above, the Liquor Tax Law divides all liquors into ten categories, some of which are divided into sub-categories. Different tax rates are applied to each of the various tax categories and sub-categories defined by the Liquor Tax Law. The rates are expressed as a specific amount in Japanese Yen ("¥") per litre of beverage. For each category or sub-category, the Liquor Tax Law lays down a reference alcohol content per litre of beverage and the corresponding reference tax rate. For whisky, the reference rate uses an alcohol strength of 40 per cent; for spirits the alcohol strength is 37 per cent; for liqueurs the alcohol strength is 12 per cent; for both shochu sub-categories, an alcohol strength of 25 per cent is used. As a result, the liquors covered by the present dispute are subject to the following tax rates:

Shochu A

Alcoholic Strength	Tax Rate (per 1 kilolitre)
(1) 25 to 26 degrees	¥155,700
(2) 26 to 31 degrees	¥155,700 plus ¥9,540 for each degree above 25
(3) 31 degrees and above	¥203,400 plus ¥26,230 for each degree above 30
(4) 21 to 25 degrees	¥155,700 minus ¥9,540 for each degree below 25 (fractions are rounded up to 1 degree)
(5) below 21 degrees	¥108,000

Shochu B

Alcoholic Strength	Tax Rate (per 1 kilolitre)
(1) 25 to 26 degrees	¥102,100
(2) 26 to 31 degrees	¥102,100 plus ¥6,580 for each degree above 25
(3) 31 degrees and above	¥135,000 plus ¥14,910 for each degree above 30
(4) 21 to 25 degrees	¥102,100 minus ¥6,580 for each degree less than 25 (fractions are rounded up to 1 degree)
(5) below 21 degrees	¥69,200

Whisky

Alcoholic Strength	Tax Rate (per 1 kilolitre)
(1) 40 to 41 degrees	¥982,300
(2) 41 degrees and above	¥982,300 plus ¥24,560 for every degree above 40
(3) 38 to 40 degrees	¥982,300 minus ¥24,560 for each degree below 40 (fractions are rounded up to 1 degree)
(4) below 38 degrees	¥908,620

Spirits

Alcoholic Strength	Tax Rate (per 1 kilolitre)
(1) below 38 degrees	¥367,300
(2) 38 degrees and above	¥367,300 plus ¥9,930 for each degree above 37

Liqueurs

Alcoholic Strength	Tax Rate (per 1 kilolitre)
(1) below 13 degrees	¥98,600
(2) 13 degrees and above	¥98,600 plus ¥8,220 for each degree over 12

2.4   A special formula is applied to determine the rate applicable to beverages having an alcohol content below 13 per cent or, in the case of "liqueurs", below 12 per cent (as a general rule, pre-mixes combining a liquor with water or with other non-alcoholic beverages). This formula yields the result that the tax rate per litre of pure alcohol levied on these beverages is the same as the tax per litre of pure alcohol that would be borne by a liquor of the same category at the legal standard strength.

B.   The 1987 Panel Report on Japan - Customs Duties, Taxes and
      Labelling Practices on Imported Wines and Alcoholic
      Beverages ("1987 Panel Report")

2.5   In 1986, the Community requested consultations with Japan in respect of
Japan's Liquor Tax Law, as it then existed. The consultations failed to resolve the
matter and in 1987 a panel was established to consider, among others, the Community's claim that the Liquor Tax Law violated Article III:2.

2.6   As of 1987, the Liquor Tax Law divided the whisky/brandy category into
whisky and brandy, and subdivided whisky into three grades, i.e., Special Grade,
First Grade and Second Grade. The category shochu was sub-divided into
Groups A and B. Specific tax rates were provided for each category and sub-
category of alcoholic beverages. In addition, an *ad valorem* tax was applicable to
inter alia, Special, First and Second Grade whiskies where the price exceeded a
certain threshold. This tax was not applicable to either shochu group.

2.7   The 1987 Panel Report concluded that some aspects of the Liquor Tax
Law were inconsistent with Article III:2, first and second sentences, and suggested that the CONTRACTING PARTIES recommend that Japan bring its taxes on
whiskies, brandies, other distilled spirits (such as gin and vodka), liqueurs, still
wines and sparkling wines into conformity with its obligations under the General
Agreement. In particular, the Panel reached the following conclusions:

> "5.5   ... The Panel concluded that the ordinary meaning of Article
> III:2 in its context and in the light of its object and purpose sup-
> ported the past GATT practice of examining the conformity of in-
> ternal taxes with Article III:2 by determining, firstly, whether the
> taxed imported and domestic products are 'like' or 'directly com-
> petitive or substitutable' and, secondly whether the taxation is dis-
> criminatory (first sentence) or protective (second sentence of Arti-
> cle III:2). The Panel decided to proceed accordingly also in this
> case.
>
> 5.6   ... The Panel found that the following alcoholic beverages
> should be considered as "like products" in terms of Article III:2 in
> view of their similar properties, end-uses and usually uniform clas-
> sification in tariff nomenclatures: imported and Japanese-made *gin*;
> imported and Japanese-made *vodka*; imported and Japanese-made
> whisky (including all grades classified as 'whisky' in the Japanese
> Liquor Tax Law) and 'spirits similar to whisky in colour, flavour
> and other properties' as described in the Japanese Liquor Tax Law;
> imported and Japanese-made *grape brandy* (including all grades
> classified as 'brandy' in the Japanese Liquor Tax Law); imported
> and Japanese-made *fruit brandy* (including all grades classified as
> 'brandy' in the Japanese Liquor Tax Law); imported and Japa-
> nese-made 'classic' liqueurs (not including, for instance, medicinal
> liqueurs); imported and Japanese-made unsweetened *still wine*; im-
> ported and Japanese-made *sparkling wines*.
>
> 5.7   The Panel did not exclude that also other alcoholic bever-
> ages could be considered as 'like' products. Thus, even though the

Panel was of the view that the 'likeness' of products must be examined taking into account not only objective criteria (such as composition and manufacturing processes of products) but also the more subjective consumers' viewpoint (such as consumption and use by consumers), the Panel agreed with the arguments submitted to it by the European Communities, Finland and the United States that Japanese shochu (Group A) and vodka could be considered as 'like' products in terms of Article III:2 because they were both white/clean spirits, made of similar raw materials, and their end-uses were virtually identical (either as straight 'schnaps' type of drinks or in various mixtures). Since consumer habits are variable in time and space and the aim of Article III:2 of ensuring neutrality of internal taxation as regards competition between imported and domestic like products could not be achieved if differential taxes could be used to crystallize consumer preferences for traditional domestic products, the Panel found that the traditional Japanese consumer habits with regard to shochu provided no reason for not considering vodka to be a "like" product. The Panel decided not to examine the 'likeness' of alcoholic beverages beyond the requests specified in the complaint by the European Communities (see ...). The Panel felt justified in doing so also for the following reasons: Alcoholic drinks might be drunk straight, with water, or as mixes. Even if imported alcoholic beverages (e.g. vodka) were not considered to be 'like' to Japanese alcoholic beverages (e.g. shochu Group A), the flexibility in the use of alcoholic drinks and their common characteristics often offered an alternative choice for consumers leading to a competitive relationship. In the view of the Panel there existed - even if not necessarily in respect of all the economic uses to which the product may be put - direct competition or substitutability among the various distilled liquors, among various liqueurs, among unsweetened and sweetened wines, and among sparkling wines. The increasing imports of 'Western-style' alcoholic beverages into Japan bore witness to this lasting competitive relationship and to the potential products substitution through trade among various alcoholic beverages. Since consumer habits *vis-à-vis* these products varied in response to their respective prices, their availability through trade and their other competitive inter-relationships, the Panel concluded that the following alcoholic beverages could be considered to be '*directly competitive or substitutable products*' in terms of Article III:2, second sentence:

-       imported and Japanese-made distilled liquors, including all grades of whiskies/brandies, vodka and shochu Groups A and B, among each other;

-       imported and Japanese-made liqueurs among each other;

-       imported and Japanese-made unsweetened and sweetened wines among each other; and

- imported and Japanese-made sparkling wines among each other.

...

5.9 a) ... The Panel concluded ... that (special and first grade) whiskies/brandies imported from the EEC were subject to internal Japanese taxes 'in excess of those applied ... to like domestic products' (i.e. first and second grade whiskies/brandies) in the sense of Article III:2, first sentence.

b) ... The Panel concluded ... that ... the imposition of *ad valorem* taxes on wines, spirits and liqueurs imported from the EEC, which are considerably higher than the specific taxes on 'like' domestic wines, spirits and liqueurs, was inconsistent with Article III:2, first sentence.

...

d) ... The Panel concluded that this imposition of higher taxes on 'classic' liqueurs and sparkling wines with higher raw material content was inconsistent with Article III:2, first sentence.

...

5.11 The Panel recalled its findings that distilled liquors, including all grades of shochu types A and B, were 'directly competitive or substitutable products' in terms of the interpretative note to Article III:2 (see above paragraph 5.7). The Panel noted that shochu was not subject to *ad valorem* taxes and that the specific tax rates on shochu were many times lower than the specific tax rates on whiskies, brandies and other spirits. The Panel noted that, whereas under the first sentence of Article III:2 the tax on the imported product and the tax on the like domestic product had to be equal in effect, Article III:1 and 2, second sentence, prohibited only the application of internal taxes to imported or domestic products in a manner 'so as to afford protection to domestic production'. The Panel was of the view that also small tax differences could influence the competitive relationship between directly competing distilled liquors, but the existence of protective taxation could be established only in the light of the particular circumstances of each case and there could be a *de minimis* level below which a tax difference ceased to have the protective effect prohibited by Article III:2, second sentence. The Panel found that the following factors were sufficient evidence of fiscal distortions of the competitive relationship between imported distilled liquors and domestic shochu affording protection to the domestic production of shochu:

- the considerably lower specific tax rates on shochu than on imported whiskies, brandies and other spirits ... ;

-    the imposition of high *ad valorem* taxes on imported whiskies, brandies and other spirits and the absence of *ad valorem* taxes on shochu;

-    the fact that shochu was almost exclusively produced in Japan and that the lower taxation of shochu did 'afford protection to domestic production' (Article III:1) rather than to the production of a product produced in many countries (say, butter) in relation to another product (say, oleomargarine, as in the example referred to by Japan in paragraph 3.11 above);

-    the mutual substitutability of these distilled liquors, as illustrated by the increasing imports into Japan of 'Western-style' distilled liquors and by the consumer use of shochu blended in various proportions with whisky, brandy or other drinks.

Since it has been recognized in GATT practice that Article III:2 protects expectations on the competitive relationship between imported and domestic products rather than expectations on trade volumes (see L/6175, paragraph 5.1.9), the Panel did not consider it necessary to examine the quantitative trade effects of this considerably different taxation for its conclusion that the application of considerably lower internal taxes by Japan on shochu than on other directly competitive or substitutable distilled liquors had trade-distorting effects affording protection to domestic production of shochu contrary to Article III:1 and 2, second sentence.

...

5.13   ... The Panel noted the Japanese submission that, for instance, the grading system for whisky was 'based on the circumstances of production and consumption of whiskies in Japan', and that generally 'taxes on liquors are levied according to the tax-bearing ability on the part of consumers of each category of liquor'. The Panel was of the view that the use of product and tax differentiations with the view of maintaining or promoting certain production and consumption patterns could easily distort price-competition among like or directly competitive products by creating price differences and price-related consumer preferences which would not exist in case of non-discriminatory internal taxation consistent with Article III:2. The Panel noted that the General Agreement did not make provision for such a far-reaching exception to Article III:2, and that the concept of "taxation according to tax-bearing ability of prospective consumers" of a product did not offer an objective criterion because it relied on necessarily subjective assumptions about future competition and inevitably uncertain consumer responses. The Panel was of the view that a national policy of 'taxation according to tax-bearing ability' did not necessitate discriminatory or protective taxation of imported products and could be pursued by each contracting party in many ways in compliance with Article III:2. A national policy of promoting the domestic production of certain goods could likewise be pursued in conformity with the General Agreement (*e.g.*, by means of production subsidies) without discriminatory or protective taxation of imported goods. The Panel concluded therefore from the text, system and objectives of the General Agreement that, even though each contracting party retained broad freedom as to its internal tax policy also in respect of its internal taxation of goods, the General Agreement did not provide for the possibility of justifying discriminatory or protective taxes inconsistent with Article III:2 on the ground that they had been introduced for the purpose of 'taxation according to the tax-bearing ability' of domestic consumers of imported and directly competitive domestic liquors."[3]

2.8   On 2 February 1989, the Government of Japan informed the CONTRACTING PARTIES that the *ad valorem* tax and the grading system had been abolished, resulting in a single rate for all grades of whisky/brandies, and that the existing differences in taxation of whisky/brandies and shochu had been considerably reduced by decreasing the specific tax rate for whisky/brandies and raising that on shochu. According to Japan, these changes had been instituted "with a view to implementing the recommendations adopted by the GATT Council on 10 November 1987 on the basis of the panel report on the Japanese customs duties, taxes and labelling practices on imported wines and alcoholic beverages".[4] Also in 1989, an interim measure was introduced under the Special Taxation Measures Law to ease the adjustment pain for small scale manufacturers of shochu up to an annual ceiling of 1,300 kl. Under the measure which was to expire within 5 years, small producers are eligible for a 30 per cent reduction in the liquor tax they pay for the first 200 kl of the products they produce. On 1 May 1994, the Liquor Tax Law was further amended to raise tax rates on shochu and on spirits, while tax rates on whisky remained unchanged. The application of the interim measure under the Special Taxation Measures Law was also extended by 3 years at the same time.

III.   CLAIMS OF THE PARTIES

The three complaining parties, namely the Community, Canada and the United States submitted the following claims against Japan:

3.1   The **Community** claimed that since "spirits" (in particular vodka, gin, (white) rum, genever) are like products to the two categories of shochu, the Liquor Tax Law violates GATT Article III:2, first sentence, by applying a higher tax rate on the category of spirits than on each of the two like products, namely, the two sub-categories of shochu. In the alternative, in the event that all or some of

---

[3]   Panel Report on "Japan - Customs Duties, Taxes and Labelling Practices on Imported Wines and Alcoholic Beverages", adopted on 10 November 19877, BISD 34S/83.

[4]   Follow up on the panel report on "Japan - Customs Duties, Taxes and Labelling Practices on Imported Wines and Alcoholic Beverages", communication by Japan dated 27 January 1989, circulated on 2 February 1989, GATT Document L/6465.

the liquors falling within the category of spirits (mentioned above) were found by the Panel not to be like products to shochu within the meaning of the first sentence of Article III:2, the Community claimed that the Liquor Tax Law violates Article III:2, second sentence, by applying a higher tax rate on all or some of the liquors falling within the category of spirits than on each of the two directly competitive and substitutable products, the two sub-categories of shochu. The Community further claimed that since whisky/brandy and liqueurs are also "directly competitive and substitutable products" to both categories of "shochu", the Liquor Tax Law violates Article III:2, second sentence of GATT 1994, by applying a higher tax rate on the categories of whisky/brandy and liqueurs than on each of the two sub-categories of shochu.

3.2   **Canada** claimed that whisky is a "directly competitive and substitutable product" to both categories of "shochu", that by applying a higher tax rate on the categories of whisky/brandy than on each of the two sub-categories of shochu, the Liquor Tax Law distorts the relative prices of whisky and shochu, that in so doing the Liquor Tax Law distorts consumer choice between these categories of alcoholic beverages and thus distorts their competitive relationship. Canada claimed that consequently, the Liquor Tax Law is inconsistent with Article III:2, second sentence, of GATT 1994.

3.3   The **United States** claimed that the Japanese tax system applicable to distilled spirits has been devised so as to afford protection to production of shochu. For this reason and because "white spirits" and "brown spirits" have similar physical characteristics and end-uses, the United States claimed that "white spirits" and "brown spirits" are "like products" in the sense of the first sentence of Article III:2, and therefore the difference in tax treatment between shochu and vodka, rum, gin, other "white spirits", whisky/brandy and other "brown spirits" is inconsistent with Article III:2, first sentence. If the Panel were not able to make such a finding, the United States requested, in the alternative, that the Panel find that all "white spirits" are "like products" in terms of Article III:2 first sentence, and that all distilled spirits are "directly competitive and substitutable" in terms of Article III:2, second sentence for the same reasons. The United States concluded that irrespective of the legal analysis the Panel adopts, the Liquor Tax Law should be found to be inconsistent with Article III:2.

3.4   The defending party, **Japan**, responded to the claims from the three complaining parties. Japan claimed that the purpose of the tax classification under the Liquor Tax Law is not to afford protection and does not have the effect of protecting domestic production. Therefore, Japan argued that the Liquor Tax Law does not violate Article III:2. According to Japan, spirits, whisky/brandy and liqueurs are not "like products" to either category of shochu, within the meaning of Article III:2, first sentence, nor are they "directly competitive and substitutable products" to shochu, within the meaning of Article III:2, second sentence. Consequently, Japan claimed that the Liquor Tax Law cannot violate Article III:2.

IV. ARGUMENTS OF THE PARTIES

A. Preliminary Objection of Japan

4.1   The **United States** requested the Panel to declare that the reduction in excise taxes for small-volume producers, contained in the 1989 legislation,[5] discriminates on its face against imported shochu, sake and wine and therefore violates Article III:2, first sentence. The operative provision of the 1989 legislation is phrased in terms of "shipment from the factory", terms which, under the Liquor Tax Law, refer exclusively to factories in Japan. These measures apply to producers of such alcoholic beverages whose taxable shipments from the factory do not exceed 1300 kilolitres in a given fiscal year; in the following fiscal year, such producers are entitled to a 30 per cent reduction in the excise tax otherwise due on their first 200 kilolitre shipped from the factory. This provision, in the US view, was provided as compensation to small domestic producers for the 1988 law reducing the other protection afforded by the tax differential between these alcoholic beverages and competing imports. In the 1994 amendment of the Liquor Tax Law, the tax relief measures for small producers of shochu A, shochu B, refined sake and wines were extended, so that the entire time period covered by the tax relief measures is 1 April 1988 through 31 March 1997.

4.2   In support of its claim, the **United States** referred the Panel to the Panel Report on "United States - Measures Affecting Alcoholic and Malt Beverages" ("1992 *Malt Beverages*"),[6] which examined a similar provision which provided for an excise tax on beer of $18 per barrel in general, but for a reduced tax of $7 per barrel for the first 60,000 barrels produced by US breweries with annual production of not more than 2 million barrels. In the 1992 *Malt Beverages* case, the panel found that the application of a lower rate of excise tax on beer, which was not available in the case of imported beer, constituted less favourable treatment of the imported product in respect of internal taxes and was therefore inconsistent with Article III:2, first sentence. The United States concluded that even if the present Panel were not to find that the tax reduction programme was inconsistent with the first sentence of Article III:2 because of the preliminary objection of Japan, this measure was a fact and must be taken into account in the Panel's evaluation of tax/price ratios and in its evaluation of protectionist purpose and effect. This measure was a significant element of the Japanese tax policy with regard to shochu and provided important evidence of the essentially protectionist nature and effect of that policy.

4.3   **Japan** responded that WTO Members who request consultations in accordance with the provisions of Article 4.4 of the DSU must identify the "measure(s)" at issue. However, the request of the United States did not mention the specific measure for small-volume producers described in paragraph 4.1 above. Nor did the United States raise this issue with Japan in the course of the bilateral

---

[5]   Article 87 of the Taxation Special Measure Law, Law No. 26 of 1957, as amended; provision applying to producers of refined sake, shochu A, shochu B or certain types of wine.
[6]   Panel report adopted on 19 June 1992, BISD 39S/208, para. 2.7.

consultations. The lack of identification of this measure in the request for consultations, as well as the failure to raise the issue in the bilateral consultations, constituted a case of non-compliance with Article 4 of the DSU. Japan submitted further that Article 6.2 of the DSU requires that the request for the establishment of a panel must identify the specific measures at issue. The lack of identification of this measure in the US request for the establishment of the present Panel also constituted failure to abide by the DSU. Japan noted also that it is a GATT practice that a panel would not render judgment on matters not raised during consultations or not included in the request to establish the panel. This practice, in Japan's view, should not be ignored because it is intended to encourage the parties to a dispute to attempt to obtain satisfactory adjustment before having recourse to the panel procedure and because it is important also for the interests that third parties may have in the dispute. Japan, therefore, requested the Panel to consider the interim measure under the Special Taxation Measures Law as being beyond the terms of reference of the present Panel.

4.4   In case the Panel decides to rule on this issue, **Japan** submitted that the Panel should find the measure to be a temporary measure to ensure compliance with the recommendations of the 1987 Panel Report, and therefore consistent with Japan's obligations under GATT 1994. Historically, this interim measure was introduced as part of the overall package for compliance with the recommendations of the 1987 Panel Report. It has served to alleviate adjustment costs felt by small scale manufacturers. The measure was extended in 1994 in order to facilitate the amendment which removed distortions arising out of price changes since the 1989 amendment. In other words, Japan suggested that this interim measure is part of the process to ensure and maintain compliance with Article III, and has no distortional effect or protective intent. In response to the reference by the United States to the 1992 *Malt Beverages* report, Japan responded that in that case, the federal and state measures found inconsistent with Article III were permanent measures, inherently distortional to trade. Japan noted, however, that most of these measures are still in place. Similarly, Japan noted that the Community has a permanent mechanism to reduce the tax rate applicable to small breweries. By virtue of this mechanism, Austria, Belgium, Denmark, Finland, Germany, Luxembourg and the Netherlands apply a reduced tax rate to small breweries, and Austria, Germany and Spain give a tax benefit to small manufacturers of distilled liquors. The United States noted in response that Japan's measure was hardly "interim" at this point, and had been routinely renewed in 1994: there were no guarantees that it would not be renewed repeatedly into the indefinite future.

B.   The Legal Value of the 1987 Panel Report

4.5   For the **Community**, since the specific tax rates applied to shochu have remained at a much lower level than the rates applicable to other "like" or "directly competitive or substitutable" products, Japan has failed to implement in full the recommendations of the 1987 Panel Report. Consequently, the Community claimed that the Liquor Tax Law is inconsistent with Article III:2, first and second sentences, of GATT 1994 (worded identically to Article III:2 of GATT 1947). In view of the time already elapsed since the adoption of the 1987 Panel

Report and of the regulatory changes implemented in the meantime, the Community argued that it was more appropriate to request the establishment of a new panel to examine and find that the Liquor Tax Law, as it stands now, is inconsistent with the obligations of Japan under GATT 1994 rather than requesting the full implementation of the 1987 Panel Report under GATT 1947. Nonetheless, to the extent that the claims contained in the Community request reiterate some of the claims already examined by the 1987 Panel Report, the findings of that panel report should be accorded a special precedential value. According to the Community, the following findings of the 1987 Panel Report, in particular, should provide decisive guidance to this Panel:

- vodka and shochu A are "like products" within the meaning of Article III:2, first sentence. Other distilled spirits may also be "like products";

- all distilled spirits are "directly competitive and substitutable" among each other within the meaning of the Note to the second sentence of Article III:2;

- the differences in taxation between shochu and the other distilled spirits afford protection to the Japanese production of shochu.

4.6 For **Canada**, Article 3.2 of the DSU makes clear that a panel "serves ... to clarify existing provisions of [covered] agreements". In so clarifying these provisions, Canada considers that Article XVI:1 of the Agreement Establishing the WTO ("WTO Agreement") provides clear guidance to a panel and the DSB respecting the legal value of reports adopted by the CONTRACTING PARTIES under GATT 1947. Article XVI:1 of the WTO Agreement provides:

"Except as otherwise provided under this Agreement or the Multilateral Trade Agreements, the WTO shall be guided by the decisions, procedures and customary practices followed by the CONTRACTING PARTIES to GATT 1947 and the bodies established in the framework of GATT 1947."

For Canada, in this case, neither the WTO Agreement nor the Multilateral Trade Agreements "otherwise provide". Canada considers that there is a strong factual nexus between the 1987 Panel Report and the current dispute. Accordingly, for Canada, in determining the consistency of the Liquor Tax Law with Article III:2, second sentence, the Panel and the DSB are, at a minimum, to be directed by the 1987 Panel Report. In Canada's view, the 1987 Panel Report is particularly authoritative in determining the consistency of the Liquor Tax Law with Article III:2 second sentence. In addition, in Canada's view, it can be argued that since the 1987 Panel Report was adopted by the CONTRACTING PARTIES, it forms now an integral part of the WTO Agreement through Article 1(b)(iv) of GATT 1994.[7] Consequently, for Canada, while previous panel reports do not constitute

---

[7] Article 1 of GATT 1994 reads as follows:
"1. The General Agreement on Tariffs and Trade 1994 ('GATT 1994') shall consist of:

"legislative text", there is an argument to be made, in the circumstances of this case, that since the Liquor Tax Law still contains provisions identical to those found inconsistent with Article III by the 1987 Panel Report now integrated into GATT 1994, and since that panel considered the same products which are at issue in the current dispute, examined the same enactment that regulates the taxation of alcoholic beverages and considered the same issue of whether different specific rates of tax imposed on different categories of distilled liquors is consistent with Article III:2, second sentence, the factors articulated in the 1987 Panel Report are determinative of whether the Liquor Tax Law is inconsistent with Article III:2, second sentence, of GATT 1994.

4.7   The **United States** argued that in drawing up their findings, GATT 1947 panels had determined the relevant facts, interpreted the law and applied the law to the facts before them. Their findings were relevant therefore to the particular facts that were presented to the Panel during its proceedings. They might not be relevant at some later date if the facts had changed, and the interpretation of the law might also change over time due to improved understanding or other factors. For instance, the panel report on "EEC - Restrictions on Imports of Dessert Apples - Complaint by Chile made in 1980",[8] detailed findings concerning the supply-management régime for apples in the Community. In 1989, a related panel[9] examined the same supply-management régime, re-analyzed the facts and the law, and came to rather different conclusions. As another example, one panel has found that tomato paste was "perishable" in the sense of the Note ad Article XI(2)(c),[10] and another found that tomato ketchup and sauce were not.[11] In the GATT 1947 system, panel reports were an input for the interpretative process, but not an independent source of binding norms. Panels were not authorized to, and did not, legislate. If the conclusions and reasoning of the first panel report on apples from Chile had become absolutely binding by virtue of its adoption by the CONTRACTING PARTIES, the second panel report would have been precluded. This view was confirmed by paragraph (x) of the 1982 Ministerial Decision on

---

(a)   the provisions in the General Agreement on Tariffs and Trade, dated 30 October 1947, ...;

(b)   the provisions of the legal instruments set forth below that have entered into force under GATT 1947 before the date of entry into force of the WTO Agreement:

    (i)   protocols and certifications relating to tariff concessions;

    (ii)   protocols of accession .... ;

    (iii)   decisions on waivers granted under Article XXV of GATT 1947 and still in force on the date of entry into force of the WTO Agreement;

    (iv)   other decisions of the CONTRACTING PARTIES to GATT 1947;

(c)   the Understandings set forth below: ... ; and,

(d)   the Marrakesh Protocol to GATT 1994."

[8]   Panel report adopted on 10 November 1980, BISD 27S/98.

[9]   Panel report on "EEC - Restrictions on Imports of Dessert Apples Complaint by Chile" adopted on 22 June 1989, BISD 36S/93.

[10]   Panel report on "EEC - Programme of Minimum Import Prices, Licences and Surety Deposits for Certain Processed Fruits and Vegetables", adopted 18 October 1978, BISD 25S/68, 100, para. 4.10.

[11]   Panel report on "Japan - Restrictions on Imports of Certain Agricultural Products", adopted 22 March 1988, BISD 35S/163, 240, para. 5.3.12.3.

Dispute Settlement: "It is understood that decisions in this process cannot add to or diminish the rights and obligations provided in the General Agreement."[12] This mandate was recognized and incorporated in the last sentence of Article 3.2 of the WTO Dispute Settlement Understanding: "Recommendations and rulings of the DSB cannot add to or diminish the rights and obligations provided in the covered agreements". It would be unnecessary for the Panel to find that GATT 1947 panel reports are just as binding as the text of the GATT 1994 itself, and such a finding would have far-reaching and unpredictable consequences. It would provoke needless controversy and constitutional argument. The Panel could accomplish all that it needed simply by drawing on the 1987 report, not by using it as a source of binding norms. For the United States, the 1987 Panel Report did offer excellent guidance on the facts of the present dispute, and its legal analysis had been completed by the 1992 *Malt Beverages* panel. The United States urged the Panel to complete the job started by the 1987 panel: to find that Japan's taxes are discriminatory and inconsistent with Article III:2 and to recommend that Japan remove the full extent of the discrimination.

4.8   **Japan** submitted that the 1987 Panel Report should not guide the deliberations of the present Panel. First, for Japan, the purpose of Article 1(b)(iv) of GATT 1994 is for GATT 1994 to inherit the provisions and other legal structure of GATT 1947. Consequently, the legal status of the 1987 Panel Report remains the same as any adopted panel report under GATT 1947; Japan noted the limited precedential effect of panel reports under GATT 1947. According to Japan, this limited precedential value is best described in the panel reports on "EEC - Restrictions on Imports of Dessert Apples - Complaint by Chile"[13] and "EEC - Restrictions on Imports of Dessert Apples - Complaint by the United States".[14] In the case initiated by Chile, the panel noted: "[The Panel] would take into account the 1980 Panel report and the legitimate expectations created by the adoption of this report, but also other circumstances of this complaint. The Panel, therefore, did not feel it was legally bound by all the details and legal reasoning of the 1980 Panel report. ... [Earlier panel reports did not] relieve it of the responsibility under its terms of reference, to carry out its own thorough examination".[15]

4.9   Second, **Japan** argued that the interpretation of Article III by the 1987 Panel Report has been overturned by a later panel in the 1992 *Malt Beverages* report and Japan submitted that the Community and Canada strongly supported the adoption of the report at the time. Specifically, this later report introduced a new test, that of "aim and effect", into the determination of the likeness between product categories. This *Malt Beverages* report abandoned the analysis of the 1987 Panel Report which relied heavily on the physical similarities and the end-use of products. On the issue of "like" products, the 1992 *Malt Beverages* report concluded that the issue should be judged ultimately by referring to the purpose of Article III; it laid down criteria that are evidently different from those used in

---

[12]   BISD 29S/13.
[13]   Panel report adopted on 22 June 1989, BISD 36S/93.
[14]   Panel report adopted on 22 June 1989, BISD 36S/135.
[15]   See note 13, para. 12.1 of the report.

the 1987 Panel Report's interpretation of Article III:2. As the 1992 *Malt Beverages* report was adopted in the form of a decision by the CONTRACTING PARTIES, Japan argued that the previous interpretations of Article III were modified and thus the 1987 Panel Report does not provide appropriate guidance for the interpretation of Article III today. For Japan, the 1992 *Malt Beverages* report agreed, in its paragraph 5.26, with the 1987 Panel Report only to the extent of examining physical properties and customs classifications of the products concerned as part of its overall consideration of the like products issue. Then the 1992 *Malt Beverages* report decided that the "like product" determination should be made considering whether a tax system is applied "so as to afford protection to domestic production".

4.10   Third, **Japan** submitted that the subject matter of the present dispute is different from the one considered by the 1987 Panel Report. As other parties to the dispute recognize, the Liquor Tax Law was amended after 1987, and the present structure of the legislation is fundamentally different from the pre-1989 régime. Fourth, Japan argued further that the 1987 Panel Report based its key findings on incorrect or irrelevant assumptions. For Japan, the problem is most pronounced in the following part of the findings, which was quoted by all other parties to the present dispute:

> "The Panel found that the following factors were sufficient evidence of fiscal distortions of the competitive relationship between imported distilled liquors and domestic shochu affording protection to the domestic production of shochu: a) the considerably lower specific tax rates on shochu than on imported whiskies, brandies and other spirits ... ; b) the imposition of high *ad valorem* taxes on imported whiskies, brandies and other spirits and the absence of *ad valorem* taxes on shochu; c) the fact that shochu was almost exclusively produced in Japan and that the lower taxation of shochu did "afford protection to domestic production"... rather than to the production of a product produced in many countries ... ; d) the mutual substitutability of these distilled liquors, as illustrated by the increasing imports into Japan of Western-style distilled liquors and by the consumer use of shochu blended in various proportions with whisky, brandy or other drink".[16]

Japan submitted that the first and second factors no longer exist in the current law and that the statements of the Panel in the third and fourth points were not based on facts. First, it was not true that shochu was produced almost exclusively in Japan. Nor is Japan the largest manufacturer of shochu. Shochu is widely produced in Southeast and East Asia. Second, consumers do not mix shochu with whisky or brandy under normal circumstances. Moreover, the increase in imports of Western-style liquors does not by itself prove the existence of substitutability, or the cross-price elasticity of demand, between shochu and other distilled liq-

---

[16]   1987 Panel Report, para. 5.11.

uors. For all these reasons, Japan argued that the present Panel cannot rely on the reasoning and conclusions of the 1987 Panel Report.

4.11   The **Community** submitted that it agreed with Japan's views on the precedential value of panel reports. However, the Community argued that Japan had taken the position that subsequent panel reports should be analyzed on the basis of the *lex posterior* principle because panel reports are adopted by the CONTRACTING PARTIES. In the Community's view, this was a thoroughly misguided view of such decisions. For the Community, panel reports do not lose their character of decisions on individual cases because they have become part of the "*acquis gattien*" under Section 1 (b) (iv) of GATT 1994. Nor should panel reports lose this trait because they have been adopted by the CONTRACTING PARTIES. Moreover, as there is no rule of *stare decisis* as between panel reports, the present panel would not be bound by the 1992 *Malt Beverages* report in any case.

C.   General Presentation of the Arguments of the Parties on Article III:2

4.12   The **Community** argued that assessing compliance with Article III:2 imposes two different tests for the first and second sentences. Under the first sentence of Article III:2, the examination of the conformity of a system of internal taxation involves a two-step analysis: first, it must be determined whether the domestic product and the imported product are "like", having regard to their physical characteristics and end-uses; and second, it must be ascertained whether the imported product is subject to internal taxes in excess of those applied to the domestic product. For the Community, once it has been established that the two products are "like" and that the imported product is subject to higher taxes, a finding that Article III:2, first sentence, has been infringed is automatic. It is not necessary to show that the difference in taxation affords protection to the domestic product; under the first sentence, unlike the second sentence of Article III:2, such protective effect is irrefutably presumed in all cases. For the Community this was in accordance with the 1987 Panel Report. Whether or not the tax differential has a protectionist aim is also irrelevant. The examination of the aim of the measure only becomes relevant in order to determine whether the infringement of Article III:2, first sentence, may be justified under one of the general exceptions of GATT Article XX.

4.13   In this context and in response to the suggestion that an aim-and-effect test is to be favoured under Article III, the **Community** responded that the aim-and-effect test is inconsistent with the ordinary meaning of the words and the specific purpose of Article III:2 and with the general objectives of Article III. Nor does the aim-and-effect test incorporate any proportionality requirement. Moreover, the burden of proof, which in GATT Article XX and the WTO Agreement on Technical Barriers to Trade ("TBT Agreement") lies with the respondent, is subtly but effectively shifted to the complainant. Given the extreme difficulty of positively proving a protectionist purpose (as opposed to refuting the proof that a measure does not have a specific non-protectionist purpose), the mere invocation by a defendant of a non protectionist purpose may suffice in practice to exclude the application of Article III:2. In this context, and unlike situations which would be dealt with through exceptions under Article XX, the aim-and-effect test would confront panels with the situation of having to adjudicate a dispute without a clearly defined standard of review. In response to the allegation that such a strict reading of the first sentence of Article III:2 would result in legitimate, non-protectionist policies being found inconsistent with Article III:2, the Community argued that it may be possible to introduce two kinds of flexibility into the interpretation of Article III:2. The first flexibility is formed by the notion of discrimination in the case of graduated systems of taxation of like products. This form of flexibility seems to have been envisaged by the 1987 Panel Report. The second flexibility is formed by the dividing line between like products and directly competitive and substitutable products. These two flexibilities, together with the general exceptions of Article XX, may offer sufficient scope to deal adequately with all situations covered by Article III:2, first sentence. In the present case, no such reference to any of the two flexibilities is necessary. The Community concluded that spirits are like products to shochu A and B, and since the Liquor Tax Law applies a higher tax rate on the category of spirits than on each of the two like products, it automatically violates GATT Article III:2, first sentence.

4.14   For the **Community,** the application of the second sentence of Article III:2 involves a different test: first, it must be determined whether the imported product and the domestic product are "substitutable or directly competitive" in the light not only of their physical characteristics and end-uses, but also of other criteria such as their cross-price elasticity, their availability in the same trade channels, etc., determined in an *ex-post* manner (i.e., by taking into account not only actual competition but also potential competition); second, it must be established whether an internal tax is applied "so as to afford protection to domestic production", which does not involve any application of the so-called aim-and-effect test. The Community considers that the aim-and-effect test is not warranted by the ordinary meaning of the words "so as to afford protection", and is contrary to the purpose of Article III:2 and, more generally, to the basic objective of Article III. For the Community, the existence of a protectionist purpose is never a necessary condition for a finding that Article III:2 has been infringed. The aim of the measure only becomes relevant under the first sentence of Article III:2, in order to determine whether it may be justified under Article XX. For the Community, the protectionist effect of a measure is the only relevant criteria for assessing whether the measure is "so as to afford protection". A protectionist purpose only becomes relevant to the extent that it may provide an indication of protectionist effect. The Community therefore concluded that (1) shochu and other distilled spirits are directly competitive and substitutable products, and (2) since Japan does not dispute that the tax rates on shochu A and shochu B are much lower than the rates on spirits, whisky/brandy and liqueur, in terms of taxation per litre of beverage and of taxation per litre of pure alcohol, and since a comparison of tax/price ratios is irrelevant and not a proof of tax neutrality, then the Liquor Tax Law has the effect of affording protection to shochu and therefore is inconsistent with the second sentence of Article III:2.

4.15   **Canada** considers that at its core, Article III:2, second sentence, is designed to protect the competitive relationship between imported and domestic products. In Canada's view, this is made clear in the "United States - Taxes on Petroleum and Certain Imported Substances" ("*Superfund*")[17] report, the 1987 Panel Report and the 1992 *Malt Beverages* report. Canada considers that these reports make clear that an organizing principle in considering whether a measure affords protection to domestic production is whether the internal fiscal measure at issue distorts the competitive relationship between imported and domestic products. For Canada, Article III:2 second sentence, together with Article III:1 and the Interpretative Note ad Article III, Paragraph 2, set out four tests that must be met for a panel to determine that in its application to Canadian whisky and sochu, the Liquor Tax Law is inconsistent with Article III:2, second sentence. These four criteria are: (1) whether whisky is a "directly competitive or substitutable product" with shochu; (2) whether the taxes levied pursuant to the Liquor Tax Law are "internal taxes or other internal charges"; (3) whether whisky and shochu are "not similarly taxed", even in using the tax/price ratio yardstick suggested by Japan; and (4) whether the taxes levied pursuant to the Liquor Tax Law afford protection to domestic production of shochu.

4.16   The **United States** began its discussion of Article III:2 with the observation that GATT panels had addressed taxes or regulations like those at issue in the present case, which are origin-neutral on their face, only on a very few occasions. In each such case, the analysis of whether a violation had occurred, had turned not on the tax's trade effects, but, on whether the tax was targeting imports as such. GATT panel findings over the years had confirmed that the first sentence of Article III:2 requires that imports be provided equivalent opportunities; the second sentence addressed situations where the targeting of imports is more subtle. The United States emphasized that WTO Members retain the right to enact and maintain taxes and regulations that do not, on their face, discriminate against imports, and which classify similar products into distinct categories, but only if the categories are objective and based on neutral fiscal or regulatory policies. The central concern of Article III was the targeting of imports as such for special treatment. Therefore, in determining whether two products subject to different treatment are "like products", it was necessary to consider whether such product differentiation is being made "so as to afford protection to domestic production" as provided in Article III:1. If the aim and effect, or purpose and effect, of the distinction was to target imports as such, the imported and domestic products should be deemed to be "like products" and a tax measure which treats the imported product less favourably than the domestic product would be inconsistent with Article III:2, first sentence. The United States further emphasized that this aim-and-effect test would apply only in the small subset of Article III cases that involve origin-neutral legislation. The aim-and-effect test would have no application in cases that involve measures that discriminate on the basis of origin.

4.17   The **United States** suggested that an examination of a measure's aim or purpose should focus, *inter alia*, on the legislation's wording and stated rationale, its preparatory work if any, statements by legislators, structural incentives, the treatment of products distinguished, the arbitrariness of distinctions drawn and *ex*

---

[17]   Panel report adopted on 17 June 1987, BISD 34S/136.

ante knowledge that the distinction would discriminate between domestic and imported products. The United States argued that a measure could be said to have the aim of affording protection if analysis of the circumstances in which it was adopted, in particular an analysis of the instruments available to achieve the declared policy goal, demonstrated that a change in competitive opportunities in favour of domestic products was a desired outcome and not merely an incidental consequence of the pursuit of a legitimate policy goal. The examination of the effects should focus on the qualitative alteration of the conditions of competition, such as targeting of imports and evidence of cross-elasticity of demand between the favoured and disfavoured categories. The United States pointed out that Article III was one element of an interlocking system of obligations under GATT, the implications of which had been developed with great consistency in interpretations in panel reports of the previous ten years. This system included a number of basic propositions: a) the equivalence imparted to national treatment obligations under Article III:2 and Article III:4, which meant that a Member could not accomplish with regulation what it could not legally accomplish with taxation, or vice versa; b) the equivalence between "like product" in Article III and in Article I:1; c) the ban on border adjustment of taxes (such as direct taxes) or regulations not imposed on a product as such; and d) the restrictive interpretation given to the exceptions contained in Article XX. Within the context of this system, the aim-and-effect test offered the only acceptable approach to the legal analysis of origin-neutral taxation or regulation. The present case, which was limited to Article III:2 and included no claims under Article III:4 or Article XX, was the wrong occasion for a Panel to reopen and reconsider the aim-and-effect test and the complex of interlocking legal interpretations in this area.

4.18   Drawing on the analysis of origin-neutral taxation followed in the 1992 *Malt Beverages* report and in the panel report on "United States - Taxes on Automobiles" ("*US Auto Taxes*"),[18] the **United States** argued that Japan's taxes on distilled spirits had the aim and effect of affording protection to domestic production of shochu. Citing writings by those who had drafted the present definition of shochu for the 1962 amendment of the Liquor Tax Law, the United States argued that in 1962 the definition of shochu was drafted so as to exclude imported distilled spirits and formed part of a system favouring shochu through the tax rate. Moreover, no neutral justification for the distinctions in taxation had been offered by Japan. For this reason and because white and brown spirits have similar physical characteristics and end-uses, the United States argued that white and brown spirits are "like products" in the sense of the first sentence of Article III:2, and therefore the difference in tax treatment between shochu and vodka, rum, gin, and other white spirits and whisky/brandy and other brown spirits is inconsistent with Article III:2, first sentence. In the alternative, the United States argued that all white spirits are "like products" in terms of Article III:2, first sentence, and all distilled spirits are "directly competitive and substitutable" in terms of Article III:2, second sentence, for the same reasons. In the latter case, the United States submitted that the difference in taxation exceeds any *de minimis*

---

[18]   Panel report dated 11 October 1994, DS31/R (not adopted).

level because that difference materially alters the conditions of competition between domestic and imported products. In the present case the change in conditions of competition is illustrated by factors such as the demonstrated effect on
consumption choices and cross-price elasticity of demand. Since domestic shochu
has such a large share of the domestic market for distilled spirits, the protection
given to shochu has had the effect of protection for domestic production. In the
US view, there is also cross-price elasticity of demand between shochu and other
distilled spirits. There was clear evidence of the discriminatory effect of the tax
favouritism shown to shochu by the Japanese political system: the tax differential
causes a change *ceteris paribus* in the conditions of competition; it also has a
negative impact on trading opportunities for imported whisky, other brown spirits
and non-shochu white spirits. Consequently, the difference in the tax treatment
between shochu and other distilled liquors in the Liquor Tax Law is inconsistent
with Article III:2.

4.19 **Japan**, based its argumentation on the test provided by the adopted 1992
Malt Beverages panel report, as well as the unadopted *US Auto Taxes* panel report, that the consistency with Article III:2 of a different treatment of products
should be judged in light of paragraph 1 of the Article, in particular the language
"not be applied ... so as to afford protection to domestic production", and that
whether or not the tax at issue is designed "so as to afford protection to domestic
production" should then be judged by the "aim" and "effect" of affording protection, and stated that since the Liquor Tax Law has neither the aim nor effect of
affording protection to domestic production, the law is not inconsistent with Article III:2. With the 1989 reform, the priority in policy purposes of Japan's distilled
liquor taxation system was shifted from "vertical equity" to "neutrality" and
"horizontal equity" with a view to broadly equalize tax/price ratios across liquor
categories. In pursuit of these two trade-neutral policy purposes, the 1989 tax
reform does not have the aim or effect of protecting domestic production. The
aim and the intent of the legislation are not protectionist: they are to equalize the
tax burden across tax categories. Nor does the Liquor Tax Law have the effect of
protecting domestic production. In Japan's view, the "effect" of protection must
be judged by whether the tax distorts the competitive relationship between imported and domestic products. For Japan, the Liquor Tax Law does not distort the
competitive relationship between imported and domestic products for the following reasons. First, the tax/price ratio of all tax categories are roughly the
same. In terms of the examination of the tax burden, the tax/price ratios is the
superior yardstick because it better indicates the impact on consumers' choice
than the ratio of tax over a certain quantity of products or alcohol contained and
it is common practice to employ a tax/price ratio in comparing the burden of an
excise tax. Second, shochu is produced outside Japan in large quantities. Indeed
in examining whether or not the category in question is almost exclusively domestic, what needs to be examined is not import ratios but rather whether the
domestic product is produced in other countries, and whether the imported product is also domestically produced. Third, there is no directly competitive or substitutable relationship (no cross-price elasticity) between shochu and imported
liquors, precluding, therefore, any possibility of protective effects. Moreover,
Japan added that protective distortion exists only when the three above men-

tioned cumulative requirements are met, which, in Japan's view, is not the case with the Liquor Tax Law. Therefore, the Liquor Tax Law does not distort any competitive relationship and does not have any protective effect. Japan concluded that the regulatory distinctions made by the Liquor Tax Law do not have the aim or effect of affording protection to domestic production. Consequently, the Liquor Tax Law is not inconsistent with Article III:2. Japan argued that it was not asking the Panel to grant an exception for legitimate domestic purposes to an otherwise non-neutral tax. Japan is requesting the Panel to find that the mechanism Japan has chosen to pursue trade neutrality is within the scope of freedom each WTO Member has in choosing a taxation system of its own under GATT Article III:2.

D.   Article III:2, First Sentence

1.   The Different Legal Analyses Suggested by the Parties for the Interpretation of Article III:2, First Sentence

a)   The Test Suggested by the Community

4.20   In the view of the **Community,** the examination of the conformity of a system of internal taxation with Article III:2, first sentence, involves a two-step analysis:[19] Firstly, it must be determined whether the taxed imported and domestic products are "like"; secondly, it is necessary to establish whether the taxation is "discriminatory".

4.21   For the **Community,** based on the 1987 Panel Report, "like products" in terms of Article III:2 are not confined to identical products but may cover also other products, for instance if they serve substantially identical end-uses.[20] More particularly, "minor differences in taste, colour and other properties (including different alcohol contents) do not prevent products from qualifying as "like products".[21] Differences in extract content level among alcoholic beverages have also been considered as minor.[22] The Community notes that the following criteria have been considered relevant in determining whether two products are like products: (1) the products' properties, nature and quality; (2) the products' end-uses in a given market; (3) the consumers' tastes and habits; and (4) the products' classification in the Harmonized System nomenclature. Factors such as differences in prices between the products or differences in local consumer traditions within a country have been found irrelevant for a like product" determination.[23] The notion of "like products" is an objective one, exclusively related to the char-

---

[19]   1987 Panel Report para. 5.5. See also *Superfund*, para. 5.1 and the panel report on "EEC - Measures on Animal Feed Proteins", adopted on 14 March 1978, BISD 25S/49, paras. 4.1 - 4.2.
[20]   1987 Panel Report, para. 5.5, referring to *Superfund*, para. 5.1.1, where the panel found that some of the imported and domestic products, albeit not identical, were like products since they served substantially the same uses.
[21]   1987 Panel Report, paras. 5.6 and 5.9, referring to the panel report on "Spain - Tariff Treatment of Imports of Unroasted Coffee", adopted on 11 June 1981, BISD 28S/102.
[22]   1987 Panel Report, para. 5.9 d).
[23]   1987 Panel Report, para. 5.9.b).

acteristics of the products. The purpose and the effects of a regulatory measure are totally alien to that notion.

4.22   The **Community** submitted that a system of taxation is "discriminatory" within the meaning of the first sentence of Article III:2 if, *inter alia,* the tax rate applied to the domestic product is lower than the tax rate applied to the like imported product. Any difference, however small, between the tax applied to the imported product and the tax applied to a domestic product violates Article III:2, first sentence, regardless of its effects on the volume of trade. Once it has been established that the two products are like and that the imported product is subject to higher taxes, a finding that Article III:2, first sentence, has been infringed is automatic. Unlike under the second sentence of Article III:2, it is not necessary to show that the difference in taxation affords protection to the domestic product because such protective effect is irrefutably presumed in all cases. In the Community's view, whether the tax differential has a protectionist aim is also irrelevant. The first sentence of Article III:2 thus lays down the evidentiary rule that tax discrimination between like products constitutes automatically a violation of Article III:2, first sentence. The examination of the aim of the measure only becomes relevant in order to determine whether the infringement of Article III:2, first sentence, may be justified under any of the general exceptions of Article XX. As further argued hereafter in paragraph 4.36 and following, in the Community's view the aim-and-effect test is inconsistent with the ordinary meaning of Article III:2, first sentence, and is contrary to the specific purpose of this provision as well as with the general objectives of Article III. Moreover, the aim-and-effect test effaces the clear textual difference between the first and the second sentences of Article III:2. The ordinary meaning of Article III:2 is that the first and the second sentences of this provision set out different legal requirements and that only the second sentence refers to the first paragraph of Article III. This results clearly from the use of the word *moreover* at the beginning of the second sentence as well as from the Note ad Article III:2, which provides that:

> "A tax conforming to the requirements of the first sentence of paragraph 2 would be considered to be inconsistent with the provisions of the second *sentence* only in cases where competition was involved between, on the one hand, the taxed product and, on the other hand, a directly competitive or substitutable product which was not similarly taxed".

For the Community, this does not mean that the first sentence of Article III:2 has a purpose contrary to the general principle set forth in Article III:1. The reason why the first sentence of Article III:2 does not refer to Article III:1, is because the imposition of taxes on imported products in excess of those imposed on domestic products is presumed inherently protective and therefore contrary in all cases to the general principle set forth in Article III:1: in the case of tax discrimination between like products a demonstration of protectionist effect is not required. The aim-and-effect test nullifies this rule through the subterfuge of forcing the requirement "so as to afford protection" into the definition of "like product".

b)   The Test Suggested by Canada

4.23   **Canada** did not raise any claim under Article III:2, first sentence. However, in response to questions from the Panel on the legal test arising out of Article III:2, first sentence, Canada stated that the negotiating history, the first Working Party Report on Brazilian Internal Taxes,[24] and a plain reading of the wording of Article III:2, and the Note ad Article III, Paragraph 2, makes clear that unlike Article III:2, second sentence, Article III:2 first sentence does not refer to Article III:1 and is thus a self-contained obligation. Canada thus considers that Article III:1 should not be "read into" Article III:2, first sentence. For Canada, to interpret Article III:2, first sentence, by adding as a separate legal requirement the provisions of Article III:1 does not clarify a Member's rights and obligations but rather goes against the explicit wording of Article III:1 and Article III:2, first sentence, of GATT 1994. Canada further argued that a fair reading of the first sentence of Article III:2 as well as the object and purpose of Article III:2, make it clear that the sentence does not authorize permissible regulatory distinctions respecting discriminatory taxation on imported products that are "otherwise" "like" products. Canada thus considers that the words "aim and effect" should not ultimately be read into an analysis of Article III:2, first sentence. Article III:2, first sentence, is singularly designed to ensure that internal taxes are not applied discriminatorily on "like" products. Therefore it does not authorize permissible regulatory distinctions on products that are otherwise like to justify discriminatory internal taxation. The structure of GATT 1994 is equally useful in considering the context of Article III:2 in relation to the WTO Agreement. This structure shows, in Canada's view, that derogations from particular obligations for domestic policy reasons are permissible only when expressly stated. Thus, for example, Article II:2, Article III:3 and Article XI:2 of GATT each set out explicit permissible regulatory derogations from stated obligations.

c)   The Test Suggested by the United States

4.24   The **United States** began by pointing out that GATT panel reports over the years have confirmed that the first sentence of Article III:2 requires that imports be provided equivalent opportunities. The central concern of Article III:2 is the targeting of imports as such for a special treatment. For the United States, in examining whether two products subjected to different regulatory or tax treatment are "like" or "directly competitive or substitutable", it is necessary to determine first whether the product differentiation is being made "so as to afford protection to domestic production". This determination requires a determination whether the distinction has the "aim and effect" of affording such protection. Physical characteristics are only a small sub-set of the legitimate distinctions that exist. However, in the US view, when a panel merely goes by its own perceptions of physical resemblance, uses, etc., it is implicitly, and non-transparently, judging the appropriateness of the tax or regulatory policies embodied in distinctions between products. Thus, the notion of "likeness" cannot be separated from the

---

[24]   GATT/CP.3/42, adopted 30 June 1949, BISD II/181.

purpose with respect to which products are "like", and the objectives of the regulatory scheme that draws a distinction between two otherwise similar products.

4.25   The **United States** noted that the WTO Agreement recognizes that origin-neutral regulatory distinctions can be compatible with WTO principles even if these distinctions do not appear in Article XX of GATT 1994. Under the WTO Agreement on Technical Barriers to Trade ("TBT Agreement"), technical regulations are permitted where they fulfil "legitimate objectives". Technical regulations by their nature differentiate among otherwise like products. "Legitimate objectives" are not exhaustively defined in the TBT Agreement, but Article 2.2 of the TBT Agreement provides a partial list (i.e., national security requirements, prevention of deceptive practices, protection of human health or safety, animal or plant life or health, or the environment). There are many other legitimate objectives, and even those specifically listed in the TBT Agreement are not all found in Article XX. The TBT Agreement was about measures that make regulatory distinctions among what may otherwise be like products. In the US view, no one could read the TBT Agreement as prohibiting technical regulations, or find that they are *per se* inconsistent with Article III of GATT 1994 whenever imports are disproportionately affected, simply because the regulations in question are based on criteria other than those in Article XX. The United States further noted that the TBT Agreement is not an exception to GATT 1994.

4.26   As a result, argued the **United States**, WTO Members are permitted to make regulatory distinctions among products that might otherwise be considered "like", in pursuance of a legitimate objective other than trade protection. This is what the 1992 *Malt Beverages* report recognized in analyzing the regulatory regime for low alcohol and high alcohol beer. In the US view, that panel sought to avoid a result that would make even an unintentional coincidence between domestic regulation and the presence or absence of foreign competition in the market amount to a violation of Article III:2. Such a result would force policy harmonization and encroach on the policy options available to legislators and regulators to an extent unanticipated when GATT was drafted. The United States also pointed out that the European Court of Justice (ECJ) had reached similar conclusions in interpreting Article 95 of the EC Treaty. In its cases on fiscal incentives, the ECJ has determined that

> "... at the present stage of the development of Community law and in the absence of any unification or harmonization of the relevant provisions, Community law does not prevent Member States from granting tax advantages, in the form of exemption from or reduction of duties, to certain products or to certain classes of producers. Indeed, tax advantages of this kind may serve legitimate economic or social purposes, such as the use of certain raw materials by the distilling industry, the continued production of spirits of high qual-

ity, or the continuation of certain undertakings such as agricultural distilleries".[25]

The Court has limited permissible differentiation to cases in which the distinction drawn

"... pursues objectives of economic policy which are themselves compatible with the requirements of the Treaty and its secondary legislation, [and] the detailed rules are such as to avoid any form of discrimination, direct or indirect, in regard to imports from other member States or any form of protection of competing domestic products."[26]

4.27   The **United States** saw this analysis by the ECJ as remarkably similar to that in the 1992 *Malt Beverages* panel report. In specific cases, the ECJ had applied the rule permitting preferential tax treatment for the pursuit of "legitimate economic and social aims" to permit, for instance, tax exemptions for beer from small-volume breweries,[27] preferential treatment of fruit-based spirits distilled by small cooperatives that use their own raw materials,[28] higher taxes imposed on luxury goods,[29] higher taxes on cars with larger engine displacement,[30] lower taxes on natural sweet wines the production of which is traditional and customary[31] and lower taxes on game machines typically used by children.[32] The ECJ has in this way been able to draw the line between Community integration and member State fiscal sovereignty. It is therefore possible for an international tribunal to examine origin-neutral legislation and determine on the facts of each case, whether the measures in question are "such as to avoid ... protection of competing products".

4.28   On this comparison between the ECJ case law and GATT Article III, the **Community** argued that it is important to begin by pointing to a basic difference between GATT Article III:2 and the corresponding tax discrimination provision of the EC Treaty (Article 95). Article III:2 is covered by the general exception of GATT Article XX; Article 95 is not subject to any exception. The latter situation has certainly contributed to the ECJ's acceptance of the EC Treaty's regulatory distinctions for tax purposes of its own invention (but largely corresponding to treaty exceptions to Article 30, which prohibits quantitative restrictions). For the Community, the WTO legislator has provided a number of exceptions in Article XX, to which panels can refer, and, indeed, regulatory distinctions for tax purposes between products which would normally be considered like should not be made on grounds other than those included in GATT Article XX.

---

[25]   H. Hansen jun. and O.C. Balle GmbH & Co. v. Hauptzollamt Flensburg, Case 148/77, [1978] ECR 1806; cited, e.g., in Commission v. Italian Republic (regenerated petroleum products), Case 21/79, [1980] ECR 1, 12.

[26]   John Walker & Sons Ltd v. Ministeriet for Skatter og Afgifter, Case 243/84, [1986] ECR 875.

[27]   Bobie Getränkevertrieb GmbH v. Hauptzollamt Aachen-Nord, Case 127/75, [1976] ECR 1079.

[28]   Hansen & Balle, note 22 above.

[29]   Commission v. Italy, Case 319/81, [1983] ECR 601, paras. 14, 21.

[30]   Commission v. Italian Republic, Case 200/85, [1986] ECR 3953.

[31]   Commission v. France (natural sweet wines), Case 196/85, [1988] CMLR 851.

[32]   Gabriel Bergandi v. Directeur général des impôts, Case 252/86, [1988] ECR 1343.

4.29   For its aim-and-effect test, the **United States** referred the Panel to the reasoning of the 1992 *Malt Beverages* panel report, as it specifically addressed the issue of product differentiation based on facially-neutral criteria:

> "The purpose of Article III is ... not to prevent contracting parties from using their fiscal and regulatory powers for purposes other than to afford protection to domestic production. Specifically, the purpose of Article III is not to prevent contracting parties from differentiating between different product categories for policy purposes unrelated to the protection of domestic production. The panel considered that the limited purpose of Article III has to be taken into account in interpreting the term 'like products' in this Article. Consequently in determining whether two products subject to different treatment are like products, it is necessary to consider whether such product differentiation is being made 'so as to afford protection to domestic production'."[33]

In that case, the panel considered that the category of wine produced from a particular variety of grape which could be grown only locally and in the Mediterranean region was "a rather exceptional basis for a tax distinction,"[34] and that it was not based on any legitimate objective. It concluded that this wine was a "like product" relative to other still wines, and that the measure was inconsistent with Article III:2. The United States argued that the same approach was used by the panel when determining that for the purpose of Article III:4, low and high alcohol beer need not be considered like products. That panel noted that both Canadian and US manufacturers produced high and low alcohol beer, and that on the basis of their physical characteristics, low and high alcohol beer are similar. However, the panel observed that the laws and regulations in question were on their face origin-neutral. Examining the policy basis for the regulatory distinction, the panel further found that both the statements of the parties and the legislative history suggested that the alcohol content of beer "has not been singled out as a means of favouring domestic producers over foreign producers".[35] The panel further noted that no evidence had been submitted to it that the choice of the particular level at which the state measures distinguished between low and high alcohol had the purpose or effect of affording protection to domestic production. The United States then argued that a similar approach was taken, though less explicitly, in the 1987 Panel Report, in which the panel addressed the Community's complaint that the numerous categories and sub-categories created by Japan's scheme for taxing alcoholic beverages were based on a distinction between "traditional" and "Western-style" beverages. Japanese products "had been differentiated for tax purposes as carefully defined separate product categories on the pretext of their traditional character. As a result, 'traditional' had become virtually synonymous for 'domestic'."[36] The practical effect of this scheme was to subject

---

[33]   1992 *Malt Beverages* panel report, op., cit., para. 5.25.
[34]   Idem., para. 5.26.
[35]   Idem., para. 5.74
[36]   1987 Panel Report, para. 3.2.

Community imports to much higher rates of tax; the tax alone on certain Western alcoholic beverages was twice the retail price of a Japanese product with similar qualities. In some instances, the panel found that different subjective criteria were applied to distinguish imported and domestic products, respectively; in others, the panel found that the apparently trade-neutral categorization did not form part of a "general system of internal taxation equally applied in a trade-neutral manner to all like or directly competitive liquors",[37] but was intended to afford protection to domestic production. For the United States, the common element in the findings of the 1987 Panel Report and 1992 *Malt Beverages* panel report, is that where government measures draw distinctions between similar products based on irrelevant, immutable physical characteristics, rather than on objective criteria based on a legitimate policy, this categorization deprives imports of equivalent competitive opportunities. In the US view, drawing distinctions on "an exceptional basis", such as whether wine has been made from a variety of grape that can only be grown in a limited geographical area (1992 *Malt Beverages*), or the amount of non-volatile ingredient necessary to create the traditional formula of a liqueur (1987 Panel Report); or the exclusion from the lower tax rate of a spirit based on the very filtering method that gives it its product identity (vodka, in the 1987 Panel Report); was strong evidence that the differentiation was intrinsically intended to protect domestic production.

4.30   The **United States** also referred the Panel to the statement of the panel in the *US Auto Taxes* report:

> "Article III deals with differences in treatment between products. These differences in treatment resulted from regulatory distinctions made by governments. If regulatory distinctions were drawn explicitly with respect to the origin of the product, or with respect to manifestly different products, then the consistency with Article III:2 or 4 could be determined in a straightforward manner. If the regulatory distinctions were not drawn explicitly with respect to origin, then it had to be determined whether the products were 'like'."[38]

Recognizing that two individual products could never be exactly the same in all aspects, the panel observed that:

> "... the practical interpretative issue under paragraphs 2 and 4 of Article III was: which differences between products may form the basis of regulatory distinctions by governments that accord less favourable treatment to imported products? Or, conversely, which similarities between products prevent regulatory distinctions by governments that accord less favourable treatment to imported products?"[39]

---

[37]   1987 Panel Report, para. 5.9(b).
[38]   *US Auto Taxes* panel report, op. cit., para. 5.5.
[39]   Idem, para. 5.6.

The *US Auto Taxes* panel report recalled the purpose of Article III in Article III:1, and reasoned that what Article III prohibits is "regulatory distinctions between products applied so as to afford protection to domestic production".

> "The Panel noted that the term 'so as to' suggested both aim and effect. Thus, the phrase 'so as to afford protection to domestic production' called for an analysis of elements including the aim of the measure and the resulting effects. A measure could be said to have the aim of affording protection if an analysis of the circumstances in which it was adopted, in particular an analysis of the instruments available to the contracting party to achieve the declared domestic policy goal, demonstrated that a change in competitive opportunities in favour of domestic products was a desired outcome and not merely an incidental consequence of the pursuit of a legitimate policy goal. A measure could be said to have the effect of affording protection to domestic production if it accorded greater competitive opportunities to domestic products than to imported products. ... [the] central objective of the analysis remained the determination of whether the regulatory distinction was made 'so as to afford protection to domestic production.' The analysis of aims and effects of the measure were elements that contributed to that determination."[40]

In examining whether distinctions have the aim of affording protection, the United States noted that the *US Auto Taxes* panel report looked at the stated policy objective for the tax or legislative measure in question, the statements by legislators, preparatory work and the wording of legislation as a whole. It also looked at the treatment of products on either side of the regulatory distinction drawn, and whether it was known at the time the legislation was enacted that it would draw a line between one group of products that would be foreign and another group that would be domestic. The panel also examined the incentives created by the legislation, and whether these incentives would lead to a result consistent with the stated policy behind the legislation. In connection with its examination whether the measure had the effect of affording protection, the panel found that the distinction drawn for the luxury tax (between automobiles above and below $30,000 in value) "did not appear arbitrary or contrived in the context of the policies pursued".[41] The *US Auto Taxes* panel report then examined for each of the measures at issue whether the distinctions drawn had the effect of affording protection to domestic production, in terms of conditions of competition. The panel examined data on sales and trade flows for evidence of a change in the conditions of competition favouring domestic products. It also examined other data, including whether the characteristics distinguished were inherent to domestic products or foreign products, and whether there was a large difference in tax rates at the threshold.

---

[40]   *US Auto Taxes* panel report, op. cit., para. 5.10.
[41]   Idem, para. 5.14.

4.31   The **United States** went on to argue that the same analysis that was developed in the *US Auto Taxes* panel report should be applied to the Japanese taxes at issue here. The United States argued that Japan's tax system applicable to distilled spirits has the aim and effect of affording protection to domestic production of shochu. For this reason, and because white and brown spirits have similar physical characteristics and end-uses, the United States requested the Panel to find that white and brown spirits are "like products" in the sense of the first sentence of Article III:2, and therefore that the difference in tax treatment between shochu and vodka, rum, gin, other white spirits, and whisky, brandy and other brown spirits is inconsistent with Article III:2, first sentence.

4.32   On the issue of the burden of proof, the **United States** argued that it is up to the complainant to produce a *prima facie* case that an origin-neutral measure has both the aim and effect of affording protection to domestic production. Once the complainant has demonstrated that this is the case, then it would be up to the defending party to present evidence to rebut the claim. The panel would decide whether it were more likely than not that the measure is applied so as to afford protection. As in the usual panel proceeding, only the respondent would have an interest in showing that one of its (origin-neutral) domestic measures did not have protective aim or effect.

d)   The Test Suggested by Japan

4.33   **Japan**, argued that the consistency with Article III:2, both the first and the second sentences, of a different treatment of products should be judged in light of paragraph 1 of the Article, in particular the language "not be applied ... so as to afford protection to domestic production", and that whether or not the tax at issue is designed "so as to afford protection to domestic production" should then be judged by whether it had the "aim" and "effect" of affording protection. Japan submitted that the more recent criteria of "like products" can be found in the 1992 *Malt Beverages* panel report which stated that "the Panel considered that the limited purpose of Article III has to be taken into account in interpreting the term 'like products' in Article III. It established that Article III:2 does not prohibit classification of products for a legitimate policy goal:

> "The purpose of Article III is thus not to prevent contracting parties from using their fiscal and regulatory powers for purposes other than to afford protection to domestic production. Specifically, the purpose of Article III is not to prevent contracting parties from differentiating between different product categories for policy purposes unrelated to the protection of domestic production".[42]

That panel found under this criteria that beer with high alcoholic content is not like beer with low alcoholic content.

4.34   **Japan** continued in stating that these more recent criteria are in contrast to the 1987 Panel Report which found "likeness" on the basis of physical similari-

---

[42]   1992 *Malt Beverages* panel report, op. cit. 5, para. 5.25.

ties, identical end-uses and customs classifications, and did not allow difference in treatment between like products. Japan also referred to the *US Auto Taxes* report which also applied the aim-and-effect test in respect of taxation:

> "The Panel noted that the purpose of Article III is set out in paragraph 1 of the article ... The Panel considered that paragraphs 2 and 4 of Article III had to be read in the light of this central purpose. The Panel reasoned therefore that Article III serves only to prohibit regulatory distinctions between products applied so as to afford protection to domestic production".[43]
>
> ...
>
> "The Panel noted that the term 'so as to' suggested both aim and effect. Thus the phrase 'so as to afford protection' called for an analysis of elements including the aim of the measure and the resulting effects."[44]

For Japan, in determining whether two products subject to different treatment are like products, it is necessary to consider whether such product differentiation is being made "so as to afford protection to domestic production". In Japan's view, the 1987 Panel Report would not allow differentiated treatment for socially legitimate policy goals (e.g., unleaded gasoline and leaded gasoline) between physically like products. The subsequent overruling of this approach proves the weakness of the reasoning of the 1987 Panel Report. Japan also emphasized that the 1987 Panel Report failed to deliver a clear-cut conclusion on the issue of "likeness" between shochu A and vodka. Although the 1987 Panel Report noted that these "could be considered as 'like' products", the analysis ended in a discussion of directly competitive or substitutable products. Nor do these products appear on the list of pairs of like products in that report. Japan concluded that the Liquor Tax Law does not apply taxes "so as to afford protection to domestic production", and under the new criteria (*US Auto Taxes* and 1992 *Malt Beverages*), shochu A and shochu B are not "like" products to whisky, brandy, liqueur or spirits.

4.35   Developing further the criteria to be used under this aim-and-effect test, **Japan** argued that the aim of the Liquor Tax Law is not so as to afford protection or protectionist. The legislation pertains to neutrality and horizontal equality in equalizing the tax/price ratio burden across tax categories. Nor does the Liquor Tax Law have the effect of protecting domestic production since it does not distort the competitive relationships between imported and domestic products based on the three following cumulative criteria: 1) the neutrality of the tax burden among categories of the legislation under examination, 2) the production of the allegedly protected products outside the imported country and of the allegedly "imported" products in the country, and 3) the absence of a directly competitive or substitutable relationship (cross-price elasticity) between the imported and domestically-produced products. Japan argued that if there is no difference in tax

---

[43]   *US Auto Taxes* panel report, op.cit., para. 5.7.
[44]   Idem, para. 5.10

burden, the system does not distort trade; if directly competitive and substitutable relationships do not exist, differences in tax burden do not matter; if the products at issue are produced in and out of the country, the tax differentiation should not be construed to afford protection to domestic production. Protective distortion can be shown only when all of the three requirements are met. Japan further argued that as one examines the relative tax burden between the products in question, the tax burden should be measured by the tax/price ratio, a yardstick which best captures the impact on consumers' behaviour. In examining whether or not the category in question is almost exclusively domestic, what needs to be examined is not import ratios, but whether or not an allegedly "domestic" category is produced in other countries and whether or not "imported" products in question are also domestically produced.

4.36   The **Community** responded that the aim-and-effect test is inconsistent with the ordinary meaning of Article III:2, first sentence, and contrary to the specific purpose of this provision. Previous panels have taken the view that the interpretation of the term "like product" should be made on a case-by-case basis as this term may have a different scope in each of GATT provisions in which it is used. For instance, the notion of "like product" has traditionally been given a broader interpretation in the context of Article I:1 or Article III:2 than in the context of Article VI. Nonetheless, it remains that, in conformity with the ordinary meaning of the word "like", the notion of "like product" is in all cases an objective one, exclusively related to the characteristics of the product. The "purpose (or aims) and the effect" of a regulatory measure are totally alien to that notion. An apple does not cease to be an apple only because the legislator does not pursue evil intentions when decreeing that it is an orange. Moreover, the aim-and-effect test effaces the clear textual difference between the first and the second sentences of Article III:2. For the Community, the ordinary meaning of Article III:2 is that the first and the second sentences of this provision set out different legal requirements and that only the second sentence refers to the first paragraph of Article III. This results clearly from the use of the word "moreover" at the beginning of the second sentence as well as from the Note ad Article III:2. This does not mean that the first sentence of Article III:2 has a purpose contrary to the general principle set forth in Article III:1. The Community argued that the reason why the first sentence of Article III:2 does not refer to Article III:1 is because the imposition of taxes on imported products in excess of those imposed on domestic products is presumed inherently protective and therefore contrary in all cases to the general principle set forth in Article III:1; and this presumption is an irrefutable one. The first sentence of Article III:2 thus lays down the evidentiary rule that in the case of tax discrimination between like products, a demonstration of protectionist effect is not required. In the Community's view, the aim-and-effect test nullifies this rule through the subterfuge of forcing the requirement "so as to afford protection" into the definition of "like product".

4.37   Moreover, the **Community** argued that the interpretation of "so as to afford protection" as requiring both a protectionist purpose and a protectionist effect is by no means mandated by the ordinary meaning of these terms. For instance, the Shorter Oxford Dictionary defines the conjunction "so as" in the following terms: "followed by an infinitive, denoting result or consequence". In turn, the French words "de manière à" are defined by the Dictionnaire Petit Robert as "propre à obtenir telle conséquence". Moreover, this interpretation is incompatible with the specific purpose of Article III:2 and, more generally, with the basic objective of Article III, which, in the Community's view, has been variedly but consistently defined as: ensuring "that internal taxes on goods should not be used as means of protection"; the "ensuring of a certain trade neutrality"; "to provide equal conditions of competition once goods had been cleared through customs"; "promoting non-discriminatory competition among imported and like domestic products"; and obliging the Members "to establish certain competitive conditions for imported products in relation to domestic products". The obligation to provide equal conditions of competition to imported like products is an obligation to ensure a certain result. The nature of the policy objectives pursued by Members cannot have any bearing on whether this result is or is not attained. The purpose of Article III:2 would be defeated if measures which have a clearly protectionist effect had to be tolerated simply because such effect is not deliberately pursued. For this reason, the Community submits that even if the requirement "so as to afford protection ..." was a valid criterion for a like product determination under Article III:2, first sentence, the purpose of the measure would still be irrelevant. The Community also added that the aim of a system of internal taxation only becomes relevant in order to determine whether an infringement of Article III:2 may be justified under Article XX. Thus, a finding that a tax measure is inconsistent with Article III:2 does not necessarily entail a finding that such measure is contrary to GATT.

4.38   The **Community** argued that the interpretation of Article III:2, first sentence, made by the 1992 *Malt Beverages* panel report reflects the panel's concerns that the traditional interpretation of this provision could be excessively rigid and lead to the automatic condemnation of innocuous regulatory distinctions. In the Community's view, these concerns were exaggerated. In the first place, Article III:2, first sentence, is subject to the general exceptions provided for in Article XX. Second, as noted in paragraph 4.13, it seems possible, without abandoning the traditional interpretation of Article III:2, first sentence, to introduce two kinds of flexibility in its interpretation. Moreover, according to the Community, the concerns expressed by the 1992 *Malt Beverages* panel seem to have been motivated by the application of Article III:4 rather than by the application of Article III:2. Indeed, the reliance by the panel on the aim-and-effect test was unnecessary to reach the conclusion that Mississippi wine made from a specific grape was "like" wine made from other grape varieties. This conclusion could have been easily reached through the application of the traditional criteria based on the physical characteristics and end-uses. In contrast, in the case of the non-fiscal regulatory distinctions between low and high alcohol beer, the panel was confronted with the difficulty that while these two products are clearly similar in terms of physical characteristics and end-uses (albeit not identical), this distinction did not have a clear protectionist purpose or effect. Unlike Article III:2, Article III:4 does not include a second sentence dealing with substitutable or directly competing products and referring to the "so as to afford protection test" of Article III:1. Thus, unlike in Article III:2 cases, the panel did not have the possibility to hold that low and high alcohol beer were competitive products, rather than like products, in order to decide the claim in the light of the 'so as to afford protection' test. Instead, the panel turned this test into an element of the definition of like product. On the premise that the notion of like product must be interpreted identically in Article III:4 and Article III:2, this approach was then mechanically applied to the Mississippi wine issue, even though it was unnecessary. This discussion, according to the Community, shows that, although both Article III:2, first sentence, and Article III:4 are concerned with discrimination between like products, there are important differences between the two provisions.

4.39   In support of its arguments, the **Community** stressed the differences between Articles III:2 and III:4 of GATT 1994.

(1)   Unlike Article III:2, first sentence, Article III:4 is not complemented by a second sentence dealing with substitutable and directly competing products and referring to the principle set forth in Article III:1. Thus, unlike the ordinary meaning of Article III:2, first sentence, the ordinary meaning of Article III:4 does not preclude the possibility of reading an implicit reference to the "so as to afford protection ..." test.

(2)   Article III:2, first sentence, lays down a specific and well defined obligation: not to impose higher taxes on imported products than on domestic like products. As explained above, the rationale for this unqualified prohibition is that discriminatory taxation is considered as inherently protectionist. In contrast, the scope of the obligation laid down in Article III:4 is much less precise: to accord "treatment no less favourable" (and not equal treatment). In practice, a determination of what constitutes "less favourable treatment" can only be made in light of the principle set forth in Article III:1, i.e., by assessing the protectionist effect of the measure.

(3)   As explained above, other panels have acknowledged that the scope of the term "like product" may differ from one GATT provision to the other. In light of the different scope of the obligations laid down in Article III:2, first sentence, and Article III:4, it might be justified to adopt a narrower view of what constitutes a "like product" under Article III:4 than under Article III:2 by requiring that in order to qualify as "like products" under Article III:4, two products be more "like" in terms of physical characteristics and end-uses than it would be required under Article III:2, first sentence.

4.40   On the relationship between Articles III and XX, the **United States** suggested that the Panel refrain from an approach that would condemn all origin-neutral regulatory distinctions other than those founded on an objective listed in Article XX. Laws and regulations routinely draw distinctions between products which in some cases are treated equally, but are in other circumstances treated differently in order to carry out domestic social, cultural, religious, political and other policies unrelated to an Article XX objective. The United States submitted examples relating to a number of such policies, such as policies protecting historic buildings not in the "national treasure" class, policies against *lèse majesté*, policies protecting foreign art, non-protectionist food labelling rules and Sunday closing laws.[45] Sunday closing laws could disproportionately affect supermarkets and other large retail businesses which distribute goods of foreign origin. These stores sell exactly the same products on Sunday and on the other days of the week. The United States asked whether such measures should be deemed to be violations of Article III simply because of the disproportionate impact of Sunday closing laws on imports. The United States emphasized that governments make regulatory distinctions for many reasons that have nothing to do with trade protection. For the United States, this is what the panel in the 1992 *Malt Beverages* case recognized in analyzing the regulatory regime for low alcohol and high alcohol beer. That panel wisely sought to avoid a result that would make even an unintentional coincidence between domestic regulation and the presence or absence of foreign competition in the market amount to a violation of Article III:2. Such a result would encroach on the policy options available to legislators and regulators to an extent unanticipated when GATT was drafted. Moreover, the United States submitted that the recognition that regulatory distinctions other than those listed in Article XX are compatible with WTO principles can be found in the TBT Agreement as further detailed in paragraph 4.25 above. The United States further submitted that if national treatment obligations in GATT and the General Agreement on Trade and Services ("GATS") were to be interpreted consistently, a discrimination test linked only to enumerated general exceptions would lead to difficult conclusions in the case of GATS which has a narrower exceptions list than GATT's. Many laws and regulations governing the behaviour of services providers draw distinctions between categories of otherwise "like or competitive" providers based on objectives wholly unrelated to the general exceptions set out in GATS Article XIV. The United States concluded that WTO Members are permitted to make regulatory distinctions among products that might otherwise be considered "like", but they must have a legitimate objective for doing so.

4.41   For the **Community**, the parallelism drawn by the United States to the application by panels of Article XX or the TBT Agreement was misleading. Arti-

---

[45]   A city might forbid destruction of historic buildings and require owners of such buildings to use only certain categories of original materials in their restoration. In many cases, those materials may only be found in the domestic market and other, competitive products may be excluded for use on the ground that they are not authentic. There is no exception in GATT for the preservation of historic buildings. The United States questioned whether such a measure would run afoul of Article III merely because the products in question are substitutable for other purposes and because the measure may tend to favour domestic products over imported ones.

A country might prohibit the sale of objects, books, or representations disrespectful to its monarchy. This prohibition by nature disproportionately affects imports. The United States noted that there is no exception in Article XX for *lèse majesté*.

A European country might ban the sale of Pre-Columbian art to cooperate in international efforts to prevent pillaging of archaeological sites. The exception in Article XX(f) only relates to "national" (i.e. one's own) treasures. The United States asked whether, since the art in question is all imported, this measure should be deemed to be a violation of Article III.

Many countries provide exemptions from their food labelling, grading and inspection laws for farm produce sold directly by the farmer, or products produced for private use (mushrooms or game harvested for private consumption), or food grown by aboriginal groups. The United States noted that these exemptions may favour domestic production, but have no protectionist intent.

cle XX lays down a limited list of exceptions. Moreover, the application of the exceptions is subject to a number of requirements defined in the chapeau of Article XX, as well as in each of the specific grounds of justification. Likewise, the TBT Agreement contains a list of grounds of justification. Even if the list is open, it provides panels with some guidance in order to determine what may constitute a "legitimate policy objective". Further, the TBT Agreement lays down strict requirements concerning, *inter alia*, proportionality, risk assessment, duration, compatibility with existing international standards, transparency and recognition of equivalent standards. For the Community, all these safeguards are absent in the aim-and-effect test. Under this approach, any non-protectionist ground may provide a valid justification for discriminatory taxation. Moreover, the aim-and-effect test does not incorporate any proportionality requirement. Last but not least, under this approach public policy objectives are not exceptions to an obligation but the criteria for defining the scope of the obligation. As a result, the burden of proof, which in Article XX and the TBT Agreement lies with the respondent, is subtly but effectively shifted to the complainant. Given the extreme difficulty of positively proving a protectionist purpose (as opposed to refuting the proof that a measure does not have a specific non-protectionist purpose), the mere invocation by a defendant of a non-protectionist purpose may suffice in practice to exclude the application of Article III:2. For the above reasons, the aim-and-effect test could have the perverse effect of rendering Article XX redundant with respect to Article III:2. The grounds of justification listed in Article XX can also be invoked under the aim-and-effect test (why should legitimate policy objectives already recognized by GATT be deemed less worthy than non-recognised ones?). Since the conditions for the application of Article XX are more restrictive, no Member would bother to invoke Article XX. Indeed, why would any Member go through the pain of arguing that a discriminatory measure is "necessary" to protect human health, if it could simply argue that because the measure has no protectionist purpose, the products concerned are not 'like' and the prohibition of discrimination does not apply? Concerning the reference to GATS made by the United States, the Community argued that GATS Article XVII differs substantially from GATT Article III:2, first sentence. While a finding that Article III:2, first sentence, has been infringed does not require proof of protectionist effect, GATS Article XVII provides that formally identical or formally different treatment shall be deemed to be less favourable only if it modifies the conditions of competition in favour of like domestic services or service suppliers. Moreover, GATS Article XVII only applies to the sectors inscribed in the Member's schedule and subject to any conditions and qualifications set out therein. In contrast, the national treatment obligation in GATT Article III applies in respect of all sectors and may not be subject to any conditions or qualifications.

4.42   The **Community** also pointed out that the Panel should be advised of the risks involved in the aim-and-effect approach. For example, the aim-and-effect test could open the door to claims that the extraterritorial application of environmental regulations concerning non-product related processes and production methods is not contrary to Article III.[46] Likewise, under the aim-and-effect test, one could argue that the imposition of a higher sales tax rate on products which have been manufactured by workers whose wages are below a certain level or who are required to work on Sundays does not infringe Article III:2 (even if the taxes have a disproportionate impact on imported products) because the tax differential is based on non-protectionist social considerations.[47] Moreover, there is a risk that the aim-and-effect test could contaminate other GATT provisions and, more generally, the entire WTO system by substituting for some of the hard-and-fast rules at the heart of the system the unpredictable balancing of ill defined "legitimate policy objectives". The Community concluded that if the general opinion were that the exceptions provided for in Article XX are not sufficient in relation to Article III:2, first sentence, the only approach consistent with the WTO Agreement would be to amend Article XX in order to add new grounds of justification and/or to relax the conditions for their application. Articles 3.2 and 19.2 of the DSU make clear that panels cannot add to or diminish the rights and the obligations of the Members under GATT. Thus, panels are precluded from engaging in the creation of new exceptions to existing obligations even when this appears to be necessary in order to fill GATT lacunae. For all these reasons, the Community requested the Panel not to consider the aim-and-effect test for the application of the first sentence of Article III:2.

4.43   **Japan** argued that in its view even the Community has come to agree that the analysis of the phrase "so as to afford protection to domestic production" requires the analysis of both purpose (i.e. aim) and effect despite its argument to the contrary, and that, therefore, the Community should accept that the aim of the measure should not be irrelevant if and when the phrase "so as to afford protection to domestic production" needs to be examined in regard to the first sentence of Article III:2. Japan further argued that there is no reason to require the "aim" of the tax difference in question to fall under one of the exceptions in Article XX. The 1992 *Malt Beverages* panel report concluded that the regulatory distinction was not so as to afford protection and reached this conclusion as a matter of the interpretation of Article III; the panel did not apply Article XX to a measure which is otherwise inconsistent with Article III. There is no reason, therefore, to restrict justifying "purposes" to those listed under Article XX. This issue ought to be interpreted on a case-by-case basis in light of the purpose of Article III. Moreover, for Japan, the Community's concern over the burden of proof of the

---

[46]   According to the Community, the generally accepted view is that an imported product and a domestic product manufactured in accordance with different non-product related PPMs (processes and production methods) are still "like" and cannot therefore be treated differently under internal regulations. This interpretation is supported by the two unadopted panel reports on "US - Restrictions on Imports of Tuna" (see Tuna I, panel report dated 3 September 1991, not adopted but published in BISD 39S/155, and Tuna II, panel report dated 10 June 1994, DS29/R, not adopted). Under the aim-and-effect test one could argue that tuna harvested with a high rate of incidental dolphin killing is not like to other tuna because the distinction does not have a protectionist purpose.

[47]   Under the traditional interpretation, this would be contrary to Article III because the more taxed products are "like" products manufactured by workers who are paid above the minimum wage level and do not work on Sundays. See panel report on "Belgium - Family Allowances", adopted on 7 November 1952, BISD 1S/59.

"aim" is unfounded. Japan does not believe that a mere claim of "legitimate purpose" can, or should, automatically override obligations under Article III. The practice of GATT dispute settlement is that both parties play the alternate role of claim and rebuttal. Under such practice, the defending party will be expected to present evidence to prove that there is legitimate rationale other than protection, which the complaining party or parties will rebut. The complaining party or parties, in turn, will present evidence of protectiveness, to which the defending party will make its rebuttal. On the basis of evidence thus available, panels can and should render judgment on protectiveness in the "aim" of a disputed measure. Therefore, Japan does not believe that the aim-and-effect test would lead to loss of discipline under Article III:2.

4.44   The **Community** replied that in the end panels would have to put the burden of proof on one of the parties. If the legitimate purpose is integrated into Article III of GATT as it is in Article 2.2 of the TBT Agreement, the final assessment of a panel would be along the following lines: The complaining party has offered no convincing proof that the legitimate purpose mentioned by the defendant was not the real purpose but protectionism. Whereas in an Article XX situation, the final assessment would be: The defendant party has not been able to show that the measures was necessary for, e.g., animal health. In the final analysis, the difference is important and the shift of burden of proof is important. In Article 2.2 of the TBT Agreement this was clearly desired by the Uruguay Round negotiators; in respect of GATT Article III:2 it was not.

4.45   The **Community** went on to argue that, without abandoning the traditional interpretation of Article III:2, first sentence, two kinds of flexibility could be read into its wording. The first flexibility is found in the interpretation of the notion of discrimination in the case of graduated systems of taxation of like products. For example, if all cars are considered like products, it may be possible to accept that a system of graduated taxes based on engine displacement or weight is not discriminatory as long as the tax increases proportionally to engine displacement or weight and applies equally to domestic cars with the same engine displacement or weight. This requires a review of the tax system as a whole as applied to a broad category of like products (here: cars). The Community argued that this form of flexibility seems to have been envisaged by the 1987 Panel Report which, after noting that the specific tax rates on special grade whisky/brandy were considerably higher than the specific tax rates on first and second grade whisky/brandy (all of which had been previously found to be like products), observed that

> "... [it] was unable to find that these tax differentials corresponded to objective differences of the various distilled liquors, for instance that they could be explained as a non-discriminatory taxation of their respective alcohol contents".[48]

The second flexibility is found in the definition of the dividing line between like products and directly competitive and substitutable products. In the above-mentioned example of cars, one can take the view that cars with different engine

---

[48]   1987 Panel Report, para. 5.9(a).

displacement are not like, but rather directly competitive and substitutable products. In that case it is possible to let the "so as to afford protection" criterion play a role. For the Community, differences in taxation based on alcohol content might be covered by the first flexibility; differences in taxation between leaded and unleaded gasoline or between recyclable and non-recyclable containers might be justified under the second flexibility; regulatory distinctions between cups made from a material producing toxic gas when incinerated and cups made from other materials might be covered by the second flexibility or, alternatively, by Article XX (b); the preservation of historical buildings is covered by Article XX(f); Sunday closing laws could be analyzed by panels in the same way as the ECJ, i.e., by laying down a distinction between those requirements that affect directly the distribution and sale of products as such and those which concern the regulation of commercial activities and have only an incidental impact on the sale of goods. The Community concluded that these two flexibilities, together with the general exceptions of Article XX, may offer sufficient scope to deal adequately with the examples of worthy regulatory distinctions between products cited by Japan and the United States.

4.46   The **United States** reiterated that the plain language of Article III:2, first sentence, condemns measures that explicitly target foreign products and accord them less favourable treatment. This, in the US view, makes sense because the discriminatory aim of such measures is apparent. However, when a measure is origin-neutral and therefore such an aim cannot be presumed, it does not make sense to say that the purpose of the measure becomes irrelevant. The United States noted that Article III is designed to protect against discrimination, not to create a *per se* rule of absolute liability for any greater burden or restriction on international trade. All direct and indirect regulation of goods has domestic and international trade-restricting effects, because by its nature regulation imposes burdens. For the United States, the rule proposed by the Community would mean that a government could not adopt any measure, irrespective of its purpose, if the measure had the effect at some point of burdening foreign more than domestic products. Such a "pure effects" test would give no guidance or certainty to legislators or to their legal advisers, because in any situation its application could change from day to day based on international and domestic factors that could not be anticipated at the time a measure is adopted. In the US view, the Community has recognized that its "effects" rule would position perfectly desirable, non-discriminatory governmental regulations - including measures maintained by the Community and its member States - under a legal guillotine. To address the obvious overbreadth of its own legal theory, the Community had invented two arbitrary "flexibilities". The United States asked the following questions: What if two automobiles with different engine displacement have identical fuel economy and emissions - why should not these automobiles be "like"? In the US view, this demonstrates that the Community, while claiming to disregard the issue of legitimacy of policy purpose, cannot really do it. The Community simply wants panels to make an *ad hoc* judgment that the engine displacement criterion used in EC auto tax schemes would remove these taxes from the "guillotine rule" of the first sentence of Article III:2. How many more flexibilities would future panels need to invent to deal with the fact that the EC rule simply overreaches, asked the United States?

4.47   For **Japan**, in introducing two kinds of "flexibility" into the first sentence of Article III:2, which qualifies the application of the "two-step" approach, the Community seems to recognize that the application of the "two-step" approach does encounter situations in which such an additional concept as "flexibility" is needed in order to make its application more relevant and applicable to reality. As a result, in Japan's view, the Community's approach appears to have much in common with the aim-and-effect test approach which, in Japan's view, can deal with such situations in a logical, systematic manner. Japan notes that the Community argues that "graduated taxation" applied "proportionally" based on "objective differences" may be consistent with Article III:2, first sentence. Japan argued that the Community fails to explain why such a differentiation is not discriminatory when applied to "like" products; a "graduated" taxation based on alcoholic strength for liquors or engine displacement or weight for cars can still result in a tax on imported products in excess of that on domestic products which may be considered as "like" in terms of physical characteristics, end-uses or consumers' habits. Japan submitted that it is because of this problem that the Community had to introduce an element of "flexibility" alien to its two-step approach. For Japan, if the "graduated taxation" is consistent with Article III: 2, first sentence, it must be because such a taxation system, being based on objective differences among products, has no "aim" to distort competitive relationships between imported goods and domestic products, nor the "effect" of distorting the competitive relationship. The second flexibility advanced by the Community poses another problem, according to Japan, because the Community is not able to establish criteria by which automobiles with different engine displacement cease to be "like" and become "directly competitive or substitutable". Japan argued that the Community would judge automobiles with different engine displacement "unlike", in introducing criteria other than physical characteristics, end-uses and consumers' habits. Third, in support of its argument that the purpose of the measure would be irrelevant in applying the test of "so as to afford protection to domestic production", the Community claims that the language "so as to" connotes "result or consequence". However, the language "so as to" normally means "with the intent or result" according to the Concise Oxford Dictionary of Current English or "for the purpose" according to the American Heritage Dictionary, 2nd edition. It should certainly include "aim" as well. For Japan, this confirmed that Article III:2, including its first sentence, should be interpreted in light of the test of "so as to afford protection to domestic production", and that this language should be applied by judging whether or not the measure in question has the "aim" and the "effect" of protection.

4.48   The **Community** responded that the first flexibility was not alien to the two-step approach. It simply would require a panel to look at a whole category of imported like products (such as white spirits) and determine whether the category as a whole is taxed in excess of the corresponding category of domestic products. This would not be the case if the proportional variations in taxation on the basis of, e.g., alcohol content, are equally and uniformly applied to this category of like product, both domestic and imported. First the group of like products is determined, next whether they are taxed equally is examined. The ultimate consequence of this approach would be that two shochus of different degrees of alcohol would have to be regarded as products which are not "like" but merely as "competitive and substitutable". As regards the second flexibility, the Community argued that a line must be drawn somewhere between "like" products and "competitive or substitutable" products. It is obvious that this is done, contrary to Japan's assertions, on the basis of physical characteristics and end-uses. On that basis, panels must decide whether differences in engine displacement between cars are a matter of gradual difference within a category of "like" products, or if the difference between a 1000 cubic centimetres utility car and a four-litre racing car is such that they are merely competitive and substitutable. Such physical differences are the reason why the Community has admitted that shochu and brandy are not "like" but merely "competitive and substitutable".

4.49 **Canada** also responded to Japan's argument that the 1992 *Malt Beverages* panel report sets out an aim-and-effect test under GATT Article III:2, second sentence. Canada recalled that as authority for this argument, Japan cites the statement by the panel, in examining the issue of "like products" under Article III:4, that "[t]here was no evidence ... that the choice of the particular [alcohol] level has the purpose or effect of affording protection to domestic production".[49] For Canada, however, even a cursory reading of the panel's statement clearly shows that the words "aim and effect" are not used by this panel. The panel wording cited by Japan refers to purpose "or" effect. In fact, Canada argued that the words "aim and effect" do not appear anywhere in the 1992 *Malt Beverages* panel report. These words rather appeared for the first time in the unadopted *US Auto Taxes* panel report that, pursuant to paragraph 1(b)(iv) of GATT 1994, has not been "integrated" into GATT 1994. According to Canada, if one would follow Japan's interpretation that the express wording of the 1992 *Malt Beverages* panel report applies to Article III:2 second sentence, the Liquor Tax Law would be inconsistent with Article III:2, second sentence, if it had either the purpose or the effect of affording protection to domestic shochu production.

4.50 The **United States** responded to the Canadian argument that in the 1992 *Malt Beverages* panel report the formulation was "aim *or* effect", not "aim *and* effect." The United States first made the grammatical point that the reference to "aim or effect" cited by Canada, from paragraph 5.74 of the 1992 *Malt Beverages* panel report, is phrased in the negative: that "there was no evidence submitted to the Panel that the choice of the particular [alcohol] level has the purpose or effect of affording protection to domestic production." As a matter of grammar, if an "or" appears in a negative statement, the positive version of the same statement could well have an "and". The internal and external evidence indicates that there was no inconsistency intended between the 1992 *Malt Beverages* and the *US Auto Taxes* panel reports. The test, for the United States, is not purpose "or" effect, but purpose "and" effect; in the US view, "aim" and "purpose" are interchangeable. "Purpose or effect" would mean that an origin-neutral regulation could be condemned solely on the basis of its purpose. The United

---

[49] See in para. 5.74.

States does not agree with this interpretation because it believes that the "effect" of legislation matters. An examination of the effects can tell if a measure is targeting imports, and if there is cross-price elasticity of demand between the relevant products. Moreover, as the United States had argued in relation to the Community's discussion of "effects", an "effects only" test is also a poor idea and unimplementable. For the United States, all taxation or regulation causes some degree of market distortion, and often it is not possible to know in advance what the effect of a tax or regulation on the market or the economy will be. Domestic products and imported products are different groupings of goods with differing characteristics. In the US view, the "effects only" test would imply that all internal measures maintained by the Community and its Member States should be reviewed and judged solely in relation to whether they happen to disadvantage imports, a position which would have sweeping effects. Since it is generally accepted that imported products have an income elasticity greater than one, and domestic goods have an income elasticity less than one, adoption of an "effects test" as posited by the Community would mean that every time the Bundesbank, or any other central bank, takes actions that reduce economic growth, these measures would be inconsistent with Article III.

2.   *Application to the Present Case of the Legal Analysis Suggested by the Community for Article III:2, First Sentence*

a)   The First Step of the Test: Like Products

4.51   In referring to the first step of the legal test it suggested for the first sentence of Article III:2 -- the like product assessment, the **Community** argued that the physical characteristics and manufacturing process of spirits and shochu A and B are similar: The two categories of shochu and most of the liquors falling within the category "spirits" are white/clear beverages with a relatively high alcoholic content made by distillation from the same large variety of raw materials (e.g., grains, potatoes ...). A comparison of the legal definitions of shochu and of the category of "spirits" contained in articles 3.5 and 3.10 of the Liquor Tax Law demonstrates that the only differences between these two categories are that shochu cannot (1) be made from sugar cane and distilled at less than 95 per cent of alcohol (such as rum); (2) have other ingredients added at the time of distillation (such as gin); (3) be filtered with charcoal of white birch (such as vodka); (4) have an alcoholic content in excess of 45 per cent, in the case of shochu B, or 36 per cent, in the case of shochu A. In practice, as mentioned above, both types of shochu typically have an alcoholic strength of 20 per cent to 35 per cent, with 25 per cent being the most common strength. The legal definition of the category of "spirits" does not provide for a maximum alcohol content but in practice, the average alcohol content of the liquors falling within this category is 40 per cent. For the Community, the above differences between shochu and each of the main types of "spirits" are clearly minor and do not prevent all of them from qualifying as like products. Similar differences (if not more significant ones) exist also among the various types of western-style distilled spirits, despite of which all of them have been included into a single category of "spirits" and taxed at a uniform rate. The Community submitted that the differences in alcoholic strength are moreover rendered irrelevant by the drinking habits of the Japanese consumers: both shochu and the liquors falling within the category of "spirits" tend to be drunk heavily diluted with water or other non-alcoholic beverages and end up at roughly the same strength.

4.52   In support of its allegation, that shochu and spirits are like products, the **Community** also argued that shochu and spirits have essentially the same consumers' uses and customs classification. Shochu and "spirits" have essentially the same end-uses. All of them are drunk "straight", "on the rocks" or, more frequently, diluted with water or other non-alcoholic beverages. Moreover, both shochu and "spirits" are widely drunk by all categories of consumers, regardless of age, sex or occupation. In support of its argument, the Community submitted two market studies.[50] Moreover, shochu and all "spirits" other than gin and rum fall within the same HS sub-heading (HS 2208.90). This confirms that the differences between shochu and the category of "spirits" may be less significant than the differences among the various types of liquors falling within the category of "spirits".

4.53   The **Community** then submitted that a striking illustration of the "likeness" between shochu and "spirits" and, at the same time, of the arbitrariness and artificiality which are inherent to the criteria on the basis of which the Liquor Tax Law attempts to distinguish them, has been recently provided by the change in the tax categorization of the brand "Juhyo". This brand had been traditionally sold by the local manufacturer Suntory as vodka and accounted for almost half of the Japanese production of that liquor. However, as from June 1993, Suntory started to market the same product as "Juhyo shochu". All that was required in order to obtain this change in tax category was to discontinue the use of charcoal of white birch as a filtering material.[51] The Community argued that the change was made with the aim of escaping the higher taxes levied on "spirits" and was followed by an immediate and substantial reduction in the retail prices of "Juhyo". In support of its argument, the Community submitted an article from the Teiin Shkuryo Shinbun. The Community concluded by referring the Panel to the findings of the 1987 Panel Report where it was stated that "Japanese shochu (Group A) and vodka could be considered as like products in terms of Article III:2 because they were both white/clear spirits, made of similar raw materials, and their end-uses were virtually identical (either as straight schnaps type of drinks or in various mixtures)"[52] and that other types of spirits, in addition to shochu A and vodka, could also be like products. For the Community therefore, the liquors falling within the category "spirits" and the two sub-categories of sho-

---

[50]   A market survey conducted by the Japan Market Research Bureau in December 1994 and a market survey conducted by an ependent research company in May 1994.

[51]   In addition, barley and rice were added as raw materials in order to alter the taste of the product. Nevertheless, this change was not required by the Liquor Tax Law in order to make "Juhyo" qualify as shochu.

[52]   1987 Panel Report, para. 5.7.

chu are, in light of all the criteria that have been identified above as relevant, "like products" within the meaning of the first sentence of Article III:2.

4.54   **Japan** argued that in its view the Community acknowledged that the differences in physical characteristics between whisky/brandy and shochu are sufficiently large to prevent the two categories from qualifying as like products. It also noted that the Community's claim of likeness applies only between the category of "spirits" and shochu A and B. Japan argued that, in examining the "likeness" of "spirits" and shochu, the Community looked at the following four criteria: (i) the product's properties, nature and quality, (ii) its end-uses, (iii) consumers' tastes and habits, and (iv) the HS classification. Japan argued that if the Community's four criteria were correctly applied to the facts, "spirits" and shochu A and B would not be "like products", because:

as to (i) the product's properties, nature and quality:

-    The alcoholic strength of shochu (mostly 20 to 25 per cent) is closer to wine and sake (12 to 15 per cent) than to "spirits" (around 40 per cent).

-    Most shochu does not undergo a post-distillation value-adding process (over 99 per cent is not aged in wooden casks) while "spirits" are characterized by value-addition through flavouring, purification with white birch charcoal or aging; picking a few examples from the vast array of shochu brands should not cloud the overall picture.

-    Bulky plastic, glass and paper bottles over 1.8 litres are the most popular containers for shochu while 0.7 litre glass bottles are common for "spirits".

as to (i) end-uses and (ii) consumers' tastes and habits:

-    60 per cent of consumers drink shochu during meals but 63 per cent drink "spirits" after meals.

-    42 per cent of shochu consumers, but only 4 per cent, 1 per cent, and none of vodka, gin, and rum consumers, respectively, drink the product in question with hot water; and none of shochu consumers but 26 per cent, 32 per cent, and 15 per cent of vodka, gin and rum consumers, respectively, drink the product in question with tonic water, according to the data submitted by the Community.

-    The study by ASI Market Research Inc. submitted by the complaining parties concludes that "(s)hochu is not seen as so much of a competitor (i.e., substitutable product) in the eyes of the consumers".

-    According to a study, only 6 per cent of shochu consumers responded that they would drink "spirits" if shochu is not available.

-    Contrary to the Community's allegation, the evidence submitted by the Community shows that shochu consumers are only as often (not more often) found in the "regular consumers" of premium brands of spirits and liqueurs as are found in all respondents.

and as to iv) classification in the HS:

-    The 1996 version of the HS gives separate headings for rum (2208.40), gin (2208.50) and vodka (2208.60), as opposed to shochu (2208.90, "other"). Japan submitted that the HS is established for purposes other than internal taxation and does not offer appropriate criteria by which to judge "likeness" in terms of Article III, but even if "likeness" should be examined on the basis of identity of the HS heading, as the Community and the 1987 Panel Report suggest, shochu and vodka would not be "like" under the 1996 version of the HS.

4.55   The **Community** responded that as far as shochu and "spirits" are concerned, Japan had been able to identify only two main differences in physical characteristics: the alcohol content and the packaging. According to the Community, the differences in alcohol content between shochu and "spirits" are not reflected in their respective legal definitions and, therefore, cannot provide a valid justification for applying different tax rates. There is nothing in the Liquor Tax Law preventing the manufacture of vodka of 25 per cent. In practice, some brands of vodka do have an alcohol strength of 25 per cent as illustrated by the case of Juhyo. On the other hand, shochu B may have an alcoholic strength of up to 45 per cent, whilst the maximum alcohol content of shochu A is set at 36 per cent, i.e., only four degrees below the average strength for spirits. High alcohol shochu is by no means a rarity. In 1994, the sales volume of shochu of 35 per cent was larger than the total sales volume of all types of "spirits". The alleged differences in packaging are irrelevant for a like product determination. The physical properties of shochu remain the same irrespective of the size and the material of the packages in which it is sold.

4.56   **Japan** submitted that such commonality of sales outlets and advertising styles between "spirits" and shochu as pointed out by the Community are also observed among all alcoholic and non-alcoholic beverages and thus fails to demonstrate that products are "like". Though the Community points out similarity in the shochu-based pre-mixes and the pre-mixes made from other liquors, for Japan, such would not be evidence of "likeness" of shochu and "spirits", just as the similarity among tequila-based, wine-based and beer-based "margaritas" in the United States would not render tequila, wine and beer "like". For Japan, "Juhyo Vodka" and "Juhyo Shochu" are two distinct products with different raw materials and different production methods sold under the same established brand name, and are not "like products". Japan also noted that the 1987 Panel Report failed to deliver a clear-cut conclusion on the issue of "likeness" between shochu A and vodka. Although the panel noted that these "could be considered as like products", these products do not appear on the list of pairs of like products in the Report.

4.57   The **Community** replied that the survey on drinking styles which it had submitted to the Panel confirmed that the end-uses of shochu and "spirits" were almost the same. Shochu was found in all the end-use categories, with only the exception of tonic water. The examples mentioned by Japan merely pointed to the fact that a limited number of specific end-uses are more typical of certain categories of distilled spirits (e.g., shochu and warm water, rum and cola or gin and tonic). Nevertheless, these end-uses are not exclusive of the liquors in question. Vodka, gin and rum are also consumed with warm water, even if in smaller percentages. On the other hand, there are other end-uses which are as common for shochu as for "spirits". For example, while the percentage of drinkers of shochu and soda is 32 per cent, the percentage of consumers of vodka, rum and gin with soda is 32 per cent, 36 per cent and 21 per cent, respectively. Furthermore, there is a substantial coincidence among the most frequent end-uses of shochu and of each of the main categories of "spirits". The Community also argued that the study submitted by Japan on "Alcohol consumption and meals" was flawed because consumers were asked about their preferences and not about how they had actually drunk each category, which led them to favour in their responses the most traditional consumption patterns. Moreover, the evidence was misleading because, according to the explanations provided orally by Japan, the percentages were not percentages of consumers but percentages of replies. The Community noted that, despite these shortcomings, the survey confirmed that both shochu and spirits were consumed before, during and after meals in substantial quantities.

4.58   The **United States** stated that under the analysis of origin-neutral taxation in the 1992 *Malt Beverages* and *US Auto Taxes* panel reports, Japan's taxes on distilled spirits are inconsistent with Article III:2, because the products are otherwise similar in terms of their physical properties, production method and end-use by consumers, and the distinction made by the Liquor Tax Law between shochu and other distilled spirits has the aim and effect of affording protection to domestic production of shochu. Since the Community and Canada had presented detailed expositions of the evidence of similarity of physical properties, production method and end-use by consumers, the United States would concentrate on the other elements. The United States noted, however, that shochu A is a colourless, odourless product, typically of 25 degrees alcohol content, resembling vodka. According to US exporters, 100 per cent of shochu A is manufactured by adding water to imported ethyl alcohol and redistilling it in Japan. The United States noted that Japan had confirmed that the ratio of imported material in shochu A has been increasing since the 1960s and is over 90 per cent. Thus, shochu A could be characterized as a product composed of ethyl alcohol imported under a duty-free tariff quota for manufacturers, plus water, made primarily by six large firms, protected by a 17.9 per cent applied tariff and benefiting from excise tax discrimination. The ensemble of government measures ensured that the effective protection for production would be maximized. Shochu B is distilled from fermented rice, sweet potatoes, barley or potatoes.[53] The shochu B industry is composed of a large number of small to medium-sized firms and a few of the larger beverage firms. Geographically concentrated in Kyushu, they have mobilized politically to obtain protection in the form of subsidies and tax discrimination. The United States also contested Japan's allegation that "the crucial difference between whisky and shochu in terms of raw materials is the use of malts", since

---

[53]   The shochu sample submitted by the United States is a barley-based shochu B and the sample from the EC is a sweet-potato-based shochu B.

Bourbon whisky and Tennessee whisky are made from corn and contain no malt. As to Japan's claim that whisky and shochu "differ in the production process of aging in wooden casks", the United States noted that a number of premium brands of shochu B are aged in casks.

b) The Second Step of the Test: Discriminatory Taxes

4.59   Concerning the second step of the test it suggested for the application of the first sentence of Article III:2, the assessment of discriminatory taxation, the **Community** submitted evidence according to which the tax rate per litre of shochu B is always lower than the rate on the category of "spirits". The tax rate per litre of shochu A is also lower than the rate per litre of "spirits" for beverages below 36 per cent - 37 per cent. Above that strength, the rate on shochu A is higher. Nevertheless, Article 3.5 of the Liquor Tax Law excludes from the definition of shochu A beverages with an alcohol content of more than 36 per cent. Thus, in practice, the rate on shochu A is always lower than the rate on the category of "spirits". More specifically, the Community argued that the tax discrimination index between shochu B of the most common strength (25 per cent) and "spirits" of the most common strength (40 per cent) is 389 per cent. If the tax rates per litre of pure alcohol, instead of the rates per litre of each beverage, are compared, the tax rate applied to the category of "spirits" is still much higher and the tax discrimination index reached 243 per cent. The Community therefore concluded that the liquors falling within the category of "spirits" and the two sub-categories of shochu being "like products", the Liquor Tax Law violates Article III:2, first sentence, by applying a tax rate to the category of "spirits" which is in excess of the tax rates applied to each of the two sub-categories of shochu.

4.60   The **United States** argued that since Japan's tax system applicable to distilled spirits has been devised so as to protect domestic production of shochu (in application of the aim-and-effect test detailed in paragraphs 4.24 to 4.32 above and further supported by an additional factual discussion detailed in Section F below) and because white and brown spirits have similar physical characteristics and end-uses, white and brown spirits are "like products" in the sense of the first sentence of Article III:2, and therefore the difference in tax treatment between shochu and vodka, rum, gin, other white spirits, whisky, brandy and other brown spirits is inconsistent with Article III:2, first sentence.

4.61   **Japan** called the legal test suggested by the Community a "two-step approach", and disagreed with it. It further argued that even if the "two-step approach" should be adopted, the examination of the second step (discriminatory or not) should be made by the comparison of tax/price ratio between imported "spirits" and domestic shochu. For Japan, the tax/price ratio is the superior yardstick for an examination of the tax burden since it indicates better the impact on consumer choice (and therefore discrimination) than the ratio of tax over volume product or alcohol content. A consumer usually does not buy a product exclusively on the basis of the size of the bottle or on the basis of the alcoholic strength. Consumers choose products by comparing the price and the overall value of a product, which rests upon the taste, flavour and other features and is not confined to the volume and strength. This is why, Japan argued, the tax/price ratio is a better criterion to evaluate the effects of taxes on competitive conditions; and neutrality is achieved when the tax/price ratio is equalized, as is the case with the Japanese tax. Japan submitted that the weighted average of liquor-tax/price ratios for the 20 best-selling brands of domestic shochu A, shochu B, imported vodka, imported rum, and imported gin are 22 per cent, 13 per cent, 18 per cent, 12 per cent, and 18 per cent, respectively. Japan concluded that, even under the "two-step approach", taxes on "spirits" would not be found discriminatory against shochu when an appropriate yardstick is applied.

E.   *Article III:2, Second Sentence*

1.   *The Different Legal Analyses Suggested by the Parties for the Interpretation of Article III:2, Second Sentence*

a)   The Test Suggested by the Community

4.62   The **Community** argued that the 1987 Panel Report, Article III:2, second sentence, the first paragraph of Article III to which reference is made in the second sentence of Article III:2; and the Note ad Article III:2, all establish a two-step test for the examination of the conformity of a system of internal taxation with Article III:2, second sentence. First, it must be determined whether the taxed imported and domestic products are "directly competitive or substitutable"; and secondly, it must be established whether the taxation is "protective". For the Community, all liquors falling within the categories of "whisky/brandy" and of "liqueurs" and the two sub-categories of "shochu" are "directly competitive or substitutable" among each other. Should any of the liquors falling within the category of "spirits" be found by the Panel not to be a "like product" to shochu, the Community submitted that shochu and "spirits" are, at the very least, "directly competitive or substitutable" products. By applying higher tax rates to the categories of "whisky/brandy", "liqueurs" and "spirits" than to each of the two shochu sub-categories, the Liquor Tax Law affords protection to the domestic production of shochu, thereby violating Article III:2, second sentence.

4.63   For the **Community**, the concept of "directly competitive or substitutable product" - the first step of the test - is wider than the concept of "like product" and may include products with different physical characteristics but substitutable in terms of uses such as, for instance, skimmed milk powder and vegetable proteins;[54] apples and oranges;[55] butter and oleomargarine;[56] tung oil and linseed oil;[57] or natural rubber and synthetic rubber.[58] In order to determine whether two products are directly competitive or substitutable, the following criteria may be relevant: the aptitude of the two products to serve the same uses (it is not neces-

---

[54]   Panel report op. cit note 16 (EEC - Measures on Animal Feed Proteins), adopted on 14 March 1978, BISD 25S/49, para. 4.3.

[55]   EPCT/A/PV/9, p.7.

[56]   Reports of Committees and Principal Subcommittees, UN Conference on Trade and Employment, 1948, p. 61.

[57]   E/CONF.2/C.3/SR.11, p. 1 and Corr.2.

[58]   E/CONF.2/C.3/SR.11, p. 3.

sary, however, that the two products are substitutable in respect of all their potential uses); the extent and the form in which the two products are available to the public; the respective prices of the products and the responsiveness of the demand for one of the products to the changes in the price of the other.

4.64   As for the second step of the test it suggested for the second sentence of Article III:2, the **Community** argued that the following criteria may be relevant in order to determine whether a difference in taxation is "protective" of domestic production. (1) The level of the tax differential, but contrary to the first sentence of Article III:2, a tax difference does not lead automatically to a violation of the second sentence of Article III:2. On the other hand, even small tax differences may be protective. Nonetheless a *de minimis* differential may, in certain cases, be found not to afford protection. (2) The degree of substitutability and competition between the two products. Logically, the protective effect of a system of taxation increases with the degree of substitutability and competition. (3) Whether the less taxed product is produced in other countries. A system of taxation is protective of the domestic production if the less taxed category is almost exclusively produced in the country imposing the taxes. In contrast, the fact that the more taxed product is produced also in the country applying the internal taxes is irrelevant. The Community also submitted that since Article III:2 protects trade expectations on the competitive relationship between imported and domestic products rather than expectations on trade volumes, it is not necessary, in order to establish a violation of Article III:2, second sentence, to show that the difference in taxation has had an actual effect on the volume of trade.

b)   The Test Suggested by Canada

4.65   **Canada**'s claim was limited to the second sentence of Article III:2. Canada submitted that taxes imposed on Canadian whisky as compared to those imposed on domestically-produced shochu are inconsistent with the provisions of Article III:2, second sentence. For Canada, the Liquor Tax Law that in 1987 was determined to be inconsistent with Article III:2, second sentence, continues, even as amended, to be inconsistent with Article III:2, second sentence.

4.66   For **Canada**, Article 3.2 of the DSU makes clear that it is the express wording of the WTO Agreement that ultimately defines the rights and obligations of Members and thus, whether the Liquor Tax Law is inconsistent with Article III:2. To the same effect, Canada cited Professor Lauterpacht regarding the role of treaties in defining the rights and obligations of States:

> "The rights and duties of States are determined in the first instance by their agreement as expressed in treaties - just as in the case of individuals their rights are specifically determined by any contract which is binding upon them. When a controversy arises between two or more States with regard to a matter regulated by a treaty, it is natural that the parties should invoke and that the adjudicating

agency should apply, in the first instance, the provisions of the treaty in question".[59]

Canada submitted that the relevant "rights and obligations of Members under the covered agreements", i.e., the "provisions of the treaty in question", respecting Japan's Liquor Tax Law are set out in Article III:1; Article III:2, second sentence, and Note ad Article III, paragraph 2.

4.67 **Canada** referred the Panel to the exact wording of Article III:2, second sentence, which provides that "No Member shall otherwise apply internal taxes or other internal charges to imported or domestic products in a manner contrary to the principles set forth in paragraph III:1". The "principles set forth in Article III:1" provide that "Members recognize that internal taxes and other internal charges ... should not be applied to imported or domestic products so as to afford protection to domestic production". Canada recalled that the Note ad Article III, Paragraph 2 to Article III:2, second sentence, was added pursuant to the Havana Conference Report of Sub-Committee A of the Third Committee on Tariff Negotiations, Internal Taxation and Regulation "so that it would be easier for Members to ascertain the precise scope of their obligations under this Article".[60] The report stated that "A tax conforming to the requirements of the first sentence of paragraph 2 would be considered to be inconsistent with the provisions of the second sentence only in cases where competition was involved between, on the one hand, the taxed product and, on the other hand, a directly competitive or substitutable product which was not "similarly taxed". Canada argued, therefore, that a clear reading of these provisions establishes that under Article III:2 second sentence, four criteria must be satisfied for Japan's Liquor Tax Law to be found to be inconsistent with this provision:

(1)   the taxes levied pursuant to the Liquor Tax Law are internal taxes or other internal charges;

(2)   whisky is a directly competitive or substitutable product with shochu Group A and shochu Group B;

(3)   whisky and shochu Group A and shochu Group B are not similarly taxed; and

(4)   the taxes levied pursuant to the Liquor Tax Law afford protection to domestic production of shochu Group A and shochu Group B.

For Canada, these criteria are based on the general principle, enunciated in the Havana Reports[61] and confirmed in the 1989 panel report on "United States - Section 337 of the Tariff Act of 1930",[62] that internal taxes should not be applied in such a manner so as to afford protection to domestic production. The Working Party Report on Border Tax Adjustments[63] and the 1987 Panel Report confirmed that Article III:2 gives effect to this general principle by ensuring the trade "neu-

---

[59]   Lauterpacht, International Law: Collected Papers, 86-87 (1970).
[60]   Havana Reports, at p. 61, para. 36.
[61]   Ibid, at p. 41, para. 7.
[62]   Panel report adopted on 7 November 1989, BISD 36S/345, para. 5.10.
[63]   Panel report adopted on 2 December 1970, BISD 18S/97, para. 9.

trality" of internal taxation measures that are applied to imported and domestic products. Internal taxation measures that are not trade neutral distort the conditions of competition between imported and domestic products thereby affording protection to domestic production. To assess whether an internal taxation system affords protection, Canada noted that the 1987 Panel Report sets out three variables that are applicable in the present case: (i) whether there is a considerably lower tax rate on shochu than on imported whisky, (ii) whether the shochu consumed is almost exclusively produced in Japan, and (iii) whether shochu and whisky are mutually substitutable.

c)   The Test Suggested by the United States

4.68   The **United States** submitted that since Japan's tax system applicable to distilled spirits has been devised so as to protect domestic production of shochu and because all distilled spirits have similar physical characteristics and end-uses, they are "directly competitive and substitutable" in terms of Article III:2, second sentence. Therefore, the United States considered that the difference in taxation between distilled spirits exceeds any *de minimis* level because that difference materially alters the conditions of competition between domestic and imported products. In the present case, the United States submitted that the change in conditions of competition is illustrated by factors such as the demonstrated effect on consumption choices and the cross-price elasticity of demand discussed further below.

4.69   The **United States** reiterated that the plain language of Article III:2, first sentence, condemns measures that explicitly target foreign products and accord less favourable treatment. This, in the US view, makes sense because the discriminatory aim of such measures is apparent. However, when a measure is origin-neutral and therefore such an aim cannot be presumed, it does not make sense to say that the purpose of the measure becomes irrelevant. The United States noted that Article III is designed to protect against discrimination, not to create a *per se* rule of absolute liability for any greater burden or restriction on international trade. All direct and indirect regulation of goods has domestic and international trade-restricting effects, because by its nature regulation imposes burdens. For the United States, the rule proposed by the Community would mean that a government could not adopt any measure, irrespective of its purpose, if the measure had the effect at some point of burdening foreign more than domestic products. Such a "pure effects" test would give no guidance or certainty to legislators or to their legal advisers, because in any situation its application could change from day to day based on international and domestic factors that could not be anticipated at the time a measure is adopted.

4.70   In the view of the **United States**, the Community had recognized that its "effects" rule would position perfectly desirable, non-discriminatory governmental regulation - including measures maintained by the Community and its member States - under a legal guillotine. To address the obvious overbreadth of its own legal theory, the Community had invented two arbitrary "flexibilities". The United States asked the following questions: What if two automobiles with different engine displacement have identical fuel economy and emissions - why should not these automobiles be "like"? In the US view, this demonstrates that the Community, while claiming to disregard the issue of legitimacy of policy purpose, cannot really do it. The Community simply wants panels to make an *ad hoc* judgment that the engine displacement criterion used in EC auto tax schemes would remove these taxes from the "guillotine rule" of the first sentence of Article III:2. How many more flexibilities would future panels need to invent to deal with the fact that the EC rule simply overreaches, asked the United States. As for the Community's analysis of the second sentence, the United States argued that the second sentence does not involve a "straight effects test". For the United States the effect of a legislation may be determined based on various elements, as further detailed in paragraphs 4.24 to 4.32 above and in Section F below.

d)   The Test Suggested by Japan

4.71   **Japan** suggested, as similarly argued with regard to the first sentence of Article III:2 in paragraphs 4.33 and following, that the consistency of a different treatment of products with Article III:2, second sentence, should be judged in light of paragraph 1 of the Article, in particular the language "not be applied ... so as to afford protection to domestic production", and that whether or not the tax at issue is designed "so as to afford protection to domestic production" should then be judged by the "aim" and "effect" of affording protection. Japan further argued that all the parties to the dispute agree that the second sentence of Article III:2 should be interpreted in the light of whether a measure at issue is applied "so as to afford protection to domestic production", and that the crucial difference between its approach, or the aim-and-effect test approach, and the approach taken by the Community and Canada, or the "two-step" approach with regard to the second sentence of Article III:2, exists in relation to the interpretation of the language "so as to afford protection to domestic production" of paragraph 1 of Article III. The latter approach's criterion is the protective effect alone, while Japan's approach considers not only the effect but also the aim of the measure in question. Japan added that even the Community had come to agree that the analysis, according to the text of the second sentence of Article III:2, should also proceed on the basis of protective purpose and effect. For Japan, the aim of the tax distinction made among categories of distilled liquors by the Liquor Tax Law is neutrality attained through a constant tax/price ratio amongst tax categories. Japan reiterated that the Liquor Tax Law does not have the effect of protecting domestic production of shochu since it does not distort the competitive relationships between imported and domestic products based on the following three cumulative criteria: (1) the neutrality of the tax burden among categories of the legislation under examination, (2) the production of the allegedly protected products outside the imported country and of the allegedly "imported" products in the country, and (3) the absence of directly competitive and substitutable relationship (cross-price elasticity) between the imported and domestically produced products. Japan argued that if there is no difference in tax burden, the system does not distort trade; if there does not exist directly competitive and substitutable relationships, differences in tax burden do not matter; if the products at issue are produced in and out of the country, the tax differentiation should not be construed to afford protection to domestic production; and thus protective distortion can be shown only when all of the three requirements are met. Japan further argued that as one examines the relative tax burden between products in question, the tax burden should be measured by the tax/price ratio, a yardstick which best captures the impact on consumers' behaviour, and in examining whether or not the category in question is almost exclusively domestic, what needs to be examined is not import ratios, but whether or not an allegedly "domestic" category is produced in other countries and whether or not "imported" products in question are also domestically produced.

2. *Application to the Present Case of the Legal Analysis Suggested by the Community and Canada*

a) The First Step of the Tests Suggested by the Community and Canada: Directly Competitive and Substitutable Goods

i) Physical characteristics, end-uses, tariff line and availability to the public

4.72   For the **Community**, the two categories of shochu and the liquors falling within the categories of "spirits", "whisky/brandy" and "liqueurs" are directly competitive and substitutable since they share the same essential physical characteristics, have similar end-uses, are similarly available to the public and are marketed in a similar way. Furthermore the prices of shochu and of the other distilled spirits and liqueurs are within a close range, once the liquor taxes are deducted. Moreover, there is evidence that, despite the distorting effects on competition of the Liquor Tax Law, the demand for shochu is largely influenced by the fluctuations in the prices of other types of distilled spirits and liqueurs.

4.73   **Canada** and the **Community** referred the Panel to the 1987 Panel Report where it was determined that shochu Groups A and B were directly competitive or substitutable with all grades of whisky, including high-quality, high-priced whisky products, for the following reasons:

"The Panel decided not to examine the 'likeness' of alcoholic beverages beyond the requests specified in the complaint by the European Communities [i.e., vodka and shochu Group A]. The Panel felt justified in doing so also for the following reasons: Alcoholic drinks might be drunk straight, with water, or as mixes. Even if imported alcoholic beverages ... were not considered to be 'like' to Japanese alcoholic beverages ... , the flexibility in the use of alcoholic drinks and their common characteristics often offered an alternative choice for consumers leading to a competitive relationship. In the view of the Panel there existed - even if not necessarily in respect of all the economic uses to which the product may be put - direct competition or substitutability among the various distilled liquors ... . The increasing imports of 'Western-style' alcoholic beverages into Japan bore witness to this lasting competitive relationship and to the potential products substitution through trade among various alcoholic beverages. Since consumer habits *vis-à-vis* these products varied in response to their respective prices, their availability through trade and their other competitive inter-relationships, [the following products, *inter alia*, were] 'directly competitive or substitutable' products: Imported and Japanese-made distilled liquors, including all grades of whisky/brandies, vodka and shochu Groups A and B, among each other".[64]

4.74 The **Community** argued that the differences in physical characteristics and manufacturing methods between the two categories of shochu and the liquors falling within the category of "spirits" are minor. The differences between the physical properties of shochu and of "whisky/brandy" are somewhat more marked. Nonetheless, these two categories share the same essential characteristics: both shochu and "whisky/brandy" are spirits obtained by distillation and with a relatively high alcoholic content. The main differences between the two categories are thus restricted to the fact that neither malted grains nor grapes can be used in the production of shochu. For the Community, this difference is only relative, as most shochu is made, like whisky, from different types of grain, albeit not malted. Other differences are that shochu is, as a general rule, a white/clear spirit, while whisky and brandy are brown-coloured; whisky and brandy are matured/aged and, as a general rule, blended, while shochu is not. These last two differences are becoming irrelevant as an increasing number of shochu brands claim to be blended and aged in barrels and are brown coloured. For the Community, the absence of any fundamental differences between shochu and "whisky/brandy" is attested by the fact that the advertising of many shochu brands tends to emphasize their similarities with whisky and/or brandy in terms of raw materials, ingredients, manufacturing process and tradition. In some cases, this policy has been pursued to the extreme of modifying the traditional manufacturing methods of shochu in a deliberate attempt to confer upon it a whisky-like appearance and taste.[65] Concerning "liqueurs", this category is comprised of a very heterogeneous variety of liquors which have as their only common characteristic an extract content in excess of two per cent. The 1987 Panel Report found that differences concerning the level of extract content were minor and did not prevent two products from being like products. *A fortiori*, differences in the extract content are not sufficient in themselves to prevent liquors falling within the category of "liqueurs" from being considered as "directly substitutable and competitive" with "shochu", "spirits" and "whisky/brandy". Moreover, it must be recalled that a major portion of the sales in this category consists of bottled or

---

[64] 1987 Panel Report, para. 5.7.

[65] Thus, in May 1988 (i.e., shortly after the adoption of the 1987 Panel Report), the Japanese manufacturer Takara started marketing "Jun Legend", a light amber coloured brand of shochu produced by blending two types of alcohol distilled from barley and corn and maturing them in charred white oak barrels for one to five years. According to Takara, "the most noticeable characteristic of this brand is a flavour and taste similar to whisky". When the new brand was launched, Takara announced its expectations that the new product would appeal to former consumers of second grade whisky which, as a result of the 1987 Panel Report, was expected to become subject to much higher tax rates as from 1989.

canned pre-mixes made from "shochu", "spirits" or "whisky/brandy" which are, therefore, identical to home-made mixed beverages from the same liquors.

4.75   The **Community** argued that the fact that all distilled spirits and liqueurs have the same basic properties and are objectively apt to serve the same end-uses is confirmed by the consumption patterns observed in the Japanese market. In support of its allegation, the Community submitted the results of a research conducted by the Japanese whisky industry on the presence of shochu and whisky in "snack bars". All of them are drunk "straight", "on the rocks" or, more frequently, diluted with water or other non-alcoholic beverages. The drinking styles of the various distilled spirits (including shochu) and liqueurs are virtually the same. Furthermore, the advertising of the different types of spirits and liquors tends to promote the same drinking styles. Both shochu and the other types of distilled spirits and liqueurs are widely drunk across all categories of consumers, regardless of their age, sex and occupation. A very high proportion of shochu consumers are also regular consumers of whisky and other spirits and liqueurs and this proportion is higher than among consumers of alcoholic beverages in general. The same pattern has been observed with respect to the consumption of premium brands of western-style spirits and liqueurs sold at the highest prices. In the last few years, a new market has emerged, especially among young consumers, for bottled or canned pre-mixed drinks combining spirits and soft drinks. As shown by the advertising materials submitted by the Community, the executional style, target market and drinking style of the shochu based pre-mixes and the pre-mixes made from other liquors are identical.

4.76   The **Community** further argued that shochu and the other types of spirits and liqueurs are directly competitive since they are available in the same trade channels and are promoted and advertised in a similar way. All of them are sold at the same outlets, both for on-premise consumption and for home consumption. Although in the past, there may have been a certain specialization among on-premise outlets, in recent years this specialisation has disappeared. The Community submitted that the results of a recent survey shows that in the Tokyo area 71 per cent of the "snack bars" (a category of outlet where western-style liquors were traditionally predominant and which represents approximately 40 per cent of the total on-premise market) now serve both whisky and shochu. Similarly, an increasing number of "izakayas" (a once "traditional" shochu/sake/beer style of outlet which accounts for approximately 20 per cent of the on-premise market) are now serving whisky and other western-style spirits and liqueurs. Both at on-premise outlets and at outlets selling for home consumption, shochu is positioned and promoted side-by-side with the other types of spirits and liqueurs, thus evidencing that both the retailers and the public regard them as substitutable and competitive products. The level of advertising spending on shochu brands is comparable to the advertising spending on the brands of other spirits and liqueurs. The advertising of shochu and of other spirits and liqueurs is very similar in executional style, is targeted towards the same categories of customers (young consumers and "salarymen") and aims at projecting similar images, regardless of whether the products are of "traditional Japanese origin", like shochu, or western-style. The distribution of advertising spending among the different media is similar for shochu and other spirits and liqueurs, a sign that similar markets are being targeted.

4.77   For **Canada,** the evidence makes abundantly clear that in Japan, shochu and whisky continue to be directly competitive or substitutable products in that shochu and whisky have many common characteristics and are commonly consumed at similar diluted alcoholic strengths and manufacturers of shochu in Japan capitalize on these common characteristics by marketing some shochu products on the strength of their similarity to whisky and on the basis that they can be consumed in the same manner as whisky. Canada suggested that the processes and raw materials used in the production of shochu and Canadian whisky are very similar. Canada submitted that both Canadian whisky and shochu are produced from a variety of grain sources such as wheat, barley, rye and corn, although a slightly broader range of agricultural raw materials, such as rice, can be used to manufacture shochu. Many varieties of shochu use exactly the same raw grains that are used in whisky production. The enzymes and yeasts used in the production of whisky and shochu are also similar. With respect to production methods, the processes of milling, cooking and conversion are common to both whisky and shochu. The same equipment is used and the fermentation processes are similar. Whisky and shochu are both produced using continuous and pot distillation methods, or through a blend of the two methods. Up to the end of the distillation process, Canadian whisky and shochu can be identical. The main distinction between Canadian whisky and shochu is that Canadian whisky must be aged. This is not so for shochu, although some shochu is currently being aged.[66]

4.78   **Canada** also argued that in Japan, both whisky and shochu can be consumed in common styles, i.e., "straight", with water or "on ice", and submitted evidence of current liquor advertising in Japan. As distilled liquors, whisky and shochu are both sold to the public at alcohol strengths significantly above the strengths common for other liquors such as beer and wine. Canadian whisky is sold at the retail level in Japan at an alcohol strength of at least 40 per cent. Shochu can be sold at the retail level up to an alcohol strength of 36 per cent for shochu Group A and 45 per cent for shochu Group B, (although the most common retail strength is 25 per cent for both shochu groups). Distilled liquors such as whisky and shochu are commonly consumed in a diluted style, with the resulting alcohol content being similar for both products. Pre-mixed, i.e., diluted, products sold in Japan contain whisky at an alcoholic strength of between five per cent and eight per cent and contain shochu at an alcoholic strength of between four per cent and six per cent. Advertisements for the sale of shochu refer variously to the similarity in the raw materials used to produce whisky and the advertised shochu, the similarity in the production processes that produce whisky and the advertised shochu product and the similarity in the physical appearance (e.g., coloration) of

---

[66]   In support of its allegation Canada submitted a letter from Hiram Walker & Sons Ltd which confirmed: "The process of milling, cooking and conversion are common to both spirits. The same equipment, grains, and enzymes are used in the production of both shochu and Canadian whisky. The details of these processes will vary by distiller and formula but the basic process is the same for both types of spirits. The same similarities hold true for the fermentation process".

whisky and the advertised shochu product. In addition, Canada argued that recently, recognizing consumer perceptions that whisky and shochu are alternative choices, the Japan Spirits and Liquor Maker's Association stated that "the drinking patterns of whisky/brandy and shochu [are] becoming alike and [that] they are competing with each other [in the] market".

4.79   **Japan** argued that "spirits" and "shochu" differ in physical characteristics, end-use, and in tariff lines as is described in paragraph 4.54 above. Japan also argued that whisky/brandy and shochu differ in materials (with malts versus without malts; Bourbon, Tennessee, and Canadian whiskies without malts are classified as "spirits" under the Liquor Tax Law), in the post-distillation processing (aged in wooden casks versus over 99 per cent not aged in wooden casks), in alcoholic strength (around 40 per cent versus 20 to 25 per cent), in colour (0.2 to 0.8 of optical density versus 0.08 of optical density) and in containers (0.7 litre glass bottles versus bulky plastic, glass and paper bottles over 1.8 litres). For Japan, they also differ in end-uses: according to a study in Japan, 60 per cent of shochu consumers drink shochu during meals, while 72 per cent of whisky consumers drink whisky after meals; and according to a study submitted by the Community, only eight per cent of consumers of shochu drink the beverage "on the rocks" while 68 per cent of bourbon whisky consumers do. None of bourbon whisky consumers mix such whisky with hot water or juice, while 42 per cent and 37 per cent of shochu consumers do respectively. They also differ in tariff lines: whisky is classified as "2208.30 whisky" while shochu is classified as "2208.90 Other". Japan also argued that the commonality in availability to the public mentioned by the Community exists only to the extent applicable to all alcoholic and non-alcoholic beverages: the menus and promotion leaflets submitted by the Community list not only whisky(ies) and shochu but also sake, wine, beer, juice, coffee and tea side by side. As to the Canada's comment that pre-mixed shochu and pre-mixed whisky are taxed at the same rate in Japan, Japan argued that the fact that pre-mixed wine and pre-mixed spirits are taxed at the same rate in Canada does not imply a directly competitive or substitutable relationship between wine and spirits, the two products taxed at completely different rates in Canada.

4.80   **Japan** also noted that the aptitude of the two products to serve the same uses raises the issue of the extent of the sameness. Since the use for quenching the thirst, for example, is common to all beverages, and since the use for enjoying alcohol is common to all alcoholic beverages, the concept of "sameness" should be understood in a narrower sense. According to Japan, the Community argues that sameness in drinking habits between shochu and other distilled liquors is sufficient to meet the criteria. However, Japan's evidence shows a good degree of divergence in drinking habits not only between shochu and spirits but between shochu and Bourbon whisky as well. The aptitude to serve the same uses does not seem to exist beyond what would apply to all alcoholic beverages.

4.81   The **Community** argued that Japan's criticisms were unfounded. The study on drinking styles submitted to the panel showed that the end-uses of shochu and bourbon whisky were the same except that shochu is not drunk with tonic water and bourbon is not mixed with warm water or juices. Moreover, the study showed that three out of the five most frequent end-uses of shochu were also found among the five most frequent end-uses of bourbon.

ii) Cross-price elasticity

4.82   Continuing on the issue as to whether shochu and other imported liquors are directly competitive and substitutable, the **Community** argued that the retail prices of shochu and of the other distilled spirits and liqueurs are within a relatively short range once the liquor taxes and the *ad valorem* consumption taxes are deducted. This, in the Community's view, confirms that all of them are, at least potentially, competitive in terms of price. The retail prices net of taxes per litre of pure alcohol of most western-style liquors are much lower than the corresponding prices for shochu but both shochu and western-style liquors are frequently diluted with non-alcoholic beverages and drunk at roughly the same strength. Therefore, it may be concluded that, but for the discriminatory taxes imposed pursuant to the Liquor Tax Law, many western-style liquors would be less expensive than shochu in real terms. Price competition between shochu and the other spirits and liqueurs is therefore distorted by the lower taxes applied to shochu. Despite these distortions, there are clear indications that the demand for shochu is largely influenced by the fluctuations in the prices of the other distilled spirits and liqueurs. The Community argued that this is demonstrated, in particular, by the evolution of the sales of shochu and of the other categories of liquors following the drastic changes in prices provoked by the 1989 tax reform: The tax reform of 1989 abolished the sub-categorization of whisky into "premium whisky", "first grade whisky" and "second grade whisky" and introduced a single tax rate for all types of whisky. As a result, the tax rate applicable to those brands which until then had been classified as second grade increased more than threefold and their retail prices almost doubled. No separate market share data are available for second grade whisky. Nevertheless, the impact of the 1989 reform is reflected in the market share of domestically-produced whisky, which includes virtually all brands previously classified as second grade whisky. The market share of domestically-produced whisky fell from 26.7 per cent in 1988 to 19.6 per cent in 1990, i.e., by more than seven percentage points in only two years. This downward trend has persisted after the 1989 tax reform. In 1994 the market share of domestically produced whisky dropped to only 13.2 per cent. In contrast, the 1994 tax reform provided for only a very modest increase in the taxes on shochu. This allowed the manufacturers of shochu to take advantage of the dramatic increase in the price of whisky brands formerly classified as second grade. As a result, sales of shochu, which had been declining during the preceding years, started to grow again in 1990. Since then, sales of shochu have continued to increase in both absolute and relative terms. Thus, in 1994 the market share of shochu reached 74.2 per cent compared to 61.6 per cent in 1989. The 1989 tax reform lowered the taxes applied to "whisky/brandy" (other than second grade), "spirits" and "authentic liqueurs", thus making possible a substantial reduction of the retail prices of these categories. Thereafter, the sales of these categories enjoyed an instant but short-ived increase. In 1992 the Japanese economy entered into a deep recession that made consumers much more price sensitive and provoked a shift of demand towards the less expensive categories of liquors. This development has hit hardest the sales of "whisky/brandy" (of all grades), "spirits" and "authentic liqueurs" which continue to be much more heavily taxed and, for this reason, still retail at higher prices despite substantial further price reductions.

As a result, since 1992 sales of these categories have fallen in both absolute and relative terms. In contrast, sales of the considerably less taxed shochu have continued to grow during the same period at the expense of the sales of the more heavily taxed categories.

4.83   In response to the Community's allegation of cross-price elasticity, supported by Canada and the United States' claims, **Japan** submitted a rebuttal to the Community's arguments on the changes in consumption of whisky and shochu since 1989, the response of consumers to questions asked by Shakai-Chosa Kenkyujo (Institute for Social Studies), and the result of the econometric analysis of national household survey statistics. Japan raised the following points in its rebuttal to the Community's arguments on the changes in the consumption of whisky and shochu since 1989. First, Japan responded to the Community's argument in stating that the decline of whisky consumption and the rising shochu price, a phenomenon since 1992 (Japan referred to the Community's own submission), indicates the lack of responsiveness of demand for one to the price of the other. Second, Japan submitted that when the complainants discuss market shares of product categories in the sales volume of all distilled liquors, they refer to distilled liquor sales as the denominator, which, according to Japan, rests on an a priori assumption of a competitive or substitutable relationship between these distilled categories.[67] Third, Japan also argued that some of the evidence submitted by the Community does not demonstrate the cross-price elasticity of demand between shochu and whisky (i.e., the responsiveness of the demand for one product to the price of another), but merely points to the responsiveness of the demand for imported whisky in Japan to changes in its own price. The fact that the demand curve for imported whisky shows a downward slope does not prove it is competing with shochu. Fourth, non-price factors such as the recent consumer tendency toward drinks of less alcoholic strength ought to be considered as well. Fifth, for Japan, the recent decline in whisky consumption seems to result, at least partly, from a pricing policy of the Scotch whisky industry which expanded its profit margin following the liquor tax reduction. While the import of whisky from the United States increased from 7,000 kl to 15,000 kl, and the import from Canada from 1,000 kl to 2,000 kl during 1987 to 1994, the figure for the United Kingdom stayed roughly the same at 23,000 kl to 24,000 kl, after a temporary surge in 1989. The temporary surge in 1989 and the ensuing decline is apparently a result of the liquor tax reduction in 1989 and the increase in the Cost-Insurance-Freight (CIF) prices in 1990. As the export prices increased, the manufacturers' profit margin doubled from 10 pounds sterling per case in 1989 to 20.

---

[67]   Japan submitted an example: For the sake of illustration, let us assume that there is no competitive relationship between products A and B. If you introduce a concept P which is the sum of the sales of the two products and calculate the shares of the products in P, you can readily create an impression that A and B are competing with each other. For example, if the price of A increase and its sales decrease, the market share of B in P will increase even if its sales column is not affected at all. Then you have a result which ostensibly indicates the responsiveness in B's share to an increase in A's price. Japan concluded that this kind of argument is, to say the least, inappropriate".

4.84   The **Community** responded that this assertion was unwarranted. The Community argued that it had shown that the fall in sales of former second grade whisky in the wake of the 1989 tax reform was accompanied by a simultaneous increase in the market share of shochu. Likewise, the decrease in sales of whisky (other than former second grade), brandy, spirits and authentic liqueurs after 1992 took place in parallel with an increase in sales of shochu. Moreover, sales of shochu did in fact decrease in absolute terms during 1989 and 1990, in the context of an overall decline in demand for distilled spirits. In relative terms, the market share of shochu increased from 61.2 per cent in 1989 to 63.1 per cent in 1991. During the same period, the share of domestic whisky (which includes virtually all former second grade whisky) fell from 23.4 per cent to 19.6 per cent. In the Community's view, the combinations described by Japan are the result of the deep recession which has affected the Japanese economy since 1992. The recession has made consumers more price sensitive and provoked a shift of demand towards less expensive liquors. Despite substantial reductions in the prices of "whisky/brandy", "spirits" and "authentic liqueur", shochu still retails at lower prices due to the differences in taxation. This has enabled shochu manufacturers to take advantage of the shift in demand notwithstanding a modest price increase.

4.85   **Japan** also cited the response of the consumers to questions asked by Shakai-Chosa Kenkyujo (Institute for Social Studies). Japan argued that according to the survey, if whisky were not available, 32 per cent of the consumers would choose beer, 32 per cent would choose brandy and only 10 per cent would choose shochu. If shochu were not available, 35 per cent would choose beer, 30 per cent would choose sake and only six per cent and four per cent, respectively, would choose "spirits" (e.g., gin, rum, vodka) and Scotch whisky. Japan also submitted the result of the econometric analysis of national household survey statistics. The study applied the statistical method used in the Bossard study commissioned by the European Commission in 1994,[68] to Japanese consumption data for the past 20 years, based on household surveys by the Bureau of Statistics of the Japanese Management and Coordination Agency. Using prices of shochu, whisky, beer, wine and sake, the household consumption expenditures, and the trend factor as seven explanatory variables, 16 equations were developed in order to explain the shochu consumption and the whisky consumption, respectively. The result was striking. Neither the impact of the whisky price on the shochu consumption nor the impact of the shochu price on the whisky consumption was proven significant: the whisky price cannot logically explain the shochu demand; equations containing this variable lead to either the relationship that the higher is

---

[68]   On the question of the cross-price elasticity of demand between alcoholic beverages, Japan had referred the Panel to a statistical analysis made by Bossard Consultants, Competition Between Difference Categories of Alcoholic Drinks (1994) which was commissioned by the European Commission in 1994. This study by Bossard Consultants resulted in a series of findings for the European markets: 1) When the price of wine rises 1%, the consumption of distilled liquors will increase 1.4%, 0.55-0.9% and 0.4%, respectively, in Spain, the United Kingdom and West Germany. 2) One percentage rise in the beer price will lead to the expansion of the distilled liquors by 1.3%, 1.2% and 0.9% respectively, in West Germany, the Netherlands and Denmark.

the shochu price, the larger is the shochu consumption or that of the higher is the whisky price, the lower is the shochu consumption. In contrast, prices of shochu and beer explain the shochu demand in a highly significant manner. Whisky consumption equations containing the shochu price as an explanatory variable either lead to the non-logical relationship that the higher the shochu price, the lower the whisky consumption, or result in a lower absolute value of t-statistics, or the lack of significance. In other words, shochu and whisky are not competing with each other in the Japanese market. Thus, the distinction between shochu and whisky in Japan should be less distortional to the market than the distinction between beer, wine and distilled liquors in the European markets.

4.86   The **United States** criticised the Japanese econometric study. The first point related to the conclusions of the Japanese study. Using the volume of shochu consumed as the dependent variable, the Japanese model found that shochu's own price elasticity is positive and the cross-price elasticity with whisky is negative; it suggested that when the price of shochu goes up the volume consumed proportionately increases by two to three times as much, and when the price of whisky increases the consumption of shochu decreases. The t-statistics corresponding to the model's estimated coefficients were greater than 2 or less than -2, meaning that the model as specified attaches a high degree of statistical significance to these results. Yet a finding that consumers react to an increase in the price of a product by increasing consumption is contrary to one of the fundamental tenets of microeconomic theory -- a downward sloping demand curve. No credence could be given to a model that states, with a high degree of statistical robustness, that demand for a good increases because its price increases; at a minimum such a counter-intuitive result casts serious doubts on the validity of the regression procedure. Secondly, looking further at the regression results in the Japanese study, the United States noted that although the model generally produced elasticities of the expected sign (i.e., negative own elasticity and positive cross-elasticity), the low t-statistics for the cross-elasticity estimates indicated that the variables, as specified, do not significantly explain movements in the consumption of whisky. The United States concluded that in no way does the model support the conclusions cited by Japan. To the contrary, in the US view, the results of the regression analysis only showed that the underlying model is mis-specified and the methodology is flawed. Thirdly, the United States pointed out the Japanese model's failure to correct for basic problems in estimation of time-series models, such as serial correlation and auto-correlation. Because serial correlation biases the standard error of the regression, a naive analysis will draw two erroneous conclusions: (1) the conclusion that the parameter estimates are more precise than they actually are -- the t-statistics will be higher than they should be in a correctly specified model, and (2) a high R^2 statistic that gives an overly optimistic picture of the success of the regression model in estimating relationships between variables. Japan had failed to use well-recognized techniques for correcting these problems such as "first-differencing" (using the change in a variable from the preceding period) or the Cochrane-Orcutt estimation procedure (used in the Bossard study referred to by Japan). In a correctly specified model, a trend variable would not be needed because the effect of increased consumption due to increased income would be picked up by the coefficient of the consumption function variable. An additional benefit of specifying the model in this form is that the coefficients of the price variables would be the actual own- and cross-price elasticities. Finally, the United States raised concerns with the Japanese data itself. The model utilized annual data since 1974. The implicit assumption that no other factors have affected the consumption of shochu or whisky (such as a change in consumer tastes) was unwarranted. For the United States, it would be preferable to use monthly or quarterly data over a shorter time period. Finally, Japan had failed to use real (i.e., inflation-adjusted) prices to avoid an inflationary bias. The United States concluded that the results of the regression study cited by Japan do not support the Japanese Government's contention that whisky and shochu are not directly competitive or substitutable products. The methodology used in the study was flawed, differing from both the Bossard study and accepted econometric practice. The model should be re-estimated as outlined above, preferably utilizing more detailed consumption and pricing data.

4.87   **Japan** responded that this first criticism is equal to saying that it is improbable that shochu consumption is not explained by prices of shochu and whisky but by prices of shochu and beer. Similarly, in response to the Community's criticism that it was improbable that many regressions did not yield a valid result whilst one variable less or more suddenly produced very strong results in one or two regressions, Japan argued that if the beer price is a real factor and the whisky price is a mere noise, "one variable less or more" should totally alter the result. According to Japan, what the Community and the United States are requesting is the result "any hypothesis can explain shochu consumption", a result which is truly improbable. Japan submitted that it is a basic econometrics principle that the level of significance depends on the combination of explanatory variables. In the present analysis, the level of significance attained by an identical set of explanatory variables did not fluctuate widely depending on methods of conversion or estimation. For Japan, the aim of an econometric analysis is to examine the validity of hypotheses. If a hypothesis led to a finding contrary to accepted economic theory under any of the standard models and methods -- linear, log-inverse, log-log, Cochrane-Orcutt, maximum likelihood -- and another led to a meaningful result, what should be rejected is not the models but the former hypothesis. Japan explained that it rejected the hypothesis that "the consumption of shochu is affected by the shochu price and the whisky price" because it produced a result contrary to accepted economic theory. It chose instead the "shochu price and the beer price" hypothesis, because the result accorded with general economic principles. In response to the US criticism that the Japanese study failed to follow the basic point of econometrics technique by failing to use log-linear transformation, which the Bossard study used, Japan noted that there is no reference in the Bossard study to the use of log-linear models, although its use of the linear models, log-log models and log-inverse models is noted. The Japanese study also used linear models, log-log models and log-inverse models, but did not use log-linear models. This is because log-linear models are regarded as more appropriate at the initial stage of introduction of new products into a given market, and are not effective for the analysis of established products such as liquor. Contrary to the US criticism that the Bossard study used the Cochrane-Orcutt method of estimation to correct for autocorrelation and that the Japanese study did not, Japan responded that the Japanese study used not only the ordinary least squares but the Cochrane-Orcutt method as well. Additionally, the maximum likelihood method, which is believed to be a better corrector for autocorrelation, was used. In response to the US criticism against Japan's use of nominal prices, Japan submitted that the Bossard study used nominal price indices. Moreover, Japan submitted that reliability of conversion of nominal prices into real prices by the use of the Consumer Price index (CPI), for example, hinges on whether or not a change in the CPI affects consumption to the same extent as a change in the nominal price of the product at issue. If consumers tend to be influenced more heavily by a change in the price of the product than a change in the price level in general, nominal price indices are more reliable. Moreover, introduction of the CPI could add noise to the analysis because of the issues of weight given to product categories or the reference year. Since prices were generally stable during the years used for the study, it is more appropriate to explain consumer behaviour on the basis of nominal prices. Japan additionally submitted an analysis using real (deflated) prices, which, according to Japan, led to similar results as the analysis using nominal prices. Japan also noted that according to the analysis submitted by the United States, which utilized real (deflated) prices and the technique of "first-differentiating", "the annual price indices of whisky and shochu and annual household expenditures do not account for movements in the quantity consumed of these products". Japan argued that this result also supports Japan's rejection of the hypothesis that the prices of shochu and whisky affect the shochu consumption. Japan thus concluded that the criticism raised by the United States was off the mark.

4.88   The expert for the **Community** further challenged the Japanese econometric study. According to this expert, time series which are used in Japan study, are inherently difficult to analyze as they tend to be beset by at least three types of problems that make a statistical analysis difficult. Concerning the trends, this means that the development of the different variables is driven by factors that cannot be explained by an econometric model, but happen due to autonomous factors. For instance, consumption of a product may change simply due to fashion, economic growth, population growth, etc. When a large part of the changes in consumption is influenced by factors of this nature, it will be difficult to separate statistically the influence of price movements from that of trends. Concerning autocorrelation, this means that extraordinary influences on the variables in one year are likely to be present in the following year. An advertising campaign in one year that pushed up consumption of the product will also have an impact on consumption of the following year. If it is not corrected, autocorrelation decreases the precision of the econometric estimates, if it is corrected (e.g. by using the Cochrane-Orcutt method), it will reduce the number of available data points. Concerning multicollinearity, this means that for the case at hand, changes in the consumption of one type of liquor are related to changes in the consumption of another liquor. A hot summer, for instance, will increase the consumption of all beverages. Again, the results show how difficult it is to statistically separate the influence of one variable from that of another. According to the Community expert, the data set used for the Japanese statistical analysis is fraught with all three problems, which would make it difficult to prove any statistical connection between shochu and whisky consumption. In addition to these problems that occur naturally in time series analysis, the date set suffers from two further limitations: first, there are breaks in the data series. During the time period analyzed there have been several tax reforms that affected the structure of liquor prices and consumption. Such breaks in the data series have, as a consequence, that what is measured at the beginning of the time period is not identical with what is measured at the end of a time period. Second, there is illegitimate aggregation of product groups. There are major shifts within a product group such as whisky. Although domestic and foreign whisky are inherently close products, the aggregation into one category hides the fact that up to 1989 the tax system treated them differently. Because the tax reform has affected domestic and foreign whisky in an opposite direction, an aggregation of the two types will lead to misleading statistical results. The Community expert submitted also that the importance of the tax reform of 1989 can be seen graphically. As the reform made domestic whisky more expensive and imported whisky less expensive, for 1989 and 1990 the statistics show a major increase in imported and a decrease in domestic whisky. After this period, the two whisky varieties start moving in line with each other. This is to be expected as they are identical products and are affected by the same external factors. For the Community, the inspection of the graph therefore leads to two evident conclusions: Firstly, it can be seen very clearly that a reduction in tax for imported whisky has a substantial impact on its consumption. Secondly, any statistical analysis that fails to take account of the structural break in the time series will come to misleading conclusions, because what is measured with the aggregate whisky consumption before and after 1989 is evidently not the same. Spurious statistical results are the natural outcome. According to the Community expert, it will be difficult for a statistical analysis to establish the impact of the whisky market on the market for shochu, because the influence here tends to be overwhelmed by other factors that happened at the same time. On the other hand, when shochu consumption increased, that of whisky fell and vice versa. While certainly such a graph does not provide an ultimate proof, it appears, however, highly suggestive of a substitution relationship between the two types of products.

4.89   **Japan** reiterated that it applied the statistical method used in the Bossard study commissioned by the European Commission, which used time series similar to Japan's household survey statistics. The Commission submitted a report citing the study to the European Council and to the European Parliament last September, and convened a conference of manufacturers and consumers in Lisbon last November to discuss the report. In Japan's view, the Community's criticism of the Japanese study applies equally to the Community's study. Moreover, although the Commission presented a graph of yearly consumption amount of shochu and whisky to assess the impact of the 1989 tax reform, Japan also presented a graph indicating the annual changes in the consumption amount of shochu and former second grade whisky. Japan submitted a chart of the "Annual Changes in Sales of Former Second Grade Whisky and Shochu" (See Annex II). In 1989 and 1990, in the wake of the 1989 reform, consumption of both former second grade whisky and shochu showed a marked decline. The issue to be examined here, for Japan, is how those consumers who drank second grade whisky in 1988 behaved in 1989 and in 1990. Unless they cease to drink alcoholic beverages (Japan argued that Canada's lagged response theory means several years of temperance, which Japan regarded as implausible), the decrease in the absolute amount of former second grade whisky consumption should have worked to increase the absolute amount of other alcoholic beverages. Thus the decline in the absolute amount of consumption of both former second grade whisky and shochu led Japan to conclude that it was more reasonable to assume that consumption shifted from former second grade whisky to alcoholic beverages other than shochu. For Japan, the share of shochu in the total amount of distilled liquor consumption in Japan increased in 1989 and 1990, only because the decrease of absolute amount of shochu consumption was smaller than that of former second grade whisky and had nothing to do with the shift between the two products.

4.90   On the issue of whether liquors are directly competitive and substitutable products in Japan, **Canada** argued that the market confirms the cross-price elasticity between Canadian whisky and shochu. Since 1987, on-shelf retail prices for distilled liquors sold in Japan have undergone significant price movements. During this period, prices of imported whisky have declined considerably, while prices for some domestic whisky, particularly formerly Second Grade whisky, have increased significantly. Sample on-shelf retail prices listed in surveys covering each of the years 1992 through 1994 conducted by the Japan External Trade Organization ("JETRO")[69] make clear the rapid decline in prices for imported whisky. For example, the reported average retail price of the bourbon whisky "Four Roses" declined from ¥2,740 in 1992 to ¥2,090 in 1994 while "Ballantines" Scotch declined in the same period from ¥2,480 to ¥2,195. Sample on-shelf prices for Canadian whisky, like the imported whisky prices quoted in the JETRO surveys, have similarly declined. For example, the price for Canadian Club 6 Year Old fell from ¥2,500 during the years 1991-1993 to ¥1,900 in 1995, a decline of 24.0 per cent. During the same period, prices for Canadian Club Classic 12 Year Old fell from a median price of ¥3,750 between 1991-1993 to ¥2,900 in 1995, a decline of 22.7 per cent. Prices for Seagrams V.O. also fell from a median price of ¥2,680 in 1990 to ¥1,730 in 1995, a decline of 35.4 per cent. Seagrams Crown Royal declined from a median price of ¥3,330 in 1990 to ¥2,230 in 1995, a decline of 33.0 per cent.

4.91   **Canada** submitted another on-shelf retail price survey for the years 1987, 1989 and 1995 of sales of former Special Grade whisky, former Second Grade whisky and shochu Group A which it claims confirms the rapid decline in the retail price of imported whisky during this time. Pursuant to this survey, retail prices in Japan for imported former Special Grade whisky fell during the period of the study. This trend applied to both premium and standard labels. Retail prices for formerly Special Grade imported whisky (standard labels) declined from a range of ¥2,800-3,200/750ml in 1987 to ¥2,400-2,800 in 1989 and to

---

[69]   JETRO is, according to Canada, a Japanese government agency affiliated with the Ministry of International Trade and Industry (MITI). According to Japan, JETRO is not a Japanese government agency but rather a non-profit, government-related organization affiliated with the Ministry of International Trade and Industry (MITI).

¥1,700-2,100 in 1995. Retail prices of formerly Special Grade imported whisky (premium labels) declined from a range of ¥4,000-5,000/750ml in 1987 to ¥3,500-4,500 in 1989 and to ¥2,500-3,500 in 1995. On the basis of the median price for these ranges, retail prices for formerly Special Grade imported whisky (standard) declined 36.7 per cent during this period (11.5 per cent after 1989); and formerly Special Grade imported whisky (premium) declined 33.3 per cent (25.0 per cent after 1989). In contrast, retail prices for domestic formerly Second Grade whisky increased from a range of ¥1,600-1750/1.8 litre in 1987 to ¥3,100-3,270 in 1989 and to ¥2,900-3,270 in 1995, resulting in a median price increase of 84 per cent during this period. At the same time, retail prices for shochu Group A increased from a range of ¥580-600/720ml in 1987 to ¥620-640 in 1989 and to ¥650-700 in 1995. Thus, median prices for shochu increased, but at a relatively more modest 14.3 per cent. Thus, between 1987 and 1995, the price differential between shochu and formerly Second Grade whisky significantly increased, while the price differential between shochu Group A and imported whisky decreased. The JETRO survey of 1993 states that there are several reasons for the retail price decline on imported whisky, including a decline in the specific tax rates for this product:

> "The types of whisky on the market have increased, and retail prices have decreased as a result of the lowering of liquor tax and tariff rates, the appreciating yen, and the dissemination of parallel imports. At one time, the prices of imported whisky fell to one-half of previous levels. For this reason, general household demand for imported whisky increased, and demand for whisky for gift-giving has declined annually as it has lost its appeal as an expensive item with rarity value. On the other hand, demand has tended to shift towards premium type whisky, which can now be purchased for prices previously paid for standard type whisky".

Thus, this JETRO survey makes clear that as prices for imported whisky fall, household demand for these products increases.

4.92   For **Canada**, as the JETRO 1993 survey implies, the narrowing price differential between imported whisky and shochu Group A has improved the price competitiveness of imported whisky *vis-à-vis* shochu. On the other hand, the median retail price ranges it had submitted previously indicate that retail prices for imported whisky continue to remain well above retail prices for shochu and thus hinder whisky's ability to compete with shochu. This is made clear in the Japan Spirits and Liquors Makers' Association submission to the Japanese Ministry of Finance of October, 1995:

> "Especially in whisky/brandy, as the liquor tax is too high and the tax differences between shochu is too large, it is too difficult for whisky/brandy to compete equally with shochu at market and are forced to disadvantages.

> Therefore, in order to make equal conditions of competition between distilled spirits, we would like to ask you to make a large reduction in liquor taxes on western-style liquors and, by doing so, to minimize the tax differences between distilled spirits.

...

> These large tax differences have no option for whisky/brandy but to set its sale price relatively higher, and this leads not only to decrease in consumers' support to whisky/brandy, but also to narrow consumers' freedom of choice. As a result, coupled with the present consumers' price-oriented attitude, the consumption of whisky/brandy has remarkably declined".

Thus, Canada argued, the lower the price of imported whisky the greater its competitiveness with shochu an alternative choice and consequently the greater its domestic consumption. Canada concluded that consumer choice between shochu and whisky is price responsive.

4.93 In addition to their arguments and counter arguments suggested in the present section, the **Community**, **Canada**, the **United States** and **Japan** submitted further evidence on cross-price elasticity of shochu and other imported distilled spirits in their discussions of the application of the aim-and-effect test, when arguing, more specifically, whether the Liquor Tax Law has the effect of distorting the competitive relationship between shochu and other imported liquors so as to afford protection (see Sections F and G below).

b) The Second Step of the Test suggested by the Community for Article III:2, Second Sentence: " ... So as to Afford Protection"

4.94 As to the second step of the legal test it suggested for the second sentence of GATT Article III:2 in assessing whether a measure imposed on substitutable or directly competitive products is "so as to afford protection", the **Community** reiterated that the following criteria may be relevant in order to determine whether a difference in taxation is "so as to afford protection" to domestic production: 1) The level of the tax differential (but contrary to the first sentence of Article III:2, a tax difference does not lead automatically to a violation of the second sentence of Article III:2); 2) The degree of substitutability and competition between the two products; 3) Whether the less taxed product is produced in other countries. In this context the Community recalled the conclusion of the 1987 Panel Report which found that the following factors were sufficient evidence of fiscal distortions between imported distilled liquors and domestic shochu affording protection to the domestic production of shochu:

- the considerably lower specific tax rates on shochu than on imported whiskies, brandies and other spirits ...;

- the imposition of high *ad valorem* taxes on imported whiskies, brandies and other spirits and the absence of *ad valorem* taxes on shochu;

- the fact that shochu was almost exclusively produced in Japan and that the lower taxation of shochu "did afford protection to domestic production" (Article III:1) rather than to the production of a product produced in many countries (say butter) in relation to another product (say oleo margarine as in the example referred to by Japan ...);

- the mutual substitutability of these distilled liquors, as illustrated by the increasing imports into Japan of Western-style distilled liquors and by the consumer use of shochu blended in various proportions with whisky, brandy or other drinks.

4.95 For the **Community**, the above factors are still present and, therefore, continue to warrant the conclusion that the Liquor Tax Law affords protection to the Japanese domestic production of shochu:

(1) Despite the 1989 and the 1994 tax reforms, the tax rates on shochu A and shochu B are still much lower than the rates on "spirits", "whisky/brandy" and "liqueurs". The taxes on shochu are from 2.45 to 9.6 times lower in terms of rates per litre of beverage and from 2 to 6 times lower in terms of rates per litre of pure alcohol and these differences can thus hardly be considered as *de minimis*. Even though the tax differentials have been reduced in absolute terms since the adoption of the 1987 Panel Report, their protectionist effect has actually become more acute in the context of the current recessionary economy which has made Japanese consumers much more price sensitive.

(2) Shochu continues to be produced almost exclusively in Japan. In 1994 imports of shochu represented 1.7 per cent of the total sales of shochu and barely 1 per cent of the total sales of distilled spirits and "authentic liqueurs". In contrast, during the same year, imports from third countries accounted for 27 per cent of the total sales of whisky, 29 per cent of the total sales of brandy, 18 per cent of the total sales of "spirits" and 78 per cent of the total sales of "authentic liqueurs". Sales of domestically produced shochu account for almost 80 per cent of the total sales of domestically produced distilled spirits and "authentic liqueurs". Thus, by affording protection to shochu, Japan is in fact affording protection to the majority of its domestic production of spirits and liqueurs.

(3) Shochu and other imported liquors are mutually substitutable as evidenced by their cross-price elasticity, argued in paragraphs 4.82 and following above in the Community's discussion of the first step of the legal test it suggested for the second sentence of Article III:2.

The Community also recalled that since Article III:2 protects trade expectations on the competitive relationship between imported and domestic products rather than expectations on trade volumes, it is not necessary, in order to establish a violation of Article III:2, second sentence, to show that the difference in taxation has had an actual effect on the volume of trade.

4.96 **Japan** responded to the Community's arguments on the three criteria. First, concerning the potential protective effect, Japan submitted that the tax differential should be measured on the basis of the tax/price ratio, as it is a criterion to judge whether or not a tax affords protection, and for Japan, there is no differential in the tax/price ratios. Secondly, for Japan, shochu and other distilled liquors do not show the aptitude of the two products to serve the same uses, and differ in the extent and the form in which the two products are available to the public, beyond what would apply to all alcoholic beverages. Cross-price elasticity of demand does not, therefore, exist. If a directly competitive or substitutable relationship were to be found in this case, it would have to be found between all alcoholic beverages, and, consequently, any liquor taxation currently in force would become inconsistent with Article III, unless all products show the same tax/price ratio. The degree of substitutability and competition between the products is minimal at best. Third, shochu is widely produced in Asian countries, and the third criterion is not met. Thus, Japan concluded that if the Community's interpretation is applied to the facts, one inevitably reaches a conclusion that Japan's liquor tax is consistent with Article III:2, second sentence.

4.97 **Japan** argued that the Community is criticizing Japan's tax distinction among distilled liquors while dividing wine into six categories in its liquor tax directive and legitimizing Germany's application of four completely different rates to categories of wines. For Japan, a position which holds that champagne and sherry may be distinguished from other wine while shochu and whisky should be treated alike, is equal to turning Article III into an instrument of harmonization of internal taxes with a system of a particular group of countries. Japan reiterated that the purpose of Article III is not to require Members to adopt a particular system of taxes or regulations, nor to harmonize taxation systems. Japan argued that only a small number of WTO Members apply a flat rate to all categories of distilled liquors and a larger number of Members apply more than one rate in one way or another. In Japan's view, the conclusion advocated by the Community in the present case would substantially affect other countries as well. Japan referred the Panel to its chart on worldwide "Taxation on Distilled Liquors" (see Annex III).

4.98 The **Community** agreed that Article III does not require Members to adopt a particular system of taxes or regulations, or to harmonize with a system of a particular Member. Nonetheless, the Community believed that the fiscal autonomy of Members is limited by their obligation under GATT to afford imported products equal conditions of competition, *inter alia*, with respect to internal taxes. The Community was not requesting Japan to introduce any particular system of taxation or to set the tax rates for distilled spirits at any particular level. All the Community was asking from Japan was that shochu and all other like and substitutable or directly competitive distilled spirits not be taxed in a discriminatory or protectionist manner. For the rest, the Community submitted that Japan retains full autonomy to choose its own tax system. Following the adoption of a panel report upholding the Community's claims, Japan would enjoy complete discretion to decide whether to maintain the current system of specific taxes or to replace it by, for example, a system of *ad valorem* excise taxes or by a system of *ad valorem* consumption taxes or by a mixed system combining specific and *ad valorem* taxes. The Community reiterated that Japan also retained complete freedom to decide not to impose any tax at all on distilled spirits. Japan would also be able to choose the level of the tax rates. If, for example, Japan decided to maintain a system of specific excise taxes, the rates for all distilled spirits could be set at or above the current level for "whisky/brandy" (the highest) or at or below the current level for shochu B (the lowest), as well as at any level in between. As it stands, the Liquor Tax Law is inconsistent with the second sentence of Article III:2. The Community also added that the taxation systems of countries other than Japan are not covered by the terms of reference of the present dispute.

c)   Application of the Second, Third and Fourth Criteria of
          the Legal Test Suggested by Canada for Article III:2,
          Second Sentence

4.99   In its discussion of its legal test for the second sentence of Article III:2,
Canada also referred the Panel to the 1987 Panel Report which set out four factors that established "sufficient evidence of fiscal distortions of the competitive
relationship between imported distilled liquors and domestic shochu" so as to
"afford protection to the domestic production of shochu": (1) the considerably
lower specific tax rates on shochu than on imported whisky; (2) the almost exclusive production in Japan of shochu; (3) the mutual substitutability of distilled
liquors like whisky and shochu as illustrated by the increasing imports into Japan
of "Western-style" distilled liquors; and (4) the imposition of an *ad valorem* tax
on imported whisky but not on shochu.

4.100   For **Canada**, the application of the three relevant criteria (omitting the
fourth one) mentioned above to the current Liquor Tax Law confirms its inconsistency with the second sentence of Article III:2, in distorting the competitive
relationship between Canadian whisky and domestically produced shochu:

(1)   Canada argued that even a cursory examination of the Liquor Tax Law
shows that whisky and shochu are not similarly taxed. The reference tax rate for
whisky is set 6.3 times higher than the reference tax rate for shochu A and 9.6
times that for shochu B. And even the lowest tax rate on whisky is still 2.5 times
higher than the maximum tax rate on shochu. More importantly, Canada argued
that even using Japan's suggested basis for analysis -- the tax/price ratio which is
the proportion of the retail price of whisky and shochu represented by the liquor
tax levied under the Liquor Tax Law -- the evidence does not support Japan's
claim that the tax differential between distilled liquors under the Liquor Tax Law
yields "roughly" equivalent tax/price ratios. Moreover, the evidence submitted by
Japan is based on manufacturers' suggested retail prices, not actual retail prices.
Yet in the Japanese distilled liquor market, suggested retail prices are merely
notional figures that bear little relationship to actual on-shelf retail prices paid by
consumers. On the other hand, Japan recognizes that the key determinant in assessing tax/price equivalency is the price that the consumer actually pays, not a
notional price obtained from a manufacturer's pamphlet that suggests a retail
price. Thus, notional retail prices of distilled liquor do not reflect the reality of
the consumer marketplace and consequently do not accurately reflect tax/price
ratios arising from the tax differentials under the Liquor Tax Act. In any event,
the tax/price ratios submitted by Japan do not come close to being "roughly the
same at around 20 per cent of the expense for the tax". In fact, the ratios for the
various categories of distilled liquors encompass a widely divergent range of
ratios. Thus, for example, the tax/price ratio for Shochu B is a claimed 13 per
cent, almost one third lower than the claimed tax-price ratio for imported whisky
of 19 per cent. For Canada, Japan's assertion that the tax differentials under the
Liquor Tax Law yield equal tax/price ratios is simply without foundation.

(2)   Canada argued that the evidence is equally unambiguous on the source of
shochu production. In 1987, 99.3 per cent of domestic sales of shochu Group A
were derived from domestic production. In 1994, that amount declined modestly

to 96.9 per cent. Regarding shochu B, 99.9 per cent of sales were derived from domestic production. In 1994, the figure remained unchanged. Accordingly, shochu continues to be almost exclusively produced in Japan. The evidence also indicates that shochu and whisky are mutually substitutable. Therefore, Canada argued the Liquor Tax Law "affords protection to domestic production" of shochu Group A and shochu Group B within the meaning of Article III:2, second sentence.

(3)   On the cross-price elasticity, Canada referred to its argumentation developed under the first step of its legal test in paragraphs 4.90 and following, namely that shochu and Canadian whisky are substitutable and directly competitive.

4.101 **Canada** argued that an examination of the relationship between the differential specific tax rates on whisky and shochu and the resulting effects on price competitiveness between the two products makes it manifestly clear that the Liquor Tax Law is inconsistent with the observation of the Working Party Report on Border Tax Adjustments and confirmed in the 1987 Panel Report, that internal taxes must be trade neutral. The Liquor Tax Law is not trade neutral. It distorts the relative prices of whisky and shochu. It, thereby, distorts the competitive relationship between these two products and consequently affords protection to shochu production in contravention of Article III:2, second sentence. Canada submitted that price is a crucial element in determining the competitive relationship between shochu and whisky. Thus, it is significant that retail prices of imported whisky are responsive to changes in liquor tax rates. Accordingly, in Japan, the specific tax rates imposed pursuant to the Liquor Tax Law have a direct effect on the prices of imported whisky and, consequently, on the competitive relationship between this product category and shochu.

4.102 **Canada** added that given the findings in the 1987 Panel Report that even small tax differences can influence the competitive relationship between directly competing distilled liquors, the significant differences in the tax burdens imposed by the tax differentials under the current Liquor Tax Law affecting the price of imported whisky, *a fortiori* magnify the distortions in the competitive relationship between shochu and whiskies. Indeed, given the nexus between specific tax rates, the price of imported whisky and, ultimately, the competitive relationship between shochu and whisky, the significance of these large tax differentials in distorting the competitive relationship between shochu and whisky is made clear when considered against the retail price of imported whisky and shochu and thus, the domestic market "value" ascribed to these products. Since 1989, the tax rate on whisky has remained constant. During this period of time, and indeed since 1987, the retail price on imported whisky has rapidly declined. Thus, for whisky, the tax rate has not responded to changes in domestic market value. By contrast, Canada submitted that in 1994 there was a modest increase in the tax rate levied on shochu corresponding to a small increase since 1987 in the retail price of this product. Unlike shochu, the net result of the specific tax rates imposed on whisky pursuant to the Liquor Tax Law is that as the retail price, and thus the domestic market value, of imported whisky has fallen, the tax portion of the retail price has increased. Canada argued that, since 1989, the liquor tax on imported whisky is consuming an ever-increasing portion of the retail price. As described in one survey of retail prices in Japan, even though the retail price of formerly Special

Grade imported whisky has proportionately decreased by an amount greater than the increase in the retail price of shochu, the tax burden levied pursuant to the Liquor Tax Law on this whisky product has proportionately increased by an amount greater than that imposed on shochu. Given the fact that price is a crucial element in determining the competitive relationship between whisky and shochu, the tax burden levied on imported whisky, not reflecting its market "value", hinders the price movement of imported whisky and hence the ability of imported whisky to compete with shochu. Canada submitted that to render neutral the proportionate differential tax burdens imposed on shochu and whiskies, the retail price of imported whisky would have to increase by a proportionate amount thereby decreasing the ability of imported whisky to compete with shochu in Japan's domestic market. In short, Canada argued that by imposing differential tax burdens on shochu and whisky that do not reflect the market value of imported whisky, the tax rates imposed on shochu and whisky pursuant to the Liquor Tax Law distort the competitive relationship between these two product categories and thus, cannot be claimed to be trade neutral.

4.103 **Japan** responded that Canada did not satisfy the three last criteria for its legal test under Article III:2, second sentence. Japan admitted that the liquor tax is an internal tax (first criterion of Canada's test). For Japan, as argued with the Community, shochu and whisky are not directly competitive or substitutable (second criterion). In discussing whether or not the products are similarly taxed (third criterion), Canada compares the amount of the tax per one litre of the products or per alcohol contained. However, Japan argued that in light of the emphasis Canada repeatedly attached to the price as a crucial element in determining the competitive relationship between shochu and whisky, the comparison ought to be made on the basis of the tax burden in relation to the price. By this standard, Japan argued that shochu and whisky are similarly taxed. Canada's fourth criterion "of affording protection" is, again, not met, in Japan's view, since tax/price ratios are roughly equal between imported whisky and domestic shochu: In restoring the balance in tax/price ratio between whisky and shochu in the 1994 reform, Japan chose to increase tax on shochu, not to reduce tax on whisky, for fiscal reasons, but both methods are equally effective in restoring the balance. Japan stressed that what is relevant to the purpose of neutrality and equity is relative relations of tax/price ratios among categories, not the absolute level of the ratios *per se*.

4.104 In addition, **Canada** argued that the *Superfund* panel report has established the principle that a finding of fiscal distortion in the competitive relationship between imported and domestic products constitutes an "irrefutable presumption" of nullification and impairment of benefits. While the *Superfund* panel report spoke in terms of Article III:2, first sentence, the 1987 Panel Report and the 1992 *Malt Beverages* panel report established that the same principle applies equally to Article III:2, second sentence. For Canada, this principle has been codified in Article 3:8 of the DSU, which provides:

> "In cases where there is an infringement of the obligations assumed under a covered agreement, the action is considered *prima facie* to constitute a case of nullification or impairment. This means that there is normally a presumption that a breach of the rules has an

adverse impact on other Members parties to that covered agreement, and in such case, it shall be up to the Member against whom
the complaint has been brought to rebut the charge".

Of the presumption of "an adverse impact", the panel report in the *Superfund*[70]
case and the 1987 Panel Report[71] enunciate the principle that overall increases in
market share for imports of the products in issue does not constitute a rebuttal.
Indeed, the *Superfund* case articulates the principle that a finding of fiscal distortion in the competitive relationship between imported and domestic products
constitutes an "irrefutable presumption" of nullification and impairment of benefits. The 1987 Panel Report determined that the factors set out in paragraph 4.94
above *ipso facto* constitute "sufficient evidence of fiscal distortions of the competitive relationship between imported distilled liquors and domestic shochu". In
view of the conclusive evidence described in paragraphs 4.72 to 4.93, including,
more specifically, the positive evidence of cross-price elasticity between shochu
and other imported distilled liquors, it necessarily follows, in Canada's view, that
the Liquor Tax Law distorts the competitive relationship between imported distilled liquors and domestically produced shochu, and therefore is inconsistent
with the second sentence of Article III:2. Canada noted that indeed, Japan's Deregulation Subcommittee of the Administrative Reform Council, an independent
advisory body whose members are appointed by Japan's Prime Minister and approved by the Diet, stated that the tax rates under the Liquor Tax Law constitute
"virtual restrictions on the buyer's activities" and are not "neutral in relation to
consumer choice".

4.105 **Japan** responded that the criterion unique to Canada's test is distortion of
the competitive relationship and that it is noteworthy that Canada's argument rests
on distortion of relative prices. Accurate data show, however, that the Liquor Tax
Law does not distort relative prices between whisky and shochu, and, accordingly, this criterion of distortive effects is not met. In order to reach a finding of
inconsistency with Article III, all of Canada's criteria would have to be met, but it
was not the case, since Canada had not proven that shochu and Canadian whisky
are directly competitive, that shochu and Canadian whisky are not similarly
taxed, or that the Liquor Tax Law affords protection to domestic production. For
Japan, Canada had, therefore, not proven that the Liquor Tax Law is inconsistent
with Article III:2, even under Canada's interpretation of the provision.

---

[70] Thus, in the *Superfund* case, para. 5.19, the panel stated: "A demonstration that a measure inconsistent with Article III:2, first sentence, has no or insignificant effects would therefore in the view
of the Panel not be a sufficient demonstration that the benefits accruing under the provision had not
been nullified or impaired even if such rebuttal were in principle permitted".
[71] The 1987 Panel Report stated in para. 5.16: " [A]n increase in imports could not refute the presumption that discriminatory or protective taxes inconsistent with Article III:2 had impaired the
competitive benefits protected under Article III:2 because, *inter alia*, an increase in imports did say
nothing about what the trade might have been in the absence of the inconsistent trade restrictions".

F.   *Application to the Present Case of the Legal Analysis Suggested by the United States for the Interpretation of Article III:2*

4.106 As argued in paragraphs 4.24 to 4.32 above, the **United States** submitted that the central concern of Article III is to prohibit the targeting of imports and suggested that application to the Liquor Tax Law of the aim-and-effect test of earlier panel reports would confirm the inconsistency of that measure with the provisions of Article III:2, second sentence, in that the regulatory distinctions made by the legislation are so as to afford protection.

1.   *The Aim of the Legislation*

4.107 The **United States** argued that the protective aim of the Liquor Tax Law structure is apparent from (1) the stated policy objective and whether it was known at the time the legislation was enacted that it would draw a line between one group of products that would be foreign and another group that would be domestic (*ex-ante* knowledge), (2) the internal inconsistencies of the legislation and its structural incentives, (3) legislative statements and the preparatory work, as well as from (4) the arbitrary and irrational categories of the legislation under scrutiny. The United States continued by stating that:

(1)   During the consultations, the Japanese Government asserted that the policy objective of the Liquor Tax Law system was to maximize tax revenue while ensuring that the tax is distributed among consumers in accordance with their "tax-bearing ability". However, this objective is nowhere stated in the law, which has no general statement of purpose other than "Taxes shall be imposed on alcoholic beverages in accordance with this law". The taxes provided for by the Liquor Tax Law are specific taxes, with no link between the tax rate and the actual price of the alcoholic beverage in question; their structure does not support the claim that they are designed to effectuate equity between categories of spirits. To base tax rates on consumers' tax-bearing ability assumes that some products are consumed by the masses and should be low-priced, and other products are exotic luxuries consumed by the rich who can afford to be taxed heavily; this proposition was specifically rejected by the 1987 Panel Report. For the United States, statements connected with the 1994 revision of the Liquor Tax Law also offer a sample of the motivations behind enactment of this legislation. The official records of deliberations in the Finance Committee of the Diet in March 1994 show that Ministry of Finance Tax Bureau Director Ogawa testified that the reason for the difference in tax treatment was "out of consideration for the higher material costs etc" of shochu B. He also testified that particular attention had been made to coordinate the tax increases with the increased costs of raw materials associated with factors such as the poor rice harvest in the case of refined sake and shochu, especially shochu B. The legislation raising taxes included as well an extension of tax reductions for small-volume producers of shochu A and B, and provision for a subsidy fund for shochu producers. The package in context demonstrates that the operative consideration in passing the legislation was the economic well-being of domestic shochu producers, not a neutral tax policy.

(2)   According to an article in a Ministry of Finance publication written by one of the Ministry drafters explaining the 1962 revisions,[72] the definitions were changed at that time in order to clarify and reinforce the distinction between shochu, whisky, brandy and spirits. The purpose of the change and the related exception was (a) to exclude certain products which would be classified as whisky, brandy, and spirits, but since dates were already being used as a raw material for shochu in Japan, these would be permitted as a fruit raw material for shochu; (b) to exclude vodka; (c) to exclude rum from the category of shochu, but permit Okinawan awamori made with barrel molasses to remain as shochu; (d) to exclude gin and similar genever-type drinks.

(3)   The lack of any policy rationale other than protection is apparent from the otherwise-arbitrary distinctions drawn in the product categories. The only difference between vodka and shochu A is that according to the definition in the Liquor Tax Law, shochu A cannot be filtered with white birch charcoal, although it can be filtered with any other material. Yet the tax rate on vodka is 2.55 times higher than the tax rate on shochu A. The Japanese government has never claimed that the ban on the use of white birch charcoal in filtering shochu was based on health reasons or any other policy. Thus the distinction cannot have any purpose other than excluding imported vodka from the tax benefits granted to the producers of shochu.

(4)   It is also arbitrary to set the maximum alcohol content for shochu made by continuous distillation methods (shochu A) at 36 per cent and the maximum alcohol content for shochu distilled otherwise (shochu B) at 45 per cent. All alcoholic beverages falling within the categories of "shochu", "whisky/brandy" and "spirits" are classified as "liqueurs" and taxed at a uniform rate whenever they are pre-mixed with a sugared non-alcoholic beverage. However, the same alcoholic beverages, when sold undiluted, are classified within different tax categories and taxed at widely differing rates, even though they are often consumed in home-made mixes made with similar non-alcoholic beverages. Again, in the US view, the Japanese government has claimed no policy justification for this difference in taxation. The only rational explanation for it is that pre-mixes, unlike undiluted alcoholic beverages, are produced almost exclusively in Japan. For the United States, the arbitrariness of the distinction drawn between "spirits" and shochu can be seen in the recent move by Suntory, the producer of "Juhyo" brand vodka, to re-characterize it as shochu A. Before June 1993, Juhyo was sold as vodka, and accounted for almost half of Japanese vodka production. After June 1993, Suntory ceased using birch charcoal as a filtering material, and began selling Juhyo as shochu A, simply in order to reduce the tax burden on the product. Suntory was then able to, and did, reduce the retail price of Juhyo. Of course, because of the substantial tariffs on shochu, it is not possible for foreign vodka producers to do the same. Thus, for the United States, the distinction drawn by the system of

---

[72]   Tan Hirosho, "Shuzeiho to no ichibu o kaisei suru horitsu" (The Law Partially Revising the Liquor Tax Law), in *Zeisei Tsushin* (Tax Policy News), June 1962, p. 23ff. The article identifies the author as the Deputy Director of the Ministry of Finance, Second Tax Policy Division.

Japanese liquor taxation between shochu and all other distilled spirits is arbitrary and contrived.

4.108 **Japan** responded that the complaining parties seemed to confuse the present Japanese policy, as explained in the bilateral consultation, with that of 1987. Japan argued that it had not referred to the notion of the tax-bearing ability in bilateral consultation. The essence of the policy in 1987 was: "Since whisky consumers have a greater tax-bearing ability than shochu consumers, the tax/price ratio ought to be higher for whisky than for shochu." In contrast, the present tax policy since the 1989 amendment is: "Tax/price ratio should be roughly constant between whisky and shochu for the sake of ensuring neutrality to consumers' choice and of equity in between consumers of these products". Examining excise taxes in view of the three criteria of neutrality, horizontal equity and vertical equity is common practice among tax authorities in the world, though which of the three is prioritized may differ according to prevailing socio-economic conditions: for example, the report on excise taxes issued by the United States' Congressional Budget Office in 1990 starts its discussion with the examination of the three criteria. The lack of statements of policy goals in the Liquor Tax Law is only a standard practice of tax legislation in Japan, and, for example, introducing the 1989 amendment before the National Diet, the Minister of Finance stated, "The fundamental principles of the present amendment are to ensure equity in distribution of the tax burden and to maintain neutrality toward economic activities". Japan further argued that the evidence cited by the United States is part of the record of Diet deliberations of the 1994 amendment. The amendments cannot conceivably have had a protective intent, however; it raised the tax rate for shochu A by 30 per cent, that for shochu B by 44 per cent, while raising the tax on "spirits" by a mere 11 per cent, but maintained the tax on whisky/brandy at the same level. The 1962 material written by the person who prepared the Liquor Tax Law merely referred to the problem common to any product classification and so did other alleged evidence of arbitrariness. The amendments of 1989 and 1994 which substantially raised the tax on shochu B refute, *ipso facto*, the allegation of policy distortion by local political forces. This led Japan to conclude that speculative inside stories are not appropriate as the basis for panel findings. Most whisky, brandy and spirits consumed in Japan are manufactured locally. For example, the rate of domestic production of whisky is 75 per cent, that of brandy, 72 per cent, and that of "spirits", 82 per cent. These categories cannot be equated with imports as such. Categorization of these products, therefore, is not the targeting of imports as the United States claims. The tariff on shochu (currently 17.9 per cent, same as that on vodka and lower than that on rum) is irrelevant to the issues of Article III. Moreover, for Japan, the categories are not exceptional or arbitrary. It is arbitrary, according to the US submission, to distinguish vodka from shochu on the basis of filtration with white birch charcoal, but Japan responded that any legal definition of a product encounters similar difficulty in translating a socially accepted concept. It is no more indicative of protective intent than the Community definition of sparkling wine on the basis of mushroom stoppers. Japan continued in asserting that different rates of ceiling on the alcoholic strength of shochu A and B result similarly from the task of defining products. Eight different threshold levels of strength are established for various product categories in the Community definition directive. Japan did not believe that this renders the Community rule protectionist.

4.109 **Japan** continued its counter argument on the aims of the legislation, in stating that it is not arbitrary to apply the same tax rate to pre-mixes, while subjecting unmixed original products to different rates; Canada while applying different rates on distilled liquors and wine, applies the same rate on distilled liquor based pre-mixes and on wine based pre-mixes. The recharacterization of the "Juhyo" brand vodka into shochu by the manufacturer is, in essence, marketing of two different products under the same brand name, and does not indicate arbitrariness in categorization. The shochu product is produced from a different set of materials and is marketed as a New Juhyo. For Japan, this should be looked at as an attempt to take advantage of a popular brand name. Suntory, the manufacturer of Juhyo brand, sells Reserve whisky and Reserve wine. The Liquor Tax Law is not "the legislation that draws a line between one group of products that would be foreign and another group that would be domestic". Whisky, spirits and liqueur have been produced in large quantities in Japan, and, therefore, are not foreign, while shochu is produced in large quantities in the Asian region, and is, therefore, not domestic. Finally, the Liquor Tax Law is designed to be neutral and does not have incentives in any direction. Thus, none of the factors supporting a protective aim have been shown. For Japan, all of the evidence supplied by the United States on arbitrary or exceptional categorization is, in fact, evidence of the difficulty common to all legal definitions of social concepts.

4.110 For the **United States**, the tax rate applicable to any particular alcoholic beverage in Japan is a function of its classification, the applicable tax rate, and any available exemptions or reductions. The definition of "shochu" was devised in 1962 when all Japanese import trade was subject to BOP quotas and imported shochu was nonexistent, in order to reserve low tax rates for an exclusively-domestic product category. In the US view, it was absolutely clear in 1962 that the definition of shochu would exclude imported distilled spirits, and would form part of a system favouring shochu through the tax rate. This categorization was designed to perpetuate the market situation of 1962. Ever since 1962, shochu A and particularly shochu B have benefited from the lowest tax rates on distilled spirits. The effect has been to cement into place distinctions made under conditions of perfect protection, and to perpetuate the closed market of the pre-liberalization period. The discrimination in tax rates was reduced but not eliminated after the 1987 Panel Report. Shochu could still be characterized as a Japanese product benefiting from discriminatory low tax rates. Indeed, the United States argued, when a system of tax classifications had been designed during such a period of absolute protection, the categorization of products based on their status during the quota period had to be re-evaluated after balance-of-payments quotas had been lifted. The tax discrimination still remained: ¥982.3 per litre for whisky and brandy versus ¥102.1 per litre for shochu B, and ¥367.3 per litre for spirits versus ¥155.7 per litre for shochu A. Japan has offered no convincing policy rationale for this differential. The United States cited a statement by the Japanese Government's own Administrative Reform Council admitting that there is at present no logical rationale for the Liquor Tax Law, and no plausible explanation for the liquor tax system including the segmentation of categories and tax rates.

4.111 The **United States** also argued that if a tax strongly favours a product of which all, or almost all, the amount consumed is produced domestically, but not another which is directly competitive or substitutable, a protective purpose may be inferred. The 1992 *Malt Beverages* panel report, in discussing the special tax treatment accorded by Mississippi to wine made from scuppernong grapes, noted that even if this wine were considered unlike other wine, the two kinds of wine would nevertheless have to be regarded as "directly competitive" products in terms of the Interpretative Note to Article III:2, second sentence, and the imposition of a higher tax on directly competing imported wine so as to afford protection to domestic production would be inconsistent with that provision. The United States also pointed to the sudden or dramatic difference in rates at the margin under the Liquor Tax Law which resulted in large differences in treatment of products on either side of the line drawn between shochu and other distilled spirits. The rates on shochu A and B are still much lower than the rates on other distilled spirits. There is still a 9.6 to 1 tax differential between whisky and shochu B, a 6.3 to 1 differential between whisky and shochu A, and a 2.4 to 1 differential between spirits and shochu A, at the respective reference alcoholic strength for each. The United States stated that the Liquor Tax Law targets the inherent characteristics of the product so that foreign manufacturers of gin or rum cannot make a product that has access to the lower tax rate without changing the nature of their product.

4.112 **Japan** responded that the tax rates currently applied to distilled liquors are completely different from those in 1962. Japan also argued that the Administrative Reform Committee's comment concerns the taxation of alcoholic beverages as a whole, and contains no specific reference to distilled liquors. For Japan, their critique of shortcomings in Japan's taxation of alcoholic beverages as a whole would be in fact valid for any liquor tax in the world. It is true that there is room for improvement, but no tax is perfect. In response to the United States condemnation on "the sudden or dramatic difference in rates at the margin", Japan argued that such difference is common to most tax distinctions: the rate of the US tax on wine jumps from $1.07 to $3.40 when the carbon dioxide in the wine crosses the threshold of 0.392g per 100 ml. Japan further argued that 75 per cent of whisky, 72 per cent of brandy, 82 per cent of spirits and 97 per cent of liqueur consumed in Japan is produced domestically. It is, therefore, farfetched to assume an element of targeting of imports behind these categories or taxes. With respect to whisky, in particular, Japan is the fifth largest producer in the world. Japan suggested that it cannot possibly target imports by taxing the category. Japan submitted that imports are not targeted and if the central concern of Article III:2 is the targeting of imports, as the United States argues, the lack of targeting is enough to establish that Japan's Liquor Tax Law is consistent with Article III. In support of its argument Japan referred the Panel to a chart showing the "Share of Domestic Production of Liquors in Total Sales in Japan" (see Annex IV).

2. The Effect of the Legislation

4.113 The **United States** went on to argue that the distinction drawn by the Liquor Tax Law also has the effect of affording protection to domestic production. In this regard, data on sales and trade flows are relevant to show changes in the conditions of competition favouring domestic products. Other factors, including the creation of inherently domestic products and foreign products, and whether there is a large difference in rates between categories, also support the conclusion of a protective effect. In this context, the United States referred the Panel to some of the conclusions of the 1987 Panel Report which found that: 1) consumer habits varied in response to the respective prices of shochu and other distilled spirits, their availability through trade and their other competitive inter-relationships (i.e., substantial cross-elasticity of demand existed between these products); 2) the increasing imports of Western-style alcoholic beverages into Japan bore witness to this lasting competitive relationship and to the potential product substitution through trade among various alcoholic beverages; and 3) there existed direct competition or substitutability among imported and Japanese-made distilled liquors, including all grades of whiskies/brandies, vodka and shochu A and B, in terms of Article III:2, second sentence. The 1987 Panel Report found as well that the following factors were "sufficient evidence of fiscal distortions of the competitive relationship between imported distilled liquors and domestic shochu affording protection to the domestic production of shochu": a) the large difference in specific tax rates between the taxes on shochu and the taxes on imported distilled spirits; b) the fact that shochu was almost exclusively produced in Japan and that the lower taxation of shochu afforded protection to domestic production, rather than to a product produced in many countries; and c) the mutual substitutability of distilled liquors, as demonstrated by the increasing imports into Japan of distilled spirits and the consumer use of shochu in mixed drinks. For the United States an examination of the effect of the Liquor Tax Law in this present case should focus on qualitative alteration of conditions of competition such as targeting of imports, and evidence of cross-elasticity of demand between the favoured and disfavoured categories.

4.114 The **United States** pointed out that shochu consumed in Japan continues to be made almost exclusively in Japan. In 1994, imports of shochu were 1.7 per cent of total sales and 1 per cent of total sales of distilled spirits and "authentic distilled spirits". Also, in 1994, imports from third countries accounted for 27 per cent of the total sales of whisky, 29 per cent of the total sales of brandy, 18 per cent of the total sales of spirits and 78 per cent of the total sales of "authentic liqueurs". At the same time, domestically-made shochu accounted for over 80 per cent of all domestic sales of distilled spirits and authentic liqueurs. Thus, the protection given to shochu has had the effect of protection for domestic production.

4.115 On the market shares of shochu and the price-cross elasticity of shochu, the **United States**, in addition to the arguments detailed in paragraphs 4.82 to 4.93 above, noted that there were clear indications that the demand for shochu is largely influenced by fluctuations in demand for other distilled spirits and liqueurs. This could be seen in the rearrangement of the market place for distilled spirits after the 1989 tax reform. The 1989 reform unified tax rates on whisky, abolished the classification of whisky into three classes, and consequently more than tripled the tax rate on second-class whisky while lowering the taxes on other whisky, authentic liqueurs and spirits. The 1989 law also raised the tax on shochu by a small amount. In particular the United States submitted that:

- Retail prices for second-class whisky almost doubled, and the market share for domestic whisky declined from 27 per cent in 1988 to 19.6 per cent in 1990. This trend has continued: in 1994 the market share of domestic whisky sank further, to only 13.2 per cent. Shochu makers were able to move into the place in the market formerly held by second-class whisky. Sales of shochu have steadily increased and reached 74.2 per cent of distilled spirits in 1994.

- The prices of imported whisky, liqueurs and spirits declined and their sales rose. However, Japan entered a recession in 1992. The highest-taxed categories, whisky/brandy, authentic liqueurs and spirits, were hit worst and have lost sales both relatively and absolutely since 1992, while the market share of shochu continues to grow at their expense.

- Because the prices of shochu and other distilled spirits have partially converged, their cross-elasticity of demand has risen.

- Shochu continues to be made almost exclusively in Japan. In 1994, imports of shochu were 1.7 per cent of total sales and 1 per cent of total sales of distilled spirits and "authentic distilled spirits". Also in 1994, imports from third countries accounted for 27 per cent of the total sales of whisky, 29 per cent of the total sales of brandy, 18 per cent of the total sales of spirits and 78 per cent of the total sales of "authentic liqueurs". At the same time domestically-made shochu accounted for over 80 per cent of all domestic sales of distilled spirits and authentic liqueurs. Thus, the protection given to shochu has had the effect of protection for domestic production.

4.116 In support of its allegation of the protective effect of the Liquor Tax Law, the **United States** argued that there is a sudden or dramatic difference in rates at the margin. The rates on shochu A and B are still much lower than the rates on other distilled spirits. The United States noted that there is still a 9.6 to 1 tax differential between whisky and shochu B, a 6.3 to 1 differential between whisky and shochu A, and a 2.4 to 1 differential between spirits and shochu A, at the respective reference values for each. The United States added that the Liquor Tax Law targets inherent characteristics of the product. Foreign manufacturers of gin or rum cannot make a product that has access to the lower tax rate without changing the nature of the product.[73]

---

[73] The United States added that this is fundamentally different from, for example, a tax incentive for adding catalytic converters to automobiles: an automobile can qualify for the incentive without changing its nature.

4.117 The **United States** further argued that the protective effect of the tax distinction can also be seen in the attempts of Japanese shochu producers to make their products resemble whisky or to emphasize the points of similarity between the raw materials, ingredients, manufacturing process, appearance and tradition of their shochu and whisky or brandy. In May 1988, the shochu manufacturer Takara began to market "Jun Legend", a light amber coloured brand of shochu produced by blending two types of alcohol distilled from barley and corn and aging them in charred oak barrels for one to five years. Takara's claim was that "the most noticeable characteristic of this brand is a flavour and taste similar to whisky". When the new brand was launched, Takara announced its expectation that the new brand would appeal to former consumers of second-class whisky, the tax rates on which were expected to increase with unification of tax rates on all classes of whisky. The favourable treatment of shochu is a classic instance of use of a tax system to perpetuate existing consumer preferences. Foreign manufacturers of gin or rum cannot make a product that has access to the lower tax rate accorded to shochu unless they change the nature of the product. Therefore, the United States concluded that the regulatory tax distinction made by the Liquor Tax Law between shochu and other imported liquor targets imports and has the aim and effect so as to afford protection, in contravention of the second sentence of Article III:2 (as well as the first sentence of Article III:2 for which the United States suggested the same test).

4.118 **Japan** responded to the US claim that the Liquor Tax Law had a protective effect. For Japan, among the four reasons why the 1987 Panel Report found Japan's liquor tax protective, the first one (large specific tax rate differential) is non-existent now under the appropriate yardstick of comparison, the second one (*ad valorem* tax on imported liquors) is already abolished, the third one (exclusive production of shochu in Japan) is incorrect, and the last one (increased imports of western style liquors, and consumer use of shochu blended with whisky etc.) is a combination of an irrelevant fact and an incorrect assumption. As argued with the Community, for Japan, "directly competitive or substitutable relationship" between domestic shochu and imported distilled liquors of other categories is not proven. Alleged "sudden or dramatic difference in rates at the margin" is common to many tax systems including taxes on wine in the US and in the Community, and is not evidence of protectiveness. The product "Jun Legend" is a case of experiment at the margin which, Japan argued, accompanies any product categories with tax differentials. Shochu, for which Japan is only the second or third largest producer in the world, is not an "inherently domestic product", and whisky, for which Japan is the fifth largest producer in the world, is not an "inherently foreign product". For Japan, none of the US criteria are met.

G.   Application to the Present Case of the Legal Analysis suggested by Japan for the Interpretation of Article III:2

4.119 **Japan** submitted that the Liquor Tax Law generally and the very nature of its tax classification system do not have the aim or the effect "so as to afford protection". For Japan, the absence of protective aims and effect of the regulatory distinction contained in the Liquor Tax Law, confirms that shochu and other imported liquors are not like products and that the legislation is not inconsistent with Article III:2, first and second sentences. Japan submitted three criteria to demonstrate that the regulatory distinction of the Liquor Tax Law is consistent with Article III:2: a) the nature of the categorization, b) the aims of the legislation, and more particularly the new policies of horizontal equity and neutrality, and c) the absence of protective effect evidenced by the fact that there is no competitive relationship between shochu and other imported liquors (no cross-price elasticity), the fact that shochu is produced abroad and the very neutrality of the Liquor Tax Law.

1.   Categorization of the Liquor Tax Law

4.120 **Japan** submitted that shochu is readily distinguishable from the rest of the distilled liquors and these differences have resulted in different net-of-tax prices in relation to which tax rates are adjusted according to the tax categories of the Liquor Tax Law. Indeed, the categorization of distilled liquors under the Liquor Tax Law is not protectionist because it is based on three objective criteria: (i) the cost of the raw materials; (ii) the alcoholic strength; and (iii) the value added through the post distillation process. More specifically, the distinctions between the categories are the following:

-       shochu A and B have a low alcohol content, are produced from inexpensive materials and are "normally consumed without post distillation processing";

-       "spirits" are also produced from inexpensive raw materials but have a high alcohol content as well as a "higher value added in post-distillation process" (in the case of vodka, through a "specialized filtering process"; in the case of rum, through aging; and in the case of gin "through the flavour-adding process");

-       "whisky/brandy" has a high alcohol content and is produced from expensive raw materials. Moreover it has a "higher added value in post-distillation" (through "wooden cask aging");

-       "liqueur", as described by the Community: "[T]his category includes two well differentiated groups of products: on the one hand, so-called single item liqueurs or authentic liqueurs with a relatively high alcohol content (often 40 per cent, although in some cases it may be only 16 per cent - 24 per cent) such as brandy liqueurs, orange liqueurs, anisette, cream liqueurs, emulsion liqueurs and certain bitters; and, on the other hand, cocktails and sparkling pre-mixes combining one or more liquors with non-alcoholic beverages and with an overall alcohol content between 4 per cent and 12 per cent". The two groups of products, which previously were two separate tax categories, were merged into a single tax category of "liqueur" by the 1989 amendment because of the recommendation of the 1987 Panel Report.

Japan summarized the above categorization in the following diagram:

Raw Materials	Distillation	Post-Distillation	Product
Malts, Grapes-----------------Distillation--------------------------Aging. . . . .**Whisky/Brandy**			
	{Pot Still--Shochu A }	{Add extracts.. . . . . **Liqueur**	
Grain Potatoes	{ }	{	
	{Patent Still-Shochu B }	{Purification, Add Flavour}	
			}. . . . ."Spirits"
Molasses----------------------Distillation--------------------------Aging------------------ }			

Then Japan explained to the Panel that the related tax categories were established in light of the following three criteria: 1) the tax categories are based on socially established boundaries; 2) the level of consumption warrants an independent category; and 3) the tax categories are consistent with the policy goals. In particular Japan argued that:

(1)   A variety of combinations of materials, production methods and strengths must have been experimented within the past, but most of them have been weeded out through a competitive process. After a long history of such trials and errors, only particular combinations have survived and come to be favoured by consumers. For Japan, there emerges socially established product categories in the form of whisky, brandy, gin and others. Shochu, too, has emerged as a distinct category widely recognized as such in Southeast to East Asia. Indeed, Japan argued that a consumer survey in Japan demonstrates that there is a readily discernable difference, in the consumers' perception, between shochu and other distilled liquors. These socially established product boundaries have their roots in history, and they remain basically stable over the years. As the liquor tax categories affect a large number of consumers, it is desirable that they are readily understandable, and this consideration favours tax categories based on socially established product boundaries. Japan also argued that a competitive relationship tends to be weaker between two products which are recognized by consumers to be different than between those belonging to the same category. For the purpose of neutrality, accordingly, a line had better be drawn along such boundaries. There are various levels of generalization in socially established concepts, and "beverages", "alcoholic beverages", whisky and "malt whisky" are all socially established concepts. Criteria are needed to choose from these concepts and to combine them into tax categories, and for Japan, consistency of the categorization with the policy goal and the level of consumption to warrant an independent category are used as criteria. Under the existing tax categories, socially established concepts, such as whisky, brandy, and gin, were grouped according to commonality in relative expensiveness of raw materials, the degree of value-adding and the alcoholic strength, and thus their net-of-tax prices. The resulting tax categories were judged to suit the policy goal of equalized tax/price ratios, while remaining consistent with the socially established product boundaries. Japan added that one problem recognized when preparing the 1989 reform was the difference in the prices of materials and the net-of-tax prices between whisky and brandy, which were combined in a single tax category. In the end, the categoriza-

tion was maintained because brandy was not consumed enough to be treated as an independent tax category.

(2)   In addition, Japan submitted that the requirement of simplicity dictates that a certain level of consumption be achieved for an independent category to be established. For example, the "whisky/brandy" category was taken out of the "miscellaneous" category in 1962 in light of expansion of consumption. Similarly, the difference in categorization of grape and fruit wines between Japan, which treats them in one category, and the Community, which establishes six categories for them, seems to result from a large disparity in the amount of consumption. Japan reiterated that categorization along socially established product boundaries testified to its objectivity and thus to its non-protective policy goal. Japan insisted that it was not arguing, contrary to the allegation of the Community, that socially established criteria be the guide to the interpretation of the Article.

(3)   Japan also submitted that the result of such selection and grouping, discussed in the previous paragraph, must suit the policy goal. The 1987 tax was accompanied by a large disparity in the tax/price ratio, but such a disparity was eliminated by the rate changes under the 1989 amendment. In light of the overriding emphasis attached to neutrality and horizontal equity under the 1989 amendment, the tax/price ratio needs to be equalized across the categories of distilled liquors. For this purpose, it is desirable that the categorization reflects differences in net-of-tax prices between types of products and Japan submitted that the Liquor Tax Law does this. Shifts in prices since the 1989 amendment led Japan to amend the law for the second time in 1994; the tax/price ratio in December 1995 was in the proximity of what was achieved right after the 1989 amendment. In sum, since the 1989 amendment, tax rates are set to roughly equalize the average tax/price ratio for shochu and other categories. Japan argued that an excise tax is trade-neutral when it equalizes the tax/price ratio. The Japanese tax is trade-neutral and has no effect of protecting domestic production.

4.121 **Japan** emphasized that the classifications of the Liquor Tax Law as amended correspond to the classifications of the Harmonized System (HS) nomenclature, as amended by the 1993 decision of the Customs Co-operation Council. As described above, shochu, as defined by the Liquor Tax Law, is a category of product which falls under HS 2208.90 (Other) and has a lower alcoholic strength. Japan argued that as a striking similarity, the HS nomenclature picks out brandy, whisky, rum, gin, vodka and liqueur as distinct categories. If the HS nomenclature is not protective, then, Japan argued, the Liquor Tax Law classification should not be regarded as protective either.

1996 HS Nomenclature		Liquor Tax Law
2208	Distilled Liquors	
2208.20	Brandy	Whisky/Brandy
2208.30	Whisky	
2208.40	Rum	"Spirits"
2208.50	Gin	
2208.60	Vodka	
2208.70	Liqueur	Liqueur
2208.90	Others	Shochu (with lower alcoholic strength)
		"Spirits" (with higher alcoholic strength)

The HS nomenclature does not define whisky, vodka or liqueur. Japan submitted that under a principle common to civilized constitutions, however, any statute which imposes a fiscal burden on the people needs to be spelled out as clearly as possible. Such drafting work would inevitably involve an exercise of drawing a line between various concepts. It is certainly not an easy task, and involves a degree of judgment, because socially accepted concepts are not necessarily based on a scientific analysis but may result from a historical development. For instance, the criteria of purification by white birch charcoal in the vodka definition is, in Japan's view of the US argument, arbitrary. Is it not arbitrary, then, asked Japan, to define a sparkling wine by its mushroom stoppers held in place by ties or fasteners as in the Liquor Tax Directive of the Community. For Japan, the Community's argument against the Japanese criteria does not indicate arbitrariness inherent in the Liquor Tax Law, but rather the difficulty common to all product definitions. For Japan, despite allegations by other parties to the present dispute, there is nothing arbitrary in identifying these popular categories according to socially accepted concepts.

4.122 **Japan** then responded to another alleged arbitrariness in the Liquor Tax Law which is the ceiling on the alcoholic strength of shochu A (35 per cent) and B (45 per cent). The perceived arbitrariness, however, reflects the difficulty inherent in defining a historically developed concept. As an illustration of such common difficulty, Japan noted the following minimum alcoholic strengths for various products under the European definitions:

40 %	whisky, pastis
37.5 %	rum, gin, vodka, ouzo, Kornbrand
36 %	brandy
35 %	grain spirit
32 %	Korn
30 %	caraway-flavoured spirit drinks
25 %	fruit spirit drinks
15 %	aniseed-flavoured spirit drinks

For Japan, these floor rates are by no means arbitrary; they merely capture basic features of historically developed and socially accepted concepts. As stated earlier, the relatively low alcoholic ceiling for shochu reflects the fundamental features of this type of low-cost alcoholic beverage. The Liquor Tax Law does leave room for experimentation at the margin, as demonstrated by examples of Juhyo vodka or Jun Legend. Japan insisted that this is not inherent in the Japanese taxation system. As long as there is a tax differential between product categories, the opportunity for experimentation arises. This is an issue of optimal tax policy and not of GATT rules. Japan argued, for example, that Juhyo vodka contained only 20 per cent alcohol and would not meet the criteria of alcoholic strength for vodka in either Europe (37.5 per cent) or the United States (40 per cent). Although the filtering method of vodka was used, it was shochu in terms of alcoholic strength. This borderline product was consumed in much the same way as shochu and was subsequently reformulated into genuine shochu with alteration of raw materials to give a typical shochu taste.

4.123 For the **Community**, neither the Liquor Tax Law nor economic reality bear out Japan's exercise of *ex-post facto* rationalization since

-        alcoholic strength is not a classification criterion under the Liquor Tax Law. Alcoholic strength is not an element of the legal definitions of either "whisky" or "spirits". These categories may be manufactured and sold at any strength. On the other hand, the maximum legal strength of shochu A and of shochu B is 36 per cent and 45 per cent which can hardly be described as low alcohol content. Therefore, in the Community's view, Japan cannot claim that differences in tax rates are based in differences in alcohol content.

-        the cost of a particular raw material may vary considerably from one country to the other as well as seasonally. Grapes, for instance, may be an expensive product in Japan, where there is hardly any production, but not in the Mediterranean region, where they are commonly used to produce industrial alcohol. Dates (one of the products that may be legally used in the manufacture of shochu) are not necessarily less expensive than malt. The Community argued that the comparison of the raw material costs is totally irrelevant since the price of rice fluctuates according to other tariff and non tariff barriers. In any event, there is no indication that the rates for shochu are regularly adjusted so as to take account of the movements in the price of rice in the Chicago futures market. The minutes of the Diet's debate on the 1994 tax reform rather suggest that the rates on shochu are only adjusted to take into account the results of the rice harvest in Japan.

-        aging, whether in wooden casks or in other containers, is not an element of the legal definition of either whisky or rum. On the other hand, the definition of shochu does not exclude the aging of this product. Therefore, Japan cannot claim that aging is a valid criterion for applying different tax rates. As regards other white spirits, one may wonder what is the value added by filtering vodka through charcoal of white birch, instead of any other material, or by adding to gin some flavouring substances. Do any of these manufacturing processes have the effect of multiplying the value of the liquor concerned by 3.22 (the current difference in taxation between "spirits" and shochu B)?

The Community recalled that according to Japan, shochu A and shochu B share the same characteristics: both have a low alcohol content; both are made from inexpensive raw materials; and both have "a lower value added in post-distillation process". However, the tax rate on shochu A is 1.52 times higher than on shochu B.

4.124 In response to the Community's argument, **Japan** pointed out that similar differentials in net of tax prices between categories do exist in countries which apply a flat-rate tax on distilled liquors as well: For Japan, the Community claimed similarity of prices of brandy and gin based on the promotional leaflet of a Belgian supermarket, picking the least expensive item out of five brandy brands advertised in the leaflet (armagnac, calvados and cognac) and the most expensive gin brand from the six on the leaflet (gin and geneva, most expensive when adjusted for differences in bottle size). Japan called it a classical case of a selective reference, saying that calculation of the average net-of-tax prices of all items appearing on the leaflet results in a significant price differential. Against the Community's argument that grapes are very inexpensive and are used to produce industrial alcohol in the Mediterranean area, Japan questioned why is it then that brandy brands are more expensive than other distilled liquors in the Belgian supermarket. Moreover, according to a survey done by Business International, Inc., an affiliate of The Economist magazine, brandy is more expensive than whisky and whisky is more expensive than gin in 32 cities of the world where a flat tax rate is applied. Against the Community's claim that no category of distilled spirits is inherently more expensive than others, Japan questioned why is it then that such price differentials prevail across the world. For Japan, the Community tends to ignore the fact that differences in the market value of distilled liquors correspond to subtle product differences.

4.125 The **Community** reiterated that the prices and taxation systems of whisky in countries other than Japan are outside the terms of reference of the present dispute.

4.126 The **Community** also referred the Panel to a recent recommendation of the Administrative Reform Council, a public law advisory body attached to Japan's Prime Minister's office, which passed the following judgement on the alleged rationality of the Liquor Tax Law:

> "The current liquor tax law divides spirits into 16 products, each with a different tax rate. Even if there were reasons for setting different tax rates for each individual liquor in the past, it may not be possible to provide a consistent explanation to justify those reasons and the liquor tax structure as a whole at the present time.
>
> ... Therefore, it would be advisable, upon determining the categories and rates, to ensure that the rationale behind the decisions is logical and can be easily understood by consumers as well".

4.127 **Japan** argued that the above translation provided by the Community and Canada, which says "the Liquor Tax Law classifies spirits into 16 products" deviates sharply from the original which says "The current liquor tax law divides liquors into 16 categories". The Administrative Reform Committee's comment concerns the taxation of alcoholic beverages as a whole, and contains no specific reference to distilled liquors. Japan admitted that there is still room for improvement in the tax as a whole, including taxation of brewed beverages. For example, sake and wine are both brewed and have a similar strength. Yet the specific tax rate, and the tax/price ratio, of sake is more than twice the rate or ratio of wine. Japan argued that the Committee's critique of shortcomings in Japan's taxation of alcoholic beverages as a whole would be in fact valid for any liquor tax in the world, citing the United States Congressional Budget Office's report on the United States excise taxes and the European Commission's report on taxes on alcoholic beverages in Europe. It is true that there is room for improvement; but no tax is perfect.

4.128 The **Community** and **Canada** responded that the prices and taxation systems of liquors in countries other than Japan were outside the terms of reference of the present dispute.

4.129 **Japan** continued its explanation of the neutrality of the categorization in stating that the tax rates are set corresponding to the average net-of-tax price of each category. While net-of-tax prices vary from one category to another, the ratio of the tax over the retail price stays roughly constant between categories. Looking at the figures contained in Annex IV, one can see that on the basis of the weighted average of the suggested retail prices of some of the 20 best selling brands, per quantity containing the same amount of alcohol as a 750 ml, 40 per cent bottle, the amount of tax burden on each category varies substantially. The ratio of the tax burden over the retail price, on the other hand, is roughly the same; as measured in December 1995 *vis-à-vis* average suggested retail prices, at around 20 per cent. According to the figures, a consumer of any category, on average, paid roughly 20 per cent of the price for tax. Japan referred the Panel to 20 individual prices, the tax/price ratio of which is distributed within a similar range. If these categories were subject to the same tax rate per alcoholic content as currently applied to whisky, any shochu would bear a heavier tax burden than any imported whisky.

4.130 In support of its argument that the categorization of the Liquor Tax Law is reasonable, **Japan** submitted to the Panel that EU members, Canada and the United States apply significantly different tax rates between distilled liquors, wine, beer and intermediate products. Moreover, in eight Community Member States and the United States, the tax applicable to still wine is different from that applied to sparkling wine. In Japan's view, this treatment of different categories is apparently not based on the degree of competitive relationship between products. For example, there seems to be little competition, if any, between cream liqueur and vodka, while the study by Bossard Consultants found a strong competitive relationship between wine and distilled liquors, and between beer and distilled liquors. In Japan's view, the other parties to the dispute reject tax distinctions between whisky and shochu, a pair of products which have not been demonstrated to be competing against each other. On the other hand, Japan submitted that the complainants take for granted tax differentiation among beer, wine and distilled liquors, categories which the Bossard study found to be competitive products. Japan suggested to the Panel that if Japan should not apply different rates to distilled liquors by virtue of GATT rules, wine-producing France should not tax distilled liquors more heavily, nor should Germany impose a higher tax on distilled liquors than on beer. Japan added that seven Community Member States apply different rates to distilled liquors. Japan argued that not all of these practices are inconsistent with GATT rules and that Article III is not an instrument for harmonization of internal taxes.

4.131 The **complainant parties** responded that the taxation systems in countries other than Japan were not included in the terms of reference of the present dispute, and, in any event, were not relevant to the issue of whether Japan's Liquor Tax Law is consistent with GATT rules.

2.   The Aim of the Legislation

4.132 For **Japan**, the classification of the Liquor Tax Law is for purposes other than protection of domestic production. Categorization of distilled liquors under the Law is indeed for the purpose of a legitimate policy to ensure neutrality and equity, and not for the purpose of protection. There has been a shift in the policy objective of legislation in the 1989 amendment: from vertical equity to neutrality and horizontal equity, or from the pursuit of differentiation in the tax/price ratio to equalization. Until 1987, the taxation placed the greatest emphasis on achieving "vertical equity". "Vertical equity" requires a greater tax burden be born by those who have a greater tax-bearing ability, compared to those who are less able to pay. This principle emphasizes the income redistribution function of taxation, and forms the basis of "progressive taxation", which applies a higher rate of tax to a higher income level. In contrast, the "horizontal equity" requires the same burden for those similarly situated. The value added tax achieves horizontal equity better by imposing an equal amount of tax on the same amount of consumption, although it does not redistribute income or achieve progressivity. Although a tax authority would never ignore any of the three goals of neutrality, horizontal equity and vertical equity, relative emphasis among the three may vary in response to prevailing economic and social circumstances and kinds of taxes at issue. Japan submitted, as an example, the US Congressional Budget Office's report on excise taxes, which starts the analysis by examining the three criteria. The taxation on distilled liquors at the time of the 1987 Panel Report was designed with the utmost priority put on vertical equity. With the 1989 reform, however, a higher priority was given to neutrality than to equity in general, and to horizontal equity than to vertical equity. For Japan, the Community and the United States erred in ignoring the policy shift.

4.133 **Japan** reiterated that the primary objective of the policy adopted since the 1989 amendment is to achieve neutrality and horizontal equity to consumers' choice or minimization of distortions in competitive conditions among products. Japan argued that the Liquor Tax Law succeeded in doing so in ensuring that the ratio of the tax over the retail price stays roughly constant between categories of distilled liquors. Japan therefore argued that the complainants failed to prove the existence of protective intent. Concerning the lack of a statement on the purpose of the Liquor Tax Law, Japan responded that omission is only a standard practice of tax legislation and that the government representatives cited neutrality and equity repeatedly before the National Diet and on other occasions. The legislative record shows that neutrality and equity were cited as primary objectives of the current Law. For example, the Minister of Finance stated at the National Diet that the fundamental principles of the 1989 amendments were to ensure equity in distribution of the tax burden and to maintain neutrality toward economic activities, under the recognition that the tax should spread the common cost in a broad, fair manner among the people, and to simplify the tax system. With respect to the 1994 amendment, the Director General in charge explained its objective and purpose in the following manner: "The present amendment reflects the last year's recommendation by the Tax Commission to appropriately rearrange the level of the taxation burden which has been declining for some categories. The amendment intends to redress the burden, and to readjust the tax rates in light of changing consumption patterns, in order to equalize the tax burden among various categories". Japan argued that the 1994 amendment was not for the purpose of implementing the recommendations of the 1987 Panel report, but to redress the decline of the tax/price ratio of shochu and spirits which resulted from the rising prices to maintain the consistency with the recommendation already attained by the 1989 amendment. The amendment raised the tax rates for all categories, except whisky/brandy. For example, the tax rate for shochu A has been raised 30 per cent and that for shochu B by 44 per cent. For Japan, these statements confirm that the policy intent of the Liquor Tax Law was and is to ensure neutrality and equity taking the tax/price ratio as a principal indicator.

4.134 **Japan** explained that two factors prompted this shift in policy priorities. First, the policy considerations behind Japanese taxation in general were shifting since 1986 towards putting more emphasis on horizontal equity, as opposed to vertical equity, and on neutrality. The Tax Commission issued the following recommendations:

> "The importance of the redistributional aspect of taxation is relatively declining over the years; instead, the need to ensure horizontal equity in the allocation of the tax burden... has become a higher priority". (October 1986)

> "It is extremely important for the vigour of the whole economy that taxation avoids interference in the consumption and business activities by individuals and corporations to the extent practicable, and that it maintains neutrality to industries and the economy". (April 1988)

Japan submitted that this shift resulted in the tax reform package which was enacted at the end of 1988 and entered into force in 1989. The package, which lessened progressivity in the income tax and introduced the consumption tax (a VAT), is indeed a milestone from the structure overwhelmingly led by vertical equity toward a new structure which emphasizes neutrality and horizontal equity. The 1989 amendment to the Liquor Tax Law formed part of this package.

4.135 **Japan** went on to argue that the 1987 Panel Report was the second motivation. It was as a result of Japan's commitment to faithfully fulfil the recommendation of the panel report to "eliminate protective effects prohibited by Article III:2 of GATT", that the tax/price ratio was equalized across categories of distilled liquor. Neutrality and horizontal equity, the two purposes prioritized in the whole reform package, were pursued with special vigour for distilled liquor taxation because of the 1987 Panel Report. In fact, the Tax Commission's recommendation of December 1987 referred to the "requirement to faithfully implement GATT recommendation", and that of April 1988 specifically recommended that "the tax disparity be minimized between various alcoholic beverages". Based on these two factors, the amendment to the Liquor Tax Law minimized the tax disparity between alcoholic beverages in general, and, with respect to distilled liquors, equalized the tax/price ratio across categories of distilled liquors in stricter pursuit of neutrality. It also intends to attain equity, or fair distribution of the tax burden among consumers, to the extent compatible with the neutrality requirement.

4.136 In response to Japan's statement that between 1986 and 1988 the tax policy underlying the Liquor Tax Law shifted from "vertical equity" to "horizontal equity" and that this shift led to an amendment to the Liquor Tax Law in 1989 that, according to Japan, "emphasizes neutrality", **Canada** referred the Panel to the Deregulation Subcommittee of the Administrative Reform Council which stated the opposite. The function of the Council, which is an independent body and whose members are appointed by Japan's Prime Minister and approved by the Diet, is to promote "rational" reform of Japan's "administrative system". In December, 1995, the Subcommittee recommended fundamental changes to the Liquor Tax Law. According to the Subcommittee, the different tax rates levied on the various categories pursuant to the Liquor Tax Law have a wide impact on consumer choice at the time of purchase, constitute "virtual restrictions on buyer's activities"; are not based on logical taxation standards; are not based on "fairness of the tax burden"; are not neutral in relation to consumer choice. Thus, Canada argued, contrary to Japan's assertion that "the liquor tax is similar to VAT in terms of "tax discrimination indices" and thus is not "trade-distortive", the Administrative Reform Council concludes otherwise, and considers that as currently structured, the Liquor Tax Law distorts neutrality in relation to consumer choice.

4.137 **Japan** argued that what Canada read from the Subcommittee's recommendation differed from the language of the Subcommittee report. Japan then submitted a chart which compares the relative tax burden between shochu A and imported vodka and whisky under the three yardsticks. For example, the left column indicates that the liquor tax per litre of vodka is 2.7 times higher than that of shochu A, and that of whisky, 7 times higher than that of shochu.

Figure: Comparison of "Tax Discrimination Indices"

	Per Litre of Beverage		Per Litre of Pure Alcohol		Tax/Price Ratio	
	Liquor Tax	VAT	Liquor Tax	VAT	Liquor Tax	VAT
Shochu A	1.0	1.0	1.0	1.0	1.0	1.0
Imported Vodka	2.7	3.4	1.6	2.0	0.8	1.0
Imported Whisky	7.0	8.0	4.0	4.7	0.9	1.0

Note: Calculated on the basis of weighted average of 20 most selling brands.

4.138 **Japan** argued that this figure demonstrates that i) the liquor tax is similar to VAT in terms of "tax discrimination indices", and that ii) VAT would be regarded more "trade-distortive" than the liquor tax as long as a comparison is made on the basis of the taxes by the tax amount per litre of beverage or of pure alcohol. Japan submitted that VAT is regarded as one of the most trade-neutral indirect taxes and its introduction is one of the conditions to join the European Union. On the other hand, a comparison made with the amount of tax per litre of beverage or of pure alcohol would find such VAT as trade-distortive. In fact it is the use of those two yardsticks as tools of comparing taxes which is problematic, rather than the tax itself. Japan emphasized that a consumer usually does not buy a product exclusively on the basis of the size of the bottle or on the basis of the alcoholic strength. Consumers choose products by comparing the price and the overall value of a product, which depends upon the taste, flavour and other features and is not confined to the volume and strength. Japan argued that this is why the tax/price ratio is a better criterion to evaluate the effects of taxes on competitive conditions, and neutrality is achieved when the tax/price ratio is equalized, as is the case with the Japanese tax.

4.139 The **Community** submitted that the system established by the Liquor Tax Law was radically different from an *ad valorem* tax system. In a true *ad valorem* system, taxes are proportional to the actual sales value of each shipment and, therefore, neutral, provided that the rates are the same for all the categories. In contrast, under the Liquor Tax Law system, the tax amount is unrelated to the actual sales price. Instead, the assumption is made that certain categories of liquors are a priori more expensive than others. The tax rates are then set so as to reflect this "assumed value" and uniformly applied to all shipments, regardless of their actual price. The outcome of this system is not "neutrality" but arbitrariness because no category of distilled spirits is inherently more expensive than others. The evidence provided to the Panel shows that, even under the current tax system, the pre-tax price of some brands of whisky is lower than the equivalent price for some brands of shochu.

4.140 **Japan** argued that the lack of plausible alternatives further testifies to the lack of protective intent. Conceivable alternatives to ensure neutrality and equity are: (i) to raise the *ad valorem* value-added tax to a level comparable to that of the European Union, which applies not only to liquor consumption but to almost all consumption or (ii) to alter the liquor tax into an *ad valorem* tax. However, for Japan, neither of these is practical. First, the decision to raise the *ad valorem* consumption tax from the present three per cent to five per cent beginning April 1997 was made in 1994 only after a prolonged, heated debate. It is not very likely that the rate would be raised to the Community level in the near future. Second, an *ad valorem* excise tax could easily invite tax evasion by way of transfer-pricing, particularly if applied at the shipping stage. Canada's Federal Manufacturers Sales Tax suffered from the same difficulty and was abolished in 1991. On the other hand, enforcement cost of an *ad valorem* tax would be very substantial if applied at the retail level.

4.141 The **Community** responded that the reasons given by Japan for not pursuing the alleged objective of neutrality through the application of an *ad valorem* tax system are groundless. In the Community's view, Japan's definition of neutrality assumes that specific excise taxes are passed on in full to consumers. Thus, if the current tax system was truly neutral, there should be no reason for the Diet to object to its replacement by an *ad valorem* consumption tax. The Diet's opposition merely reflects the fact that under the current system shochu is much less taxed than it would under a truly neutral *ad valorem* consumption tax. In any event, internal political difficulties may not provide a valid justification for infringing GATT rules. For the Community, the tax evasion problems invoked by Japan are common to the application of all *ad valorem* systems. Similar issues arise, for instance, in connection with the application of *ad valorem* customs duties to import transactions between related parties. It is therefore suggested that any tax evasion problems related to transfer pricing could be appropriately tackled by using any of the alternative methods for the calculation of transaction values provided for in the Agreement on Implementation of Article VII of GATT 1994 (the Customs Valuation Code). In this respect, it is worth noting that Japan currently applies *ad valorem* customs duties on imports of a fair number of liquors, apparently without this giving rise to any major duty evasion problems. Moreover, until 1989, Japan applied *ad valorem* excise duties to certain liquors. These duties were abolished because they were found inconsistent with Article III:2 by the 1987 Panel Report and not because they were an invitation to tax evasion. *Ad valorem* excise duties on alcoholic beverages are currently applied by other WTO Members (e.g., in Denmark). Contrary to Japan's assertions, the application of a flat rate tax to all distilled spirits would not necessarily render the Japanese system less "neutral" (according to Japan's own definition of neutrality). For the Community, the scenario depicted by Japan is unrealistic because it does not take into account the likely dynamic effects of a tax readjustment. If shochu was taxed at the same rate as whisky, the cheapest brands of shochu would be expelled from the market, just like former second grade whisky was wiped out of the market by the 1989 tax reform. This would have the consequence of lowering the average tax/price ratio for the remaining brands of shochu. On the other hand, an increase of the rates on shochu would allow the entry into the market of cheaper brands of the other categories of liquors, thus driving up their respective average tax/price ratios. Moreover, there is no reason why a flat tax rate should be applied at the level of the current rate for whisky. It could as well be set at the level of the current rate for shochu or at any intermediate level between the current rates for shochu and "whisky/brandy". The tax systems of other WTO Members which apply a flat tax rate to all distilled spirits are not less "neutral" in terms of tax/price ratios than the current Japanese system but rather the opposite.

4.142 In response to the Community's argument that the evasion problems are manageable since there are other cases of the *ad valorem* tax, **Japan** made the following counterarguments. First, the Danish *ad valorem* tax is expected to be abolished shortly. According to Japan, the abolition was prompted by the fact that, as prices are determined on a case-by-case basis, the system became enormously confusing, and that, in particular, it was easy to manipulate prices while such manoeuvres were hard to detect. The Community now prohibits members from adopting an *ad valorem* tax. Second, although it is true that an *ad valorem* tax used to be part of the Japanese liquor tax before the 1989 amendment, detection of transfer pricing was possible then because retail prices were stable at the suggested retail prices and the margin rates for retailers and wholesalers were broadly constant. However, liquors are now traded, in some cases, at prices substantially different from suggested retail prices and it has become virtually impossible to distinguish manipulation from normal trading. In fact there was another *ad valorem* excise tax before the 1989 amendment which applied to consumer goods such as automobiles, cameras, watches and audio equipments. However, since these items were often sold at discount, there were a series of complaints over taxable prices, and the integrity of the tax was put into question. Third, for Japan, an *ad valorem* excise tax is fundamentally different from an *ad valorem* customs duty; and the success of an *ad valorem* customs duty does not mean that an *ad valorem* excise tax is feasible. The total tax burden under Japan's liquor tax is 20 billion US dollars, and is more than 50 times greater than that of customs duties on liquor. The aggregate magnitude of incentives for tax evasion is therefore far greater for the liquor tax than for the customs duty. Nevertheless, it is far more difficult to secure compliance with the excise tax. Customs duties are charged before the goods are withdrawn, while the liquor tax is levied after they are shipped. Importers must declare the prices to the customs authorities and pay applicable duties before they are authorized to withdraw the goods. In contrast, the liquor tax is levied after the goods have been shipped, on the basis of declaration for the preceding one month. Japan argued that careful examination of the examples of *ad valorem* duties put forward by the Community demonstrates the impracticality of an *ad valorem* liquor tax. In response to the Community's claim concerning "the likely dynamic effect of a tax adjustment", Japan raised the following points. First, since 1987, the tax rate on whisky has been halved. However, the share of premium whisky in the imported Scotch whisky market expanded from 33 per cent in 1987 to 51 per cent in 1994. Japan argued that, contrary to the allegation of the Community, the decrease of tax promoted premium whisky sales. Also, during the same period, in which the shochu tax rate increased twofold, containers of shochu A shifted from a medium size to a large size. Again, contrary to the Community's allegation, higher tax has led to an increase in the share of low-cost brands. The Japanese market configuration shifted in a direction opposite to the Community's "likely dynamic effect of tax adjustment". Second, according to Japan, differentials in net of tax prices between categories similar to those in the Japanese market do exist in countries which apply a flat-rate tax on distilled liquors as well. According to a survey done by Business International, Inc., an affiliate of The Economist magazine, brandy is more expensive than whisky and whisky is more expensive than gin in 32 cities of the world where a flat tax rate is applied. The Community argued that the application of a flat rate tax to all distilled spirits would not necessarily render the Japanese system less neutral. However, Japan calculated the tax burden in Belgium on the basis of average prices quoted in the promotion leaflet of the supermarket in Brussels submitted by the Community and found that any bottle of vodka or any bottle of gin is burdened with a higher tax/price ratio than any of the bottles of brandy in the shop (left hand side of the exhibit in Annex V). On the other hand, under the Japanese system, tax/price ratios are broadly equal across categories (right hand side of the exhibit in Annex V). Japan concluded from the exhibit that a flat-rate tax was far inferior to the current Japanese tax in terms of neutrality, horizontal equity and vertical equity. Japan submitted two tables on "Tax/Price Ratio in Belgium and in Japan" (see Annex V).

4.143 **Japan** also submitted to the Panel charts which identified the "roughly equal" tax/price ratios, namely a chart showing the Average Retail Prices and Taxes of Liquor and another chart on the Percentage of Taxes in Retail Prices (see Annex VI). According to Japan, the Liquor Tax Law's tax rates are set corresponding to the average net-of-tax price of each category. While net-of-tax prices vary from one category to another, the ratio of the tax over the retail price stays roughly constant between categories. Japan submitted that the ratio of the tax burden over the retail price is roughly the same; as measured in December 1995 *vis-à-vis* average suggested retail prices, at around 20 per cent. A consumer of any category paid, on average, roughly 20 per cent of the price for the tax, in other words. One category which shows a substantially lower ratio is imported authentic liqueur. Japan argued that this results from the 1989 amendment's integration of authentic liqueur and other liqueur and the application of the lower tax rate. If the pre-1989 rate were applied, the ratio would be roughly in line with the other categories. The second figure uses 20 individual prices which should differ from the weighted average price. Nevertheless, the tax/price ratio of each brand is distributed within a similar range for all categories. If these categories were subject to the same tax rate per alcoholic content as currently applied to whisky, any shochu would bear a heavier tax burden than any imported whisky. Japan referred to the example of the retail prices and taxes of liquor in the UK, as an indication of the result of the abolition of tax categories. In support of its allegation, Japan submitted two charts showing the "Retail Prices and Taxes of Liquors in the UK" and another chart showing the "Percentage of Taxes in Retail Prices in the UK" (see Annex VII). Japan argued that, according to the example, the price of a bottle of whisky which originally cost 20 pounds would increase only 50 per cent to 30 pounds, while that of a bottle of gin would increase three times, from 4 pounds to 12 pounds. For Japan, this tax distorts consumers' choice in favour of whisky, to the detriment of gin. It also runs counter to the notion of equity, because gin consumers must pay two thirds of the consumption expense to the government while whisky consumers are taxed only on third of the expense. For Japan, these are the problems which Japan's liquor tax categories and different tax rates are designed to avoid. To the Community's allegation that the examples are not representative, Japan responded that, even in the promotional leaflet of a supermarket in Brussels which the Community itself submitted to the Panel, any bottle of vodka and any bottle of gin is burdened with a higher tax/price ratio than any bottle of brandy in the shop. Japan also suggested that with the recent expansion of discount operations, actual market prices are, in some cases, substantially different from the suggested prices. However, in the discount outlets, all categories, including shochu, are subject to discount, and the relationship between tax/price ratios of different categories tends to remain the same. For example, for the items listed on the promotional leaflet of a discount outlet sake Ichitba Yamada, which the Community submitted to the Panel, the ratio is 21 per cent for whisky/brandy, and 26 per cent for shochu on the basis of suggested retail prices. At discount prices, it is 35 per cent and 40 per cent, respectively, for whisky/brandy and shochu, resulting in much the same picture.

Japan submitted that as an indicator of the overall market situation in Japan, the suggested retail price seems to work better. This is because, while discounts are frequent in the Tokyo metropolitan area, the actual prices in other parts of Japan tend to be close to the suggested prices. In Japan's view, the JETRO survey cited by the Canadian submission confirms this: Old Parr (12 years; suggested retail price of ¥8,500), for example, is selling at ¥4,920 on the average in three outlets in Tokyo; its price in Nagoya and Fukuoka (the fourth and eighth largest cities in Japan) is ¥8,000. In support of its arguments, Japan also submitted its own survey of actual on-shelf prices of all of the relevant items (in aggregate, 5,130 items) displayed at 36 outlets in six cities in Japan.

4.144 **Japan** also submitted that in the complainants' assessment of the tax burden under the Liquor Tax Law, their criteria of selecting products were not objective. For instance, Japan continued, it is not meaningful to compare a brand of whisky whose tax/price ratio is the highest, and a brand of shochu whose tax/price ratio is the lowest. The complainants' analysis did not adequately capture discounts applied to shochu.

4.145 In view of the clearly protectionist effects attached to the application of lower tax rates to shochu, the **Community** argued that the aim pursued by Japan is irrelevant for this Panel to rule on the consistency of the measures concerned with Article III:2, first and second sentences. As argued, for the Community, the examination of the Liquor Tax Law's purpose would only become relevant if Japan had claimed that the infringement of Article III:2 is justified under Article XX. In any case, for the Community, the existence of a protectionist purpose is nonetheless manifest. The existence of a protectionist intent results, in the first place, from the apparent arbitrariness and lack of rationality of the product categorization, of which the following are but some of the most egregious examples:

-    the only difference between vodka and shochu A is that shochu A cannot be filtered with charcoal of white birch, even though it can be filtered with any other material. Yet the tax rate on vodka is 2.55 times higher than the tax rate on shochu A. Quite clearly, the distinction for tax purposes between vodka and shochu A on the basis of such an obviously minor difference cannot have any rational justification other than excluding imported vodka from the tax privileges granted to the local producers of shochu.

-    likewise, it is arbitrary to set the maximum alcohol content for shochu obtained by continuous distillation (i.e, shochu A) at 36 per cent and the maximum alcohol content of shochu obtained by other distillation methods (i.e., shochu B) at 45 per cent. The only rational explanation for this difference is that most western-style spirits are made by continuous distillation and have an average strength of 40 per cent.

-    all liquors falling within the categories of "shochu", "whisky/brandy" and "spirits" are, when pre-mixed with a sugared non-alcoholic beverage, classified as "liqueurs" and taxed at a uniform rate. However, the same liquors, when sold undiluted, are classified within different tax categories and taxed at hugely diverging rates, despite the fact that they are often consumed in home-made mixes made from similar non-alcoholic beverages. This difference in taxation only becomes rational in light of the fact that, unlike undiluted liquors, pre-mixes are produced almost exclusively in Japan.

4.146 **Japan** responded that the complaining parties' allegation of arbitrariness in categorization is evidence of the difficulty common to all legal definition of socially accepted concepts. It is difficult, since socially accepted concepts are not necessarily based on a scientific analysis but may result from historical development. The Community's directives classify wine into six complex tax categories in their attempt to reconcile social notions such as sherry, champagne, or cider with the definition in the directive, define sparkling wine by its mushroom stoppers, determine eight minimum alcoholic strengths for various categories of distilled liquors, and emphasize the relations among product value, traditional quality, definition and minimum alcoholic strength. For Japan, the taxation authorities are facing a similar difficulty everywhere and the attempt to overcome such difficulties should not be considered arbitrary. Japan argued that tax categories must be designed respecting the market reality, and the market is keen on the differences in materials, the production methods and the alcoholic strength, as is demonstrated by the price differentials among categories observed around the world. Japan also argued that Canada applies the same tax rate to wine-based and spirits-based pre-mixes, while taxing wine and spirits differently. For Japan, it indicates that pre-mixes present a tax issue common to all countries and the points raised by the Community and the United States do not prove the arbitrariness of categorization.

4.147 The **Community** submitted that it is a commonly held view in Japan that the concessionary tax rates applied to shochu are specifically aimed at protecting the small producers of shochu, even though over 50 per cent of the shochu sold in Japan is now produced by six major companies. Thus, the Japanese media often reflect the view that the lower taxes applied to shochu respond to the pressure exerted by the small manufacturers of shochu, which tend to be concentrated in a few prefectures and enjoy for this reason a disproportionate political influence. A recent confirmation of this was provided by the vigorous opposition of some Japanese legislators to the very modest increase in the tax on shochu proposed by the Government as part of the 1994 tax reform bill. According to a member of the Diet, that increase would have been "a blow to the more than 30% of shochu makers who show a deficit". In order to appease this criticism, the Japanese Government was forced to admit that the tax increases had been kept "to the minimum level possible". Contrary to the Japanese Government's claim that the only public policy objective pursued by applying lower tax rates to shochu is to maximize the tax revenue while ensuring that the tax burden is distributed among the different categories of consumers in accordance with their respective tax bearing ability, the amount of the tax is unrelated to the actual price of the liquors: a liquor falling within a certain category and having a certain alcoholic content is always taxed at the same rate, regardless of its sales price. Instead, the Japanese authorities make the *a priori* assumption that certain categories of liquors are more expensive than others and are consumed by more affluent consumers. As a result, it is the amount of the tax that the Japanese authorities arbitrarily decide to impose on each category of liquors which determines its sales price and ultimately its consumption pattern, and not the opposite.

4.148 Against the Community's allegation of political influences based on media articles, **Japan** referred the panel to a newspaper article conveying a contrary view and submitted that speculative inside stories were not appropriate as the basis of Panel findings. For Japan, the record of Diet deliberation of the 1994 amendment cannot be evidence of a protective intent, as the amendment raised the tax rate on shochu A by 30 per cent and that for shochu B by 44 per cent, while raising the tax on "spirits" by mere 11 per cent and maintaining the tax on whisky/brandy at the same level. Japan also argued that the complaining parties seem to confuse the present Japanese policy with that of 1987. Japan stressed that its current distilled liquor taxation prioritizes neutrality and horizontal equity over vertical equity, and that Japan is not saying that a pursuit of vertical equity can justify a non-trade neutral tax. For Japan, what it is saying is that in so far as a tax system satisfies the trade-neutral requirement, the less regressive it is, the better. In explaining the notion of vertical equity, Japan argued that tax inequity among consumers of different liquors can have a distributional impact when different income groups prefer different categories of liquor. Japan submitted evidence that compares the income, the consumption tax payments, the liquor tax burden in respect of distilled liquor under the current Liquor Tax Law and the hypothetical liquor tax burden under a flat specific rate, of an average household in income quintiles. Under the current Liquor Tax Law, the consumption tax burden or the present liquor tax burden track roughly the income level and are fairly proportional. However, the tax becomes highly regressive under the flat-rate regime.

4.149 For **Japan**, one of the possible factors contributing to the introduction of the flat-rate tax in Europe and North America seems to be the importance in the tax policy attached to the prevention of alcoholic dependence. Community documents prepared in the course of drafting the Community Council Directives of 1992 indicate that the impact on health has been an important factor. Similarly, the local liquor tax laws of the United States were introduced in the wake of the Prohibition, and some of them earmark the tax revenue specifically for fighting alcoholism. Another possible factor is the high *ad valorem* consumption tax. The proportionality of the *ad valorem* consumption tax (e.g., VAT, the state sales tax) could mitigate the overall regressiveness of taxes on liquor. For example in the Community member States' VAT rates range from 15 per cent to 25 per cent. The Canadian federal government imposes a VAT of 7 per cent, and Ontario levies a 12 per cent sales tax. The rate of State and local sales tax in New York is 8.25 per cent. These taxes serve to ensure equity, enabling the liquor tax to focus on alcohol. These factors are not present in Japan. At the rate of 3 per cent, the *ad valorem* consumption tax alone cannot ensure the equitable distribution of tax burden among liquor consumers under a flat rate liquor tax system. Japan submitted that the National Diet demands annually an estimate of the ratio of the liquor tax burden relative to the income level for each income group. Japan argued that it was against this background of acute concern over the issue of distributional equity that the Liquor Tax Law incorporated an element of distributional equity in its structure. Different specific rates apply to a variety of products, depending on the degree of value-added. However, Japan argued, the present policy pursues the goal of distributional equity only to the extent compatible with neutrality. For Japan, while the pre-1989 policy assumed that a consumer of imported whisky had a greater tax-bearing ability, and therefore should bear a greater tax burden, Japan's taxation of distilled liquors made a clear departure from that policy with the 1989 amendment following the 1987 Panel Report. Contrary to the claims by other parties to the dispute, the present policy requires an equal burden to be shared among consumers of imported whisky and shochu. For Japan, distortional effects of a tax on consumer choice are most pronounced in the case of flat-rate specific taxes, as currently applied in some countries of Europe and North America. For example, different categories of liquors are produced by different manufacturing processes; some are stored in wooden casks for many years, and others are consumed immediately after distillation. Their value or net-of-tax price differs accordingly. However, the flat-rate tax imposes the same amount of tax across various categories of distilled liquors if the amount of alcohol contained is the same, regardless of product differences. Under the flat-rate taxation, where the amount of tax is the same for all categories of distilled spirits, a bottle of gin the value of which is 4 pounds sterling will cost 12 pounds to purchase after tax. In contrast, a bottle of whisky the value of which is 20 pounds sterling will be priced at 30 pounds. In other words, the tax makes the price of gin three times higher than its value, while making the whisky price only 50 per cent higher. This kind of taxation prejudices consumers' choices against gin in favour of whisky because consumers choose products by comparing their price and their overall value.

4.150 **Japan** further argued that in order to ensure neutrality to consumers' choice, a liquor tax should not be based exclusively on one element of the overall value: alcoholic strength. The Liquor Tax Law, on the other hand, captures other elements of value by classifying liquors on the basis of the difference in value added by post-distillation processing. Indeed, this results in a broadly constant value/price ratio across categories (80 per cent, as measured in December 1995 vis-à-vis average suggested retail prices) and a tax/price ratio (20 per cent as measured in the same manner). For example, prices of a bottle of whisky (¥3,000) and of a bottle of shochu (¥1,000) increase by a similar percentage after tax. Categorization of distilled liquors under the Liquor Tax Law thus serves the goal of neutrality, a legitimate tax policy objective. In fact, this role of varied specific rates is not peculiar to Japan. Eight countries out of 15 Member States of the Community apply a tax rate to sparkling wine several times higher than the one levied on still wine. Japan also submitted that the US tax on sparkling wine per litre of alcohol is 3.2 times higher than that on still wine, compared with the 3.9-to-1 tax differential per litre of alcohol between whisky and shochu A in Japan. Also, the import ratio of still wine in the United States is lower than that of sparkling wine, as is the import ratio of shochu, which is lower than that for whisky. Moreover, in Japan, wine is wine and the same tax rate is applied to both sparkling and still wines, whereas in the United States, alcohol is alcohol and the same tax rate is applied to all distilled liquors.

4.151 The **Community**, **Canada** and the **United States** reiterated that the taxation systems of the countries other than Japan were outside the terms of reference of the present Panel.

4.152 The **Community** stated that although Japan argued that "equity" requires a "fair distribution of the tax burden among consumers", it did not provide any clear explanation of what is considered as a "fair distribution" of the tax burden. In the Community's view, Japan argues that "equity" means that tax rates on distilled spirits should be progressive or at least proportional to the consumers' income level: "Tax inequity among consumers of different categories can have a distributional impact when different income groups prefer different categories of liquors". The Community submitted that different income groups do not have fixed and inherently different tastes. Consumers with lower incomes drink less than consumers with higher incomes simply because whisky is more expensive. In turn, it is more expensive because it bears higher taxes. Thus, through the application of higher tax rates on the categories of liquors deemed a priori to be preferred by the rich, a groundless assumption is turned into a self-fulfilling prophecy. The assumption that certain income groups prefer certain liquors was also at the heart of the "tax bearing ability" principle invoked by Japan as a justification before 1987. This justification was rejected by the 1987 Panel Report. "Equity" is but another tag name for "tax bearing ability" and should be condemned on identical grounds. The Community concluded by stating that the above considerations led the 1987 Panel Report to dismiss in categorical terms a similar justification advanced by the Japanese Government:

> "The Panel was of the view that the use of product and tax differentiations with the view of maintaining or promoting certain production and consumption patterns could easily distort price-competition among like or directly competing products by creating price differences and price-related consumer preferences which would not exist in case of non-discriminatory internal taxation consistent with Article III:2. The Panel noted that the General Agreement did not make provision for such a far-reaching exception to Article III:2 and that the concept of taxation according to tax-bearing ability of prospective consumers of a product did not offer an objective criterion because it relied on necessarily subjective assumptions about future competition and inevitably uncertain consumer responses".[74]

3. The Effect of the Legislation

4.153 **Japan** reiterated that the "effect" of "so as to afford protection" must be judged by whether the tax distorts the competitive relationship between imported and domestic products. For Japan, the Liquor Tax Law does not distort the competitive relation between imported and domestic products for the following rea-

---

[74] 1987 Panel Report, para. 5.13.

sons. 1) The tax/price ratios of all tax categories are roughly the same. In terms of the examination of the tax burden, the tax/price ratio is the superior yardstick and better indicates the impact on consumers' choice than the ratio of tax over product volume or alcohol content and it is common practice to employ a tax/price ratio in comparing the burden of an excise tax. 2) Shochu is produced outside Japan; indeed in examining whether or not the category in question is almost exclusively domestic, what needs to be examined is not import ratios but rather whether the "domestic" product is produced in other countries, and whether the "imported product" is also domestically produced. 3) There is no directly competitive or substitutable relationship between domestic products and imports, precluding therefore any possibility of protective effects. Since in Japan's view, protective distortion exists only when the three above-mentioned cumulative requirements are met, it is clear that the Liquor Tax Law does not distort any competitive relationship and is therefore consistent with Article III:2.

a) The Tax/Price Ratio Rates under the Legislation are Neutral)

4.154 For **Japan** the lack of protective effect of the Law is demonstrated by the neutrality of the tax. The application of varying rates dependent on average net-of-tax prices of distilled liquor categories results in a fairly stable tax/price ratio. Thus the liquor tax is far less distortional than taxes of other countries, and far less likely to alter consumer choice.

4.155 The **Community** responded more specifically that the Liquor Tax Law is not, de facto, "neutral" even according to the standard of "neutrality" defined by Japan. The tax/price ratios, as calculated by Japan, are far from being "roughly constant". Moreover, the calculation method followed by Japan leads to the systematic overestimation of the ratios for shochu and the underestimation of the ratios for the other categories. Even if the tax/retail prices were exactly the same (*quod non*), the Japanese tax system would still not be truly neutral. The specific tax rates on a litre of whisky/brandy, spirits and liqueurs are from three to nine times higher than the specific tax rates on a litre of shochu. For example, the specific tax rate on a 0.75 litre bottle of whisky of 40 per cent is ¥737, i.e., more than the weighted average retail price net of taxes for an equivalent bottle of shochu A which, according to Japan's own calculations, is ¥631. As a result, whisky is bound to be much more expensive than shochu, regardless of whether its pre-tax price is lower or higher. The considerably much higher taxes imposed on "whisky/brandy", "spirits" and "liqueurs" have excluded the less expensive brands of these categories from the lower segments of the Japanese market for distilled spirits where price is the main competition factor. On the other hand, these brands cannot compete in the upper segments where quality and brand image are as important as price. Confirmation of this is provided by the spectacular decline in the sales of former second grade whisky in the wake of the 1989 tax reform. The distorting effects of the Liquor Tax Law are also evident in the composition of Community exports. Premium brands of scotch such as Chivas or Johnnie Walker Black Label represent a disproportionate share of imports. Likewise, imports of Community brandy consist almost exclusively of very expensive brands of X.O. and V.S.O.P cognac. For the Community, the exclusion of the less expensive brands of "whisky/brandy", "spirits" and "liqueurs" from the Japanese market has the consequence that the overall tax/price ratio for these categories is much lower than it would be if the possibility to sell these brands was not precluded through dissuasive taxation. For this reason, even if the tax/price ratios for shochu and the other categories of distilled spirits were "roughly constant", this would not be proof that the Japanese tax system is "neutral". Rather, it would be the consequence of its lack of neutrality.

4.156 In response to the Community's claim that differences in net-of-tax prices among categories are the results of tax differences, **Japan** raised the following points. First, since 1987, the tax rate on whisky has been halved, but the share of premium whisky in the imported Scotch whisky market expanded from 33 per cent in 1987 to 51 per cent in 1994. Japan argued that, contrary to the allegation of the Community, the decrease of tax promoted premium whisky sales. Also, during the same period, in which the shochu tax rate was increased twofold, containers of shochu A shifted from a medium size to a large size. Again, contrary to the Community's allegation, the higher tax has led to an increase in the share of low-cost brands. The Japanese market configuration shifted in a direction opposite to the Community's hypothesis. Second, according to Japan, differentials in net-of-tax prices between categories similar to those in the Japanese market do exist in countries which apply a flat-rate tax on distilled liquors as well. For example, calculation of the average net-of-tax prices of all items appearing in the leaflet of a supermarket in Brussels, which the Community submitted to the Panel, results in significant price differentials among the categories of distilled liquors. Also, according to a survey done by Business International, Inc., an affiliate of The Economist magazine, brandy is more expensive than whisky and whisky is more expensive than gin in 32 cities of the world where a flat tax rate is applied. For Japan, net of tax prices of distilled liquor differ from one category to another, reflecting differences in such factors as materials, production methods and alcoholic strength, as agreed by a delegate from the Community during the Panel deliberations. Japan argued that the price differences exist under a flat rate excise tax as well as under multiple rates, and that the tax cannot be responsible for the universal phenomenon.

4.157 The **Community** submitted that for the purposes of applying Article III:2, taxes must be compared on the same basis as they are levied. Accordingly, in the present case the only relevant comparison is the comparison of rates per volume of beverage. A comparison of rates per volume of alcohol might also be relevant if the specific taxes, though assessed on the volume of beverage, were aimed at taxing the alcohol content. However, Japan has not claimed that the tax rates are proportional to the alcohol content. According to Japan, alcoholic strength is only one of the criteria for classifying distilled spirits under the Liquor Tax Law. However, alcoholic content is not even mentioned in the legal definitions of categories other than shochu. Moreover, a comparison of tax/price ratios, as suggested by Japan, is irrelevant. An accurate comparison of tax price/ratios is, in practice, unfeasible. Unlike tax/volume ratios or *ad valorem* tax rates, tax/price ratios are not transparent. They are not known in advance to the producers, the consumers or even the Government. They can only be estimated retrospectively on the basis of necessarily selective price data which can be easily manipulated.

Furthermore, tax/price ratios are subject to constant change due to variations in prices. The Community argued that an adjustment *a posteriori* of the tax rates to take into account the variations in tax/price ratios, even if carried out on a regular and consistent basis, would not render the Liquor Tax Law neutral. If a higher rate is imposed on a certain category, the less expensive products within that category will be excluded from the market. This will drive down the ratios for the entire category, thus creating the false impression that an upward adjustment, instead of a downward adjustment, is warranted. In any event, there is no legal provision requiring the Japanese authorities to readjust the rates to take into account changes in prices. The Japanese Government is not even required to survey periodically the evolution of the ratios. The periodical readjustment of rates has merely been envisaged by two non-binding recommendations of the Tax Commission, an advisory body, the first of which dates from 1993 only. In practice, the readjustment of rates has been carried out sporadically and in response to foreign pressure. Thus, in order to keep pace with price changes and preserve the neutrality of the system, it would be necessary to readjust the tax rates continuously. This would not only deprive international trade of necessary stability but, in addition, would risk turning the application of the Liquor Tax Law into a matter subject for permanent review by WTO panels. The Community submitted further that the argument that the Liquor Tax Law is "neutral" in terms of tax/price ratios is not new. It was put forward by Japan before the 1987 Panel Report in order to justify the differences in taxation between, on the one hand, special grade whisky and, on the other hand, first and second grade whisky. This argument was rightly disregarded by the 1987 Panel Report which only took into account the differences between the rates per volume.

4.158 In response to a question how one can be assured that the tax/price ratios would be roughly constant across the categories in the future as well, **Japan** argued that one can be assured of it since i) equalization of tax/price ratios across the categories of distilled liquors is firmly rooted in the fundamental principles and philosophy of Japan's tax policy; ii) the Tax Commission in its reports repeatedly requested the Prime Minister to watch tax/price ratios as a continuous exercise, and iii) the division in charge carefully monitors the price developments. Japan argued further that it is a common practice to employ the tax/price ratio in comparing the burden of an excise tax: the British Chancellor of the Exchequer, Mr. Clark, based his tax rate decisions on the "share of the tax in costs" in his budget address; the European Commission's "Excise Duty Rate Tables" - compares the "tax burden in the retail price"; the US Congressional Budget Office report on excise taxes (August 1990) includes a section titled "Federal Tax Rates in Relation to Product Prices"; the Community documents prepared in the course of drafting the liquor tax directive state that a higher tax is necessary for sparkling wine, which is more expensive than still wine, in order not to distort competitive conditions between the two products; and a cartoon indicating the tax ratio in the retail price plays a prominent role in the Scotch Whisky Association's call for a lower tax. Japan noted that the Community initially rejected this approach and embraced both "tax per litre of beverage" and "tax per litre of pure alcohol". For Japan, the Community has thereafter changed its position and argues now that the "tax per litre of beverage" is the only meaningful yardstick because the Japanese tax is levied on the basis of volume of the beverage. The Community's new approach, which allows comparison only on the same basis as taxes are levied, however, would deny any effort to compare those taxes which have different bases. For example, the UK beer tax, which is levied on the basis of the volume of pure alcohol, cannot be compared with the UK wine tax, which is levied on the basis of the volume of beverage. Taxes per tax base cannot be the only yardstick to measure the relative tax burden. Japan reiterated that the purpose of comparing the tax burden here is to judge whether or not the tax has a distortive effect on competitive conditions. The terms of comparison ought to be, therefore, such that would correctly capture the tax's impact on consumer behaviour. Japan submitted the example of a bottle of imported whisky and a bottle of domestic shochu both priced at ¥2,000 before tax. The whisky is contained in a 0.7 litre bottle at 40 per cent alcohol, while the shochu is marketed in a four litre plastic bottle at a 25 per cent strength. If the amount of tax per volume of beverage is equalized, the tax levied on the bottle of shochu must be 5.7 times the tax on the bottle of whisky. Thus, if the whisky is to be taxed ¥700, the shochu must be taxed ¥4,000. Alternatively, if the tax per a quantity of alcohol contained is equalized, the tax on the shochu will be ¥2,500, or 3.6 times the ¥700 tax. In either case, a potential whisky customer is likely to remain undeterred. However, a shochu customer would be forced to alter its choice toward other beverages such as beer or sake. For Japan, this tax would distort consumers' behaviour; in fact the least distortive method is to levy the identical amount if products' before-tax prices are equal; ¥700 tax both on ¥2,000 shochu and ¥2,000 whisky.

4.159 **Canada** recalled that Japan repeatedly asserts that the tax/price ratio between all alcoholic beverages is "roughly constant" and that, accordingly, the Liquor Tax Law does not distort conditions of competition between whisky and shochu. Thus, it follows, in Canada's view that tax/price ratios that are not "roughly constant" show that the Liquor Tax Law distorts conditions of competition between whisky and shochu in favour of domestic shochu production. On the basis of Japan's own evidence that ostensibly summarizes tax/price ratios using suggested retail prices, the Liquor Tax Law does not yield "roughly" equivalent tax/price ratios between distilled liquors. This is made even more clear using tax/price ratios based on on-shelf retail prices. Put simply, in the consumer marketplace where whisky and shochu compete, the tax/price ratios show that the tax differentials between whisky and shochu are clearly skewed in favour of domestic shochu production. For Canada, in stating that "[a] consumer of any category must pay roughly 20 per cent of the expense for the tax", Japan acknowledges that on-shelf retail prices -- the prices that consumers actually pay -- are the appropriate price variable in assessing tax/price equivalency between categories of distilled liquors. In Canada's view, Japan relies on the prices offered at the discount retail outlet "Sake Ichiba Yamada", to show that "at discount prices [the tax/price ratio] is 35 per cent and 40 per cent, respectively, for whisky/brandy and shochu" and thus that "the relation between tax/price ratio of different categories tends to remain the same". However, Canada argued, the prices submitted by Japan reflect only a single discount retail outlet; significantly, in comparison to the whisky and brandy sold at this store in volumes of either 700 or 750 ml sizes, eight of the nine shochu products listed by Japan are sold in very large sizes ranging from 2.7 litres to 5.0 litres that maximize volume discounts in pricing, thereby "driving down the per unit cost of shochu and consequently "grossing-up" the tax/price ratios of shochu". The one shochu product selected having a volume of 720 ml has a tax/price ratio of 25.4 per cent that compares to a tax/price ratio for whisky of similar volume that reaches a high of 52.7 per cent. Indeed, tax/price ratios based on on-shelf retail prices in Japan show that whisky and shochu are subject to a substantial tax differential in favour of shochu:

-        A survey of on-shelf retail prices of shochu Group A, formerly Special Grade whisky and formerly Second Grade whisky (standard and premium labels) shows that the current tax/price ratio for premium imported whisky is 26.4 per cent, for standard imported whisky is 41.7 per cent, for shochu A is 16.6 per cent and for Shochu B is 9.5 per cent.

-        Based on on-shelf retail prices, the tax/price ratio of Canadian whisky shows a similar pattern to the formerly Special Grade whisky and formerly Second Grade whisky surveyed.

-        A more recent survey of on-shelf retail prices of shochu in discount, supermarket and smaller shops in four cities, Tokyo, Osaka, Nagoya and Fukuoka demonstrates tax/price ratios ranging from 10.9 per cent to 23 per cent with most ratios falling between 13 per cent and 18 per cent.

Canada submitted that the tax/price ratio of whisky and shochu is consistently skewed in favour of shochu. Accordingly, whether considered in absolute terms or in terms of tax/price equivalency, the Liquor Tax Law imposes a substantial tax differential between distilled spirits. Clearly, whisky and shochu, two directly competitive or substitutable products, are not similarly taxed (see paragraphs 4.90 to 4.92 above).

4.160 The **Community** also argued that, according to the data submitted by Japan the percentage of taxes on retail prices may vary from only 5 per cent to as much as 22 per cent . Whether it is shochu or the other categories of distilled spirits that bear a higher tax/price ratio lacks any relevance. The evidence shows that the Japanese tax system is far from being "neutral" even in the terms defined by Japan and on the basis of Japan's own price data. Moreover, the method followed by Japan to calculate the tax/retail price ratios grossly and systematically underestimates the ratios for liquors other than shochu while overestimating the ratio for shochu:

-        It does not take into account sales of domestically produced "whisky/brandy", "spirits" and "authentic liqueurs". The retail prices for domestic brands of these categories tend to be lower than the prices for imported brands. As a result, the tax/price ratios of domestic brands are, as a general rule, higher than ratios of imported brands. This difference has been recognised by Japan in a previous estimate provided to the Community during the consultations which shows that, for example, the ratio for imported brands of whisky is within the range of 16.7 per cent to 29.3 per cent, while the ratio for domestic brands may vary from 30.5 per cent to 36.3 per cent. By excluding domestic brands from the calculation, Japan artificially reduces the average ratio for these categories. In the case of "whisky/brandy" and "spirits" this effect is particularly important since domestic brands account for a majority of the total sales.

- Moreover, the effects of the tax/price ratios have been calculated on the basis of weighted average prices. This basis could be considered as representative if the prices for the individual brands stood within a relatively close range. However, the prices for individual brands of "whisky/brandy" and of "spirits" vary considerably. For example, on the basis of Japan's evidence, it may be estimated that the suggested retail prices ("SRP") for whisky range from ¥2,000 to ¥7,000. When calculating the weighted average price for whisky a bottle of ¥7,000 would weigh the same as 3.5 bottles of ¥2,000. In view of this, it is very likely that a majority of the individual sales of whisky covered by Japan's calculation was in fact made below the weighted average price and, therefore, with a tax/price ratio in excess of the one submitted by Japan. Indirect confirmation of this is provided by the fact 14 out of the 20 best selling brands of imported whisky have tax/price ratios above the weighted average ratio.

- SRPs for shochu A and shochu B vary much less. On the basis of Japan's evidence, it may be estimated that 19 out of the 20 best selling brands of shochu A retail at SRPs between ¥700 and ¥1,100. The range of SRPs for shochu B is even shorter. This means that, unlike in the case of "whisky" and "spirits", the actual tax/price ratios for the majority of individual sales of shochu should be close to the weighted average ratios.

- The tax/price ratios have been calculated on the basis of SRPs and not of actual retail prices. Discounts on SRPs are widespread and substantial (in some cases they may represent as much as 70 per cent of the SRP) which renders any comparison on the basis of SRPs a purely theoretical exercise. Discount margins vary considerably from one category to the other. As a general rule, discounts are lower for shochu brands than for brands of other categories. For example, on the basis of the evidence submitted by Japan, the average discount margins for brandy, whisky and shochu offered at the outlet "Sake Ichiba Yamada" are 57.2 per cent, 42.8 per cent and 37.6 per cent respectively. As a result, and contrary to Japan's allegations, the relations between the tax/price ratios of different categories do vary substantially depending on whether the calculation is made on the basis of SRPs or of actual discounted prices. For example, at Sake Ichiba Yamada, the tax/retail prices ratios for whisky and shochu are, on the basis of SRPs, 26.6 per cent and 25.5 per cent, respectively. On the basis of discounted prices, the ratios are 42.8 per cent for whisky and 37.6 per cent for shochu, i.e., the difference, which is of one percentage point on the basis of SPRs, increases to five percentage points on the basis of actual prices.

- The charts submitted by Japan do not take into account the differences in relative prices between bottles of different sizes. Large size bottles tend to be less expensive in relative terms than small bottles and consequently have higher tax/price ratios. Shochu is more frequently sold in large size bottles than the other categories. By lumping together bottles of all sizes when calculating the average tax/prize ratios Japan conceals the fact that the ratio for shochu is much lower than the ratio for other catego-ries when only bottles of the same or similar size are compared. For ex-ample, the tax/discount price ratio for the shochu brand Triangle (the only brand sold in bottles of 0.72 litre which is included in the sample) is only 28.9 per cent. In contrast the average tax/discount price ratio for the sam-pled whisky brands (all of which are sold in 0.7 or 0.75 bottles) is 42.8 per cent, i.e., almost 14 percentage points higher.

4.161 The **United States** submitted that the tax differential today amounts to a 9.6 to 1 differential between whisky and shochu B, a 6.3 to 1 differential between whisky and shochu A, and a 2.4 to 1 differential between spirits and shochu A. At the respective reference values for each, the tax rate per degree alcohol is ¥24.88 for whisky, ¥6.2 for shochu A, and ¥4.08 for shochu B, amounting to a four-to-one differential between whisky and shochu A and a six-to-one differential be-tween whisky and shochu B. From the US point of view, Japan has not offered any convincing policy rationale for this differential. Instead, Japan has asserted that this discrimination simply does not exist. Japan has claimed repeatedly that "the Japanese tax is consistent with Article III because the tax/price ratio is roughly constant between categories, and would not distort consumer choice". Japan had asserted that the tax/price ratio is approximately 20 per cent of the pre-tax retail price but Japan's use of tax/price ratios to gauge tax incidence was mis-guided. For instance, the table used by Japan to support its argument on con-sumer neutrality was based on manufacturers' suggested retail prices for the vari-ous types of distilled spirits. There is a wide gap between those prices and actual retail prices. If the objective were to maintain neutrality with respect to the con-sumer, it is appropriate to use actual prices, not the manufacturer's suggested re-tail price, and to weight the prices per degree of alcohol, in order to account for the fact that most consumers consume distilled spirits in diluted form, diluted to approximately the same strength. The United States referred the Panel to a survey conducted by the European Business Community in Tokyo showing that the tax/price ratio for shochu is 13 to 16 per cent of actual retail prices for shochu A and a mere 9.5 per cent for shochu B. Furthermore, even though actual retail prices for imports had been declining since 1992, the Japanese Government had not reduced the tax rates on whisky, and the liquor tax rates on whisky now rep-resent as much as 35-40 per cent of retail prices. The only plausible explanation is that the Japanese Government has been maintaining a margin of protection for politically-favoured shochu producers. The evidence submitted by Japan shows that the prices for imported whisky and brandy are much more variable than the price of shochu A or B, especially if corrected for differences in alcoholic con-tent. Thus, there appears to be less active price and quality competition in the case of shochu. The Liquor Tax Law's dampening effect on competition may be a cause. In a price survey conducted by the US Embassy in Tokyo in late 1995, a 750ml bottle of Ancient Age Bourbon, sold at ¥1690 bore a tax of ¥736.725, for a tax/price ratio of 43.6 per cent. One premium Bourbon, Wild Turkey, sold for ¥2480 and paid a tax of ¥948, for a tax/price ratio of 37.5 per cent; another, Blantons, sold for ¥3790, was taxed at ¥736.725 for a tax/price ratio of 19.4 per cent. This pattern is repeated in other imported spirits categories. Tax incidence at these levels, and the consequent effect on price, will obviously have a substantial effect on consumer behaviour. Thus, while tax incidence for whiskies is variable and may be quite high, tax incidence for shochu is low and well below the effective tax rate on (imported) whisky. These results are not consistent with Japan's claim of horizontal tax equity or consumer neutrality. Finally, the United States pointed out that the charts and data on tax incidence presented by Japan do not take into account the effect of the low-volume tax exemption for domestically-produced shochu, which lowers the effective tax rate on shochu, is by definition limited to Japanese producers of shochu and further increases the discrimination in tax rates.

4.162 **Japan** responded that it is correct for the complainants to argue that there is a difference in tax/price ratios among categories and that they are not fully equalized. A discrepancy, however, does not necessarily impair competitive conditions of imported distilled liquors *vis-a-vis* domestic shochu. For example, if the ratio is to be strictly equalized at the level of shochu A, the heaviest increase in burden will fall on brandy, and then rum. Although shochu B will have to bear a greater burden, so will whisky, vodka and gin. The burden on shochu A, on the other hand, will remain unchanged. This "full equalization" will not improve competitive conditions of imported distilled liquors *vis-à-vis* domestic shochu. An inevitable fate for a tax policy maker is to make continuous effort to catch up with the market reality. Though an *ad valorem* tax is supposed to automatically reflect the market price developments, regrettably, it usually is outwitted by sophisticated tax evaders. Thus, liquor taxes are not able to fully equalize the tax/price ratio. However, the existing lack of full equalization benefits imported distilled liquors, not domestic shochu, thus resulting in no protective effect. Concerning the argument that Japan's data on tax/price ratio is based on manufacturers' suggested retail prices, which differ from actual on-shelf prices, Japan responded that on-shelf prices in major cities other than Tokyo are fairly close to suggested retail prices. In local cities of a medium to small size, little difference exists between suggested prices and on-shelf prices. After all, the number of "discount" liquor stores in Japan is estimated to be only a few thousand out of a total of 170,000 liquor stores. Moreover, these discount outlets offer both whisky and shochu at discount prices. Japan argued therefore that suggested retail prices are the reliable denominator by which tax/price ratios can be calculated and compared between beverage categories for the Japanese market as a whole. In order to examine the above point, Japan submitted the results of an additional survey which took place on February 14 to 16 of 1996:

-    Two outlets each from department stores, liquor shops, supermarkets and discount stores in each of the three cities of Tokyo, Osaka and Nagoya were selected. For Sapporo, Takamatsu and Fukuoka, one outlet each was chosen for the four channels. In total, 36 outlets were surveyed.

-    On-shelf prices of all the imported brandy, whisky, rum, vodka and gin items, as well as domestic shochu, brandy and whisky items, on display in these outlets were surveyed. The aggregate number of items surveyed amounted to 5,130.

Based on these actual on-shelf prices (some 500 pages of such prices were submitted to the Panel), Japan calculated the tax/price ratios of domestic shochu and imported distilled liquors and Japan was able to conclude that tax/price ratios are roughly equivalent. This figure is based on the actual on-shelf prices of 628 imported brandy items, 1,578 imported whisky items, 186 imported rum items, 183 imported gin items, 219 imported vodka items, 475 domestic shochu A items, and 927 domestic shochu B items.

4.163 In explaining the relevance of tax/price ratios, **Japan** referred to the example of a bottle of imported whisky (0.7 litre, 40 per cent alcohol, pre-tax price of ¥2,000) and a bottle of domestic shochu A (4 litre, 25 per cent alcohol, pre-tax price of ¥,2000). The Community criticized this example as a case of selective reference, and referring to the on-shelf price data in an exhibit submitted by Japan, requested Japan to reformulate the example into that of bottles of imported whisky and domestic shochu both containing 0.7 litre and at ¥1,000 pre-tax. Japan explained that the price shown in the exhibit is after-tax price per a quantity containing the same amount of alcohol as a 0.75 litre, 40 per cent bottle. A pre-tax price of ¥1,000 for a bottle of shochu A containing 0.7 litre at 25 per cent corresponds to ¥1,958. Among 475 items surveyed, no item was at or above ¥1,958. Similarly, among the total of 1,578 imported whisky items surveyed, only 128 bottles, or 8.1 per cent of the total, were with prices at or below the level corresponding to a 0.7 litre, 40 per cent bottle of pre-tax price of ¥1000. Japan noted that the example was used just to illustrate that tax/price ratio is a better indicator than tax per litre of beverage or alcohol, but Japan argued that it did not mean that use of one example alone can demonstrate the appropriateness of its tax rates. Japan also argued that the comparison of tax burden should be made, not by an item by item comparison, but by a comparison between the product groups created by the tax distinction, for example, between the group of imported whisky as a whole and the group of domestic shochu A as a whole. For example, under a flat rate specific tax system, a low-priced imported item has a higher tax/price ratio than a high-priced domestic item. This, however, does not mean that the tax is creating a discriminatory difference in tax burden between imported and domestic products. In the case of a flat rate tax, comparison should be made between the product group of imported distilled liquors as a whole and the product group of domestic distilled liquors as a whole. In response to the allegation by the Community and Canada that the comparison of tax/price ratios was inappropriate since it is based on average price data, Japan responded that the distribution for each category overlaps with each other, indicating roughly constant tax/price ratios across categories. Japan also responded to Canada's argument that tax/price ratios are not fully equalized. Since an *ad valorem* tax cannot be adopted due to the difficulty in securing compliance, the only available choices are 1) a multiple rate specific tax, which Japan currently uses, and 2) a flat rate specific tax, which the federal government of Canada currently uses. Under a multiple rate specific tax, the distribution of tax/price ratios for different categories substantially overlap one another, though perfect equivalence cannot be attained. Under a flat rate specific tax, most domestic shochu would be burdened with higher tax/price ratios than most imported whisky/brandy, creating an extreme discrepancy in burden across categories. According to Japan, all tax authorities can do is to choose from available alternatives the structure which they deem best, and to continue their best efforts to maintain the broad equivalence of tax/price ratios across categories.

3

4.164 The **Community**, **Canada** and the **United States** responded that they did not have enough time to study this additional survey presented to them on the day of the second meeting of the Panel with the parties. The Panel then allowed the complainants to respond in writing to the conclusions of the additional survey submitted by Japan. Then, the **Community** criticized the example used by Japan in the analytical part of its survey and requested Japan to reformulate the example into that of bottles of imported whisky and domestic shochu both containing 0.7 litre and at ¥2000 pre-tax. The Community also argued that the group of products selected for the comparison was inappropriate. The Community argued that even if it was correct that on average the tax rate on imported liquor is roughly the same as that for domestic liquor, as argued by Japan, one can show that the figure is irrelevant for purchasing decisions, and the figure is not the result of the wisdom of the Japanese government, but a simple economic process. The expert of the Community argued that the figure submitted by Japan is irrelevant, because it hides discrimination within market segments, and then submitted a figure which according to him demonstrates for instance that a bottle of shochu with a net price of ¥500 has a tax of ¥76, which implies that the tax increases the price by 15 per cent. By the same token whisky with a net price of ¥500 is burdened with an additional tax burden of 158 per cent. According to the expert of the Community, there exist a tax discrimination in every single market segment. This is true in particular for the low and medium quality brands of whisky and brandy, while for the premium brands the effect is less important. According to the expert of the Community, an important possible counter argument against the evidence submitted by the Japanese could be that the differences in taxes are justified by the different alcohol content of shochu (25 per cent), imported brandy (43 per cent) and whisky (40 per cent). This argument may not be unreasonable and could be taken to justify a tax on whisky that is 1.6 times higher than that on shochu to take this correction factor into account. This correction does not diminish the highly discriminatory nature of the tax system. For the **complainants**, the average tax rate for brandy and whisky is low not because the Japanese government set it low, but because expensive brands are what is left on the shelf, while low and medium quality brandies are driven out of the market through a tax system that very effectively discriminates against this market segment.

4.165 **Canada** argued that the portions of the survey relating to imported whisky are particularly revealing of the fundamental failures in the survey. According to Canada, the whisky samples represented in the survey cover an enormous price range, running upwards from ¥999 to over ¥15,000. Canada noted that since whisky is commonly sold in containers of similar volumes and within a similar range of alcoholic strengths, the tax applicable to each item will be very similar in most cases. Canada stated that with the applicable tax being roughly constant and the prices ranging over a magnitude of 15, the result is necessarily an equally vast range of tax/price ratios. Canada noted by way of example that a 750 ml bottle of 40 degree whisky priced at ¥1500 will have a tax/price ratio of 49 per cent whereas an equivalent premium whisky priced at ¥15000 will have a tax/price ratio of 4.9 per cent. Canada argued that the survey masks this by the artificial imposition of a single tax/price ratio of 17 per cent that purportedly applies to each and every one of the whisky samples in the survey. According to

Canada, when examined on an item-by-item basis, the degree to which tax/price ratios diverge in actual situations from Japan's claimed "rough constant" of 20 per cent becomes obvious. Canada concluded, therefore, that Japan's attempt to use the survey to support its use of suggested retail price falls apart.

4.166 **Japan** also argued that a flat tax rate runs counter to the notion of tax equity: a consumer of gin must pay most of his expenditure as liquor tax, while a consumer of whisky is taxed only a small portion of his expenditure. Similar inequity would result if Japan were to apply a flat-rate tax. Japan recalled that under the Liquor Tax Law consumers of shochu and imported whisky are both paying about one fifth of their expenditure as liquor tax. If a flat rate tax were to be applied to these products at the present whisky tax level, however, shochu consumers would be forced to pay half their expenditure as the liquor tax, while whisky consumers' burden would remain at one fifth of their expenditure. The Tax Commission's following recommendation to the Prime Minister stresses the importance of the tax/price ratio as a yardstick in achieving an appropriate level of the tax burden: "The liquor tax has specific tax rates. When the prices rise, the level of the burden becomes lower. Therefore, it is necessary to review the level from time to time, and to ensure an appropriate level of the burden".

b)   Cross-Price Elasticity)

4.167 **Japan** submitted the results of the survey mentioned in paragraphs 4.83 to 4.89 above, namely a first survey conducted in March 1995 by "Shakai-Chosa Kenkyujo" (Institute for Social Studies) as well as a Summary of Findings of Statistical Analysis based on data taken from the national household survey (a government survey conducted by the Census Bureau of the General Affairs Agency since 1962 on the Japanese household revenues and expenditures) for the 20-year period of 1975 through 1994, which, in Japan's view, confirmed that there is no cross-price elasticity between shochu and other distilled imported liquors and if shochu has any cross-price elasticity with another liquor, one may argue that there is cross-price elasticity between shochu and beer.

4.168 For the **Community**, the Japanese statistical analysis suffered from such problems relating to the data underlying it, the common trends to which they are subject and the limited number of data points (20), that statistical correction techniques reduce the degrees of freedom in the data to such an extent that it becomes highly unlikely that one could ever statistically prove that there is cross-price elasticity of demand between whisky and shochu, even if it existed in reality. The Community also argued that in these circumstances Japan should be required to disprove that there is such cross-elasticity of demand. For the Community, the most important error of the study is that it uses nominal prices instead of deflated ones. This means that statistically the analysis does not distinguish between the price of shochu in 1984 and the price in 1993, which are practically identical in the table. In real terms, however, the price in 1993 was actually substantially lower than in 1984. Taking the average Japanese inflation rate in the 1980s (=1.9 per cent p.a.), there was a real decrease in the price of shochu by roughly 20 per cent. Evidently, the failure to discern a real price change from a nominal price change can lead to spurious results. A proper analysis should therefore use real (i.e., deflated) values to correct for this problem. A major problem of time series analysis in general is that time series are dominated by trends. In the Community's view, if one looks at the raw data, one can see for instance that the consumption of sake steadily decreased while that of beer steadily increased. There could be multiple reasons for this, e.g., changes in taste or successful advertising. In the present case, price plays a relatively small role compared to those factors that are not included in the analysis, except for what is labelled under "trend". The Community continued by arguing that most time series have such an underlying trend. If one took a random time series, e.g., of cucumber production in France, the population of India and shochu consumption in Japan, a naive statistical analysis could "prove" that for the last 20 years shochu consumption in Japan was positively related to cucumber production in France. Evidently, there is no causal relationship just because all three variables follow a common trend. This type of logic is, however, to be found in the Japanese study: Because the consumption of shochu rose at the same time as its price rose (due to inflation), a naive regression will tell you that the higher the price of shochu, the higher will be shochu consumption. This is evidently economic nonsense, but is predictably the result of the regression (expressed as positive own price elasticities in the table).

4.169 In this context, the **Community** submitted a study by Ames and Reiter.[75] They found that an R^2 (the figure that roughly indicates how well the regression explains the dependent variable; a perfect match would mean an R^2 of 1) in excess of 0.5 could be obtained by selecting an economic time series and regressing it against two to six randomly selected time series. If one looks at the data of most regressions undertaken in the Japanese study, the R^2 is lower than that. Thus, most of these regressions do not produce better results than if shochu consumption had been regressed on production of cucumbers. Therefore, the Community argued, in naive time series analysis one can basically show anything. One can econometrically filter out a lot of these spurious relationships, but for every type of correction one looses a degree of freedom in the data. The more complex the analysis is, the more data points you need; 20 data points are hardly enough to correct for the following problems that appear simultaneously:

- There normally is a lagged reaction of consumption to prices. This is because it usually takes a while for consumers to find out or get used to the fact that a certain product now has a different price, and shopping goes often by habit.

- There is a problem of autocorrelation. This means basically that, if a variable is higher than average in one year, it is likely to be so in the following one. For instance, if you have low growth in one year most likely growth will be low in another one. This effect makes your regression less reliable. The Cochrane-Orcutt method is one way of correcting for this problem, if applied correctly.

---

[75] Ames, E. and S. Reiter, "Distributions of Correlation Coefficients in Economic Times Series", *Journal of the American Statistical Association*, 56, 1961, pp. 637-56

-       There is a problem of multicollinearity. This means that variables tend to move in a common direction. If, for instance, at the same time that one independent variable goes up and the other always goes down, it is statistically difficult to separate the effect of one from the other. Because all price as well as the consumption variables are determined by a similar trend, exactly this problem occurs. It is unlikely that under those circumstances the regression parameters are statistically significant.

-       Apart from inflation-caused price increases, variations in real prices appear relatively small. This is important because small variations decrease the likelihood that a parameter can be shown to be statistically significant, i.e., produce reliable estimates. Because there are only 20 data points, in combination with the type of problem listed, it should be clear that it is unlikely that the regression analysis produces significant and/or robust values.

4.170 In response to the Community's attack on Japan's econometric analysis, **Japan** recalled that hypothesis A: "the prices of beer and shochu affect the consumption of shochu" explained the actual data. However, hypothesis B: "the prices of whisky and shochu affect the consumption of shochu" led to a result inconsistent with accepted theory of economics. This is why Japan found hypothesis A reliable and hypothesis B not reliable. Japan recalled that the United States submitted the result of its own analysis of the data it used and concluded that "the annual price indices of whisky and shochu and annual household expenditures do not account for movements in the quantity consumed of these products". In Japan's view, this supports its rejection of hypothesis B. As to the Community's claim that "[t]he most important error in the study is that it uses nominal prices instead of deflated ones", Japan submitted that for further confirmation, Japan ran an additional regression analysis using the deflated prices and deflated household expenditures as variables. The results were similar to the nominal price analysis. Hypothesis A, based on the prices of beer and shochu, could explain the data in a significant manner. However, hypothesis B which attempts to explain shochu consumption by the prices of whisky and shochu once again led to a result not compatible with the accepted economic theory. In sum, for Japan, the most important alleged error does not alter the conclusion. Even though the Community insists that "in naive time series analysis one can basically show anything", neither Japan's initial method, the second method based on the suggestion by the Community itself, nor the method employed by the United States, succeeded in demonstrating that "prices of whisky and shochu affect the consumption of shochu". Japan added that the initial method it used is the one employed by Bossard Consultants in the analysis they completed under engagement by the Community.[76]

---

[76]   As mentioned before, in Japan's view, the Community's criticism of the Japanese study applies equally to the Community's study. Last September, the Commission submitted a report on excise tax to the Council and the European Parliament and convened a conference in Lisbon last November to discuss the report. In the report, the Commission refers to the Bossard study and states that "[g]iven the importance attached in the Directive to this particular issue [of competition between categories of

4.171 **Canada** argued further that the evidence that Japan cites does not refute Canada's allegation and demonstration that consumer choice between shochu and whisky is price responsive. A key pillar in Japan's defense of its claim that whisky and shochu are not directly competitive or substitutable products is a consumer survey purportedly canvassing consumer opinions regarding the alcoholic beverages participants would substitute if a particular beverage was not available. Far from demonstrating that whisky and shochu are not directly competitive or substitutable products, the survey shows that there is a sizeable percentage of Japanese consumers of shochu who would consume whisky if shochu was not available. The survey does not address the fundamental question of the impact of relative price differentials between shochu and whisky on consumer choice. Japan purported to show graphically that declines in sales for both shochu and formerly Second Grade whisky immediately following the imposition of tax rate changes in 1989 indicate that there is no cross-price elasticity between whisky and shochu and thus that the two beverages are not directly competitive or substitutable. The graph yields no such conclusion because a competitive relationship need not manifest itself as an instantaneous shift in cross-price elasticity. Indeed, when considered over the period 1989 through 1994, the graph demonstrates a marked transfer of market share from formerly Second Grade whisky to shochu, reflecting the substantial price differentials during this period of time between formerly Second Grade whisky and shochu. In fact, when the variable "price" is considered in assessing consumer preference between whisky and shochu, the results provide clear evidence that there is significant cross-price elasticity between whisky and shochu and thus that whisky and shochu are directly competitive or substitutable products.

4.172 In response to Japan's denial of a directly competitive or substitutable relationship between shochu and other distilled spirits (as well as of cross-price elasticity between shochu and other distilled spirits), the **Community**, **Canada** and the **United States** submitted the results of a study commissioned by the Liquor Committee of the European Business Community in Tokyo and carried out in February 1996 by ASI Market Research (an independent research institution). Unlike Japan's statistical analysis, the ASI study is not based on the historical analysis of the correlation between price and consumption trends, but on the contemporary reactions of a representative sample of shochu drinkers to a series of 36 different combinations of price levels for shochu and five brown spirits (Scotch Japanese whisky, cognac, Japanese brandy and North American whisky. The same exercise has been carried out with respect to three types of white spirits (gin, vodka and rum). The market research firm drew a sample of 400 drinkers (250 in Tokyo and 150 in Osaka). They selected drinkers aged 20 to 59 who had drunk shochu in the past three months. This sample was drawn for comparability with the sample in Japan's study, and excluded persons associated with the alco-

---

alcoholic beverages], the Commission engaged an independent firm of consultants to assess the extent of such competition" (COM (95) 285 final, 13.09.1995). Did the Commission submit a defective report to the Council and the European Parliament, asked Japan? Did the Commission convene a conference of manufacturers and consumers to discuss an incomplete analysis?

holic beverages industry. The survey-takers showed each person pictures of six types of alcoholic beverages and lists of prices for each, and asked which type of beverage the person would most like to buy given the prices specified. They then proposed a slightly different set of prices, and so on, working through three scenarios of relative prices and products. For the complainants, the ASI study confirms that there is a high degree of cross-price elasticity between shochu and brown spirits as well as between shochu and white spirits, as attested by the results of the following scenarios covered by the study:

-       If the current representative prices for 0.72 litre bottles of brown spirits were reduced by ¥500 (i.e., less than the current tax differential between shochu and "whisky/brandy") and the prices for 0.72 litre bottles of shochu remained fixed at the current representative level, the share of respondents that would buy 0.72 litre shochu bottles instead of equivalent brown spirits bottles would fall from 65.4 per cent to only 37 per cent;

-       A similar result is obtained when the price gap caused by the current difference in taxation is filled by increasing the price of shochu and reducing the prices of brown spirits simultaneously. For instance, if the current representative prices for 0.72 litre bottles of brown spirits fell by ¥300 and the price for 0.72 litre shochu bottles increased by ¥150, the share of shochu consumers would drop from 65.4 per cent to 40.1 per cent.

-       The degree of cross-price elasticity of demand is even higher when consumers are asked to choose between 0.72 litre brown spirit bottles and 1.8 litre shochu bottles. For example, assuming that the current representative prices for 0.72 litre bottles of brown spirits fell by ¥500 and the prices for 1.8 litre bottles of shochu remained fixed at the current representative level, the share of respondents that would buy 1.8 litre shochu bottles instead of 0.72 litre brown spirits bottles would fall from 62.4 per cent to 36.3 per cent.

Based on the foregoing, the report concludes:

"The results showed that consumer purchase preference for Shochu and other distilled spirits has a high degree of price elasticity in relative terms and in absolute terms. ... Thus, it can be inferred that a significant cross-price elasticity of demand between Shochu and brown spirits was demonstrated, suggesting that many Shochu consumers perceive these drinks to be part of a competitive and substitutable repertoire. ...

[I]t is fair to say that there is a conscious decision to consider Shochu as part of the repertoire of brown spirits shown. If it were seen by consumers as a separate drink in its own right, it is unlikely that there would be any shift to the other drinks, except perhaps at the higher price ends as, even at those prices, Shochu is still cheaper. Thus it could be inferred that a fair number of respondents perceive the Shochu and brown spirit categories to be part of a competitive and substitutable repertoire".

The three complainants, each pointed out that the results showed that actual consumer price preferences for shochu and other distilled spirits do have positive price elasticity in both relative and absolute terms. As the relative price gap between shochu and other spirits decreased in the price scenarios, consumer preferences switched progressively from shochu to other spirits. The main beneficiary was usually the lowest-priced alternative spirit in each simulation. As the price of shochu increased relative to its value for the shochu drinkers in the study, they began to switch to brown spirits of their choice, with the more price-conscious of them going for the spirit that was next-lowest in price. As the prices of non-shochu distilled spirits were moved from a level corresponding to the current tax regime for brown spirits to a level corresponding to the current tax regime for shochu, consumer preference shifted still more from shochu to other spirits. The survey shows that brown spirits and shochu have a significant cross-price-elasticity of demand, suggesting that many shochu consumers perceive these drinks as part of a competitive and substitutable repertoire. In addition, the survey found positive, although weaker, cross-price elasticity of demand between shochu and other white spirits such as gin, rum or vodka. The **United States** noted that the ASI study provided real evidence of the discriminatory effect of the tax favoritism shown to shochu by the Japanese political system; the tax differential clearly causes a change *ceteris paribus* in the conditions of competition. The differential also has a clear negative effect on trading opportunities for imported whisky, other brown spirits, and non-shochu white spirits; conversely, removal of the differential would have a clear positive effect on opportunities for these products.

4.173 **Japan** responded that there is a fundamental difference between the choices a real consumer would make and the choices a respondent of the survey is allowed to make. In the real world, consumers may choose beer or sake if the price of shochu increases. Indeed, the Institute for Social Studies found that 35 per cent and 30 per cent of respondents would choose beer and sake, respectively, if shochu were not available. As long as the demand shifts from shochu to beer or sake in response to a rise in the price of shochu, consumption of whisky could not be affected. However, respondents of the ASI survey were not allowed to choose beer, sake or wine. Their choice was confined within the alternatives of whisky, brandy and shochu, or of rum, vodka, gin and shochu. By eliminating more plausible alternatives, the survey forces consumers to consider these products as substitutes. Then Japan presented the example of a survey which would force respondents to choose between a hamburger and ice cream. One who chooses a hamburger if both cost 1 dollar may shift to ice cream if the price of the former rises to 1 dollar 50 cents. This does not prove that a higher price of hamburgers will lead to increased consumption of ice cream in reality. In the real world, consumers are likely to shift to such items as hot dogs, fried chickens, and fish and chips. According to Japan, the ASI's method deprives consumers of real choices and creates an artificial rivalry between products which may not be substitutable. It cannot determine whether or not the goods selected for a survey are competing with each other. At best, it only shows which one of the surveyed goods is relatively, and potentially, competitive with shochu. Moreover, in Japan's view, the Community admits that the differences between whisky/brandy and shochu are so large that the two cannot be regarded as "like products". On the other hand, the ASI report, after comparing the results of a brown spirits survey and a white spirits survey, concluded that "there is a suggestion that, in the white spirit segment, Shochu is not seen as so much of a competitor (i.e., substitutable product) in the eyes of the consumers". The ASI found rum, vodka, and gin are less of a competitor with shochu than whisky and brandy. This, in Japan's view, implies that even from the EC standpoints, rum, vodka and gin cannot be regarded as "like products" with shochu. Second, Japan submitted that the issue before the Panel is not the competition between domestic whisky and domestic shochu, but rather the competition between imported whisky and domestic shochu since Article III concerns itself with national treatment for imported products and not the treatment between two different products as such. The ASI report shows that the only product which will be substantially affected by a rise in the shochu price is domestic whisky, and that it is hard to find a discernible change in the consumption of imported whisky/brandy. The impact of a shochu price change on imported whisky/brandy is not discernible even though other major competitive products are eliminated from the survey. Consequently, Japan argued that it is reasonable to conclude that there is no directly competitive or substitutable relationship between imported whisky/brandy and domestic shochu.

4.174 For **Canada**, the results of the survey confirm the "macro-economic" evidence of changes in market share between shochu and whisky, reflecting relative price differentials between these two products. At the "micro-economic" level, the survey clearly shows that consumer preferences between whisky and shochu respond to the relative price differentials between the two alcoholic beverages. In response to Japan's argument that protective effects should be found if competitive conditions between domestic products and imports are distorted in favour of domestic production, Canada argued that the 1987 Panel Report set out factors that "were sufficient evidence of fiscal distortions of the competitive relationship between imported distilled liquors and domestic shochu" in favour of domestic shochu production: whether shochu and whisky are "mutually substitutable"; whether specific tax rates on shochu are considerably lower than on imported whisky; and whether shochu in Japan is almost exclusively supplied from domestic production. For Canada, the evidence it had submitted to this Panel more than meets these factors and accordingly shows that competitive conditions between domestic products and imports are distorted in favour of domestic production. Thus, applying Japan's own interpretation of the 1992 *Malt Beverages* panel report, the conclusion necessarily follows that the Liquor Tax Law, having a "protective effect", affords protection to Japanese production of shochu.

c) Production of Shochu Outside Japan

4.175 In support of its claim that there were no protective effects, **Japan** submitted that shochu is not inherently Japanese. Shochu does not have its origin in Japan. Its origin is believed to be in Southeast Asia. The product was not consumed by the Japanese until the 14th or the 15th century when it was first introduced from Southeast Asia. The oldest documented evidence of shochu consumption in Japan dates back only to 1559. Even today, consumption of this type of liquor is not an exclusively Japanese phenomenon; on the contrary, the product is widely produced and consumed in Southeast to East Asia. For example, Singapore and Malaysia produce samsoo or samsu, Korea is known for soju production, and some shaojiu in China falls under the shochu definition of the Law.

These products have the following common three features: First, they use grains or potatoes as the base material, which is readily available at low cost in this part of the world. Second, they have a relatively low alcoholic strength. The maximum alcoholic content is about 35 per cent. Third, they are consumed directly after distillation. They do not normally undergo further post-distillation processing. These features constitute essential elements of the definition of shochu under the Liquor Tax Law. For Japan, the definition is nothing more than an attempt to correctly capture these characteristics. Moreover, as more advanced technologies for distillation or post-distillation processing (e.g., aging, purification, flavouring) became available, and as more expensive materials (e.g., grapes, malts) became affordable, this simple, low-cost liquor emerged as a distinct category. The Asian consumers of this product have recognized its identity, as illustrated in their government classifications of alcoholic beverages. The identity of the product has not been artificially created by Japanese law; it exists in many Asian markets and the largest manufacturer of shochu is not Japan but the Republic of Korea. Foreign production of this magnitude facilitates international trade in this product. In 1994, for example, Japan imported 11,244 kl of shochu. The record of the first half of 1995 was 7,465 kl, and the annual volume could be as high as 14,930 kl. These figures are far larger than the 1994 annual importation by Canada of rum, gin and vodka combined (7,471 kl). The share of imports in the Japanese shochu market is increasing. Despite the disadvantage of being an inexpensive, low-margin commodity, the share rose from 0.4 per cent in 1987 to 2.4 per cent in the first half of 1995. It is noteworthy that the share of imports in the US vodka and rum markets was nil until 1975, and grew gradually to 11.6 per cent for vodka and 7.0 per cent for rum by 1993. Were vodka or rum inherently American in 1975, asked Japan?

4.176 In response to Japan's argument that one of the reasons why the Liquor Tax Law does not have a protectionist effect is because shochu is not an "inherently Japanese product" but, rather, a liquor which is "widely produced and consumed in Southeast to East Asia", the **Community** responded that whether or not shochu is produced in other countries and, if so, in how many countries, is of no relevance. The only relevant fact is that imports of shochu represent an insignificant fraction of the total sales of shochu in Japan (1.7 per cent in 1994). In contrast, during the same year, imports from third countries accounted for 27 per cent of the total sales of whisky, 29 per cent of the total sales of brandy, 18 per cent of the total sales of spirits and 78 per cent of the total sales of authentic liqueurs. Moreover, sales of domestically produced shochu account for almost 80 per cent of the total sales of domestically produced distilled spirits and authentic liqueurs. Thus, it is indisputable that by giving a privileged tax treatment to shochu, Japan affords protection to its domestic production of distilled spirits. In the Community's view, Japan's argument is based on a misreading of the 1987 Panel Report. The 1987 Panel Report did not hold that the lack of production of the less taxed product in other countries was a necessary condition for a finding of protectionist effect. The 1987 Panel Report records Japan's argument to the effect that "a certain volume [of shochu] was imported from abroad including the EC countries". This fact was not disputed by the other parties. The Panel, therefore, was aware that shochu was produced in an indeterminate number of other countries. Moreover, whether the production of shochu in other countries was significant was an issue not raised by any of the parties to the dispute. In the Community's view, the Panel, therefore, had no grounds whatsoever to infer that most of the world production of shochu was confined to Japan. In view of these contextual elements, the statement in the 1987 Panel Report that "shochu was almost exclusively produced in Japan" can only be read as meaning that the shochu sold in Japan was almost exclusively produced in that country. The Community submitted that in any event, aside from learned etymological considerations, Japan provided very little evidence in the way of proving that shochu or something resembling shochu is in fact produced in any significant quantities in other Asian countries:

- Japan admitted in a footnote that the majority of Chinese "shaojiu" has a higher alcohol content than shochu with the consequence that only a deliberately unspecified "part" of shaojiu falls within the definition of shochu. Moreover, the differences in alcohol content between shochu and shaojiu (which according to Japan are the same product) refute Japan's assertions that a low alcohol content is a "historically developed feature" of shochu and that the lack of a high alcohol content constitutes one of the "core" characteristics of shochu in the Asian market.

- No data concerning the volume of production of "samsu" in Singapore and Malaysia has been made available, which may suggest that it is not significant. Moreover, it is not specified whether all the production of Singaporean and Malaysian samsu or only "part" (as in the case of Chinese shaojiu) falls within the Japanese definition of shochu. In this connection it is worth noting that the Malaysian liquor referred to by Japan is called "likeur" (dutch for liqueur). This casts some doubt on the alleged existence of a family of shochu-like products of common Asian origin.

- Most imports of shochu into Japan seem to originate in Korea. Nonetheless, it remains uncertain whether all the Korean production qualifies as shochu under the Liquor Tax Law.

The Community further argued that in any event whether there is production of shochu outside Japan is of no relevance for the interpretation of the first sentence of Article III:2. There are imported "like products", i.e., the other white spirits, and they are taxed "in excess" of the like domestic product. If there is also imported shochu on the Japanese market this means that an infringement of Article I:1 *juncto* Article III:2 is added to the infringement of Article III:2 alone, not that the infringement of Article III:2 disappears. *A fortiori*, the infringement of Article III:2 does not disappear where there is only potential import of shochu from other sources.

4.177 **Japan** responded that the Community (as well as Canada and the United States) seemed to contradict its initial arguments. For example, the Community initially stated "the following criteria may be relevant in order to determine whether a difference in taxation is 'protective' of the domestic production: ... whether the less taxed product is produced in other countries ... ". In its second submission, it argued "the Community notes that whether or not shochu is produced in other countries and, if so, in how many countries, is of no relevance".

Arguing that the complaining parties were unanimous in their first written submission in referring to "production outside Japan" rather than to "the level of imports", Japan also submitted that Canada underpinned its complaint of protection by "the almost exclusive production in Japan of shochu" and that the United States argued "the creation of inherently domestic products" was the evidence of protective effect. In Japan's view, the Community rationalizes the Panel's recognition of shochu production outside Japan, and stated that the panel's finding to the effect "that shochu is almost exclusively produced in Japan" ought to be understood as a reference to the import ratio. Japan cited the relevant passage of the report: " ... the fact that shochu was almost exclusively produced in Japan and that the lower taxation of shochu did 'afford protection to domestic production' rather than to the production of a product produced in many countries (say, butter) in relation to another product (say, oleomargarine)".[77] For Japan, it is obvious that the contrast the panel made between a product "produced in many countries" and a product "almost exclusively produced in Japan" relates not to the import ratio but to production abroad. Japan also referred the Panel to the paragraph 5.73 of the 1992 *Malt Beverages* panel report which, in Japan's view, did not review the import ratio but focused its analysis on production abroad. Therefore, for Japan, "protectiveness" ought to be judged not by the import ratio but by foreign production. Japan argued that the import ratio depends on the marketing strategy, the exchange rate and other factors, and the level of the ratio has nothing to do with whether or not the product is inherent in a particular country. The import ratio of shochu in the first half of 1995, for example, was 2.4 per cent in Japan. This figure is equal to the import ratio of vodka in the United States in 1980. The import ratio of beer into Canada was 2.9 per cent in 1994, while that of Japan in the same year was 4.2 per cent. The level of the import ratio of shochu in Japan is comparable to those of other international products in open markets.

4.178 **Japan** reiterated that shochu's origin is in Southeast Asia. The word "shochu" is derived from Chinese. Its largest producer is either the Republic of Korea or the People's Republic of China. There is nothing inherently Japanese in materials or production methods. Germany's korn falls under the shochu definition. Shochu is also produced in Singapore, Malaysia, Vietnam, the United States, Canada and France. Over 90 per cent of the materials used in the production of shochu A are imported, and more than half the rice (smashed rice) used to produce shochu B is imported. Shochu is indeed an international product. As for the identity of Chinese "shaojiu" with shochu, the fact is, there are two categories of shaojiu with high and low alcohol content, and, out of 371 shaojiu brands on display at China's fifth national shaojiu exhibition of 1989, 135 brands, or 36 per cent of the total, belonged to the low alcohol category. The volume of shaojiu production is about 8 times larger than that of Japan's shochu production; 36 per cent of the volume dwarfs Japan's shochu production by 3 to 1 and the UK Scotch production by 2 to 1. In response to the Community's doubt on the production quantity and the identity of samsu or samsoo of Malaysia and Singapore,

---

[77]   1987 Panel Report, para. 5.11.

Japan argued that the product is given an independent tax category, and thus, the production quantity must be sufficiently large to justify such categorization. On the issue of its identity, Japan noted that the product consists of "alcohol and water" according to the label of the samsu bottle. Judging from the contents as well as the low level of alcohol strength, Japan stated that it was confident that it falls under the shochu definition. Finally, the expression of "likeur" on the bottle of Malaysia's samsu means "liquor" and not "liqueur", according to its enquiry in Malaysia. Japan also stated that the liquor tax legislation of the Republic of Korea defines soju in two sub-categories of diluted soju, which is equivalent to shochu A, and "distilled soju, which is equivalent to shochu B, in a manner similar to Japan's definition. Essentially, shochu and soju are identical products. Japan submitted that since the relationship between shochu and whisky has been discussed, reference should be made to domestic production of whisky as well. In Japan's view, the United States employs an evenhanded criterion of "whether the categorization creates an inherently domestic or foreign product". Moreover, the European Commission has argued before the ECJ, that, if a country domestically produces both of the two categories at issue, an origin-neutral taxation will not go against the national treatment obligation, and that the relationship between the two is only a matter of harmonization.[78] Japan informed the Panel that it is the world's fifth largest manufacturer of whisky. In Japan's view, the Liquor Tax Law applies an origin-neutral tax to shochu which is produced in large quantities overseas, and to other distilled liquors which are domestically produced in large quantities. The Liquor Tax Law cannot have protective effect.

4.179 The **United States** recalled that imports of shochu were nonexistent in 1962 when the Liquor Tax Law was amended to insert the present categorization of distilled spirits. This categorization was designed to perpetuate the market situation of 1962 when all imports into Japan were subject to import quotas. Shochu could still be characterized as a Japanese product benefiting from discriminatory low tax rates. Indeed, the United States argued, when a system of tax classifications had been designed during such a period of absolute protection, the categorization of products based on their status during the quota period had to be re-evaluated after balance-of-payments quotas had been lifted.

d) Import Statistics

4.180 **Japan** argued that according to the Japanese customs statistics, the import volume of Scotch whisky into Japan remained roughly equal from 23,473 kl in 1987 to 23,705 kl in 1994. In contrast, the import volume of Bourbon whisky grew 90 per cent from 5,998 kl in 1987 to 11,178 kl in 1994. Canadian whisky showed similar growth in the same period from 1,046 kl to 2,195 kl, recording a growth of 110 per cent. It is puzzling why Scotch whisky alone was not successful in exploiting such favourable conditions as the substantial decline in tax and the appreciation of the yen's value. This, in Japan's view, is not a case of failure

---

[78] The European Commission v. The United Kingdom ("Wine and Beer"), Case 170/78, 12 July 1983, [1983] ECR p. 2265.

but success in their pricing policy. Although the volume of imports remained constant, the value of the Scotch imports more than doubled from 82 million pounds sterling in 1987 to 199 million pounds sterling in 1994. Moreover, according to "The Scotch whisky Industry Review" by Alan S. Gray, the rate of gross margin in the price of Scotch whisky increased over the period from 47 per cent to 60 per cent. With such increases in revenue and in margin ratios, the amount of margin in the exportation of Scotch whisky to Japan must have grown more than threefold. The Scotch whisky industry did exploit the decline in the tax and the higher value of the yen, through a strategy emphasizing the value of imports as opposed to the volume, and successfully scooped gross profits three times the amount of 1987 out of the same volume of trade. In other words, all of the Scotch industry, the Bourbon industry and the Canadian whisky industry have been enormously successful in their trade with Japan since 1987.

4.181 **Canada** responded that the *Superfund* panel report and the 1987 Panel Report have firmly rejected the notion that the trade effects of a measure are relevant in determining the consistency of the measure with Article III:2. On the presumption of "an adverse impact", the *Superfund* panel report, the 1987 Panel Report and the 1992 *Malt Beverages* enunciated the principle that overall increases in market share for imports of the products in issue does not constitute a rebuttal. Indeed, the *Superfund* case articulates the principle that a finding of fiscal distortion in the competitive relationship between imported and domestic products constitutes an "irrefutable presumption" of nullification and impairment of benefits. Given the principle enunciated in the *Superfund* case, it is within the context of the fiscal distortion of the competitive relationship between imported and domestic alcoholic beverages that the Panel, and ultimately the DSB, must evaluate the consistency of the Liquor Tax Law with Article III:2, second sentence.

V.   INTERIM REVIEW

5.1   On 28 May 1996, Japan, United States and Canada requested the Panel to review, in accordance with Article 15.2 of the DSU, precise aspects of the interim report that had been issued to the parties on 20 May 1996; Japan and the United States requested the Panel to hold a meeting for that purpose. The Panel met with the parties on 6 June 1996 to hear their arguments concerning the interim report. The Panel carefully reviewed the arguments presented by the parties.

5.2   In approaching the interim review stage, the Panel drew guidance from Article 15.2 DSU which states that "a party may submit a written request for the panel to review precise aspects of the interim report prior to circulation of the final report to the Members". Whilst the Panel was willing to approach the interim review stage with the broadest possible interpretation of Article 15.2 DSU, it was of the view that the purpose of the review meeting is not to provide the parties with an opportunity to introduce new legal issues and evidence, or to enter into a debate with the Panel. In the view of the Panel, the purpose of the interim review stage is to consider specific and particular aspects of the interim report.

Consequently, the Panel addressed the entire range of such arguments presented by the parties which it considered to be sufficiently specific and detailed.

5.3   The United States submitted to the Panel and the parties at the review meeting copies of press reports relating to the interim report. After a brief discussion on the need to maintain confidentiality, the Panel appealed and all parties to the dispute agreed, on the utmost importance of maintaining confidentiality so as to preserve the credibility and integrity of the dispute settlement process.

5.4   With respect to the legal status of adopted panel reports, the United States argued that nothing in GATT 1994 modified the status they had enjoyed under GATT 1947 and that they thus should not be considered as subsequent practice in the sense of Article 31 of the Vienna Convention on the Law of the Treaties (VCLT). The Panel drew the attention of the United States to paragraph 6.10 of the report. In order to clarify its position, the Panel introduced some drafting modifications in the panel report.

5.5   In respect of the discussion of Article III:2 in the interim report, both Japan and the United States argued that the Panel should not have rejected their approach according to which the benchmark to evaluate whether domestic legislation is in breach of the obligations contained in Article III:2 is the aim-and-effect test that they felt had its basis in the phrase "so as to afford protection" in Article III:1. The Panel took note of the arguments of the United States and Japan which had been the subject of detailed and serious considerations throughout its deliberations, but for the reasons spelled out in paragraph 6.11ff. the Panel decided not to take any further action in this respect.

5.6   Japan argued that with respect to Article III:2, the Panel's overall approach would lead to findings of violations of Article III:2 by virtually all tax distinctions. The Panel could not subscribe to Japan's position. The Panel reiterated that its task was circumscribed by its terms of reference which required it to review the consistency of the Japanese taxation system with respect to certain alcoholic beverages *vis-à-vis* Japan's obligation under Article III:2. The Panel consequently limited its conclusions to the subject-matter circumscribed by its terms of reference.

5.7   In respect of the Panel's discussion on "like products", Japan argued that under the Harmonized System (HS) nomenclature shochu and vodka no longer appear under the same heading. The Panel took note of the statement and, whilst not sharing the legal conclusion by Japan, the Panel proceeded to make certain drafting changes in paragraph 6.22 in order to clarify its point of view.

5.8   Japan argued that the tax/price ratio for domestic shochu A is higher than that for imported vodka, and, consequently, shochu A should be excluded from the Panel's finding in paragraph 6.27 that Japan violated its obligation under Article III:2, first sentence. The Panel did not share this opinion but felt that it should further explain its position. The additional discussion by the Panel of this point is reflected in paragraph 6.25.

5.9   In respect of the distinction between "like products" on the one hand, and, "directly competitive or substitutable products" on the other, the United States argued that the Panel did not offer any clear distinguishing criteria between the two categories. In response, the Panel expanded its analysis of this distinction in paragraph 6.23.

5.10   The United States argued that the Panel did not offer any useful criteria concerning the interpretation of the term "dissimilar taxation" that the Panel uses in the report. More particularly, the United States argued that the Interpretative Note ad Article III, second paragraph, contained language that could be considered as a necessary condition in order to establish a violation of Article III:2, second sentence, but that it was questionable whether the same language could be considered as sufficient for the same purpose. The Panel added language in paragraph 6.33 to address this argument.

5.11   Japan argued that the complainants did not offer any evidence on liqueurs and that, consequently, liqueurs should be excluded from the findings in paragraph 6.33 that Japan violated its obligations under Article III:2, second sentence. The Panel was not persuaded by the arguments advanced by Japan but added language in paragraph 6.28 in order to clarify the Panel's position.

5.12   The United States argued that the Panel's analysis of the phrase "directly competitive or substitutable products" established a requirement to show adverse trade effects as a condition for establishing a violation of Article III. The Panel added language in paragraph 6.33 to make it clear that it follows the reasoning and the conclusions of previous panel reports on this issue and that the Panel felt that there is no need to examine trade effects in the context of Article III, since Article III deals with conditions of competition. A factual determination of whether two products are directly competitive or substitutable is a necessary precondition in order to apply the legal test of dissimilar taxation. In the Panel's view, this determination takes place in the marketplace and does not mean at all that Article III has been made subject to an effects test.

5.13   Japan requested the Panel to suggest specific ways to bring its measures into compliance with its obligations under Article III:2. The Panel recalled its recommendation in paragraph 7.2, which is consistent with Article 19 DSU, that Japan bring its measures into compliance with the provisions of Article III:2.

5.14   With regard to some other issues raised by the United States, the Panel recalled that the only panel report that contains an analysis of "like products" similar to that of 1992 *Malt Beverages* is an unadopted panel report that had followed the same reasoning. The Panel also recalled its findings in paragraph 6.21 where it stated that a product's description in a tariff binding is an "important criterion for confirming likeness" and that "this does not mean that the determination of whether products are 'like' should be based exclusively on the definition of products for tariff bindings".

5.15   Japan, the United States and Canada made a number of suggestions concerning language changes that the Panel accepted and introduced in its final report.

5.16   In respect of the interim report's descriptive section, Japan suggested further changes which the Panel took into account in re-examining that part of the report. The Panel revised the descriptive section of the final report where it accepted the need for these changes.

VI.   FINDINGS

A.   Claims of the Parties

6.1   The Community requests the Panel to find that vodka, gin, (white) rum, genever and shochu are like products and that Japan, by taxing the other four products in excess of shochu violates Article III:2, first sentence. In the event that the Panel does not find the aforementioned products to be like products, the Community requests the Panel to find that they are directly competitive and substitutable products and that Japan, by taxing vodka, gin, (white) rum and genever higher than shochu has failed to observe its obligations under Article III:2, second sentence. The Community further requests the Panel to find that whisky, brandy, liqueurs and shochu are directly competitive and substitutable products and that Japan, by taxing the first three products higher than the latter, violates its obligations under Article III:2, second sentence.

6.2   Canada requests the Panel to find that whisky, brandy, other distilled alcoholic beverages, and liqueurs on the one hand, and shochu, on the other, are directly competitive and substitutable products and that Japan by taxing the former higher than the latter violates its obligations under Article III:2, second sentence.

6.3   The United States requests the Panel to find that white and brown spirits are like products in the sense of Article III:2, first sentence, and, therefore, that the difference in tax treatment by Japan between shochu and vodka, gin, rum and other white spirits, as well as whisky, brandy and other brown spirits, is inconsistent with Article III:2, first sentence. If the Panel is not able to make such a finding, the United States request, in the alternative, that the Panel find that all white spirits are like products in terms of Article III:2, first sentence, and that all distilled spirits are directly competitive and substitutable products in terms of Article III:2, second sentence. In the latter case, the United States requests the Panel to find that the difference in taxation by Japan under its Liquor Tax Law in favour of shochu materially alters the conditions of competition between shochu and other distilled spirits and that Japan thus violates its obligations under Article III:2, second sentence. The United States further claims that the small-volume producer exemption from excise taxes provided under Japan's Taxation Special Measures Law is limited to Japanese producers and that Japan thus fails to respect its obligations under Article III:2, first sentence.

6.4   Japan requests the Panel to find that its taxation system does not violate Article III. Japan claims that the purpose of the tax classification under the Liquor Tax Law is not to afford protection and does not have the effect of protecting domestic production. Japan further argues that spirits, whisky/brandy and liqueurs are not "like products" to either category of shochu, within the meaning of Article III:2, first sentence, nor are they "directly competitive or substitutable products" to shochu, within the meaning of Article III:2, second sentence. Finally, Japan requests the Panel to reject the claim by the United States with respect to its Taxation Special Measures Law because it lies outside the terms of reference of the Panel.

B.   Preliminary Finding

6.5   The Panel first turned to the United States' claim with respect to the Japanese Taxation Special Measures Law. The Panel noted that Japan argued that the claim of the United States is not part of the terms of reference of the Panel. The Panel further noted that its terms of reference, following from Articles 7 and 11 DSU, are circumscribed in WT/DS8/6, WT/DS10/6 and WT/DS11/3. The Panel noted that no mention of the Japanese Taxation Special Measures Law is included in WT/DS8/6, WT/DS10/6 and WT/DS11/3. The Panel concluded that its terms of reference do not permit it to entertain the claim of the United States with respect to the Japanese Taxation Special Measures Law and it proceeded, therefore, to examine the other claims.

C.   Main Findings

6.6   The Panel noted that the complainants are essentially claiming that the Japanese Liquor Tax Law is inconsistent with GATT Article III:2 (hereinafter "Article III:2"). Article III:2 reads:

> "The products of the territory of any contracting party imported into the territory of any other contracting party shall not be subject, directly or indirectly, to internal taxes or other internal charges of any kind in excess of those applied, directly or indirectly, to like domestic products. Moreover, no contracting party shall otherwise apply internal taxes or other internal charges to imported or domestic products in a manner contrary to the principles set forth in paragraph 1*".[79]

GATT Article III:1 (hereinafter "Article III:1), which is referred to in Article III:2, reads:

> "The contracting parties recognize that internal taxes and other internal charges, and laws, regulations and requirements affecting the internal sale, offering for sale, purchase, transportation, distribution or use of products, and internal quantitative regulations requiring the mixture, processing or use of products in specified amounts or proportions, should not be applied to imported or domestic products so as to afford protection to domestic production*".[80]

In addition, the Panel noted that there is an Interpretative Note ad Article III, Paragraph 2, which is relevant to this case. The Note reads:

> "A tax conforming to the requirements of the first sentence of paragraph 2 would be considered to be inconsistent with the provisions of the second sentence only in cases where competition was involved between, on the one hand, the taxed product and, on the other hand, a directly competitive or substitutable product which was not similarly taxed".

---

[79] The asterisk in Article III:2 refers to the Interpretative Note ad Article III, Paragraph 2 that is quoted infra.

[80] The asterisk in Article III:1 refers to the Interpretative Note ad Article III, Paragraph 1 that is not quoted because it refers to an unrelated issue.

The Panel noted that the Interpretative Note ad Article III, Paragraph 2, is contained in Annex I to GATT 1994. The Panel noted, in this respect, that Article XXXIV of GATT 1994 provides:

> "The annexes to this Agreement are hereby made an integral part of this Agreement".

1. General Principles of Interpretation

6.7   The Panel understood the dispute among the parties over the appropriate legal analysis to be applied in this case required it to interpret the wording of Article III:2. The Panel recalled that Article 3:2 DSU states:

> " ... The Members recognize that [the WTO dispute settlement system] serves to preserve the rights and obligations of Members under the covered agreements, and to clarify the existing provisions of those agreements in accordance with customary rules of interpretation of public international law".

The Panel noted that the "customary rules of interpretation of public international law" are those incorporated in the Vienna Convention on the Law of Treaties (VCLT). GATT panels have previously interpreted the GATT in accordance with the VCLT.[81] The Panel noted that Article 3:2 DSU in fact codifies this previously-established practice. The Panel also noted that there is no disagreement among the parties to proceed on this basis.

6.8   In the view of the Panel, Articles 31 and 32 VCLT provide the relevant criteria in the light of which Article III:2 should be interpreted. The Panel recalled that Articles 31 and 32 VCLT state:

> *"Article 31   General rule of interpretation*
>
> 1.   A treaty shall be interpreted in good faith in accordance with the ordinary meaning to be given to the terms of the treaty in their context and in the light of its object and purpose.
>
> 2.   The context for the purpose of the interpretation of a treaty shall comprise, in addition to the text, including its preamble and annexes:
>
> (a)   any agreement relating to the treaty which was made between all the parties in connection with the conclusion of the treaty;
>
> (b)   any instrument which was made by one or more parties in connection with the conclusion of the treaty and accepted by the other parties as an instrument related to the treaty.
>
> 3.   There shall be taken into account together with the context:

---

[81]   See, for example, the panel report on "Japan - Customs Duties, Taxes and Labelling Practices on Imported Wines and Alcoholic Beverages", adopted on 10 November 1987, BISD 34S/83 (hereinafter "the 1987 Panel Report"); see also the panel report on "EC - Imposition of Anti-dumping Duties on Imports of Cotton Yarn From Brazil", ADP/137, adopted on 30 October 1995, paras. 540ff.; see also the Appellate Body report on "United States - Standards for Reformulated and Conventional Gasoline", WT/DS2/AB/R, adopted on 20 May 1996.

(a)   any subsequent agreement between the parties regarding the interpretation of the treaty or the application of its provisions;

(b)   any subsequent practice in the application of the treaty which establishes the agreement of the parties regarding its interpretation;

(c)   any relevant rules of international law applicable in the relations between the parties.

4.   A special meaning shall be given to a term if it is established that the parties so intended.

Article 32   Supplementary means of interpretation

Recourse may be had to supplementary means of interpretation, including the preparatory work of the treaty and the circumstances of its conclusion, in order to confirm the meaning resulting from the application of article 31, or to determine the meaning when the interpretation according to article 31:

(a)   leaves the meaning ambiguous or obscure; or

(b)   leads to a result which is manifestly absurd or unreasonable".

6.9   Consequently, the Panel concluded that the starting point of an interpretation of an international treaty, such as the General Agreement on Tariffs and Trade 1994, in accordance with Article 31 VCLT, is the wording of the treaty. The wording should be interpreted in its context and in the light of the object and the purpose of the treaty as a whole and subsequent practice and agreements should be taken into account. Recourse to supplementary means of interpretation should be made exceptionally only under the conditions specified in Article 32 VCLT. The Panel noted that none of the parties to the present dispute argued that recourse to supplementary means of interpretation was necessary.

6.10   In this respect, the Panel noted that no formal subsequent agreement as to the interpretation of Article III:2 exists among the WTO Members. The Panel noted that other GATT and WTO panels have interpreted Article III and that panel reports adopted by the GATT CONTRACTING PARTIES and the WTO Dispute Settlement Body constitute subsequent practice in a specific case by virtue of the decision to adopt them. Article 1(b)(iv) of GATT 1994 provides institutional recognition that adopted panel reports constitute subsequent practice. Such reports are an integral part of GATT 1994, since they constitute "other decisions of the CONTRACTING PARTIES to GATT 1947". The Panel noted that Article 1(b)(iv) does not provide a hierarchy among "other decisions of the CONTRACTING PARTIES to GATT 1947". Moreover, the Panel noted that the panel report on "European Economic Community - Restrictions on Imports of Dessert Apples - Complaint by Chile"[82] (hereinafter "the 1989 Panel") had concluded that:

"... It would take into account the 1980 Panel report and the legitimate expectations created by the adoption of this report, but also

---

[82]   Panel report adopted on 22 June 1989, BISD 36S/93, para. 12.1.

other GATT practices and panel reports adopted by the CONTRACTING PARTIES and the particular circumstances of this complaint. The Panel, therefore, did not feel it was legally bound by all the details and legal reasoning of the 1980 Panel report".

As a consequence, the 1989 Panel independently examined whether certain EEC measures restricted the marketing of products and reached a different conclusion than had the 1980 Panel.[83] In light of the foregoing, the Panel was of the view that panel reports adopted by the CONTRACTING PARTIES constitute subsequent practice in a specific case and as such have to be taken into account by subsequent panels dealing with the same or a similar issue. The Panel noted, however, that it does not necessarily have to follow their reasoning or results. The Panel further noted that unadopted panel reports have no legal status in the GATT or WTO system since they have not been endorsed through decisions by the CONTRACTING PARTIES to GATT or WTO Members. Thus, the Panel decided that it did not have to take them into account as they do not constitute subsequent practice. In the Panel's view, however, a panel could nevertheless find useful guidance in the reasoning of an unadopted panel report that it considered to be relevant.

2. *Article III*

6.11   The Panel proceeded on the basis of the interpretative rule of the VCLT by turning first to the wording of Article III:2. The Panel noted that Article III:2 is concerned with two different factual situations: Article III:2, first sentence, is concerned with the treatment of like products, whereas Article III:2, second sentence, is concerned with the treatment of directly competitive or substitutable products, i.e., products other than like products, since no mention of like products is made in Article III:2, second sentence. In the Panel's view, the inclusion of the words "moreover" and "otherwise" in the second sentence of Article III:2 makes this point clear. The Interpretative Note ad Article III:2 further clarifies this distinction by providing an example where the first sentence of Article III:2 is not violated whereas the second is, thus confirming the existence of two distinct obligations in Article III:2.

6.12   The Panel, having established the basis for interpretation of Article III:2, turned to an examination of its elements. The Panel noted that while Article III:2, second sentence, contains a reference "to the principles set forth in paragraph 1", no such reference is contained in Article III:2, first sentence. The Panel recalled that according to Article III:1, WTO Members recognize that domestic legislation "should not be applied ... so as to afford protection to domestic production". In this context, the Panel felt that it was necessary to examine the relationship between Article III:2 and Article III:1. The Panel noted that the latter contains general principles concerning the imposition of internal taxes, internal charges, and laws, regulations and requirements affecting the treatment of imported and

---

[83]   See the panel report on "EEC - Restrictions on Imports of Apples from Chile", adopted on 10 November 1980, BISD 27S/98.

domestic products, while the former provides for specific obligations regarding internal taxes and internal charges. The words "recognize" and "should" in Article III:1, as well as the wording of Article III:2, second sentence, ("the principles"), make it clear that Article III:1 does not contain a legally binding obligation but rather states general principles. In contrast, the use of the word "shall" in Article III:2, both sentences, makes it clear that Article III:2 contains two legally binding obligations. Consequently, the starting point for an interpretation of Article III:2 is Article III:2 itself and not Article III:1. Recourse to Article III:1, which constitutes part of the context of Article III:2, will be made to the extent relevant and necessary.

6.13   The Panel then turned to other contextual elements that have to be taken into account, as required by Article 31 VCLT. The Panel noted in this respect the relationship between Articles II and III of GATT 1994. The Panel concluded, as had previous panels that dealt with the same issue, that one of the main purposes of Article III is to guarantee that WTO Members will not undermine through internal measures their commitments under Article II. The Panel noted in this respect that an adopted panel report that had dealt with this issue had stated that:

> "... one of the basic purposes of Article III was to ensure that the contracting parties' internal charges and regulations were not such as to frustrate the effect of tariff concessions granted under Article II ...".[84]

The Panel further took note of the fact that another adopted panel report concluded on the same issue that:

> "...The most-favoured-nation requirement in Article I, and also tariff bindings under Article II, would become ineffective without the complementary prohibition in Article III on the use of internal taxation and regulation as a discriminatory non-tariff trade barrier".[85]

3.   Article III:2, First Sentence

a)   Overview

6.14   In light of the foregoing, the Panel then proceeded to an analysis of how the legal obligations imposed by Article III:2, first sentence, should be interpreted. In this context, the Panel recalled the divergent views of the parties to the dispute: the Panel noted that, with respect to like products, the Community essentially argued in favour of a two-step procedure whereby the Panel should establish first whether the products in question are like and, if so, then proceed to examine whether taxes imposed on foreign products are in excess of those im-

---

[84]   See the panel report on "Canada - Import, Distribution and Sale of Certain Alcoholic Drinks by Provincial Marketing Agencies", adopted on 18 February 1992, BISD 39S/27, paras. 5.30 - 5.31.
[85]   See the panel report on "United States - Measures Affecting Alcoholic and Malt Beverage", adopted on 19 June 1992, BISD 39S/206, para. 5.9 (the "1992 *Malt Beverages*" report). See also the discussion in para. 6.21.

posed on like domestic products. The Community had stated that physical characteristics of the products concerned, their end-uses, as well as consumer preferences could provide relevant criteria for the Panel to judge whether the products concerned were like. The Panel noted in this respect, that complainants have the burden of proof to show first, that products are like and second, that foreign products are taxed in excess of domestic ones.

6.15   The Panel further took note of the statements by Japan that essentially argued that the Panel should examine the contested legislation in the light of its aim and effect in order to determine whether or not it is consistent with Article III:2. According to this view, in case the aim and effect of the contested legislation do not operate so as to afford protection to domestic production, no inconsistency with Article III:2 can be established. The Panel further took note of the statement by the United States that essentially argued that, in determining whether two products that were taxed differently under a Member's origin-neutral tax measure were nonetheless "like products" for the purposes of Article III:2, the Panel should examine not only the similarity in physical characteristics and end-uses, consumer tastes and preferences, and tariff classifications for each product, but also whether the tax distinction in question was "applied ... so as to afford protection to domestic production": that is, whether the aim and effect of that distinction, considered as a whole, was to afford protection to domestic production. According to this view, if the tax distinction in question is not being applied so as to afford protection to domestic production, the products between which the distinction is drawn are not to be deemed "like products" for the purpose of Article III:2. The Panel noted that the United States and Japan reached opposite results by applying essentially the same test. Japan concluded that its legislation did not have the aim or effect of affording protection, while the United States concluded that the categorization made in that legislation did have such an aim and effect. Lastly in this context, the Panel noted that the United States also argued that independently of the legal test chosen and applied, the Panel should find that Japan in this case is in violation of its obligations under Article III:2. It was also the view of Japan that independently of the legal test chosen and applied, the Panel should find that Japan is not in violation of its obligations under Article III:2.

6.16   The Panel first turned to the test proposed by Japan and the United States. The Panel noted, in this respect, that the proposed aim-and-effect test is not consistent with the wording of Article III:2, first sentence. The Panel recalled that the basis of the aim-and-effect test is found in the words "so as to afford protection" contained in Article III:1.[86] The Panel further recalled that Article III:2, first sentence, contains no reference to those words. Moreover, the adoption of the aim-and-effect test would have important repercussions on the burden of proof imposed on the complainant. The Panel noted in this respect that the complainants, according to the aim-and-effect test, have the burden of showing not only the effect of a particular measure, which is in principle discernible, but also its aim, which sometimes can be indiscernible. The Panel also noted that very often

---

[86]   See paras. 4.16 - 4.19 and 4.24ff. of the Descriptive Part.

there is a multiplicity of aims that are sought through enactment of legislation and it would be a difficult exercise to determine which aim or aims should be determinative for applying the aim-and-effect test.[87] Moreover, access to the complete legislative history, which according to the arguments of the parties defending the aim-and-effect test, is relevant to detect protective aims, could be difficult or even impossible for a complaining party to obtain. Even if the complete legislative history is available, it would be difficult to assess which kinds of legislative history (statements in legislation, in official legislative reports, by individual legislators, or in hearings by interested parties) should be primarily determinative of the aims of the legislation.[88] The Panel recalled in this respect the argument by the United States that the aim-and-effect test should be applicable only with respect to origin-neutral measures. The Panel noted that neither the wording of Article III:2, nor that of Article III:1 support a distinction between origin-neutral and origin-specific measures.

6.17   The Panel further noted that the list of exceptions contained in Article XX of GATT 1994 could become redundant or useless because the aim-and-effect test does not contain a definitive list of grounds justifying departure from the obligations that are otherwise incorporated in Article III.[89] The purpose of Article XX is to provide a list of exceptions, subject to the conditions that they "are not applied in a manner which would constitute a means of arbitrary or unjustifiable discrimination between countries where the same conditions prevail, or a disguised restriction of international trade", that could justify deviations from the obligations imposed under GATT. Consequently, in principle, a WTO Member could, for example, invoke protection of health in the context of invoking the

---

[87]   The Panel noted, in this respect, an interesting parallel with the legal status of "supplementary means" of interpretation of treaties -- that comprise preparatory work -- and their relevance for interpreting treaties. The Panel noted that according to Article 32 VCLT recourse to supplementary means of interpretation is required only as an exception in specific circumstances. The Panel noted in this respect the commentary of the International Law Commission: "The Commission considered that the exception must be strictly limited, if it is not to weaken unduly the authority of the ordinary meaning of the terms." The Panel further noted the statement of the International Law Commission that "...the preparatory work...does not, in consequence, have the same authentic character as an element of interpretation, however valuable it may sometimes be in throwing light in the expression of the agreement in the text. Moreover, it is beyond question that the records of treaty negotiations are in many cases incomplete or misleading, so that considerable discretion has to be exercised in determining their value as an element of interpretation. D. Rauschning and R.G. Wetzel, The Vienna Convention on the Law of Treaties, Travaux Préparatoires (Frankfurt: Alfred Metzner Verlag, 1978), pp. 255, 252. The Panel noted that considerable differences exist between preparatory work of international treaties and preparatory work of domestic legislation that preclude the automatic transposition of the reasoning of the International Law Commission to the case before it. Nevertheless, in the Panel's view, the analysis and reasoning of the International Law Commission could be relevant even in the context of preparatory work of domestic legislation.

[88]   See para. 4.17 of the Descriptive Part.

[89]   In this context, the Panel noted that the Appellate Body in its report on "United States - Standards for Reformulated and Conventional Gasoline", noted that "one of the corollaries of the 'general rule of interpretation' in the Vienna Convention is that interpretation must give meaning and effect to all the terms of a treaty. An interpreter is not free to adopt a reading that would result in reducing whole clauses or paragraphs of a treaty to redundancy or inutility". WT/DS2/AB/R, DSR 1996:I, 3, at 21.

aim-and-effect test. The Panel noted that if this were the case, then the standard of proof established in Article XX would effectively be circumvented. WTO Members would not have to prove that a health measure is "necessary" to achieve its health objective.[90] Moreover, proponents of the aim-and-effect test even shift the burden of proof, arguing that it would be up to the complainant to produce a *prima facie* case that a measure has both the aim and effect of affording protection to domestic production and, once the complainant has demonstrated that this is the case, only then would the defending party have to present evidence to rebut the claim.[91] In sum, the Panel concluded that for reasons relating to the wording of Article III as well as its context, the aim-and-effect test proposed by Japan and the United States should be rejected.

6.18   The Panel turned at this point to the relevance of the two GATT panel reports that, according to the arguments of Japan and the United States, have espoused the aim-and-effect test. With respect to the panel report on "United States - Taxes on Automobiles" (*US Auto Taxes*),[92] the Panel noted that the report remains unadopted and that, for the reasons stated in paragraph 6.10, it did not have to take it into account since it does not constitute subsequent practice. At any rate, for the reasons mentioned in paragraphs 6.16 and 6.17, the Panel was not persuaded by the reasoning contained in the panel report on *US Auto Taxes*. With respect to the 1992 *Malt Beverages* report, the Panel first noted that it interpreted the term "like product" as it appears in Article III:2 in a manner largely consistent with the interpretation of the 1987 Panel Report that had previously interpreted the same term. The Panel noted that the 1992 *Malt Beverages* report, when interpreting the term "like product", took into account the product's end-uses, consumer tastes and habits, and the product's properties, nature and quality. However, the 1992 *Malt Beverages* report also considered whether product differentiation is being made "so as to afford protection to domestic production".[93] The Panel was not in a position to detect how the 1992 *Malt Beverages* panel weighed the different criteria that it took into account in order to determine whether the products in dispute were like. In the Panel's view, however, an interpretation of the term "like product" as it appears in Article III:2, first sentence, that conditions likeness on the criterion whether a domestic legislation operates so as to afford protection to domestic production, is inconsistent with the wording of Article III:2, first sentence. The Panel recalled its conclusions reached in this respect in paragraphs 6.16 and 6.17. For this reason, the Panel decided not to follow the interpretation of the term "like product" as it appears in Article III:2, first sentence, advanced by the 1992 *Malt Beverages* report in so far as it incorporates the aim-and-effect test.

6.19   The Panel, having decided not to apply the aim-and-effect test proceeded to develop the legal test that it would apply in this case in order to determine

---

[90]   See, for example, the panel report on "Thailand - Restrictions on Importation of and Internal Taxes on Cigarettes", adopted on 7 November 1990, BISD 37S/200.
[91]   See para. 4.32 of the Descriptive Part.
[92]   DS31/R, report dated 11 October 1994.
[93]   See the 1992 *Malt Beverages* report, paras. 5.25 - 5.26.

whether Japan had acted inconsistently with its obligations under Article III. More specifically, in the view of the Panel, the wording of Article III:2, first sentence, requires it to make three determinations: (i) whether the products concerned are like, (ii) whether the contested measure is an "internal tax" or "other internal charge" (not an issue in this case) and (iii) if so, whether the tax imposed on foreign products is in excess of the tax imposed on like domestic products. If these three determinations are in the affirmative, such a tax would result in the WTO Member imposing it being in violation of the obligation contained in Article III:2, first sentence. Moreover, in the Panel's view, the only relevant contextual elements supported this interpretation. The Panel recalled in this respect its conclusions reached in paragraph 6.12 concerning the limited relevance of Article III:1 to the interpretation of Article III:2. The Panel further recalled that past GATT panels had followed this approach.[94] Thus, the Panel decided to proceed on the basis outlined in this paragraph.

b)   Like Products

6.20   The Panel noted that the term "like product" appears in various GATT provisions. The Panel further noted that it did not necessarily follow that the term had to be interpreted in a uniform way. In this respect, the Panel noted the discrepancy between Article III:2, on the one hand, and Article III:4 on the other: while the former referred to Article III:1 and to like, as well as to directly competitive or substitutable products (see also Article XIX of GATT), the latter referred only to like products. If the coverage[95] of Article III:2 is identical to that of Article III:4, a different interpretation of the term "like product" would be called for in the two paragraphs. Otherwise, if the term "like product" were to be interpreted in an identical way in both instances, the scope of the two paragraphs would be different. This is precisely why, in the Panel's view, its conclusions reached in this dispute are relevant only for the interpretation of the term "like product" as it appears in Article III:2.

6.21   The Panel noted that previous panel and working party reports had unanimously agreed that the term "like product" should be interpreted on a case-by-case basis.[96] The Panel further noted that previous panels had not established a particular test that had to be strictly followed in order to define likeness. Previous panels had used different criteria in order to establish likeness, such as the

---

[94]   See for example, the panel report on "United States - Taxes on Petroleum and Certain Imported Substances", adopted on 17 June 1987, BISD 34S/136; the 1987 Panel Report; see also the panel report on "United States - Standards for Reformulated and Conventional Gasoline", WT/DS2/R, adopted on 20 May 1996.

[95]   By the term "coverage", the Panel means whether Article III:4 regulates the treatment of both categories of products mentioned in Article III:2, namely both "like" and "directly competitive or substitutable" products.

[96]   See, for example, the Working Party Report on "Border Tax Adjustments", L/3464, adopted on 2 December 1970, BISD 18S/97, p. 102, para. 18 (hereinafter "the 1970 Working Party report"); the panel report on "United States - Taxes on Petroleum and Certain Imported Substances", adopted on 17 June 1987, BISD 34S/136, pp.154-155, para. 5.1.1; the 1987 Panel Report, pp.113-115, para. 5.5-5.7; the 1992 *Malt Beverages* report, pp. 276-277, paras. 5.25 - 5.26.

product's properties, nature and quality, and its end-uses; consumers' tastes and habits, which change from country to country; and the product's classification in tariff nomenclatures.[97] In the Panel's view, "like products" need not be identical in all respects. However, in the Panel's view, the term "like product" should be construed narrowly in the case of Article III:2, first sentence. This approach is dictated, in the Panel's view, by two independent reasons: (i) because Article III:2 distinguishes between like and directly competitive or substitutable products, the latter obviously being a much larger category of products than the former; and (ii) because of the Panel's conclusions reached with respect to the relationship between Articles III and II. As to the first point, the distinction between "like" and "directly competitive or substitutable products" is discussed in paragraph 6.22. As to the second point, as previous panels had noted, one of the main objectives of Article III:2 is to ensure that WTO Members do not frustrate the effect of tariff concessions granted under Article II through internal taxes and other internal charges, it follows that a parallelism should be drawn in this case between the definition of products for purposes of Article II tariff concessions and the term "like product" as it appears in Article III:2. This is so in the Panel's view, because with respect to two products subject to the same tariff binding and therefore to the same maximum border tax, there is no justification, outside of those mentioned in GATT rules, to tax them in a differentiated way through internal taxation. This does not mean that the determination of whether products are "like" should be based exclusively on the definition of products for tariff bindings, but in the Panel's view, especially where it is sufficiently detailed, a product's description for this purpose is in this case an important criterion for confirming likeness for the purposes of Article III:2. The Panel noted that its proposed interpretation does not unduly restrict the possibility offered to WTO Members to challenge internal taxes that discriminate against foreign products, since Article III:2, second sentence, effectively prohibits the taxation of "directly competitive or substitutable products" "so as to afford protection to domestic production". As explained in the next paragraph, the phrase "directly competitive or substitutable products", should be interpreted more broadly than the phrase "like products". In the Panel's view, its interpretation of Article III:2, first sentence, is in accordance with the requirements of Article 31 VCLT.

6.22   The wording of Article III and of the Interpretative Note ad Article III make it clear that a distinction must be drawn between, on the one hand, like, and, on the other, directly competitive or substitutable products. Such an approach is in conformity with the principle of "effective treaty interpretation" as laid down in the "general rule of interpretation" of the Vienna Convention on the Law of Treaties. The Panel recalled in this respect the conclusions of the Appellate Body in its report on "United States - Standards for Reformulated and Conventional Gasoline" where it stated that "an interpreter is not free to adopt a

---

[97]   See the 1970 Working Party report on "Border Tax Adjustments", op. cit., at para. 18; the 1987 Panel Report at para. 5.6; the panel report on "United States - Taxes on Petroleum and Certain Imported Substances", op. cit., at para. 5.1.1; the panel report on "EEC - Measures on Animal Feed Proteins", adopted on 14 March 1978, BISD 25S/49, at para. 4.3.

reading that would result in reducing whole clauses or paragraphs of a treaty to redundancy or inutility."[98] In the view of the Panel, like products should be viewed as a subset of directly competitive or substitutable products. The wording ("like products" as opposed to "directly competitive or substitutable products") confirmed this point, in the sense that all like products are, by definition, directly competitive or substitutable products, whereas all directly competitive or substitutable products are not necessarily like products. Giving a narrow meaning to "like products" is also justified by the inescapability of violation in case of taxation of foreign products in excess of like domestic products.[99] Moreover, in the Panel's view, the wording makes it clear that the appropriate test to define whether two products are "like" or "directly competitive or substitutable" is the marketplace. The Panel recalled in this respect the words used in the Interpretative Note ad Article III, paragraph 2, namely "where competition exists": competition exists by definition in markets. In the view of the Panel, to define a precise cut-off point that distinguishes between, on the one hand, like, and on the other, directly competitive or substitutable products requires an arbitrary decision. The Panel decided therefore, to consider criteria on a case-by-case basis in order to determine whether two products are like or directly competitive or substitutable. The Panel recalled, in this respect, that previous panels had pronounced in favour of a case-by-case approach when defining like or directly competitive or substitutable products.[100] In the view of the Panel, descriptions used in the context of tariff classifications and bindings whilst by themselves not providing decisive guidance on likeness, can be used nevertheless in considering the content of "like products" in the context of Article III:2, first sentence. Such an approach is in line with previous panel reports that concluded that the purpose of Article III was to avoid that "the value of the bindings under Article II of the Agreement and of the general rules of non-discrimination as between imported and domestic products could be easily evaded."[101] Previous panels that dealt with the same issue have used a series of criteria in order to define likeness or substitutability.[102] In the view of the Panel, the wording of the term "directly competitive or substitutable" does not suggest at all that physical resemblance is required in order to establish whether two products fall under this category. This impression, in the Panel's view, was further supported by the words "where competition exists" of the Interpretative Note; competition can and does exist among products that do not necessarily share the same physical characteristics. In the Panel's view, the decisive criterion in order to determine whether two products are directly competitive or substitutable is whether they have common end-uses, *inter alia*, as shown by elasticity of substitution. The wording of the term "like products" how-

---

[98] See WT/DS2/AB/R, at p.21.
[99] The panel report on "United States - Taxes on Petroleum and Certain Imported Substances", op. cit., at para. 5.1.9 made it clear that no *de minimis* defense can be raised in case of taxation of foreign products in excess of domestic like products. The Panel agreed with this statement.
[100] See footnote 96 and accompanying text.
[101] See the panel report on "Italian Discrimination Against Imported Agricultural Machinery", adopted on 23 October 1958, BISD 7S/60 at p.64, para. 15; see also the 1987 Panel Report op. cit.
[102] See footnote 96 and accompanying text.

ever, suggests that commonality of end-uses is a necessary but not a sufficient criterion to define likeness. In the view of the Panel, the term "like products" suggests that for two products to fall under this category they must share, apart from commonality of end-uses, essentially the same physical characteristics. In the Panel's view its suggested approach has the merit of being functional, although the definition of likeness might appear somewhat "inflexible". Flexibility is required in order to conclude whether two products are directly competitive or substitutable. In the Panel's view, the suggested approach can guarantee the flexibility required, since it permits one to take into account specific characteristics in any single market; consequently, two products could be considered to be directly competitive or substitutable in market A, but the same two products would not necessarily be considered to be directly competitive or substitutable in market B. The Panel proceeded to apply this approach to the products in dispute in the present case.

6.23   The Panel next turned to an examination of whether the products at issue in this case were like products, starting first with vodka and shochu. The Panel noted that vodka and shochu shared most physical characteristics. In the Panel's view, except for filtration, there is virtual identity in the definition of the two products. The Panel noted that a difference in the physical characteristic of alcoholic strength of two products did not preclude a finding of likeness especially since alcoholic beverages are often drunk in diluted form. The Panel then noted that essentially the same conclusion had been reached in the 1987 Panel Report, which

> "... agreed with the arguments submitted to it by the European Communities, Finland and the United States that Japanese shochu (Group A) and vodka could be considered as 'like' products in terms of Article III:2 because they were both white/clean spirits, made of similar raw materials, and the end-uses were virtually identical".[103]

Following its independent consideration of the factors mentioned in the 1987 Panel Report, the Panel agreed with this statement. The Panel then recalled its conclusions concerning the relationship between Articles II and III. In this context, it noted that (i) vodka and shochu were currently classified in the same heading in the Japanese tariffs, (although under the new Harmonized System (HS) Classification that entered into force on 1 January 1996 and that Japan plans to implement, shochu appears under tariff heading 2208.90 and vodka under tariff heading 2208.60); and (ii) vodka and shochu were covered by the same Japanese tariff binding at the time of its negotiation. Of the products at issue in this case, only shochu and vodka have the same tariff applied to them in the

---

[103]   Para. 5.7. The same paragraph further reads: "... the Panel found that the traditional Japanese consumer habits with regard to shochu provided no reason for not considering vodka to be a 'like' product. ... Even if imported alcoholic beverages (e.g vodka) were not considered to be 'like' to Japanese alcoholic beverages (e.g shochu Group A), the flexibility in the use of alcoholic drinks and their common characteristics often offered an alternative choice for consumers leading to a competitive relationship.

Japanese tariff schedule (see Annex 1). The Panel noted that, with respect to vodka, Japan offered no further convincing evidence that the conclusion reached by the 1987 Panel Report was wrong, not even that there had been a change in consumers' preferences in this respect. The Panel further noted that Japan's basic argument is not that the two products are unlike, in terms of the criteria applied in the 1987 Panel Report, but rather that they are unlike because the Japanese tax legislation does not have the aim and effect to protect shochu. The Panel noted, however, that it had already rejected the aim-and-effect test. Consequently, in light of the conclusion of the 1987 Panel Report and of its independent consideration of the issue, the Panel concluded that vodka and shochu are like products. In the Panel's view, only vodka could be considered as like product to shochu since, apart from commonality of end-uses, it shared with shochu most physical characteristics. Definitionally, the only difference is in the media used for filtration. Substantial noticeable differences in physical characteristics exist between the rest of the alcoholic beverages at dispute and shochu that would disqualify them from being regarded as like products. More specifically, the use of additives would disqualify liqueurs, gin and genever; the use of ingredients would disqualify rum; lastly, appearance (arising from manufacturing processes) would disqualify whisky and brandy. The Panel therefore decided to examine whether the rest of alcoholic beverages, other than vodka, at dispute in the present case could qualify as directly competitive or substitutable products to shochu. The Panel lastly noted that the 1987 Panel Report had also considered these products only under Article III:2, second sentence.

c)   Taxation in Excess of that Imposed on Like Domestic Products

6.24   The Panel then proceeded to examine whether vodka is taxed in excess of the tax imposed on shochu under the Japanese Liquor Tax Law. The Panel noted that what was contested in the Japanese legislation was a system of specific taxes imposed on various alcoholic drinks. In this respect, it noted that vodka was taxed at 377,230 Yen per kilolitre - for an alcoholic strength below 38° - that is 9,927 Yen per degree of alcohol, whereas shochu A was taxed at 155,700 Yen per kilolitre - for an alcoholic strength between 25° and 26° - that is 6,228 Yen per degree of alcohol.[104] The Panel further noted that Article III:2 does not contain any presumption in favour of a specific mode of taxation. Under Article III:2, first sentence, WTO Members are free to choose any system of taxation they deem appropriate provided that they do not impose on foreign products taxes in excess of those imposed on like domestic products. The phrase "not in excess of those applied ... to like domestic products" should be interpreted to mean at least identical or better tax treatment. The Japanese taxes on vodka and shochu are calculated on the basis of and vary according to the alcoholic content of the products and, on this basis, it is obvious that the taxes imposed on vodka

---

[104]   See para. 2.3 of the Descriptive Part for a complete description of the Japanese liquor tax rates.

are higher than those imposed on shochu. Accordingly, the Panel concluded that the tax imposed on vodka is in excess of the tax imposed on shochu.

6.25   The Panel then addressed the argument put forward by Japan that its legislation, by keeping the tax/price ratio "roughly constant", is trade neutral and consequently no protective aim and effect of the legislation can be detected. In this connection, the Panel recalled Japan's argument that its aim was to achieve neutrality and horizontal tax equity.[105] The Panel noted that it had already decided that the existence or non-existence of a protective aim and effect is not relevant in an analysis under Article III:2, first sentence. To the extent that Japan's argument is that its Liquor Tax Law does not impose on foreign products (i.e., vodka) a tax in excess of the tax imposed on domestic like products (i.e., shochu), the Panel rejected the argument for the following reasons:

(i)   The benchmark in Article III:2, first sentence, is that internal taxes on foreign products shall not be imposed in excess of those imposed on like domestic products. Consequently, in the context of Article III:2, first sentence, it is irrelevant whether "roughly" the same treatment through, for example, a "roughly constant" tax/price ratio is afforded to domestic and foreign like products or whether neutrality and horizontal tax equity is achieved.

(ii)   Even if it were to be accepted that a comparison of tax/price ratios of products could offset the fact that vodka was taxed significantly more heavily than shochu on a volume and alcoholic content basis, there were significant problems with the methodology for calculating tax/price ratios submitted by Japan, such that arguments based on that methodology could only be viewed as inconclusive. More particularly, although Japan had argued that the comparison of tax/price ratios should be done on a category-by-category basis, its statistics on which the tax/price ratios were based excluded domestically produced spirits from the calculation of tax/price ratios for spirits and whisky/brandy. Since the prices of the domestic spirits and whisky/brandy are much lower than the prices of the imported goods, this exclusion has the impact of reducing considerably the tax/price ratios cited by Japan for those products. In this connection, the Panel noted that one consequence of the Japanese tax system was to make it more difficult for cheaper imported brands of spirits and whisky/brandy to enter the Japanese market. Moreover, the Panel further noted that the Japanese statistics were based on suggested retail prices and there was evidence in the record[106] that these products were often sold at a discount, at least in Tokyo. To the extent that the prices were unreliable, the resultant tax/price ratios would be unreliable as well.[107]

---

[105]   See para. 4.132ff. of the Descriptive Part.
[106]   See paras. 4.100, 4.142-4, 4.159, 4.160-1 of the Descriptive Part.
[107]   See paras. 4.100, 4.159, 4.160 and 4.165 of the Descriptive Part.

(iii)   Nowhere in the contested legislation was it mentioned that its purpose was to maintain a "roughly constant" tax/price ratio. This was
rather an *ex post facto* rationalization by Japan and at any rate,
there are no guarantees in the legislation that the tax/price ratio will
always be maintained "roughly constant". Prices change over time
and unless an adjustment process is incorporated in the legislation,
the tax/price ratio will be affected. Japan admitted that no adjustment process exists in the legislation and that only *ex post facto*
adjustments can occur. The Panel lastly noted that since the modification in 1989 of Japan's Liquor Tax Law there has been only one
instance of adjustment.

6.26   The Panel then turned to the arguments put forward by Japan concerning
taxation systems in other countries. The Panel noted that its terms of reference
were strictly confined to the Japanese legislation. The Panel could not, therefore,
consider the domestic taxation systems of other countries since they lie outside its
terms of reference.

6.27   Consequently, the Panel concluded that, by taxing vodka in excess of shochu, Japan is in violation of its obligation under Article III:2, first sentence.

4.   *Article III:2, Second Sentence*

a)   Directly Competitive or Substitutable Products

6.28   The Panel then turned to an analysis of the issues arising under Article
III:2, second sentence. In the view of the Panel, the wording of Article III:2, second sentence, requires it to make two determinations: (i) whether the products
concerned (whisky, brandy, gin, genever, rum and liqueurs) are directly competitive or substitutable, and (ii) if so, whether the treatment afforded to foreign
products is contrary to the principles set forth in paragraph 1 of Article III. In the
view of the Panel, the complainants have the burden of proof to show first, that
the products concerned are directly competitive or substitutable and second, that
foreign products are taxed in such a way so as to afford protection to domestic
production. The Panel recalled that the term "directly competitive or substitutable
product", in accordance with its ordinary meaning, should be interpreted more
broadly than the term "like product". In this sense the Interpretative Note ad Article III:2, second sentence, speaks about products "where competition was involved between..." them. The Panel noted, in this respect, that independently of
similarities with respect to physical characteristics or classification in tariff nomenclatures, greater emphasis should be placed on elasticity of substitution. In
this context, factors like marketing strategies could also prove to be relevant criteria, since what is at issue is the responsiveness of consumers to the various
products offered in the market. Such responsiveness, the Panel recalled, may vary
from country to country,[108] but should not be influenced or determined by inter-

---

[108]   See the 1970 Working Party report, op. cit., at para. 18.

nal taxation.[109] The Panel noted the conclusions in the 1987 Panel Report,[110] that a tax system that discriminates against imports has the consequence of creating and even freezing preferences for domestic goods. In the Panel's view, this meant that consumer surveys in a country with such a tax system would likely understate the degree of potential competitiveness between substitutable products.

6.29   In examining whether the products at issue were directly competitive or substitutable, the Panel first noted that the 1987 Panel Report that dealt with this issue concluded that both "white" and "brown" spirits were directly competitive or substitutable products to shochu, according to Article III:2, second sentence. The Panel noted in this respect, that the 1987 Panel Report had reached its conclusion based essentially on the substitutability among the products in dispute as a result of "their respective prices, their availability through trade and their other competitive inter-relationships".[111] Turning to the evidence in this case, the Panel noted that the complainants had submitted a study (the ASI study) that concludes that there is a high degree of price-elasticity between shochu, on the one hand, and five brown spirits (Scotch whisky, Japanese whisky, Japanese brandy, cognac, North American whisky) and three white spirits (gin, vodka and rum), on the other.[112] Japan questioned the relevance of this ASI study by noting that consumers were not allowed to choose other than the mentioned eight products (for example, they were not allowed to choose, beer, sake or wine) and also argued that if choices are too limited even such disparate products as hamburger and ice cream could be argued to be directly competitive or substitutable products. In the Panel's view, however, price-elasticity between the mentioned products is not altered by the fact that consumers were presented with a limited choice. At best, the argument by Japan, if proven, could eventually lead to the conclusion that the three products mentioned by Japan have a greater degree of price-elasticity with shochu. It would not, however, in the Panel's view, amount to a rejection of the existence of a significant directly competitive or substitutable relationship between shochu and the examined eight products.

6.30   The Panel further noted that as a result of the 1989 Japanese tax reform, the distinction between "premium whisky", "first grade whisky" and "second grade whisky" was abolished. This tax reform disadvantaged domestically produced whisky, by substantially increasing the tax rate on second grade whisky compared to the other alcoholic beverages at issue in the present case.[113] The market share of domestic whisky including second grade fell from 26.7 per cent in 1988 to 19.6 per cent in 1990. This, according to the Community's evidence,

---

[109]   In this respect, note para. 5.7 of the 1987 Panel Report "since consumer habits are variable in time and space and the aim of Article III:2 of ensuring neutrality of internal taxation as regards competition between imported and domestic like products *could not be achieved if differential taxes could be used to crystallize consumer preferences* for traditional domestic products, the Panel found that the traditional Japanese consumer habits with regard to shochu provided no reason for not considering vodka to be a like product". (emphasis added).

[110]   See the 1987 Panel Report, op. cit., at para. 5.9.

[111]   See the 1987 Panel Report, op. cit., para. 5.7.

[112]   See paras. 4.171ff. of the Descriptive Part.

[113]   See para. 4.82 of the Descriptive Part.

led to a rise of both shochu's and foreign produced whisky's market shares in Japan.[114] This proves to the Community that there is elasticity of substitution between whisky and shochu. The Panel further noted that Canada and the United States provided evidence to the same effect, that is showing that elasticity of substitution between whisky and shochu was evident as a result of the 1989 Japanese tax reform.[115] The Panel took note that in its response, Japan argued that the combination of the expansion of shochu consumption and the declining whisky prices rather indicated the lack of a competitive relationship between the two commodities. In the Panel's view, Japan failed to take account of the fact that shochu and foreign whisky were in fact capturing the market share lost by domestically produced whisky. In the Panel's view, the fact that foreign produced whisky and shochu were competing for the same market is evidence that there was elasticity of substitution between them.

6.31   The Panel noted Japan's argument that there is no elasticity of substitution between shochu and the rest of the alcoholic drinks in dispute in this case. If at all, according to Japan, the evidence the complainants provided to the Panel shows elasticity of substitution between shochu and beer. Japan based its argument on a survey conducted among consumers that showed, according to Japan, that in case shochu were not available 6 per cent of the consumers would switch to spirits whereas only 4 per cent to whisky; if whisky were not available, 32 per cent of the consumers would choose brandy and only 10 per cent would choose shochu. Japan submitted this survey to the Panel. The Panel did not accept Japan's argument on the grounds that Japan, in conducting this survey, failed to take into account price distortions caused by internal taxation. In other words, consumers' choices were sought within the existing price regime (which is the subject matter of the current dispute), and not independently of it. Moreover, in the Panel's view, the inadequacies of the survey notwithstanding, in case of non-availability of shochu, 10 per cent of the consumers would switch to spirits and whisky. This, in the Panel's view, was proof of significant elasticity of substitution between shochu, on the one hand, and whisky and spirits, on the other. The Panel noted that Japan further provided an econometric study in which no elasticity of substitution could be found between shochu, on the one hand, and spirits or whisky, on the other. This study attempted to evaluate the extent to which the relevant products are directly competitive.[116] In considering the study, the Panel took account of the views of the parties and of general econometric principles. The Panel noted that the extent to which two products are competitive in economics is measured by the responsiveness of the demand for one product to the change in the demand for the other product (cross-price elasticity of demand). The more sensitive demand for one product is to changes in the price of the other product, *all other things being equal*, the more directly competitive they are. This is related to the substitutability of one product for another (elasticity of substitu-

---

[114]   The Panel noted that this rise was short-lived, since as of 1992 the Japanese economy entered into recession and there was a shift of demand towards the less expensive categories of liquors.
[115]   See paras. 4.73, 4.77-8, 4.90-2, 4.111, 4.113, 4.115, 4.117, 4.171-2, 4.174 of the Descriptive Part.
[116]   See paras. 4.83ff. of the Descriptive Part.

tion). Under national antitrust and trade law régimes, the extent to which products directly compete is measured by the elasticity of substitution. Formal statistical methods are employed to measure, with a reasonable degree of certainty, the magnitude and direction of variables, based on actual observations. The greater the number of observations, the greater the degree of certainty. In the case of product demand and product substitutability (i.e., the direct competitiveness of products), the relevant information includes prices, quantities, and incomes. Ideally, one would like to test for the relationship between the price of one product and the demand for another, *all other things being equal*. Under these conditions, relatively simple statistical methods can be employed. This is the approach taken in the Japanese econometric study. However, all other things are not equal. When working with a set of (potentially) substitutable products, it is necessary to recognize that underlying trends in the data may affect the apparent relationship between the variables examined (serial and autocorrelation). In addition, the variables may in actuality be closely related. For example, outside factors (i.e., those not measured directly) may affect the markets that are examined jointly (multicollinearity). Moreover, changes in income may affect demand in all of the product markets studied, and this effect may vary systematically across the markets. In statistical studies of related markets involving time series data (as in the present study), one could normally expect to encounter all of these problems. Relatively standard methods can be employed to control for serial and autocorrelation and multicollinearity. Failure to account for these effects can render the results of simple statistical analysis meaningless. According to the complainants, this is the case of the study submitted by Japan. The Panel accepted the validity of these criticisms and noted that Japan had not succeeded in rebutting the criticism advanced by complainants and thus Japan's study did not refute the evidence of substitutability submitted by complainants.

6.32 The Panel then concluded that in deciding whether shochu and the other products in dispute were directly competitive or substitutable products, it noted that the products concerned were all distilled spirits and it would give particular emphasis to the following factors: the findings of the 1987 Panel Report; the studies put forward by the complainants (the ASI study) that contained persuasive evidence that there is significant elasticity of substitution among the products in dispute; the survey submitted by Japan that, notwithstanding the fact that it failed to take into account price distortions caused by internal taxation, still shows elasticity of substitution among the products in dispute; and, lastly, the evidence submitted by complainants concerning the 1989 Japanese tax reform which showed that whisky and shochu are essentially competing for the same market. In the view of the Panel, the conclusions of the 1987 Panel Report, buttressed by any of the other three factors, were sufficient for the Panel to conclude that shochu and the other products subject to dispute are directly competitive or substitutable according to Article III:2, second sentence.

b) " ... So as to Afford Protection"

6.33 The Panel turned to the question whether Japan was violating its obligations under Article III:2, second sentence. In this respect, the Panel recalled the Interpretative Note ad Article III:2 that states:

"A tax conforming to the requirements of the first sentence of paragraph 2 would be considered to be inconsistent with the provisions of the second sentence only in cases where competition was involved between, on the one hand, the taxed product and, on the other hand, a directly competitive or substitutable product which was not similarly taxed".

In the Panel's view, the Interpretative Note ad Article III:2 explains how a national measure operates "so as to afford protection to domestic production" and thus runs counter to the principles set forth in Article III:1. In other words, if directly competitive or substitutable products are not "similarly taxed", and if it were found that the tax favours domestic products, then protection would be afforded to such products, and Article III:2, second sentence, is violated. Although the 1987 Panel Report did not focus on the Interpretative Note, its conclusions on the issue of "so as to afford protection" was essentially the same, as it concluded that the higher (i.e., dissimilar) Japanese taxes on imported alcoholic beverages and the existence of substitutability were "sufficient evidence of fiscal distortions of the competitive relationship between imported distilled liquors and domestic shochu affording protection to domestic producers of shochu".[117] The Panel agrees with this conclusion. In this connection, the Panel noted that for it to conclude that dissimilar taxation afforded protection, it would be sufficient for it to find that the dissimilarity in taxation is not *de minimis*.[118] In the Panel's view, it is appropriate to conclude, as have other GATT panels including the 1987 panel, that it is not necessary to show an adverse effect on the level of imports, as Article III generally is aimed at providing imports with "effective equality of opportunities" in "conditions of competition".[119] In line with these interpretations of Article III, the Panel concluded that it is not necessary for complainants to establish the purpose or aim of tax legislation in order for the Panel to conclude that dissimilar taxation affords protection to domestic production. In the Panel's view, the Interpretative Note interpreted in this respect the term "so as to afford protection" which appears in Article III:1. The Panel took the view that "similarly taxed" is the appropriate benchmark in order to determine whether a violation of Article III:2, second sentence, has occurred as opposed to "in excess of" that constitutes the appropriate benchmark to determine whether a violation of Article III:2, first sentence, has occurred. In the Panel's view, the following indicators, *inter alia*, are relevant in determining whether the products in dispute are similarly taxed in this case: tax per litre of product, tax per degree of alcohol, *ad valorem* taxation, and the tax/price ratio.

---

[117] See the 1987 Panel Report, op. cit., para. 5.11.

[118] The Panel decided that it did not have to further define "*de minimis*", because in this case the differences in taxation were significant.

[119] See the panel report on "United States - Taxes on Petroleum and Certain Imported Substances", op. cit., para. 5.1.9; see also the panel report on "Italian Discrimination Against Imported Agricultural Machinery", op. cit., para. 12.

a)   With respect to taxation per kilolitre of product the Panel noted that the amounts were:[120]

Shochu A (25°)	¥ 155,700
Shochu B (25°)	¥ 102,100
Whisky (40°)	¥ 982,300
Brandy (40°)	¥ 982,300
Spirits (38°)	¥ 377,230 (gin, rum, vodka)
Liqueurs (40°)	¥ 328,760

The Panel concluded that the amounts of tax are not similar and that the differences are not *de minimis*.

b)   With respect to taxation per degree of alcohol the Panel noted that the amounts were:[121]

Shochu A (25°)	¥ 6,228
Shochu B (25°)	¥ 4,084
Whisky (40°)	¥ 24,558
Brandy (40°)	¥ 24,558
Spirits (38°)	¥ 9,927 (gin, rum, vodka)
Liqueurs (40°)	¥ 8,219

The Panel concluded that the amounts of tax are not similar and that the differences are not *de minimis*. Since the Japanese taxes at issue were calculated on the basis of the alcohol content of the various products, the Panel considered this dissimilarity to be particularly dispositive for its analysis under Article III:2, second sentence.

c)   The Panel noted that Japan's Liquor Tax Law does not provide for *ad valorem* taxation and this criterion is, consequently, irrelevant in this case.

d)   With respect to the tax/price ratio, the Panel noted that the statistics submitted by Japan show that significant differences exist between shochu and the other directly competitive or substitutable products and also noted that there are significantly different tax/price ratios within the same product categories. Moreover, there were significant problems with the methodology for calculating tax/price ratios submitted by Japan, such that arguments based on that methodology could only be viewed as inconclusive. More particularly, although Japan had argued that the comparison of tax/price ratios should be done on a category-by-category basis, its statistics on which the tax/price ratios were based excluded domestically produced spirits and whisky/brandy from the calculation of tax/price ratios for spirits and whisky/brandy. Since the prices of the domestic spirits and whisky/brandy are much lower than the prices of the imported ones, this exclusion has the impact of reducing considerably the tax/prices ratios cited

---

[120] See para. 2.3 of the Descriptive Part.
[121] Based on calculations upon information included in para. 2.3 of the Descriptive Part.

by Japan for those products. In this connection, the Panel noted that one consequence of the Japanese tax system was to make it more difficult for cheaper imported brands of spirits and whisky/brandy to enter the market. Moreover, the Panel noted that the Japanese statistics were based on suggested retail prices and there was evidence in the record that these products were often sold at a discount, at least in Tokyo. To the extent that the prices were unreliable, the resultant tax/price ratios would be unreliable as well.

The Panel consequently concluded that the products in dispute are not similarly taxed and the taxes on shochu are lower than the taxes on the other products subject to dispute, leading the Panel to the conclusion that protection is afforded to shochu inconsistently with Japan's obligations under Article III:2, second sentence.

6.34   The Panel then addressed the argument put forward by Japan that the Japanese legislation is trade-neutral, and thus guarantees equality of competitive conditions, since it maintains a "roughly constant" tax/price ratio and no protective aim or effect of the legislation can be detected. In this connection, the Panel recalled the argument by Japan that its aim was to achieve horizontal tax equity.[122] The Panel further recalled in this context that it had already dismissed the aim-and-effect test put forward by Japan. The Panel noted that to the extent that Japan's argument could be considered as an argument that Japan's Liquor Tax Law taxed directly competitive or substitutable products similarly, in the Panel's view, the argument should be rejected for the following reasons:

(i)   The benchmark in Article III:2, second sentence, is whether internal taxes operate "so as to afford protection to domestic production", a term which has been further interpreted in the Interpretative Note ad Article III:2, paragraph 2, to mean dissimilar taxation of domestic and foreign directly competitive or substitutable products. However, in the Panel's view, it is not at all clear that maintaining a "roughly constant" tax/price ratio avoids violating this requirement.

(ii)   The statistics on the tax/price ratio show that significant differences exist between shochu and the other directly competitive or substitutable products[123] and that there are significantly different tax/price ratios within the same product categories. Therefore, the tax/price ratios could not be regarded as being "roughly constant", and horizontal equity could not be demonstrated. Moreover, as noted in paragraph 6.33 above, there were significant problems with the methodology for calculating tax/price ratios submitted by Japan, such that arguments based on that methodology could only be viewed as inconclusive. More particularly, although Japan had argued that the comparison of tax/price ratios should be done on a category-by-category basis, its statistics on which the tax/price ra-

---

[122]   See para. 4.132ff. of the Descriptive Part.
[123]   See paras. 4.100, 4.159, 4.160, 4.161 and 4.165 of the Descriptive Part.

tios were based excluded domestically produced spirits and whisky/brandy from the calculation of tax/price ratios for spirits and whisky/brandy. Since the prices of the domestic spirits and whisky/brandy are much lower than the prices of the imported ones, this exclusion has the impact of reducing considerably the tax/price ratios cited by Japan for those products. In this connection, the Panel noted that one consequence of the Japanese tax system was to make it more difficult for cheaper imported brands of spirits and whisky/brandy to enter the market. Moreover, the Panel noted that the Japanese statistics were based on suggested retail prices and there was evidence in the record that these products were often sold at a discount, at least in Tokyo. To the extent that the prices were unreliable, the resultant tax/price ratios would be unreliable as well.

(iii)   Finally, the Panel noted that nowhere in the contested legislation was it mentioned that its purpose was to maintain a constant tax/price ratio. This is rather an *ex post facto* rationalization by Japan and, at any rate, there are no guarantees in the legislation that the tax/price ratio will always be maintained at a constant (or "roughly constant") level. Prices change over time and unless an adjustment process is incorporated in the legislation, the tax/price ratio will be affected. Japan admitted that no adjustment process exists in the legislation and that only *ex post facto* adjustments can occur. The Panel lastly noted that since the modification of Japan's Liquor Tax Law there has been only one instance of adjustment.

Consequently, in the Panel's view, the argument by Japan that its legislation by keeping the tax/price ratio "roughly constant" is trade neutral and does not operate "so as to afford protection to domestic production" should be rejected.

6.35   The Panel took note, in this context, of the statement by Japan that the 1987 Panel Report erred when it concluded that shochu is essentially a Japanese product. The Panel accepted the evidence submitted by Japan according to which a shochu-like product is produced in various countries outside Japan, including the Republic of Korea, the People's Republic of China and Singapore. The Panel noted, however, that Japanese import duties on shochu are set at 17.9 per cent. At any rate what is at stake, in the Panel's view, is the market share of the domestic shochu market in Japan that was occupied by Japanese-made shochu. The high import duties on foreign-produced shochu resulted in a significant share of the Japanese shochu market held by Japanese shochu producers. Consequently, in the Panel's view, the combination of customs duties and internal taxation in Japan has the following impact: on the one hand, it makes it difficult for foreign-produced shochu to penetrate the Japanese market and, on the other, it does not guarantee equality of competitive conditions between shochu and the rest of "white" and "brown" spirits. Thus, through a combination of high import duties and differentiated internal taxes, Japan manages to "isolate" domestically produced shochu from foreign competition, be it foreign produced shochu or any other of the mentioned white and brown spirits. In the Panel's view, the table in Annex I illustrates this point.

VII. CONCLUSIONS

7.1   In light of the findings above, the Panel reached the following conclusions:

    (i)   Shochu and vodka are like products and Japan, by taxing the latter in excess of the former, is in violation of its obligation under Article III:2, first sentence, of the General Agreement on Tariffs and Trade 1994.

    (ii)   Shochu, whisky, brandy, rum, gin, genever, and liqueurs are "directly competitive or substitutable products" and Japan, by not taxing them similarly, is in violation of its obligation under Article III:2, second sentence, of the General Agreement on Tariffs and Trade 1994.

7.2   The Panel *recommends* that the Dispute Settlement Body request Japan to bring the Liquor Tax Law into conformity with its obligations under the General Agreement on Tariffs and Trade 1994.

Annex I

(1) HS 1996 Nomenclature	(2) Product Description	(3) Bound Rate 1/4/96 - 31/3/97	(4) Applied Rates	(5) Internal Taxation
2208.20	Brandy (50° or higher)	308.00 ¥/litre	193.20 ¥/litre	(40°) ¥ 982.30/litre
	Brandy (Other)	364.00 ¥/litre	227.90 ¥/litre	
2208.30	Whiskies:			
	Bourbon	19.6%*	13.7%	
	Rye	22.4%	15.7%	
	Other (over 50° or higher)	330.40¥/litre	207.20¥/litre	
	Other (Other)	274.40¥/litre	172.50¥/litre	(40°) ¥ 982.30/litre
2208.40	Rum and Tafia	36%	Free/20.2% **	(38°) ¥ 377.23/litre
2208.50	Gin and Genever	29.2%**** or 128.33 ¥/litre (whichever is the less)	19.6% or 86.20 ¥/litre (whichever is the less)	(38°) ¥ 377.23/litre
2208.60	Vodka	26.7%****	17.9%	(38°) ¥ 377.23/litre
2208.70	Liqueurs and Cordials	210 ¥/litre	141.10 ¥/litre	(40°) ¥ 328.76/litre
ex 2208.90	Shochu	26.7% ***	17.9%	A (25°) ¥ 155.70/litre
				B (25°) ¥ 102.10/litre

*   Annual percentage reduction: approximately 2.4%

**   Intended for use in distilling alcohol for making alcoholic beverages through the continuous still: for the "pooled quota" (free); other (17.9%)

***   Annual percentage reduction: approximately 2.7%

**** Annual percentage reduction: approximately 2.9%

N.B: For applied rates for whiskies, rum and tafia, gin and genever, vodka, liqueurs, and shochu, we use rates valid from 1/4/1995 to 31/3/1996.

Source: Columns (1) - (4): WTO Secretariat; Column (5): paragraph 2.3 of the Descriptive Part.

Annex II
Annual Changes in Sales of Former Second Grade Whisky and Shochu

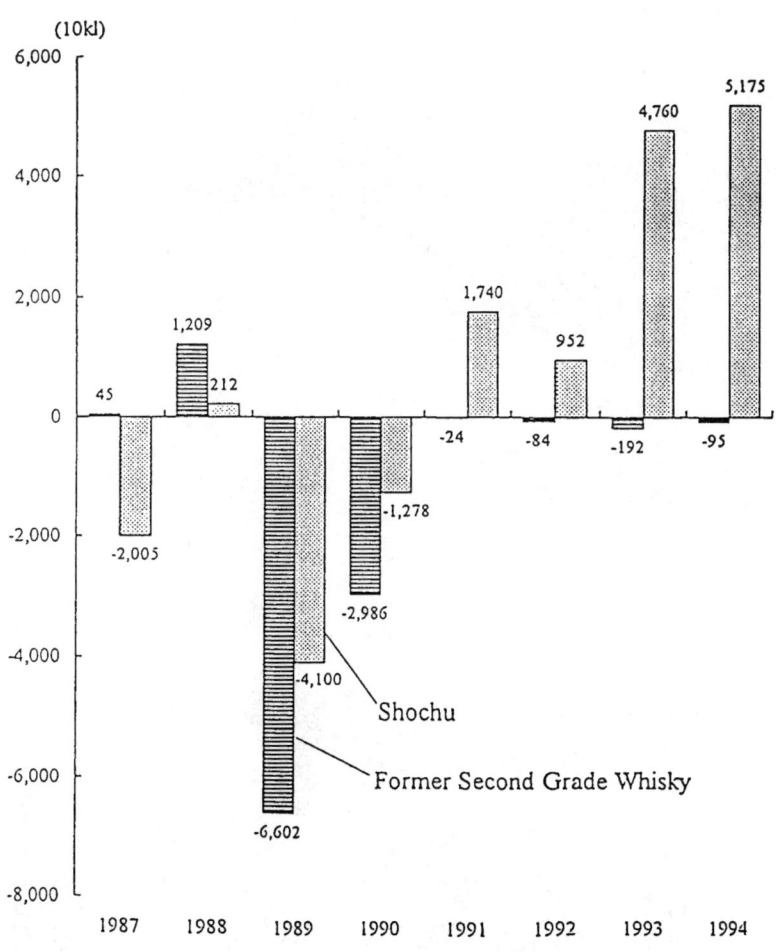

Source: National Tax Administration, except for the figures for former second grade whisky since 1989, which are based on industry statistics of the sales of whiskies below 40 vol (excluding pre-mixed).

Annex III

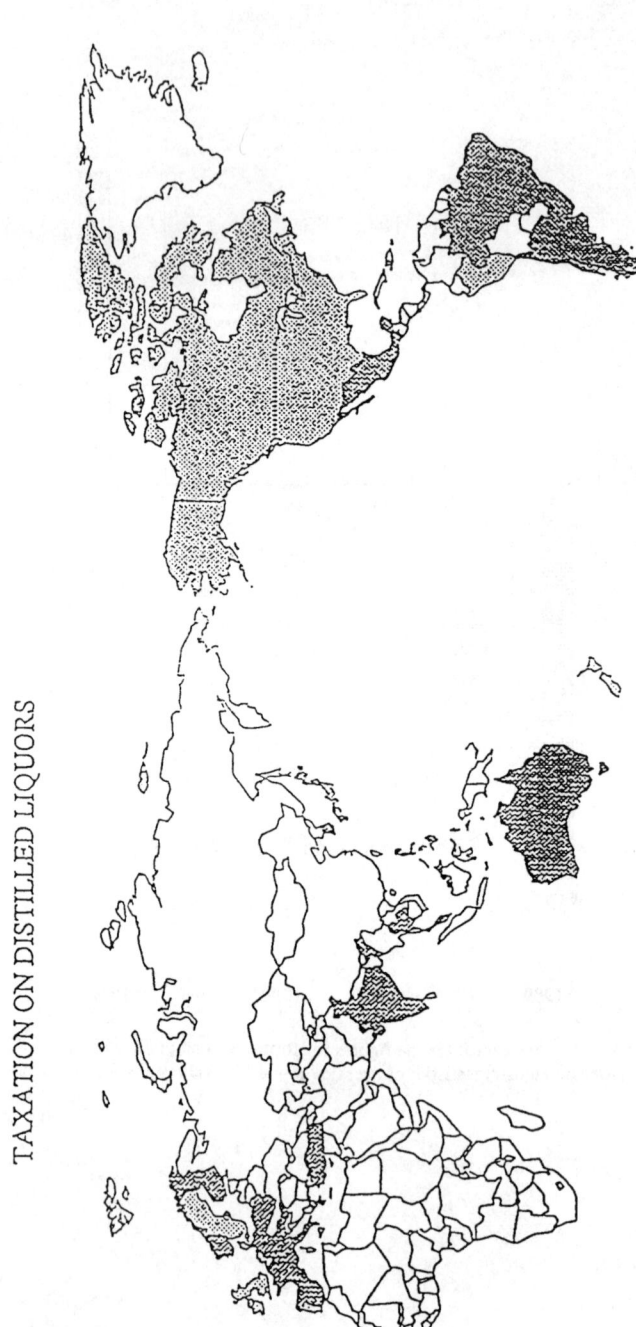

TAXATION ON DISTILLED LIQUORS

— Flat Rate

— Different Rates

Annex IV

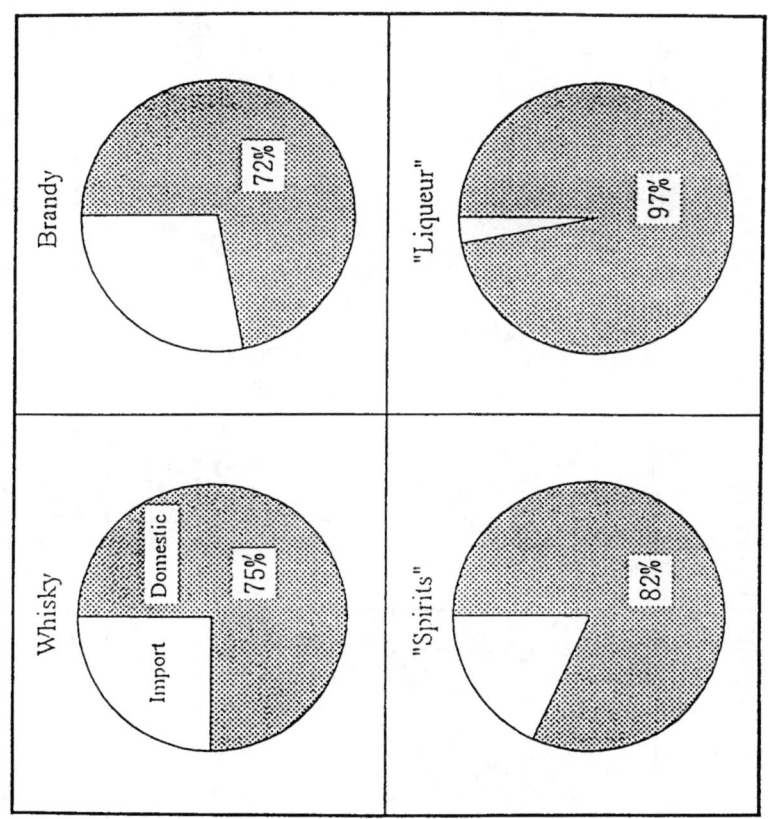

SHARE OF DOMESTIC PRODUCTION IN TOTAL SALES

Brandy — 72%

"Liqueur" — 97%

Whisky — Domestic / Import — 75%

"Spirits" — 82%

Annex V

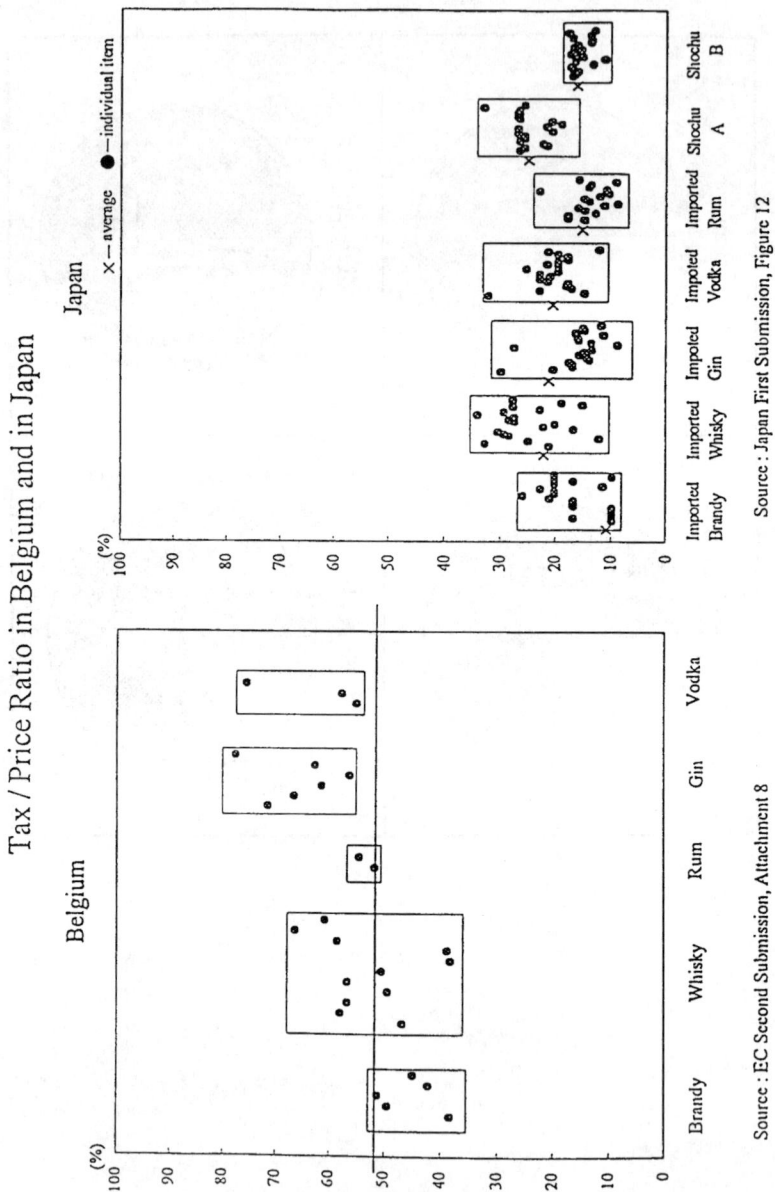

Tax / Price Ratio in Belgium and in Japan

Annex VI

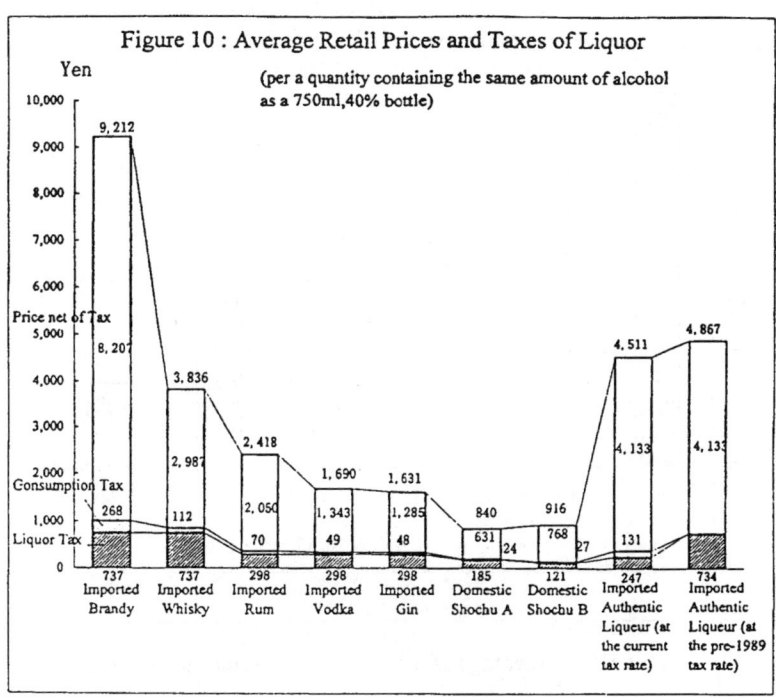

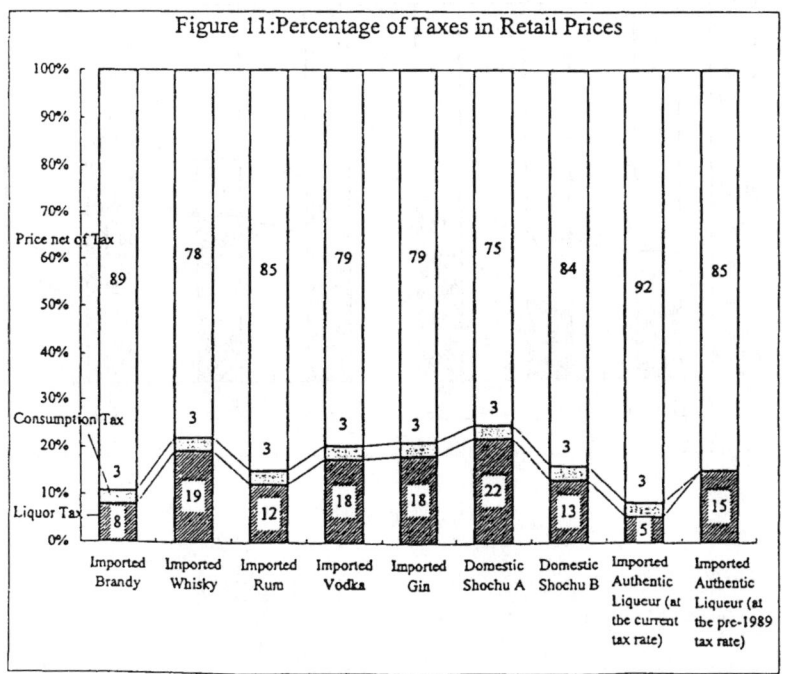

Annex VII

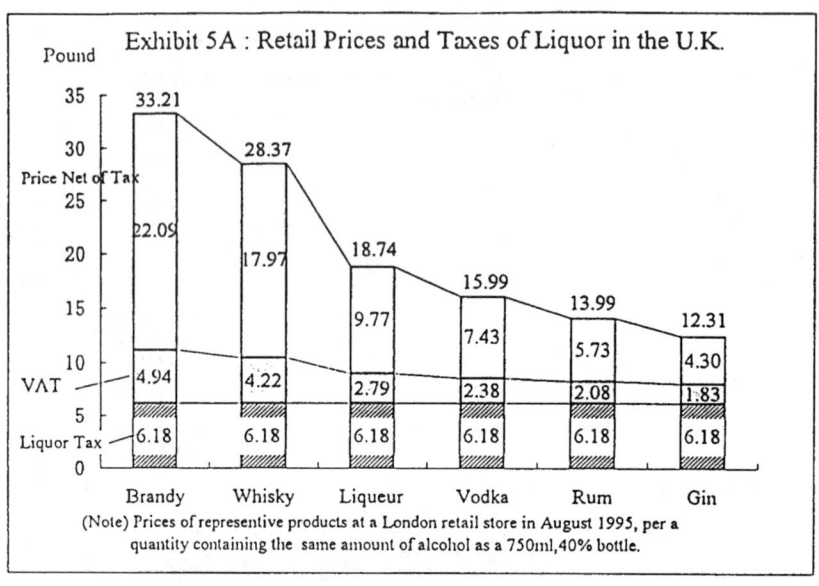

Exhibit 5A : Retail Prices and Taxes of Liquor in the U.K.

(Note) Prices of representive products at a London retail store in August 1995, per a quantity containing the same amount of alcohol as a 750ml,40% bottle.

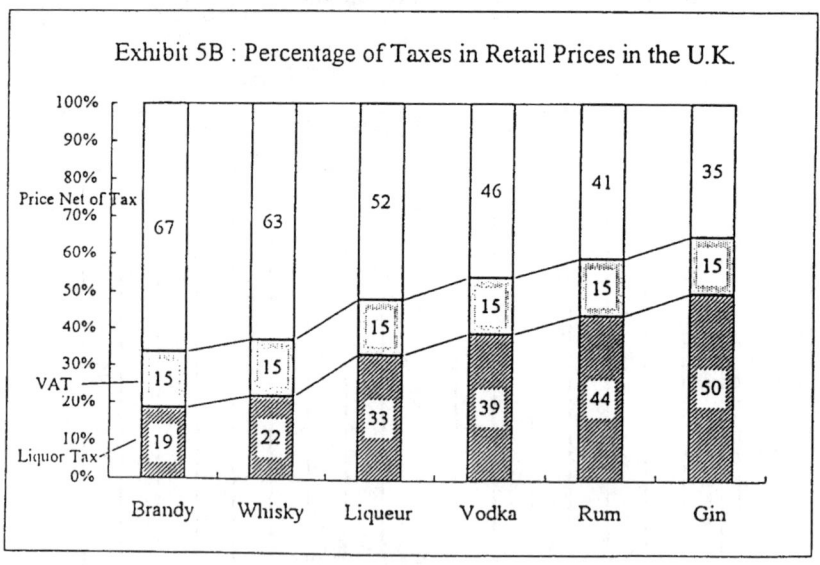

Exhibit 5B : Percentage of Taxes in Retail Prices in the U.K.